This Book Comes With Lots of
FREE Online Resources

Nolo's award-winning website has a page dedicated just to this book. Here you can:

KEEP UP TO DATE. When there are important changes to the information in this book, we'll post updates.

GET DISCOUNTS ON NOLO PRODUCTS. Get discounts on hundreds of books, forms, and software.

READ BLOGS. Get the latest info from Nolo authors' blogs.

LISTEN TO PODCASTS. Listen to authors discuss timely issues on topics that interest you.

WATCH VIDEOS. Get a quick introduction to a legal topic with our short videos.

And that's not all.
Nolo.com contains thousands of articles on everyday legal and business issues, plus a plain-English law dictionary, all written by Nolo experts and available for free. You'll also find more useful **books, software, online apps, downloadable forms,** plus a **lawyer directory.**

With
Downloadable
FORMS

Get forms and more at
www.nolo.com/back-of-book/EMHA.html

8th Edition

Create Your Own Employee Handbook

A Legal & Practical Guide for Employers

Lisa Guerin, J.D. &
Amy DelPo, J.D.

EIGHTH EDITION	MAY 2017
Editor	MARCIA STEWART
Cover Design	SUSAN PUTNEY
Book Production	SUSAN PUTNEY
Proofreading	IRENE BARNARD
Index	JULIE SHAWVAN
Printing	BANG PRINTING

Names: Guerin, Lisa, 1964- author. | DelPo, Amy, 1967- author.
Title: Create your own employee handbook : a legal & practical guide for
    employers / Lisa Guerin, J.D. & Amy DelPo, J.D.
Description: 8th Edition. | Berkeley, CA : Nolo, [2017] | Revised edition of
    the authors' Create your own employee handbook, [2015] | Includes
    bibliographical references and index.
Identifiers: LCCN 2016056189 (print) | LCCN 2017009571 (ebook) | ISBN
    9781413323979 (pbk.) | ISBN 9781413323986 (ebook)
Subjects: LCSH: Employee orientation. | Employees--Training of. | Employee
    rights. | Employee rules.
Classification: LCC HF5549.5.I53 G84 2017 (print) | LCC HF5549.5.I53 (ebook)
    | DDC 658.3/01--dc23
LC record available at https://lccn.loc.gov/2016056189

Please note

We believe accurate, plain-English legal information should help you solve many
of your own legal problems. But this text is not a substitute for personalized advice
from a knowledgeable lawyer. If you want the help of a trained professional—and
we'll always point out situations in which we think that's a good idea—consult an
attorney licensed to practice in your state.

Acknowledgments

The authors would like to thank the following people who helped to make this book possible:

- Our editor on the first edition, Ilona Bray, whose good humor and easy nature made the editing process fun—and whose words and insights never failed to improve upon what we gave her

- Our editor on the second edition, Stephanie Bornstein, whose eye for detail and consistency helped us immeasurably

- Albin Renauer for his wonderful design ideas—and his ability to think "inside the box"!

- Mary Randolph, for helping us mold and formulate our vision of this book

- Nolo jack-of-all-trades Stan Jacobson, who tirelessly haunted libraries throughout the Bay Area to meet our research needs

- Ella Hirst, for her years of hard work on the 50-state charts that appear in this book; and Alayna Schroeder, Drew Wheaton, Stephen Stine, and the rest of the Nolo legal research team, for graciously picking up where Ella left off

- Andre Zivkovich and Ellen Bitter, who managed to take our printed pages and turn them into forms that people could use on their computers, and

- Terri Hearsh, for working with us on a wonderful book design.

In addition, Amy would like to dedicate her work on this book to her daughter, Sophia, whose early birth delayed the first edition of this book by almost half a year. She is everything and more.

About the Authors

Lisa Guerin is a former Nolo editor specializing in employment and human resources issues. After graduating from the Boalt Hall School of Law at the University of California at Berkeley, Lisa practiced employment law in government, public interest, and private practice. Lisa has represented clients at all levels of federal and state court, in agency hearings, and in mediation and arbitration proceedings. She is the author or coauthor of many Nolo titles, including *The Essential Guide to Workplace Investigations, Smart Policies for Workplace Technologies,* and *The Essential Guide to Family & Medical Leave.*

Amy DelPo brings more than six years of criminal and civil litigation experience to her work at Nolo, having litigated cases at all levels of state and federal courts, including the California Supreme Court and the U.S. Supreme Court. Before joining Nolo's staff in January 2000, Amy specialized in employment law, handling a wide variety of disputes between employers and employees, including sexual harassment, discrimination, and wage-and-hour issues. She has written and edited numerous employment law titles for Nolo, including *Dealing With Problem Employees* (coauthor). Amy received her law degree with honors from the University of North Carolina at Chapel Hill. She lives in Denver, Colorado, with her husband and three children.

Together, the authors have written several books published by Nolo, including *Dealing With Problem Employees, The Manager's Legal Handbook,* and *The Essential Guide to Federal Employment Laws.*

Table of Contents

Appendixes

What an Employee Handbook Can Do for Your Organization

If you're like most managers, you (or people who work for you) probably devote a good part of every day to employee relations. If you're in human resources or own a business, you may find yourself making decisions or fielding questions about everything from benefits to vacation time to disciplinary problems. Sometimes, you may know the answer right away ("You get ten vacation days"); other times, you may have to think a bit or come up with something new ("What is our policy on paternity leave?").

In such situations, a good employee handbook is essential. Simply defined, an employee handbook is a written and/or electronic document describing the benefits and responsibilities of the employment relationship. In reality, however, the handbook's role is much more complex and powerful. While it sits quietly on the shelf (or server), the employee handbook can actually help define and manage your company's relationship with its employees. It knows all the answers and communicates them clearly to employees. Indeed, an employee handbook can do a lot for your company, including:

- save time by cutting down on the number of questions employees ask every day
- ensure that the company treats employees consistently, and
- provide legal protection when an employment relationship goes sour.

The Purposes of an Employee Handbook

An employee handbook is an indispensable workplace tool that helps your company communicate with employees, manage its workers (and managers), streamline its organization, and protect itself from lawsuits.

Communication

A handbook tells employees what the company expects from them and what they can expect from the company. "What time do I have to be at work?" "Does my employer provide health insurance?" "How do I complain about my supervisor's sexual advances?" A well-drafted handbook will answer all of these questions and many more.

In addition to relaying basic information about benefits, hours, and pay, an employee handbook imparts the company's culture, values, and history. When was the company founded? Why is it successful? What attitude should employees take toward their jobs and customers? This information can help motivate employees to work more effectively and enthusiastically on behalf of the company.

Management

Employees are not mind readers. Although you may know what the company's practices and policies are, without a handbook, other employees, managers, and supervisors have no place to turn for this information. This creates an environment ripe for trouble, both legal and practical. Employee morale will drop if employees are treated inconsistently, possibly resulting in a discrimination lawsuit if an employee thinks this different treatment is based on race, gender, or some other protected characteristic.

Handbooks promote positive employee relations by ensuring that all employees are treated consistently and fairly. They prevent misunderstandings, confusion, and complaints by giving everyone the same resource for learning company personnel practices. If there is ever any doubt or dispute about a particular policy, you can simply open the book and take a look. You don't need to have long, agonizing discussions or try to reinvent the wheel.

Planning

The process of creating (or reviewing) a handbook will force your company's management to carefully consider every aspect of its relationship with employees. Rather than doing things a certain way just because that's the way they've always been done, you can reflect on how employees have been treated and consider whether any changes are in order. For each policy, your company's decision makers should ask themselves: Do we really want to continue doing things this way? If so, why?

Creating an employee handbook necessarily requires communication with, and feedback from, employees, supervisors, and managers about the company's current personnel practices. This will help determine what works and what doesn't, what should change and what should stay the same, and what new policies or practices the company might want to adopt.

Legal Protection

Just having a handbook can help your company comply with the law and reduce its risk of lawsuits. Consider the following:

- Some laws require employers to communicate certain information to their employees. The handbook provides a convenient place to put this information.
- Even when the company isn't required to give information to employees, providing it in a handbook may create important legal protections. For example, companies aren't necessarily required to tell employees how to complain about sexual harassment, but a company that has such a policy in place can use the policy as a legal defense should an employee file a harassment lawsuit. (You can find a sexual harassment policy in Chapter 19.)
- Certain policies in a handbook can affirm a company's commitment to equal employment

opportunity laws. This is one step toward creating a tolerant and discrimination-free workplace (something that most employers are legally obligated to do). (You can find standard equal employment opportunity policies in Chapter 3.)

- In certain situations, a company will be responsible for the actions of its employees and supervisors who violate the law, even if the company did not condone or even know about the illegal conduct. Providing guidance and prohibitions in an employee handbook can cut down the risk of unlawful behavior.

Perhaps the most important reason to have an employee handbook is to protect the company's legal right to terminate employees at will. In theory, employers already have this right. Unless the company has entered into a contract with an employee promising something else, its relationship with that employee is automatically "at will." This means the employer can terminate the employment relationship at any time for any reason that is not illegal, and the employee can do the same.

However, just because an employee does not have a written contract does not necessarily guarantee that the employee is working at will. A company can inadvertently destroy its right to terminate at will by creating an implied contract with an employee, promising not to fire the employee without a legitimate business reason. Some employers with badly written handbooks have gotten burned over this issue. Courts have found that certain statements in their handbooks—including that employees will only be fired for certain reasons, that employees won't be fired if they are doing a good job, or that employees are considered "permanent" once they complete a probationary period—created implied contracts that limited the employers' right to fire at will. (For more on at-will employment and implied contracts, see Chapter 2.)

In this book, we help you avoid this trap by providing standard policies that steer clear of any promises of continued employment, as well as disclaimers specifically stating that employment relationships at your company are at will.

What an Employee Handbook Is Not

An employee handbook can do a lot, but it can't do everything, nor should it. A handbook is just one part of a company's relationship with its employees. It lays the groundwork for success in that relationship, but it's up to the company's managers to take it from there.

A Handbook Is No Substitute for Personal Interaction

Although a handbook is an important communication tool, it cannot take the place of one-on-one personal interaction between management and employees. An employee handbook can help foster trust, loyalty, and positive employee relations, but it can't do the job on its own. Employees need a human face behind the policies. They need to see, hear, and feel that the company's management is interested in them and the job they are doing.

A Handbook Is No Substitute for Good Practices

No matter how many policies you write, they won't do your company any good unless managers follow them. In fact, they might actually do some harm.

From a practical standpoint, personnel practices that are inconsistent with written policies can damage employee relations. Employees who read one thing but experience another won't trust—or feel loyal to—their employer.

From a legal standpoint, a company is courting trouble if it doesn't deliver what it promises in the handbook. Even though the handbook will include disclaimers explaining that the handbook is not a contract (these disclaimers are covered in Chapter 1), a judge or jury might think differently and try to hold the company to its words or make it pay for not following them. For these reasons, the handbook should include only those policies that your company is prepared to follow.

A Handbook Is Not a Personnel Policy Manual

Employee handbooks are written in general terms, for use by employees. A policy or procedures manual, on the other hand, is a detailed guide that sets out very specifically how supervisors and managers are to do their jobs. Usually, employees are not allowed access to policy or procedures manuals.

You may wonder why you can't just have one book for both audiences. There are a number of reasons, including:

- There might be sensitive information (trade secrets, for example) that the company doesn't necessarily want to reveal to all employees.
- Employees don't need to be bogged down by every little detail of how things are done in your company. If you throw too much information at employees at once—some of it irrelevant to their day-to-day work—they might feel overwhelmed and not read the handbook at all.
- The details of how policies are implemented are more likely to change than the general policies themselves. If you put these details in the handbook, you will need to change it frequently.

Who Can Use This Book

This book is for business owners, managers, supervisors, and human resource professionals in companies of all sizes, from small outfits with only a handful of employees to large corporations. It is also appropriate for virtually every industry, from manufacturing to sales to service provision.

As the name "Employee Handbook" indicates, you can use this book to create policies for use with employees, not independent contractors. While some of the policies might be useful for companies that hire independent contractors, you'll want to create separate documents for that purpose. If you require your independent contractors to read and agree to abide by your employee handbook, you are by definition treating them like employees. This greatly increases the risk that a government agency might later decide you misclassified them as contractors, something you want to avoid. For more information, see *Working with Independent Contractors*, by Stephen Fishman (Nolo).

There are two types of workplaces for which this book won't work: public workplaces (that is, workplaces with federal, state, or local government employees) and unionized workplaces.

Get Policies, Forms, Updates, and More on Nolo.com

All of the sample policies in this book, along with modifications, alternative language, and forms, are available for download at this book's online companion page:

www.nolo.com/back-of-book/EMHA.html

You'll find other useful information there too, including blog posts and legal updates on Obamacare and laws that affect employers—which will be especially important as the Presidency changes hands. (See Appendix A, "Creating Your Handbook," for details on this book's companion page.)

How to Use This Book

If you're eager to create an employee handbook—or modify an existing handbook—we should warn you that there is a catch. Well, two catches: Handbooks don't write themselves, and there is no such thing as a one-size-fits-all handbook. It's a bad idea to simply purchase or download a generic handbook, slap your company's name on the cover, and distribute it to employees. It won't be tailored to your company's needs, and it may even get you into legal trouble. If you want an effective and legally sound handbook, you are going to have to sit down and actually create it, with policies and language that reflect your company's culture, values, and personnel practices.

Don't despair, however. We've designed this book to make the process easy and straightforward, taking you step by step through planning, writing, and distributing a handbook. Using this book, you can create an employee handbook that's tailored to your company's needs, with minimal time and headaches.

In this chapter, we:
- explain what you'll find in the different parts of this book
- advise you on information you'll need to obtain from other sources, and
- instruct you on each phase of the handbook creation process, from gathering the information you'd like to include in the handbook to deciding how to distribute the handbook once it's complete.

What You'll Find in This Book

This book is both a workbook and a guidebook. The heart of the book (Chapters 1 through 21) contains a combination of important material. First, it contains prewritten personnel policies that you'll be able to cut and paste (and modify, if necessary), policy by policy, into the handbook you're creating. Along with prewritten policies, these chapters also provide valuable explanatory material, including:

- background information
- guidance to help you decide whether you want to include a particular policy in your handbook
- standard language that you can cut and paste into your handbook (or, if there is no standard way to word a policy, an example of what such policies look like and detailed guidance on writing your own from scratch)
- instructions on completing the standard policy with information specific to your workplace
- when appropriate, alternate modifications that you can use to complete a policy so that it accurately reflects the reality at your company
- when appropriate, additional clauses that you can add to a policy to suit your needs
- information on potential trouble spots, both practical and legal, and
- advice on when to consult an attorney for more assistance.

For each policy, you'll find a box in the margin that provides a quick look at what the policy is, whether there are any alternate modifications or additional clauses you should consider, and whether there are related policies you should review. If you like, you can use these boxes to keep track of your thoughts as you read through the book and to communicate those thoughts to anyone else in your company who may be working with you on the handbook.

When you're ready to start compiling the handbook, you'll find all of the prewritten policy language at this book's online companion page on Nolo.com, ready for cutting, pasting, and editing. The file name for the particular policy language, such as Meal and Rest Breaks, is also listed in the box in the margin. The companion page also provides legal updates, blogs, podcasts, and more. For instructions on accessing and using these materials, see Appendix A.

Appendix B gives you information on where to go for more assistance, such as your state department of labor.

What You Won't Find in This Book

This book is not a treatise on employment law. To keep it trim and to the point, we assume that our readers have personnel practices in place already. This book helps you communicate those practices to your employees; it does not help you choose those practices in the first place. For example, this book includes a policy warning employees that they might have to take a drug test, but we don't go into detail on when to conduct drug tests or how to conduct them so that they comply with your state's laws. That's up to your company to figure out through different sources, such as other books or discussions with an attorney.

Because of this, before you start creating a handbook (or modifying an existing handbook), you need to understand your company's legal obligations as an employer in your state.

RESOURCE

Employment law resources from Nolo. Nolo publishes many general resources on employment law (as well as titles that help you handle specific managerial tasks, such as giving performance appraisals, conducting investigations, or using progressive discipline). For basic information on the legal rights and obligations of the employment relationship, see *The Employer's Legal Handbook*, by Fred Steingold, and *The Essential Guide to Federal Employment Laws*, *The Manager's Legal Handbook*, and *Dealing With Problem Employees*, all by the authors of this book. Also, be sure to check out the "Employment Law Center" on Nolo.com for lots of useful articles on the legal and practical rules involved in hiring employees, covering everything from wage and hour to antidiscrimination laws.

Drafting Your Handbook

By now, you've probably gotten our message that creating a handbook requires more than simply stringing together a bunch of boilerplate paragraphs. It takes planning and research. But don't worry. It doesn't have to be a time-consuming or arduous task. With a little investigation, you can put together a handbook fairly quickly.

The very first thing you must do is decide who will be in charge of creating your company's handbook. If you own a small business, that someone might just be you, or perhaps an office manager. If you work in a larger company, it might make sense to assign this task to a group of people. Whoever is charged with this task should be familiar with your company's employment practices and should have the power to decide what to include in the handbook. When we refer to "you," we are referring to the person or people creating the handbook.

We suggest the following four-step process for creating your handbook:

1. Investigate.
2. Compile and write.
3. Review and revise.
4. Get final approval from an attorney.

Step 1: Investigate

Before you can communicate your company's policies to employees, you must know precisely what those policies are. This is often more complex than it sounds. "Policy" is really just a word for how a company treats its employees, and this is something that often happens informally and inconsistently. This is especially true if your company is a small business. Let's say, for example, that you own your own business and your secretary, whom you think the world of, was in a car accident last year. You paid her salary for the two months it took her to rehabilitate. Does this mean that everyone in your company is entitled to two months of paid sick leave? Or only people who are in car accidents? Or only people whom you like?

The situation can be even worse in large companies, where managers or supervisors are in charge of employees' day-to-day work lives. Different managers may do things differently, so a company may have as many variations of a policy as it has managers. If your company has offices in different states or countries, there may be a very good reason why your policies are inconsistent: The laws of each state or country may impose different obligations on employers who do business there.

To figure out how personnel matters are being handled, and why any inconsistencies exist, we suggest doing the following:

- Interview managers and supervisors.
- Distribute a questionnaire to managers and supervisors.
- Consult your current personnel policies manual (if you have one).
- Consult old handbooks and policy manuals (if they exist).
- Obtain handbooks from other businesses in your state (your local chamber of commerce might be a good source for this type of information).
- Distribute a questionnaire to employees.
- Talk to people in your human resources and payroll departments.
- Consult with your benefits administrator and office manager.
- Review bulletin board notices, memos, newsletters, and employee complaints.

The chapters and headings in this book can help you structure your interviews or questionnaires. We recommend scanning them to remind yourself of the various categories that you need to inquire into, from work hours to benefits to complaint procedures.

> CAUTION
>
> **Don't copy another company's handbook.** If you are able to obtain handbooks from other companies, it's perfectly fine to mine them for ideas, but do not lift their policies wholesale and cut-and-paste them into your handbook. Those policies have been created for another business and may contain information that doesn't fit your company, is outdated, or is no longer legally sound.

Step 2: Compile and Write

When you sit down to actually create the policies you want to include in your handbook, start with the standard policies and modifications provided here. The explanatory text we provide will help you decide whether to include that policy in your handbook and what the policy should address. For the most part, this will be a straightforward cut-and-paste job. However, when you need to modify policies or write them from scratch, keep these rules in mind:

- Use simple vocabulary.
- Use short sentences.
- Don't use legalese or jargon.
- Keep paragraphs short.
- Be clear and concise.
- Use language that reflects the culture of your company (for example, formal or informal).
- Write to the education and sophistication level of your employees.
- Use terms consistently.
- Emphasize the positive aspects of any policy.
- Where appropriate, briefly explain the rationale behind the policy.

For many policies, we provide you with ways to modify the policies to fit your workplace. In some cases, you must choose one of the possible modifications if you want to complete the policy; we call these "alternate modifications." Other times, you may choose whether or not to include a modification to tailor the policy to your workplace; we call these "additional clauses." In other words, if a policy provides "alternate modifications," you must pick one of the alternatives if you want to include that policy in your handbook. If a policy provides "additional clauses," you can choose to modify it or not, but the policy will work with or without the modification.

If your company has offices or employees in more than one state or country, you have some options for dealing with the fact that your policies may be different for each locale. If there are only a few differences, and you don't mind employees in one place knowing how employees in other places are treated, you can have one version of the handbook that explains the policies for each locale. If the differences are numerous or complex, however, you can create a version of your handbook for each state or country.

Step 3: Review and Revise

All managers and supervisors should read the initial draft of the handbook and give feedback. After all, they are the ones on the front lines, dealing with employees every day, and they are the ones who are going to have to actually enforce the policies you've chosen. They can alert you to inconsistencies or to policies that won't work in the real world. They can also tell you when your writing is unclear or misleading. And they might be able to recommend new or different policies.

Step 4: Get Final Approval From an Attorney

In this book, you will find advice and policies that comply with federal law and the laws of most states. That being said, each state has its own legal requirements. For example, in California, it's illegal to prohibit women from wearing pants. In Kentucky, it's illegal to discriminate against employees for smoking off duty. We provide 50-state information on a variety of basic employment topics here, but there may be additional laws that apply in your state. What's more, laws change over time: The information in this book was current when published, but your state may have amended or repealed a particular law, or passed a new law that isn't yet included here. Courts or regulatory agencies may have changed their interpretation of existing laws. Or, new workplace issues may arise that your handbook should address.

Your company may also have to comply with local laws to do business in your city or county. For example, San Francisco companies must comply with a city ordinance that requires employers to provide at least one hour of paid sick leave for every 30 hours an employee works. We don't have room in this book to cover applicable local laws.

Because of this ever-changing legal landscape, and because your company's employee handbook must be legally sound and up to date, you absolutely must have a knowledgeable local employment attorney review the final product. A good lawyer can let you know about state and local law details, developments in your state's courts, and additional policies you might want to consider. Because you will have done all of the work to put your handbook together, a final review like this shouldn't take more than a few hours.

> **CAUTION**
>
> **Don't skip the legal review!** As we go to press, employment laws are changing. When the White House changes hands (and parties), rapid shifts are possible. What will happen to Obamacare, new overtime rules, enforcement priorities at the National Labor Relations Board and Equal Employment Opportunity Commission, and more? We have some idea of what to expect, but we certainly don't have a crystal ball. Luckily, we don't need one: An experienced employment lawyer in your area is the best source of up-to-date legal information and policy guidance. Now more than ever, you must have your completed handbook reviewed by a lawyer, to make sure you stay on the right side of the law.

Looking for an Employment Lawyer?

Asking for a referral to an employment attorney from someone you trust can be a good way to find legal help. Someone looking to hire a lawyer, even if only for consultation, can also try these excellent and free resources:

- **Nolo's Lawyer Directory.** Nolo has an easy-to-use online directory of lawyers, organized by location and area of expertise, such as employment law. You can find the directory and its comprehensive profiles at www.nolo.com/lawyers.
- **Lawyers.com.** At Lawyers.com, you'll find a user-friendly search tool that allows you to tailor results by area of law and geography. You can also search for attorneys by name. Attorney profiles prominently display contact information, list topics of expertise, and show ratings—by both clients and other legal professionals.
- **Martindale.com.** Martindale.com offers an advanced search option that allows you to sort not only by practice area and location, but also by criteria like law school. Whether you look for lawyers by name or expertise, you'll find listings with detailed background information, peer and client ratings, and even profile visibility.

Formatting the Handbook

Once you have a final draft of your handbook, the next step is to decide how it should look. We suggest grouping your policies into chapters by topic (for example, your handbook might have a benefits chapter and a payroll chapter). This book presents the standard policies in this way. You can use our organization or come up with your own. Here are some other formatting tips:

- **Include a table of contents at the beginning of your handbook.** Because it is likely that your handbook's most common use will be to answer employees' specific questions, a table of contents helps ensure that they'll find the answers.
- **Include an index at the end.** This is also helpful for employees who can't find what they're looking for.
- **Start each policy on a new page.** This enables employees to insert updates and remove old policies without disturbing the surrounding policies.
- **Double-space the text of policies.** This makes them easier to read.
- **Give each policy its own boldfaced heading.** This also makes for easier reading and navigation.
- **Don't use page numbers.** Instead, number your policies by chapter (for example, a policy numbered "1:3" is the third policy in the first chapter). You'll notice that we number our policies in this way as well. This method enables employees to remove old policies and insert new ones without ruining the handbook's pagination. If you want to insert a policy where there wasn't one before, you can use letters (for example, "1:3a").
- **Put the policies in a three-ring binder.** This allows employees to insert new policies or replace old policies when instructed to do so. Not only does this method make it easy to revise policies, it saves you money, because you invest in the binder only once. One drawback of this handbook format is that it makes it difficult for you to know whether employees have actually inserted new or revised policies when they are told to do so. This creates the risk that employees have out-of-date policies

in their handbooks. To minimize this risk, require employees to give you the old policies when you distribute the new or revised ones.

Electronic Handbooks

You may be considering putting your handbook online. If so, you have a lot of issues to consider, some practical and some legal.

On the practical side of things, there are a lot of advantages to an electronic handbook, most of them monetary. You don't have to pay publication costs, nor do you have to purchase binders. Plus, you can react more quickly to changes in the law or in company policy: To update your handbook, you need only make the changes in the electronic version and then send an email to employees or post a notice on your intranet site. Electronic handbooks are not for all companies, however. If you have any employees who do not have easy access to computers or who are not skilled at using computers, it's best to stick to a paper handbook. Also, if you have concerns about the security of your website, it's nice to know that a paper handbook can't be hacked into.

The legal issues are a bit more complicated, mostly having to do with what it means for something to be "signed" or "in writing." For example, it is vitally important that employees sign the handbook acknowledgment form in a manner courts will recognize as binding. Although electronic signatures have been around for a long time, some systems still leave wiggle room for employees to argue later that their electronic signature was forged or transmitted by mistake. If you choose to make your handbook electronic, make sure your electronic signature system is state-of-the-art (and will pass legal muster, if a court has to decide whether an agreement was created). Some employers hedge their bets by asking employees to print out the acknowledgement form and sign and date it by hand.

Similarly, some laws, both federal and state, require employers to distribute certain policies to employees in writing. If you plan to use an electronic handbook, you should talk to a lawyer to find out whether you should give these policies to employees on paper or whether your handbook will suffice.

You will also have to make sure that your electronic handbook is fully accessible to employees with disabilities. The federal Americans with Disabilities Act (ADA) and similar state laws require employers to provide reasonable accommodations to allow employees to do their jobs and access work facilities.

The best strategy for employers considering an all-electronic handbook is to include that issue in your legal consultation. An experienced employment lawyer can help you figure out how best to handle acknowledgment forms, handbook updates (and acknowledgment forms for those), legal requirements that policies be in writing, and accommodations for employees with disabilities.

Revising and Updating

You have the right to revise and update your handbook at any time. We recommend reviewing it once a year to determine whether any policies need to be revised or updated. Usually, policies must be revised for one of two reasons: (1) because your personnel practices have changed, or (2) because the law has changed.

If only one or two policies need to be revised, it's easy enough to distribute the new policy to employees, with instructions to remove the old policy and insert the new one in its place. Require employees to return the old policy to you. That way, you know that they actually updated the book and didn't simply drop the new policy in the recycling bin.

Over time, you will see that more and more of the policies in your book are revised policies and not the original ones. You may also notice that the language or tone of the original policies has become outdated or stale. When this happens, it's time to consider revising the entire handbook and handing out a new edition to your employees.

Distributing Your Handbook

Once your employee handbook is complete, it's time to distribute it to employees. The best way to do this—particularly if your company has never had a handbook or hasn't had one for a long time—is to hold a meeting.

Call all of your employees together (or, if this is impossible, hold a series of meetings and require each employee to attend one). At the meeting, explain that the company has a new employee handbook to set forth the company's policies. Let employees know that you expect each of them to read the handbook and abide by its contents. And tell everyone that you want them to sign a form acknowledging that they have received the handbook (this important form is covered in Chapter 2).

Once you distribute the handbooks (or, if your handbook is online, once you tell employees how to access it), stick around for a while to answer any employee questions. And make sure to pass out the acknowledgment forms and ask employees to sign them.

When you hire new employees, give them a copy of the handbook—and ask them to sign the acknowledgment form—during their orientation meetings or when they fill out their other first-day paperwork.

Handbook Introduction

A handbook's introductory statements will be the first policies employees read, and they will set the tone for everything else to come. For this reason, they should be friendly and nonthreatening, easing employees into the drier—and sometimes less pleasant—information that will follow. Envision the handbook as an engaging tour guide, personally leading employees through the company. Employees will be more receptive to—and pay more attention to—a handbook that they perceive as warm and friendly than a handbook that feels impersonal and cold.

Start by introducing employees to the company, and its history, products or services, and goals. You'd be surprised how many long-term employees—let alone employees who have just been hired—don't know this basic information. The handbook can be an effective way of indoctrinating employees into a company's culture and values. This knowledge can inform everything employees do at the company, from dealing with customers and vendors to setting standards for their own work.

Depending on industry standards, company culture, and employee sophistication, some employers might want to make the policies in this chapter more formal, and some might want to make them more casual. Regardless of the level of formality you choose, however, try to make the tone as pleasant and friendly as possible.

1:1 Welcome to Our Company!

File Name: 01_Introduction.rtf

Include This Policy?
- ☐ Yes
- ☐ No
- ☐ Use our existing policy
- ☐ Other _____

Alternate Modifications
None

Additional Clauses
Company-Specific Information
Insert?: ☐ Yes ☐ No

Related Policies
None

Notes

_____
_____
_____
_____
_____
_____
_____
_____
_____
_____
_____
_____
_____
_____
_____
_____
_____

1:1 Welcoming Statement

Though it's not a legal requirement, we recommend you begin the handbook by welcoming employees to the company. After all, the vast majority of employees will read through the handbook only at the beginning of their employment. Thereafter, they will look at it only in bits and pieces, finding the information they need and nothing more.

A hearty welcome can quickly and effectively establish the friendly tone that you want to convey. An effective welcoming statement is positive and upbeat, and it begins the process of selling the company to your employees.

Welcome to Our Company!

It's our pleasure to welcome you to our Company. We're an energetic and creative bunch, dedicated to high standards of excellence and quality. We value each one of our employees, and we hope that you find your work here rewarding and satisfying.

This section introduces you to our Company's history, purpose, and goals. Please read it carefully so that you can better understand who we are and what we do. We think we are a special place, made all the more so by the hard work and dedication of our employees.

Additional Clause to Insert Company-Specific Information

This welcome will be even more effective if you add some concrete information about the company. Although some of this information will overlap with information you include in your introduction and history sections (see Policies 1:2 and 1:4, below), it doesn't hurt to give employees a preview here. Consider mentioning:

- How long your company has been in existence. For example: "We're an energetic and creative bunch, dedicated to high standards of excellence since 1902 when the Martinez family first opened this company's doors at 311 Main Street."
- The services or products that your company provides. For example: "Our company has dedicated itself to providing superior printing services since 1902."
- A description of your company's culture. For example: "As a family-owned company, we run a casual operation where people feel free to decorate their workspaces and wear clothes that reflect their personality. Don't let the informality fool you, however. We demand excellence from ourselves and

our employees, and we consider ourselves to be the premier printing company in the Tri-State Area."

If you do add company-specific information to this welcome statement, keep it brief. Your employees will be getting more detailed information from the policies that follow.

CAUTION

Don't make big promises in a handbook. Be careful not to say anything that could create an implied contract with your employees promising to terminate them only for cause. (See Chapter 2 for more about implied contracts and termination for cause.) Avoid statements that promise employees a long future at the company, for example.

1:2 Introduction to the Company

File Name: 01_Introduction.rtf

Include This Policy?
☐ Yes
☐ No
☐ Use our existing policy
☐ Other _____

Alternate Modifications
None

Additional Clauses
None

Related Policies
None

Notes
_____
_____
_____
_____
_____
_____
_____
_____
_____
_____
_____
_____
_____
_____
_____
_____

1:2 Introduction to the Company

The beginning pages of a handbook are a great place to briefly introduce employees to a company's background, history, and culture. (You will delve into your company's history in more detail later. See Policy 1:4, below.) In the Introduction, speak directly to employees and present the company as you want them to see it.

During employees' day-to-day work at your company, information about your company's values and goals will trickle down to them from supervisors, managers, coworkers, and customers. Unfortunately, this means that sometimes employees will hear things about your company that aren't true or that are distorted by the prejudices and personalities of the people around them. If these are an employee's first impressions of your company, they will be hard to undo. The Introduction is your opportunity to get in the first word about your company and to make a good first impression.

There is no standard policy language that we can provide to convey your company's unique personality; that's up to you. Here is an example of what an introduction might look like.

> **SAMPLE POLICY LANGUAGE**
>
> Juanita Jones founded this company in 1978 on a very basic principle: Customers will pay for exceptional service and knowledge. Using that principle as her beacon, she took a small independent bookstore and created a chain of 30 stores serving customers throughout the western United States.
>
> Here at J&J Books, we continue to believe that a knowledgeable and courteous staff can sell more books than discount prices can. For this reason, we encourage our employees to read the publishing and literary magazines that you will find in the break room, to use your employee discount to buy and read as many books as possible, and to take advantage of our tuition reimbursement program to take literature and writing classes at local colleges. When our customers come to you with questions, we want you to be able to answer them—with a smile.
>
> We know that only happy and relaxed employees can give the quality and good-natured service that our customers demand. So take all of the breaks you are scheduled for, alert your manager to any problems in your work area, and communicate any ideas you might have for making this a better place to work.
>
> At J&J Books, we want our employees to put the customer first. That's why we, in management, put our employees first. We know that we are only as good as you are.

Drafting Your Own Policy

All sorts of information can go into your Introduction, from a heartfelt description of your company's values to an inventory of the products you create and sell. When you write this policy, imagine sitting across from a single employee. What do you want this person to know about your company? What do you think the essence of your company is? What sort of attitude do you want this employee to have toward customers and clients? What information about your company would be useful to this employee in doing the job?

Consider including the following information in this policy:

- Outline the values that are most important to your company's success, such as customer service, product quality, or high-speed productivity. Be as concrete as possible. Do you always do what the customer wants, no matter how much time and effort it takes? Do you try to fill all orders within one day? Do you always redo orders, no questions asked, if a customer complains?

- Explain why these values are important to your company's success.

- Describe any goals your company has (for example, doubling sales in the next decade or lowering operating costs).

- State the values and goals that each employee should have. For example, it may be more important to your company for employees to develop friendly relationships with customers than to pressure customers into making purchases they don't really need.

- Describe your company culture.

- Give a description of the products your company produces or the services it provides.

- Provide an organizational chart for your company.

1:3 Mission Statement

File Name: 01_Introduction.rtf

Include This Policy?

☐ Yes
☐ No
☐ Use our existing policy
☐ Other _____

Alternate Modifications

None

Additional Clauses

None

Related Policies

None

Notes

_____
_____
_____
_____
_____
_____
_____
_____
_____
_____
_____
_____
_____
_____
_____
_____
_____
_____
_____
_____

1:3   Mission Statement

Most modern businesses and organizations have mission statements as part of their overall business or strategic plan. If you have a mission statement, share it with your employees in your handbook. It is yet another way to educate your employees about your company. It helps them understand why they are there and how they should act. It also helps them see the big picture of what your organization is and what it is trying to accomplish in the world.

If you do not have a mission statement, see the guidelines for drafting one, below.

> **SAMPLE POLICY LANGUAGE**
>
> The mission of *The Daily News* is to enhance and protect our community through journalism that informs, educates, and inspires.

Drafting Your Own Policy

When writing your mission statement, try to think of the essence of why your organization exists. If you run a business, you certainly want to make money, but there is always more to a business's mission than the mere desire for profit. Ask yourself: Why do I run this business? Why is it in this place? Why is this business important? This should get you in the mindset of articulating your company's mission.

Like the sample above, the mission statement should be short and to the point. Most are no longer than one sentence. Information about your company history and culture can go into other policies. The mission statement should be short enough that employees can memorize it, yet long enough to provide information about:

- what you do
- whom you do it for
- how you do it, and
- why you do it.

1:4 History of the Company

The more pride your employees take in your company as a whole, the more pride they will take in their own performance. Telling the history of your company is one way to instill this pride. It can make employees feel like they are part of something special.

In addition, knowing this history can make employees more effective in their jobs. Anecdotes about your company's noble beginnings can help your employees sell your company to customers and clients. Funny stories from your company's past can make the company seem more human and friendly.

Although you may have previewed this information in the Welcoming Statement and Introduction to the Company (see Policies 1:1 and 1:2, above), now is the time to go into more detail.

Of course, each company has its own history, and you'll have to decide how best to convey those facts. Here is an example of what this kind of policy might look like.

SAMPLE POLICY LANGUAGE

In 1855, Dante DeMarco opened this newspaper's doors at 111 Main Street—right between City Hall and the county courthouse. It was a fitting geographic location for Dante, who always kept both eyes peeled for scandal and corruption among the city's power elite. While he ran this newspaper, he lived and breathed the journalist's creed: "Afflict the comfortable and comfort the afflicted." He often said his proudest moment was the day Mayor Lou Mixon was forced to resign because of the great Black and Tan Scandal of 1925, a scandal uncovered and publicized by "DeMarco's Moles," as the reporters were then called. "I would have gotten away with it if it hadn't been for that meddling paper," Mixon was heard to say on his way up the jailhouse steps.

Here at the *Daily Conscience and News*, we still believe in the ideals that have won this newspaper three Pulitzer Prizes (the first for the Black and Tan Scandal). As Dante said, we must be the conscience of the city. We want reporters with suspicious and inquisitive minds and editors who won't breathe easy until a story is just right. We are committed to hiring the highest-quality staff. We strive to provide the resources our employees need to keep their work at the highest level. We will never bow to pressure from advertisers or civic leaders. In short, we will continue to be the daily conscience of Cedar Falls.

1:4 History of the Company

File Name: 01_Introduction.rtf

Include This Policy?
- ☐ Yes
- ☐ No
- ☐ Use our existing policy
- ☐ Other _____

Alternate Modifications

None

Additional Clauses

None

Related Policies

None

Notes

Drafting Your Own Policy

Try to entertain your employees; tell them a good story. Get them hooked on your company's past and becoming part of its future. Be as specific as possible. Use concrete details like names, dates, and amounts. If you have pictures from the early days, include them.

In writing your history, don't forget the values and goals that you laid out in the Introduction to the Company section (see Policy 1:2, above). If you can, use the history to illustrate those values and show where they came from.

1:5 Handbook Purpose

Every company should include a purpose statement in its employee handbook. From the beginning, you must make clear to employees that they are expected to read the whole handbook and to incorporate the information they read into their work. After all, what's the use of a handbook if employees don't read it?

There is also a legal reason to include this policy. As we explained in the Introduction to this book, one of the biggest risks of using an employee handbook is that a judge or jury might view it as a contract and hold the company to what it says. One way to minimize this risk is to plainly state that the handbook is not a contract and to emphasize that policies can change at any time, for any reason, and without warning.

The Purpose of This Handbook

We think that employees are happier and more valuable if they know what they can expect from our Company and what our Company expects from them. In the preceding sections, we introduced you to our Company's history, values, culture, and goals. We expect you to incorporate that information into your day-to-day job performance, striving to meet our Company's values in everything you do.

The remainder of this Handbook will familiarize you with the privileges, benefits, and responsibilities of being an employee at our Company. Please understand that this Handbook can only highlight and summarize our Company's policies and practices. For detailed information, you will have to talk to your supervisor or _____ .

In this Company, as in the rest of the world, circumstances are constantly changing. As a result, we may revise, rescind, or supplement these policies from time to time. Nothing in this Handbook is a contract or a promise. The policies can change at any time, for any reason, without warning.

We are always looking for ways to improve communications with our employees. If you have suggestions for ways to improve this Handbook in particular or employee relations in general, please feel free to bring them to _____ .

1:5 The Purpose of This Handbook

File Name: 01_Introduction.rtf

Include This Policy?
- ☐ Yes
- ☐ No
- ☐ Use our existing policy
- ☐ Other _____

Alternate Modifications

None

Additional Clauses

None

Related Policies

None

Notes

_____
_____
_____
_____
_____
_____
_____
_____
_____
_____
_____
_____
_____
_____
_____
_____
_____
_____
_____

How to Complete This Policy

Of course, no handbook can anticipate all of the questions and concerns that your employees might have. For this reason, you must designate people at your company to whom your employees can go for more information. If you have a very small company, there might be only one member of management: you. In larger companies, there might be several levels of management to choose from, or you may want to direct employees to the human resources department, if your company has one. (Policy 1:7 introduces the human resources department.) Adjust this policy to reflect the situation at your company. If possible, name two people (by position, not by name) to whom employees can turn (for example, a supervisor and a human resources director). That way, employees have a choice: If they are uncomfortable with one of their options, they can pick the other. Of course, if you have a small company, there may only be one appropriate person. That's fine, too.

1:6 Bulletin Board

Many employers use a company bulletin board to communicate with their employees about various events, laws, and rules, and to inform employees about changes to information in the handbook. Typical bulletin board postings include legally required notices (for example, about equal employment opportunity laws, wage and hour laws, and the like), flyers about special company events, and an organizational chart.

If you have a company bulletin board, include a policy in the introductory section of your handbook that alerts employees to the board's existence, instructs employees to read the board periodically, and identifies who is allowed to put things on the board.

Be Sure to Check Out Our Bulletin Board

You can find important information about this Company and your employment posted on the bulletin board located at _____

_____ .

This is also the place where we post important information regarding your legal rights, including information about equal employment opportunity laws and wage and hour laws. We expect all employees to read the information on the bulletin board periodically.

Alternate Modifications to Specify Who Can Post

To Prohibit Employees From Posting

Some companies do not want employees posting information on official bulletin boards. If that is the case at your company, add the following paragraph to your policy.

Alternate Modification A

> Because this bulletin board is our way of communicating with employees, we do not allow anyone but managers and Company officials to post information there.

To Allow Employees to Post

Some companies like to allow their employees to post information on company bulletin boards. If you would like to do so, add the following paragraph to your policy.

1:6   Be Sure to Check Out Our Bulletin Board

File Name: 01_Introduction.rtf

Include This Policy?
- ☐ Yes
- ☐ No
- ☐ Use our existing policy
- ☐ Other _____

Alternate Modifications
Specify Who Can Post
Choose one: ☐ A ☐ B

Additional Clauses
None

Related Policies
None

Notes

_____
_____
_____
_____
_____
_____
_____
_____
_____
_____
_____
_____
_____
_____
_____
_____
_____
_____

Alternate Modification B

> If you would like to communicate information to your coworkers, consider using the Company bulletin board. To post something, you must first give it to _____
>
> _____
>
> for approval. Employee notices may remain on the bulletin board for 90 days. After that period, they will be removed.

1:7 Human Resources Department

If your company has a human resources department, that is a wonderful thing. A human resources department can help ensure that your company's most important assets—its human resources—are happy and productive. The human resources department does such things as conduct trainings, field questions about benefits, and handle complaints of illegal discrimination. It also plans staff retreats and recognizes exceptional service. But your employees can't use the human resources department if they don't know about it. Your handbook is a great way to introduce the department to your employees.

Get to Know the Folks in Human Resources

We are fortunate enough to have wonderful human resources professionals who are available to answer your questions, field your complaints, and make our Company run more smoothly. In fact, the policies in this Handbook often refer you to the human resources department for more information or to obtain help. The department is located at _____

_____ ;

its phone number is _____ ;

and its email address is _____ .

1:7 Get to Know the Folks in Human Resources

File Name: 01_Introduction.rtf

Include This Policy?

☐ Yes

☐ No

☐ Use our existing policy

☐ Other _____

Alternate Modifications

None

Additional Clauses

None

Related Policies

None

Notes

_____

_____

_____

_____

_____

_____

_____

_____

_____

_____

_____

_____

_____

_____

_____

_____

_____

_____

_____

At-Will Protections

One of the first—and probably the most important—policies to include in the handbook is an at-will statement. This policy confirms that company employees work "at will": They can be fired at any time and for any reason that is not illegal, and they can quit at any time they like. This policy gives employers some very important legal protection against lawsuits. If an employee sues, claiming that the handbook, the company's unwritten personnel practices, or statements by company managers constituted a promise that he or she would not be fired except for good cause, an at-will policy in the handbook will be the employer's best defense.

The law generally presumes that employees work at will unless they can prove otherwise. As evidence, employees will need to show that they entered into an employment contract with their employer that changed the at-will relationship. If an employer enters into a written employment contract that limits its right to fire an employee—such as a contract that the employee will work for the company for a specified period of time or that the employee may only be fired for specified reasons (misconduct, criminal behavior, or good cause are common examples)— that employee no longer works at will. These written contracts won't be affected by the sample at-will policy we provide, and you don't want them to be. In those relatively rare situations when the company really wants an employee to come on board (or stay there) for a set period of time, offering an employment contract that limits the company's right to fire will help you seal the deal.

> CAUTION
>
> **Montana companies take note.** The state of Montana has greatly restricted the doctrine of at-will employment. In Montana, an employee who is fired without good cause after completing the employer's probationary period (or after six months of work, if the employer has no probationary period) has been wrongfully discharged. This means that the employee can sue for lost wages and benefits, as well as punitive damages (damages intended to punish the employer for wrongdoing) if the firing was fraudulent or malicious. What's more, an employer that violates its own written policies in firing an employee has also committed a wrongful discharge. Because of these unique rules, Montana employers should consult with a lawyer in creating their handbooks.

Even if employees don't have written employment contracts, they can still argue that they were promised, either outright or by implication, that they would not be fired without good cause. These employees might point to conversations with managers ("He said I would always have a position with the company, as long as my sales numbers were strong"), your company's personnel practices

("The company has never fired someone without a good reason"), or official company statements ("At ABC Company, we are loyal to our valued employees; because our employees know we will always be here for them, they can always be here for you") to argue that they had an unwritten contract of employment that limits the company's right to fire at will. To defeat these types of claims—"oral contract" claims if the employee argues that explicit promises were made limiting the company's right to fire, or "implied contract" claims if the employee argues that statements and actions by company decision makers limited the right to fire—you will need something more than an at-will policy. You'll also need a form for employees to sign agreeing to their at-will status. You'll find both in this chapter.

2:1 At-Will Policy

Your at-will policy should clearly state that the company retains the right to fire employees at will and that nothing in the handbook constitutes a contract or promise to the contrary. You should also designate someone (or more than one person) who is solely authorized to make employment contracts on behalf of the company. This will allow the company to relinquish its at-will rights if necessary for a particular employee.

Employment Is At Will

We are happy to welcome you to our Company. We sincerely hope that your employment here will be a positive and rewarding experience. However, we cannot make any guarantees about your continued employment at our Company. Your employment here is at will. This means that you are free to quit at any time, for any reason, just as we are free to terminate your employment at any time, for any reason—with or without notice, with or without cause.

No employee or company representative, other than _____

_____ ,

has the authority to change the at-will employment relationship or to contract with any employee for different terms of employment. Furthermore, _____

may change the at-will employment relationship only in a written contract, signed by _____

and the employee. Nothing in this Handbook constitutes a contract or promise of continued employment.

CAUTION

Check your state law for formatting requirements!
Because an at-will policy and disclaimer limit an employee's right to sue the employer, some courts consider how prominent and clear these documents are in deciding whether an employee really understood their significance. In South Carolina, for example, employers may avoid contract claims if they adopt an at-will policy as the first page of their handbook, in underlined, capital letters, and require employees to sign it. If your state has a similar law, you should modify our policy and acknowledgment as necessary to make sure you get the full benefit of the statute. Talk to a local employment lawyer to find out about requirements like these.

2:1   Employment Is At Will

File Name: 02_Employment.rtf

Include This Policy?
☐ Yes
☐ No
☐ Use our existing policy
☐ Other _____

Alternate Modifications
None

Additional Clauses
None

Related Policies
None

Notes

Who Needs This Policy

Some employers—particularly small businesses, "mom and pop" enterprises, and companies with trusted long-term employees—may wonder if they want an at-will policy. After all, they are not planning to fire employees without a good reason, so why adopt a policy that says they can? The reason is simply to hedge your bets. Even if a company never plans to act without good cause, the safest course of action is to adopt an at-will policy that preserves its right to do so, just in case. If a fired worker decides to challenge the employer's decision in a lawsuit, the employer won't have to prove that it had good cause to fire the employee; the at-will policy makes this unnecessary. Most judges will be easily convinced to throw out the employee's contract claim very early on in the lawsuit, saving the company from spending a lot of time and money justifying its decisions.

The truth is companies cannot know ahead of time that they will never have to rely on an at-will policy. Sometimes, an employee just doesn't work out, for reasons that might not conclusively add up to "good cause" to a judge or jury. If the company has a clear at-will policy, it can simply fire that worker and move on. If it does not, the safest course of action from a legal perspective might be to keep the employee on, gathering evidence and documenting problems until management can prove good cause to fire. For as long as it takes, the employee will keep on mucking up the works, while management spends time building a legal case rather than improving the company's fortunes.

Despite the benefits of an at-will policy, some companies choose not to adopt one. There are a few advantages to forgoing an at-will policy, with improved employee relations topping the list. Employees are generally not happy to open an employee handbook and read that they can be fired at any time, for any reason. A company that promises to give workers a fair shake might reap some rewards, like improved loyalty and more positive attitudes toward the company.

Every employer has to decide for itself whether to assert its at-will rights in the employee handbook. Given the clear benefits of having such a policy—and the real dangers of leaving one out—we strongly recommend that all employers adopt an at-will policy, whether they plan to rely on it or not. There are plenty of other ways to show employees that the company values their work.

How to Complete This Policy

The sample policy above provides a space where you should name a company officer who can modify the at-will relationship. This provision gives the company discretion to enter into employment contracts that limit its right to fire, while at the same time protecting its at-will rights over the rest of its employees.

Most companies will want to designate the highest company officer, such as the president, CEO, or owner of the company. Take care to select someone at the highest echelons of company management. The company should have complete control over who gets an employment contract and who doesn't. Also, be sure to designate this person by position (for example, the president of the company) rather than by name. Although you may not anticipate any changes in the company ladder, you never know what the future might bring. By omitting any names from this policy, you ensure that the policy won't require any changes if the person currently holding that position leaves the company.

Some companies designate more than one person who can make contracts. This is fine as long as you authorize only a few people, at most. The more people who have the right to make contracts, the higher the likelihood that someone will enter into a contract that important company decision makers don't know about (and may later come to regret).

CAUTION

The National Labor Relations Board is showing interest in at-will policies and acknowledgments. Starting in 2012, the National Labor Relations Board (NLRB) issued several decisions and opinion memos on at-will handbook provisions. The NLRB was concerned that requiring an employee to agree that at-will status could never be changed might discourage employees to join together, in a union or otherwise, to improve the terms and conditions of their employment or seek a collective bargaining agreement that changes their at-will status. (This right to act jointly is legally protected, whether or not a company has a union.) Thus far, the NLRB has approved of policies that, like ours, give the employer the right to change at-will status and do not require employees to agree that at-will status can never be changed. However, this issue remains in play. When you get your final legal review of the completed handbook, make sure the attorney checks the NLRB's current pronouncements on at-will policy language.

Form A: Handbook Acknowledgment Form

Companies that have an at-will policy should also ask employees to sign a form acknowledging that they understand their employment is at will. (You can find this and all other forms on this book's online companion page: See Appendix A for information on accessing it.) To anyone who isn't a lawyer, it probably seems like overkill to have both a policy and a form that essentially restates that policy. But in the legal world, redundancy is not only encouraged; it is sometimes required. In this case, using both a policy and an acknowledgment form gives the company more protection against future lawsuits.

Using an acknowledgment form offers two important benefits. First, it will prevent employees from arguing that they didn't know about or read the at-will policy in the handbook. While some courts might listen to such an argument—especially if that policy was buried deep in a thousand-page manual—all courts presume that people read a written agreement before signing it. Second, a signed, written agreement legally trumps agreements made in less-reliable forms, such as an oral agreement or an implied contract. While having a written policy helps the employer's side of the argument, it's not a contract: It will weight the scales strongly in the company's favor, but it might not deliver the knockout blow. But a signed written agreement is generally conclusive. Courts are not interested in hearing people argue, "Well yes, I signed it, but I thought it didn't apply to me." If an employee tells a court that the company entered into an oral or implied agreement not to fire him or her without good cause, having an acknowledgment form signed by that employee should put an end to the employee's claim.

The handbook acknowledgment form should explain the importance of the handbook, state that the handbook can be changed at any time and does not constitute a contract of continued employment, and explain the at-will policy again, so employees can sign the form to acknowledge their understanding of the policy.

How to Complete This Form

In the space provided, insert the position of the person who has the authority to enter into contracts on behalf of the company. This language should track the language of your at-will policy, above.

Handbook Acknowledgment Form

By signing this form, I acknowledge that I have received a copy of the Company's Employee Handbook. I understand that it contains important information about the Company's policies, that I am expected to read the Handbook and familiarize myself with its contents, and that the policies in the Handbook apply to me. I understand that nothing in the Handbook constitutes a contract or promise of continued employment and that the Company may change the policies in the Handbook at any time.

By signing this form, I acknowledge that my employment is at will. I understand that I have the right to end the employment relationship at any time and for any reason, with or without notice, with or without cause, and that the Company has the same right. I acknowledge that neither the Company nor I have entered into an employment agreement for a specified period of time, that only _____ _____ may make any agreement contrary to the at-will policy, and that any such agreement must be signed and in writing.

_____ .

_____   _____
Employee's Signature   Date

_____
Employee's Name (Print)

Reality Check: Don't Ask Employees to Acknowledge That They've Read the Whole Handbook

Many companies ask employees to agree, in the acknowledgment form, that they have already read the handbook. This is not realistic, nor is it sensible. You want employees to sign the at-will acknowledgment right away, preferably as part of the first-day paperwork. This lets employees know where they stand right from the start, so they don't feel like you waited to spring an unpleasant surprise on them. It also gives employees less time to have the kinds of conversations and interactions with others that can lead to implied or oral contract claims. In short, the sooner this form is signed, the better.

On the other hand, most employees are not going to take an hour or more out of their first day of work to read the employee handbook from cover to cover. While we hope the sample policies we provide in this book are down to earth and easy to understand, let's face it: An employee handbook just isn't thrilling reading material. Employees are more likely to skim through the handbook early on in their employment, then read particular policies in detail as the need arises. By asking the employee to acknowledge only that the handbook is important and that the company expects them to read it, you create a form that employees can sign honestly on their first day of work.

RESOURCE

For more information on at-will employment and employment contracts, see *Dealing With Problem Employees*, by Amy DelPo and Lisa Guerin (Nolo), which explains both in detail. It also contains a sample at-will offer letter that you can modify for use in your own company.

Hiring

You may wonder why you should discuss hiring in an employee handbook. After all, by the time people read the handbook, they've already been hired, right? Although this is true, your company's current employees do need to know a few things about hiring practices, both for themselves (if they choose to apply for another job within the company) and for friends and colleagues whom they might try to recruit to join the company. In addition, communicating how your company hires is yet another way to inform employees about company culture and values.

3:1 Commitment to Equal Opportunity

File Name: 03_Hiring.rtf

Include This Policy?

☐ Yes

☐ No

☐ Use our existing policy

☐ Other_____

Alternate Modifications

Specify Protected Characteristics

Choose one: ☐ A ☐ B

Additional Clauses

None

Related Policies

19:1 Antidiscrimination Policy

Notes

_____

_____

_____

_____

_____

_____

_____

_____

_____

_____

_____

_____

_____

_____

_____

_____

_____

_____

_____

3:1 Equal Opportunity

It's nice to start the handbook's hiring section with an Equal Opportunity Policy that acknowledges the existence of anti-discrimination laws and affirms your company's commitment to follow them in the hiring process. (For more information about antidiscrimination laws, see Chapter 19.)

Commitment to Equal Opportunity

Our Company believes that all people are entitled to equal employment opportunity.

Who Needs This Policy

Although neither state nor federal law requires it, all employers who are covered by any combination of state or federal antidiscrimination laws should begin the hiring section of their handbook with a statement acknowledging these laws and the company's commitment to follow them throughout the hiring process. Not only will employees appreciate hearing this, but the handbook language can also be a handy piece of evidence should a disgruntled applicant ever file a lawsuit against your company alleging discriminatory hiring practices.

If you don't know which antidiscrimination laws apply to your company, then you should find out. These laws cover every aspect of your company's relationship with its employees, and ignorance of them leaves your company vulnerable to costly and embarrassing accusations and lawsuits. (See Chapter 19 for help in finding out which laws cover your workplace.)

Alternate Modifications to Specify Protected Characteristics

To Pledge to Follow the Law

If your company is big enough to be covered by state, local, and federal antidiscrimination laws, but you do not want to list specific protected characteristics in your policy, add the following language to your policy.

Alternate Modification A

We follow state, local, and federal laws prohibiting discrimination in hiring and employment. We do not discriminate against employees or applicants in violation of those laws.

To List Specific Characteristics

If you know which state, local, and federal laws cover your workplace, and which characteristics these laws protect (for example, race, color, religion, national origin, gender, age, disability, and veteran status, among others), you can be more specific in this policy and actually list for your employees the characteristics that are protected. To do so, add the following language to your policy.

Alternate Modification B

We do not discriminate against employees or applicants on the basis of _____

_____

_____

_____

_____

_____

_____

or any other characteristic protected by state or federal law.

3:2 Recruitment

File Name: 03_Hiring.rtf

Include This Policy?
- ☐ Yes
- ☐ No
- ☐ Use our existing policy
- ☐ Other _____

Alternate Modifications

None

Additional Clauses

Encourage Current Employees to Apply

   Insert?: ☐ Yes ☐ No

Referral Bonus Program

   Insert?: ☐ Yes ☐ No

Related Policies

None

Notes

_____
_____
_____
_____
_____
_____
_____
_____
_____
_____
_____
_____
_____
_____
_____

3:2 Recruitment

If you want current employees to help in recruitment efforts, then ask for their help in the hiring section of the handbook. The following policy explains where and how your company will look for new employees (for example, referrals, advertising, or employment agencies). It also encourages current employees to help generate ideas about how to find talented people who will fit into the workplace.

Recruitment

We know that we are only as good as our employees, so we search as widely as possible for talented and motivated individuals to fill vacant positions in our Company. Our recruitment methods include _____

_____

_____ .

   Although these methods have served us well in the past, we know that the marketplace is ever changing and that finding high-quality people is an evolving process. We encourage our employees to share their ideas about what more we can do to find and recruit talented and motivated individuals.

   We conduct all recruiting in a fair and nondiscriminatory manner.

Additional Clause to Encourage Current Employees to Apply

If you would like to encourage current employees to apply for transfer or promotion to vacant positions (see Policy 3:3, below, for more on this), make the following paragraph the second-to-the-last paragraph of the policy.

Additional Clause

   In addition to looking outside the Company for new hires, we also look within. After all, we already know the value and quality of our current employees. We post all internal job openings on _____

_____

[*give the location where you will post job openings*]. If you see a posting for a job that interests you, we encourage you to apply for it by following our internal application process (see below).

Although some employers promise to give priority for vacant positions to current employees, we recommend against limiting your options in this way. Sometimes, you'll want to look outside your workplace for a new hire, even if there is someone currently on staff who could fill the position.

Additional Clause If You Have a Referral Bonus Program

If you give bonuses to employees who refer new hires to you (see Policy 3:4, below, for more on this), add this before the final paragraph of the policy.

Additional Clause

> We also encourage employees to recruit and refer external applicants for open positions. If you refer someone whom we eventually hire, we will thank you for your efforts with a referral bonus. See "Refer a New Hire; Get a Bonus!" below, for details.

3:3   Internal Application Process

File Name: 03_Hiring.rtf

Include This Policy?
- ☐ Yes
- ☐ No
- ☐ Use our existing policy
- ☐ Other _____

Alternate Modifications

None

Additional Clauses

None

Related Policies

None

Notes

_____
_____
_____
_____
_____
_____
_____
_____
_____
_____
_____
_____
_____
_____
_____
_____
_____
_____
_____
_____
_____

3:3   Internal Application Process

If you'd like to encourage current employees to apply for open positions, a good place to start is in the handbook. Allowing good employees to change jobs within your company (as opposed to looking for better jobs outside your company) is a win-win situation: Your company gets to retain good employees, while the employees stay motivated by taking jobs that interest them rather than sticking with jobs that have grown stale.

The following policy gives employees permission to apply for vacancies and tells them how to do so. Again, it's a good idea to list the position of the person to whom employees should apply rather than a particular name so that you do not have to change the policy if the person holding that position should change.

Internal Application Process

Sometimes, the best person for a job is already on our payroll. We encourage current employees to apply for vacant positions that interest them.

We post all internal job openings on _____
_____ .

To apply for a position, give a cover letter, current résumé, and copy of the job posting to _____
_____ .

3:4   Employee Referral Bonus Program

Sometimes, a company's employees are the ones best situated to find and recruit new talent on its behalf. Although some employees will do this out of dedication to the company (and their job-seeking friends), others need a little more motivation. Many employers like to sweeten the pot by promising bonuses to employees who find successful applicants for open positions.

The following policy promises a bonus to employees who successfully refer a potential employee to fill a vacant position.

Refer a New Hire; Get a Bonus!

Our employees know our needs and Company culture better than anyone else and are often the best situated to find and recruit new employees to fill open positions within our ranks.

Alternate Modifications to Specify Bonus Details

To Give One Bonus for All Positions

You will have to decide what kind of bonus to give to employees. This will depend on your company's culture and finances, as well as the standards in your industry. For example:

- Many nonprofits give one or two paid days off as a bonus.
- Small businesses often give $500 to $1,000.
- Corporate law firms give as much as $10,000.

To specify one bonus in your policy, add the language below.

Alternate Modification A

To encourage employees to act as recruiters on our behalf, and to reward employees who help make a successful match, we operate an Employee Referral Bonus Program. We will give _____ _____ to any employee who refers an individual whom we hire.

To find out more about the program, or to refer a potential applicant for an open position, contact _____ _____ .

3:4   Refer a New Hire; Get a Bonus!

File Name: 03_Hiring.rtf

Include This Policy?
- ☐ Yes
- ☐ No
- ☐ Use our existing policy
- ☐ Other _____

Alternate Modifications
Specify Bonus Details
Choose one: ☐ A   ☐ B

Additional Clauses
Exclude Some From the Policy
Insert?:   ☐ Yes   ☐ No

Related Policies
None

Notes

_____
_____
_____
_____
_____
_____
_____
_____
_____
_____
_____
_____
_____
_____
_____
_____
_____

To Offer Different Bonuses for Different Positions

Some companies would pay a king's ransom to find a top-notch professional, such as a design engineer or a chief financial officer, but not to locate a rank-and-file employee, such as an assembly line worker or a sales clerk.

If there are positions that your company values more highly than others, you can create a policy that pays a different bonus depending on the position. For example, if you operate a law firm, you might offer a bonus of $5,000 for lawyers, $2,500 for paralegals, $1,000 for secretaries, and $500 for file clerks.

You can either name the positions (as in the previous example) or you can give a category of positions (for example, professional, support staff, and so on).

If you would like to create a tiered bonus system, simply add the following language to your policy.

Alternate Modification B

To encourage employees to act as recruiters on our behalf, and to reward employees who help make a successful match, we operate an Employee Referral Bonus Program. The amount of the bonus depends on the position that you have helped to fill:

Position: _____ Bonus: _____

Position: _____ Bonus: _____

Position: _____ Bonus: _____

Position: _____ Bonus: _____

Additional Clause to Exclude Some From the Policy

If you have people in your company whose job it is to find new employees for you, their paycheck is reward enough for accomplishing the task; you don't need to add a bonus on top of that. These people usually include officers in the company (the president, the chief executive officer, and the chief financial officer), members of the human resources department, and on-staff recruiters.

If you would like to exclude people in certain positions from the bonus program, add the following paragraph to your policy.

Additional Clause

People holding the following positions may not participate in the Employee Referral Bonus Program: _____

_____ .

3:5   Employment of Relatives

File Name: 03_Hiring.rtf

Include This Policy?

☐ Yes

  Choose one: ☐ A ☐ B

☐ No

☐ Use our existing policy

☐ Other _____

Alternate Modifications

None. (Entire policy has two alternate versions from which you must choose.)

Additional Clauses

Policy B only: Current Employees Who Become Related

  Insert?:   ☐ Yes   ☐ No

Related Policies

None

Notes

_____
_____
_____
_____
_____
_____
_____
_____
_____
_____
_____
_____
_____
_____
_____

3:5 Nepotism

Many employers like to think of their company as a family. However, when actual family members of employees start filling a company's ranks, complications can arise. How does your company feel about a husband supervising a group of employees that includes his wife? What about the CEO's son taking a part-time job in the mailroom? Or siblings working side by side on the assembly line?

Even if your company doesn't have any concerns about these things, employees might. For example, it could be a little awkward for the mailroom manager to supervise and discipline his boss's son. Or downright impossible for an employee to complain to a supervisor about the behavior of the supervisor's spouse. Not to mention the troubles that can arise for coworkers when family members don't get along.

Many employers choose to allow family members to work for the same company, as long as they don't work together, or at least don't supervise each other. Other employers have a strict policy against nepotism, preferring to play it safe and keep clear of any potential conflicts or favoritism that could crop up.

Policy A, below, allows employment of relatives. Policy B, below, prohibits employment of relatives.

Policy A

Employment of Relatives

Usually, this Company will not refuse to hire someone simply because he or she is related to one of our current employees. If you have a relative who might be perfect to fill an open position in our Company, please don't hesitate to refer this person to us.

There are times, however, when employing relatives is inappropriate and has the potential to affect the morale of other employees and to create conflicts of interest for the relatives involved.

Therefore, we will not hire relatives of current employees where one relative will have to supervise the other.

If two employees become related while working for this Company, and if one of them is in a position of supervision over the other, only one of the employees will be allowed to keep his or her current position. The other will either have to transfer to another position or leave the Company.

Under this policy, the term "relatives" encompasses spouses, live-in partners, domestic partners, parents, children, siblings, in-laws, cousins, aunts, and uncles. This policy covers biological relationships, marriage relationships, and step relationships.

Policy B

Employment of Relatives

We do not allow family members of current employees to take jobs with our Company. We believe the risk of morale problems, security problems, and conflict of interest problems is too great.

Under this policy, the term "relatives" encompasses spouses, live-in partners, domestic partners, parents, children, siblings, in-laws, cousins, aunts, and uncles. This policy covers biological relationships, marriage relationships, and step relationships.

SEE AN EXPERT

If your company operates in a state that prohibits discrimination based on marriage or family status, check with a lawyer for assistance in creating and administering the nepotism policy. Some of these states view it as discriminatory to transfer, terminate, or refuse to hire someone because he or she is married or related to a coworker. Other states view a nepotism policy as an acceptable exception to the antidiscrimination law (at least in some situations). You'll need a lawyer's assistance to find out where your state stands on these issues. (To find out if you live in a state that prohibits discrimination based on marriage or family status, see the chart at the end of Chapter 19.)

Additional Clause for Current Employees Who Become Related

Sometimes, current employees become related through marriage. In such a situation, an employer with a strict antinepotism policy will have to decide whether it will make an exception for those employees or whether it will force one of the employees to quit.

Doing the latter is certainly the most consistent approach, but it has a few significant drawbacks:

- It punishes employees for marrying or moving in together rather than just dating.
- It forces an otherwise valuable employee to leave your ranks.
- It could pose a problem if your state prohibits discrimination based on marital status, as discussed above.

Only you can decide the way you want to go on this issue. If you would like to create an exception for current employees who become related, add the following paragraph to the policy.

Additional Clause

If two employees become related while working for this Company, they will both be allowed to remain with the Company. However, if one of them supervises the other, only one of the employees will be allowed to keep his or her current position. The other will either have to transfer to another position or leave the Company.

New Employee Information

Although the entire handbook will include information for both new and long-term employees, there are a few policies to include exclusively for new employees. In this section of your handbook, you can tell new employees what to expect during their initial weeks of employment. You can also advise them about information the company will collect for the government regarding their immigration status and any outstanding child support obligations.

4:1   New Employee Orientation

File Name: 04_New Employee Info.rtf

Include This Policy?

☐ Yes

☐ No

☐ Use our existing policy

☐ Other _____

Alternate Modifications

None

Additional Clauses

None

Related Policies

Form A: Handbook Acknowledgment Form should be part of every employee's first-day paperwork. (For this form and a related discussion, see Chapter 2.)

Notes

_____
_____
_____
_____
_____
_____
_____
_____
_____
_____
_____
_____
_____
_____
_____
_____
_____
_____
_____

4:1   New Employee Orientation

Some employers schedule an orientation meeting or program for new employees. This meeting can take many forms. Large employers who routinely hire many employees at a time might schedule a group gathering in a conference room, while smaller employers might simply set up a time for a new hire to get together with a benefits administrator or human resources employee. No matter what type of orientation your company uses, it serves three purposes: (1) to explain company procedures to new employees (for example, about payroll, scheduling vacations, and signing up for health insurance benefits); (2) to take care of all of that pesky first-day paperwork; and (3) to answer any questions new employees might have.

New Employee Orientation

Within a day or two of starting work, you will be scheduled for a new employee orientation meeting. During this meeting, you will receive important information about our Company's policies and procedures. You will also be asked to complete paperwork and forms relating to your employment, such as tax withholding forms, emergency contact forms, and benefits paperwork.

Please feel free to ask any questions you might have about the Company during the orientation meeting. If additional questions come up after the meeting, you can ask your supervisor or _____

_____ .

How to Complete This Policy

In the blank, insert the title or position of the person who conducts the new employee orientation meetings (for example, human resources manager, benefits administrator, or office manager).

4:2 Orientation Period

Many employers use an orientation period for their new employees. During this time, the employee can learn how to do the job and what the company expects, and the company can offer the employee extra supervision and make sure that the employee is going to make the grade. As sensible as such policies may be, they can also create a legal risk for employers. Orientation policies must be carefully drafted with an eye toward preserving the at-will employment relationship. (For more on at-will employment, see Chapter 2.)

Employers get into trouble with orientation policies that state or imply that completion of the orientation period guarantees the worker a job, makes the worker a "permanent employee," or otherwise limits the employer's right to fire the worker at will. The orientation period is a trial run of sorts: It gives both employer and employee a chance to make sure that there's a good fit between the worker and the job. But emphasizing this too strongly in an orientation policy can lead workers to expect that completing their orientation means they've "made the cut" and, thereafter, will be fired only for good cause. To avoid this potential legal pitfall, the sample policy we provide clearly states that employment is at will both during and after the orientation period.

4:2 Orientation Period

File Name: 04_New Employee Info.rtf

Include This Policy?

☐ Yes

☐ No

☐ Use our existing policy

☐ Other _____

Alternate Modifications

None

Additional Clauses

Extend Orientation Period

Insert?: ☐ Yes ☐ No

Related Policies

None

Notes

_____

_____

_____

_____

_____

_____

_____

_____

_____

_____

_____

_____

_____

_____

_____

_____

_____

CAUTION

Montana employers must follow different rules. The state of Montana has greatly limited the doctrine of at-will employment. Montana law provides that an employee who has completed the employer's probationary period—or who has worked for the employer for at least six months, if the employer has not adopted a probationary period—may be fired only for good cause. Because of this requirement, Montana employers probably won't want to adopt a probationary or orientation period of less than six months. If your company does business in Montana, get some legal advice on how best to preserve your rights while staying within the law.

Who Needs This Policy

Employers are not required to have an orientation policy or to make any special arrangements to train new employees. If your company treats new employees like everyone else, you don't need this policy.

However, many employers do use a probationary, orientation, or "new employee" period. If your company is one of them, using this policy will help you avoid jeopardizing the company's right to fire employees at will.

This orientation policy offers other benefits as well. It lets new workers know where to go with questions or concerns, and it allows the company to create a waiting period before employee benefits go into effect. (See "How to Complete This Policy," below.)

Orientation Period

The first _____ days of your employment are an orientation period. During this time, your supervisor will work with you to help you learn how to do your job successfully and what the Company expects of you. This period also provides both you and the Company with an opportunity to decide whether you are suited for the position for which you were hired.

When your employment begins, you will meet with _____ _____ , who will explain our benefits and payroll procedures and assist you in completing your employment paperwork. (For our Company's benefits policies, see Section _____ of this Handbook.) You will also meet with your supervisor to go over your job goals and performance requirements. During the orientation period, your supervisor will give you feedback on your performance and will be available to answer any questions you might have.

Employees are not eligible for the following benefits unless and until they complete the orientation period: _____

_____ .

Although we hope that you will be successful here, the Company may terminate your employment at any time, either during the orientation period or afterwards, with or without cause and with or without notice. You are also free to quit at any time and for any reason, either during the orientation period or afterwards, with or without notice. Successful completion of your orientation period does not guarantee you a job for any period of time or in any way change the at-will employment relationship. (For an explanation of at-will employment, see Section _____ of this Handbook.)

CAUTION

New employees have legal rights, too. Although employers are allowed to require new employees to work for a certain period of time before they are eligible for fringe benefits, employers must follow the law in dealing with new employees. Wage and hour laws, antidiscrimination laws, occupational safety laws, and many other workplace protections apply to workers from their very first day on the job. While employers can condition discretionary benefits on tenure at the company, they cannot place their new employees' legal rights on hold until they complete an orientation period.

How to Complete This Policy

Our sample policy leaves you a space to indicate how long the orientation period will be. Ninety days is a fairly standard length for an orientation period. It's long enough to give employees a chance to learn the ropes and show what they can do, but not so long that you'll be stuck mentoring new workers forever. However, some employers use a 60-day period or some other time frame that better fits their business model. For example, if workers have quarterly sales goals or change assignments every two months, you might want to use these time periods instead.

We also leave you space to list the benefits that won't be available to new employees during the orientation period. For example, many employers impose a waiting period for health insurance coverage (if they are allowed to; see Chapter 8) or employer contributions to a retirement fund. Some employers do not allow their employees to use sick or vacation time during the orientation period. If you plan to impose such a waiting period, list the benefits that will not be available to new employees here.

We also leave you space to designate the person who will explain benefits, payroll procedures, and other administrative matters to new employees. If you have a human resources function, you can insert someone from the human resources department here. If not, designate the position that handles these matters (for example, the payroll administrator or benefits coordinator).

Additional Clause to Extend Orientation Period

Some orientation policies provide that the orientation period can be extended at the employer's discretion. The purpose of such an addition is to provide some extra time to evaluate a worker, if necessary. For example, if the worker doesn't seem to be getting the hang of things, or if unusual circumstances during the orientation period prevented the worker from receiving sufficient training and feedback, the option of a longer period might be helpful. If you wish to include this provision, add this language to the end of the first paragraph.

Additional Clause

Your orientation period may be extended if the Company decides that such an extension is appropriate.

4:3   Work Eligibility

A federal law called the Immigration Reform and Control Act (IRCA) requires all employers to verify, within the first three days of employment, that a new hire is legally eligible to work in the United States. The employer must require each new employee to complete an I-9 Form, show identification, and present proof of employment eligibility.

The work eligibility policy should tell employees that they will have to present certain documents and complete the I-9 Form and where they can go for more information.

Proof of Work Eligibility

Within three business days of your first day of work, you must complete federal Form I-9 and show us documentation proving your identity and your eligibility to work in the United States. The federal government requires us to do this.

If you have worked for this Company previously, you need only provide this information if it has been more than three years since you last completed an I-9 Form for us or if your current I-9 Form is no longer valid.

Alternate Modifications for New Employee Orientation Procedures

For Companies That Do Not Hold Orientation Meetings

If your company does not provide forms to new employees at a new hire interview or orientation meeting, you should add language to the policy explaining who will provide the I-9 Form and examine the employee's documentation. Simply add the language below as the last paragraph of the policy. In the blank space, designate someone to be responsible for completing and answering questions about the I-9 Form. Typically, that person is the human resources manager or office manager. The same person who deals with new employees' tax and insurance forms can also handle this form.

4:3   Proof of Work Eligibility

File Name: 04_New Employee Info.rtf

Include This Policy?
- ☐ Yes
- ☐ No
- ☐ Use our existing policy
- ☐ Other _____

Alternate Modifications
New Employee Orientation Procedures
  Choose one: ☐ A   ☐ B

Additional Clauses
None

Related Policies
Your policy on personnel files should explain where employees' I-9 Forms will be kept. (For this policy and a related discussion, see Chapter 16.)

Notes

_____

_____

_____

_____

_____

_____

_____

_____

_____

_____

_____

_____

_____

_____

_____

Alternate Modification A

> _____
>
> will give you an I-9 Form and tell you what documentation you must present to us.

For Companies That Hold New Employee Orientation Meetings

If you adopt the first policy in this chapter, your company will hold new hire interviews or orientation meetings at which a designated person will give new employees all the forms they'll need to complete upon joining the company. This stack of forms often includes a Handbook Acknowledgment Form (see Chapter 2), an IRS W-4 Form, and a Form I-9. If your company uses this type of process for new employees, add the following language as the last paragraph of the policy. In the first blank, insert whatever you call this initial meeting, such as "new hire interview" or "orientation meeting." In the second blank, identify the person who is responsible for completing and answering questions about the I-9 Form. Typically, that person is the human resources manager or office manager. The same person who deals with new employees' tax forms and insurance forms can also handle this form.

Alternate Modification B

> At your _____
>
> _____ ,
>
> you should have received a blank Form I-9 and instructions on completing it and presenting the necessary documentation.
> If you did not, contact _____
> immediately.

RESOURCE

For more information on I-9 Forms and employer responsibilities under the Immigration Reform and Control Act, see *The Essential Guide to Federal Employment Laws,* by Lisa Guerin and Sachi Barreiro (Nolo). You can also get free information about the law from Citizenship and Immigration Services, a bureau of the federal Department of Homeland Security, at www.uscis.gov.

4:4 Child Support Reporting Requirements

All employers are required to report information on new employees to a government agency in their state: the State Directory of New Hires. Once the state receives this information, it checks to see whether any of these new employees appear on its list of parents who owe child support. It also forwards the information to the National Directory of New Hires, which compares it to information from other states on child support obligations. If either agency finds a match, it will send the employer a withholding order requiring that a certain amount of that employee's income be withheld and paid to the other parent.

Every state requires employers to provide at least the employee's name, address, and Social Security number, as well as the employer's name, address, and employer identification number, to this agency. Some states require additional information, such as the employee's birth date or the date of the employee's first day of work. Some states allow you to simply submit a copy of the employee's W-4 form; others require you to use a different format.

Child Support Reporting Requirements

Federal and state laws require us to report basic information about new employees, including your name, address, and Social Security number, to a state agency called the State Directory of New Hires. The state collects this information to enforce child support orders. If the state determines that you owe child support, it will send us an order requiring us to withhold money from your paycheck to pay your child support obligations.

Who Needs This Policy

You don't have to tell employees about this requirement; many employers simply gather the information and send it off, without ever mentioning it to their employees. However, an explicit policy explaining the requirement to employees can prevent hassles down the road. If a new hire owes child support and the company has to withhold money from his or her paycheck, you will have to explain the situation, including how the state found the employee in the first place. By explaining up front that the company is legally required to provide this information and obey withholding orders, you let employees know that the company isn't singling anyone out or going

4:4 Child Support Reporting Requirements

File Name: 04_New Employee Info.rtf

Include This Policy?
☐ Yes
☐ No
☐ Use our existing policy
☐ Other _____

Alternate Modifications
None

Additional Clauses
None

Related Policies
None

Notes
_____
_____
_____
_____
_____
_____
_____
_____
_____
_____
_____
_____
_____
_____
_____
_____
_____
_____

out of its way to cause problems for anyone. You also pave the way for easier conversations about any withholding orders that must be followed in the future.

We recommend that employers include a brief policy in their handbook explaining this requirement. You can also include a form for employees to fill out, giving the information your state requires.

RESOURCE

For more information on child support reporting requirements, see *The Essential Guide to Federal Employment Laws,* by Lisa Guerin and Sachi Barreiro (Nolo). You'll also find several helpful resources on these requirements at the website of the Office of Child Support Enforcement, a subdivision of the federal government's Department of Health and Human Services, at www.acf.hhs.gov/css. The website includes a list of each state's requirements and agency information; access it by going to www.acf.hhs.gov/css/employers/employer-responsibilities/new-hire-reporting, and selecting "State New Hire Reporting Contacts and Program Requirements."

Employee Classifications

In any given workplace, there might be five, ten, 30, or more classifications of employees, including such categories as "regular," "temporary," "on call," "per diem," and so on. The list is as endless as the employer's imagination.

Employers like to group workers into classifications for a wide variety of reasons, most having to do with identifying which employees are entitled to certain wages, benefits, and privileges. For example, an employer who does not want to provide benefits to employees who are scheduled to work fewer than 30 hours per week will likely classify employees as part time or full time and will have a policy that allows only full-time employees to receive benefits.

For the most part, the law does not dictate how you classify employees. For example, you can decide how many hours per week employees have to work to be considered full-time employees. (However, this is not true for health insurance if you are subject to the employer mandate under the Affordable Care Act; see Chapter 8.)

The more complicated your workplace, the more employee classifications you might have. We cannot cover all of the various categories into which different employers group their employees. Instead, we tackle the most common ones. The classifications covered by policies in this chapter will meet the needs of the vast majority of small to midsized businesses.

It is important to understand that these categories are not mutually exclusive. They divide employees up according to different criteria, so you could use all (or none) of these classifications depending on your needs. For example, an employee could be both full time and exempt. This would mean that the employee is scheduled to work at least a minimum number of hours per week (full time) and is not entitled to receive overtime under state or federal law (exempt). We discuss these possibilities further in the descriptions of the various employee classifications throughout this chapter.

5:1 Temporary Employees

File Name: 05_Employee Class.rtf

Include This Policy?
☐ Yes
☐ No
☐ Use our existing policy
☐ Other _____

Alternate Modifications
None

Additional Clauses
None

Related Policies
For information and policies about at-will employment, see Chapter 2.

For information and policies on which benefits part-time employees are and are not entitled to, see Chapters 8 and 10.

Notes
_____
_____
_____
_____
_____
_____
_____
_____
_____
_____
_____
_____
_____
_____
_____

5:1   Temporary Employees

Most companies experience times when they need a little extra help. Perhaps you run a retail shop and tend to hire more salespeople during the holidays, or maybe you operate an accounting firm and must hire additional clerical help during tax season.

If you use temporary employees, you must distinguish them from your regular employees. Most companies choose not to extend optional benefits (such as life insurance) or the ability to accrue discretionary leave to temporary employees, and they reserve their right to terminate the employees once the need for their services ends.

Depending on your state law, you may have to extend certain legally mandated benefits to all employees, whether they are hired for a temporary project or for a full-time position. Currently, for example, the District of Columbia and a handful of states (including California and Massachusetts) require employers to provide paid sick leave to their employees. These laws differ in the details, including how long employees must work for their employer before they are entitled to use their accrued paid sick time. Although you may legally preclude temporary employees from your discretionary leave programs (such as vacation time), you may have to include them in your sick leave program if you do business in one of these states.

Similarly, you may have to extend other legally mandated benefits —like workers' compensation and state disability insurance—to temporary employees. Contact your state labor department for details. (See Appendix B for contact information.)

The following policy distinguishes those employees who are working for you on a temporary basis from your regular workforce. It also explains that temporary employees are not entitled to the same benefits and privileges as are regular employees.

Reality Check: Are Those Temporary Employees Really Independent Contractors?

Someone who works for you on a temporary basis may really be an independent contractor, not a temporary employee. If possible, it will usually be to your advantage to classify a worker as an independent contractor, because independent contractors tend to be less expensive than temporary employees. For example, you don't have to provide workers' compensation insurance for them, nor do you have to withhold or pay payroll taxes for them. To learn more about independent contractors, see *Working With Independent Contractors*, by Stephen Fishman (Nolo).

Temporary Employees

Periodically, it becomes necessary for us to hire individuals to perform a job or to work on a project that has a limited duration. Typically, this happens in the event of a special project, special time of year, abnormal workload, or emergency.

Individuals whom we hire for such work are temporary employees. They are not eligible to participate in any of our Company benefit programs, nor can they earn or accrue any discretionary time off, such as vacation leave.

Of course, we will provide to temporary employees any and all benefits mandated by law.

Temporary employees cannot change from temporary status to any other employment status by such informal means as remaining in our employ for a long period of time or through oral promises made to them by coworkers, members of management, or supervisors. The only way a temporary employee's status can change is through a written notification signed by _____ .

Like all employees who work for this Company, temporary employees work on an at-will basis. This means that both they and this Company are free to terminate their employment at any time for any reason that is not illegal, even if they have not completed the temporary project for which they have been hired.

How to Complete This Policy

Sometimes, temporary employees will begin to feel that they are regular employees simply by virtue of the length of time that they have spent with a company, because of something a manager has said to them.

It is important that you don't allow the status of temporary employees to change through these informal methods. Otherwise, you may find yourself obligated to provide benefits and discretionary time off to individuals whom you never wanted to hire in the first place.

Of course, you may on occasion find that you do want to hire temporary employees on a more regular basis, so you'll need some method by which you can change the status of temporary employees.

The fourth paragraph of the sample policy, above, warns temporary employees that their status cannot change informally or by implication. It does, however, give you the ability to change their status through a written notification signed by someone within your company. You should designate by position, not by name. Choose a position that handles hiring decisions at your company or oversees employee benefit or leave programs. A human resources manager or an office manager is often a good choice.

5:2 Part-Time and Full-Time Employees

File Name: 05_Employee Class.rtf

Include This Policy?
- ☐ Yes
- ☐ No
- ☐ Use our existing policy
- ☐ Other _____

Alternate Modifications
None

Additional Clauses
None

Related Policies
None

Notes

_____
_____
_____
_____
_____
_____
_____
_____
_____
_____
_____
_____
_____
_____
_____
_____
_____
_____

5:2 Part-Time and Full-Time Employees

If you have some employees who work fewer hours than others, you may want to treat them differently in terms of benefits and other perks. To do this, it's helpful to classify employees as either part time or full time, depending on how many hours they work each week.

Be aware that under some circumstances, state or federal law will govern whether you can deny certain benefits to part-time workers. For example, the Affordable Care Act or Obamacare (the federal health care reform law) defines full-time employees as those who work at least 30 hours per week. Larger employers must either provide these employees with health insurance meeting a number of requirements or pay a penalty for each employee who isn't adequately covered.

Understanding these benefits laws can be difficult, and determining which workers must be allowed to participate can require complex calculations. Talk to your benefits administrator, accountant, or financial adviser before denying benefits to part-time employees.

Part-Time and Full-Time Employees

Depending on the number of hours per week you are regularly scheduled to work, you are either a part-time or a full-time employee. It is necessary that you understand which of these classifications you fit into, because it will be important in determining whether you are entitled to benefits and leave. (See Section _____ of this Handbook for information about who is entitled to benefits and leave.)

Part-time employees: Employees who are regularly scheduled to work fewer than _____ hours per week are part-time employees.

Full-time employees: Employees who are regularly scheduled to work at least _____ hours per week are full-time employees.

How to Complete This Policy

Your company must decide how many hours per week it requires of employees to entitle them to benefits and leave. Many employers require 40 hours; others require only 32 or 24. You also have the option of prorating benefits and leave. For example, you may call an employee who works 32 hours per week a full-time employee, thereby guaranteeing the employee some benefits and leave, but still prorate the amount of vacation that person is entitled to based on a 40-hour work week. Under such a system, if an employee who works 40 hours per week would earn five vacation days per year, then an employee who works 32 hours per week (four-fifths time) would only earn four (four-fifths of full-time vacation benefits).

5:3   Exempt and Nonexempt Employees

Depending on the type of work employees do, they may be entitled to overtime pay for any hours they work in excess of 40 hours in a week (or, in some states, in excess of eight hours in a day). Classifying workers as exempt or nonexempt is not a matter of choice for you; it is a matter of state and federal law. Most likely, you have already determined for payroll purposes which workers fall into which category.

This policy explains to employees that their right to overtime compensation depends on whether they are classified as exempt or nonexempt, and it explains the difference between the two classifications.

Exempt and Nonexempt Employees

Your entitlement to earn overtime pay depends on whether you are classified as an exempt or a nonexempt employee.

Exempt employees are those who do not earn overtime because they are exempt from the overtime provisions of the federal Fair Labor Standards Act and applicable state laws.

Nonexempt employees are those who meet the criteria for coverage by the overtime provisions of the federal Fair Labor Standards Act and applicable state laws.

If you are uncertain about which category you fall into, speak to _____ .

5:3   Exempt and Nonexempt Employees

File Name: 05_Employee Class.rtf

Include This Policy?
- ☐ Yes
- ☐ No
- ☐ Use our existing policy
- ☐ Other _____

Alternate Modifications
None

Additional Clauses
None

Related Policies
6:5   Overtime
7:6   Pay Docking

Notes

_____
_____
_____
_____
_____
_____
_____
_____
_____
_____
_____
_____
_____
_____
_____
_____
_____
_____
_____

Hours

Employers generally want to be able to dictate when their employees will work: what time they will start and finish, when they will take breaks, and how much—if any—overtime they will work. The policies in this chapter will help your company set these standards. Although some state and federal laws impose restrictions on work hours—for example, requiring employers to pay certain employees an overtime premium if they work more than a prescribed number of hours in a day or week, or mandating that employees receive certain breaks during their shifts—employers are generally free to tell their employees when they must work.

<table>
<tr><td>

6:1 Hours of Work

File Name: 06_Hours.rtf

Include This Policy?
- ☐ Yes
- ☐ No
- ☐ Use our existing policy
- ☐ Other _____

Alternate Modifications

Include Schedule Information

Choose one: ☐ A ☐ B ☐ C

Additional Clauses

None

Related Policies

None

Notes

_____
_____
_____
_____
_____
_____
_____
_____
_____
_____
_____
_____
_____
_____
_____
_____

</td></tr>
</table>

6:1 Hours of Work

Your policy on work hours should tell employees when the company is open for business and when they are expected to be at work. This policy will set the stage for company policies on absenteeism and punctuality. (See Chapter 12.) In the blanks, list the start time, end time, and days of operation (for example, "seven days a week").

Hours of Work

Our Company's regular hours of business are from _____
_____ .

Alternate Modifications to Include Schedule Information

To Have Supervisors Provide Schedule

Some employers want company supervisors to set employee work hours, particularly if employees work a variety of schedules or if employee schedules are subject to change. This allows supervisors to make staffing decisions as they see fit. To use this modification, simply add the following language to your policy.

Alternate Modification A

> Your supervisor will let you know your work schedule, including what time you will be expected to start and finish work each day.

To Specify Hours for All Employees

In some companies, all employees work the same hours. For example, if an employer has limited hours (such as a convenience store that caters to office workers or an after-hours nightclub), it may need all employees to start work at the same time and stop work at the same time. You can use this modification to set the schedule for all workers. Simply add the following language to the end of your policy.

Alternate Modification B

> All employees are expected to be here, ready to start work, when we open. Unless you make other arrangements with your supervisor, you are expected to work until closing time.

To Include Shift Schedules

A variety of businesses, from restaurants and stores to manufacturers and hospitals, operate in shifts. If your company assigns workers to shifts with set schedules, you should modify the work hours policy to let employees know when each shift starts and ends. This will not only tell workers when they are expected to work, but will also let them know what other shifts might be available, if they need or want to change their work schedules.

This modification also advises that any shift changes, whether temporary or permanent, must be approved by a supervisor. This will put employees on notice that they may not simply swap shifts with a coworker whenever they wish, which will give the company more control over work schedules.

If you want to include a shift schedule in your policy, add the following modification to the end of your policy. In the blanks, fill in the number of shifts your company uses and the start and end time of each shift. Our modification includes space for three shifts; if your company has more or fewer shifts, you will have to modify this provision accordingly.

Alternate Modification C

Our Company operates in _____ shifts: from _____ to _____ , from _____ to _____ , and from _____ to _____ . Your supervisor will let you know your shift assignment.

If you wish to change shifts permanently, talk to your supervisor. Although the Company will consider all requests to change shifts, we cannot guarantee that any particular request will be granted.

You may exchange shifts with another employee (that is, switch shifts on a one-time basis) only with the prior approval of your supervisor.

6:2 Flexible Scheduling

File Name: 06_Hours.rtf

Include This Policy?
- ☐ Yes
- ☐ No
- ☐ Use our existing policy
- ☐ Other_____

Alternate Modifications

None

Additional Clauses

None

Related Policies

None

Notes

_____
_____
_____
_____
_____
_____
_____
_____
_____
_____
_____
_____
_____
_____
_____
_____
_____
_____
_____
_____

6:2 Flexible Scheduling ("Flextime")

Many companies offer their employees some form of flexible scheduling, often to accommodate the busy lives of working parents, employees who are attending school, or those who have other pressing needs off the job.

Companies can reap many benefits from allowing their employees to work a flexible schedule. Employees who have sufficient time off work to deal with their outside concerns, be they family commitments, health problems, volunteer work, or school responsibilities, will be better able to concentrate and perform well when they are on the job. Showing concern about employees' lives outside the workplace also goes a long way toward instilling respect and commitment to the company. And some workers simply do a better job—they are more efficient or productive—during certain times of the day. If there are a lot of "morning people" on the payroll, for example, allowing them to start work earlier could boost the bottom line.

If you adopt a flexible scheduling policy, it should tell workers how to request a flexible schedule and what kinds of schedules might be allowed.

Flexible Scheduling

We understand that many employees have to balance the demands of their job with the needs of their families and other outside commitments. Therefore, we offer our employees the opportunity to request a flexible schedule.

If you would like to change your work schedule—for example, to come in and leave a couple of hours earlier or to work more hours on some days and fewer on others—please talk to your supervisor.

The Company will consider flexible scheduling requests on a case-by-case basis. When deciding whether to grant your request, we may consider the nature of your job, your work history, and our staffing needs, among other things.

Reality Check: Deciding Who Gets to Flex

Flexible scheduling can be a tremendous boon to employer and employee alike. However, employers who choose to offer this opportunity must make sure that they dole out the benefits fairly.

An employer that offers a discretionary benefit—that is, a benefit that may be granted for some employees but not for others—must be very careful to have solid business reasons for these decisions. Otherwise, the employer may face legal claims of discrimination. For example, if working mothers are routinely allowed to alter their schedules to meet child care needs but the same benefit isn't always extended to working fathers, an employer could get into trouble. Decision makers must consider each claim for flexible scheduling on its own merits: Can the company accommodate the request without substantial disruption? Does the employee's job lend itself to flexibility? Has the employee demonstrated the responsibility and self-motivation to work outside usual work hours?

CAUTION

Longer days may be costly in some states. A few states have a daily overtime standard. Typically, employers owe overtime to eligible employees who work more than 40 hours in a week. In states with a daily standard, employers owe overtime once an employee works more than eight hours (in California and Alaska) or 12 hours (in Colorado) in a day, even if their weekly hours are less than 40. If you adopt a flexible scheduling policy that allows employees to work more hours on some days and fewer hours on others, you may have to shell out daily overtime pay.

6:3 Meals and Rest Breaks

File Name: 06_Hours.rtf

Include This Policy?
- ☐ Yes
- ☐ No
- ☐ Use our existing policy
- ☐ Other _____

Alternate Modifications

Provide Paid or Unpaid Meal Breaks

Choose one: ☐ A ☐ B

Additional Clauses

None

Related Policies

None

Notes

_____
_____
_____
_____
_____
_____
_____
_____
_____
_____
_____
_____
_____
_____
_____
_____
_____
_____

6:3 Meal and Rest Breaks

Most companies offer their employees some breaks during the day. The laws in some states require employers to provide paid breaks; other states require breaks but don't require employers to pay employees for this time. You can find out what your state requires by consulting "State Meal and Rest Break Laws" at the end of this chapter.

Even if your state doesn't require any breaks, you should adopt a break policy if your company generally allows employees to take breaks. Having a written policy will reduce confusion over how much time can be taken and whether it will be paid or unpaid.

Your policy on meal and rest breaks should let employees know when they get breaks, how long they can take, and whether those breaks are paid. Your policy should also tell employees that they must take their scheduled breaks unless they have made other arrangements with their supervisor. Recently, some employers have faced lawsuits by employees claiming that they were entitled to be paid for breaks they never took (or were never allowed to take). Also, because some state laws require employers to provide breaks at particular intervals, including this language in your policy allows you to make sure your company is complying with applicable law.

Meal and Rest Breaks

Employees are allowed a _____-minute break every _____ hours. These breaks will be _____ .
In addition, all employees who work at least _____ hours in a day are entitled to take a _____-minute meal break. Your supervisor will let you know when you should take your breaks. Breaks are an opportunity to rest and eat during the workday, and they may be required by law. For this reason, employees must take their breaks, as scheduled, unless they make other arrangements with their supervisor. For example, employees may not decide to skip breaks in order to leave early or come in late.

How to Complete This Policy

Federal law doesn't require employers to offer employees breaks of any length during the workday. However, federal law does require employers to pay employees for any breaks of 20 minutes or less that they choose to provide. A handful of states—including California and Washington—currently require employers to provide paid breaks during the workday. State laws are summarized in "State Meal and Rest Break Laws" at the end of this chapter.

To complete this policy, fill in the blanks with the length and frequency of the break your state requires (or the length of the break your company offers, as long as it meets or exceeds your state's legal requirements). Also, indicate whether rest breaks will be paid or unpaid.

Alternate Modifications to Provide for Paid or Unpaid Meal Breaks

To Provide Paid Meal Breaks

Generally, state and federal law do not require paid meal breaks, as long as the employee is entirely relieved of all work during the break; employees who are required to work through a meal period are entitled to be paid for that time. Nonetheless, many employers offer paid meal breaks to employees. If your company chooses to do so, add the language below to the end of the first paragraph of the policy.

Alternate Modification A

Meal breaks will be paid.

To Provide Unpaid Meal Breaks

If your company will not pay employee for their meal breaks, add the language below to the end of the first paragraph of your policy.

Alternate Modification B

Meal breaks are generally unpaid. However, employees who are required to work or remain at their stations during the meal break will be paid for that time.

6:4 Lactation Breaks

File Name: 06_Hours.rtf

Include This Policy?
☐ Yes
☐ No
☐ Use our existing policy
☐ Other _____

Alternate Modifications
Specify Where to Breast-Feed or
Express Breast Milk
Choose one: ☐ A ☐ B

Additional Clauses
None

Related Policies
None

Notes

_____
_____
_____
_____
_____
_____
_____
_____
_____
_____
_____
_____
_____
_____
_____
_____

6:4 Lactation Breaks

The Affordable Care Act of 2010 (Obamacare) includes provisions that promote preventive health care and healthy habits. In keeping with that intent, the law requires employers to allow reasonable break time for nursing mothers to express breast milk at work for up to one year after birth. The employer must also provide private space, other than a bathroom, for this purpose.

A number of states also require employers to provide lactation breaks. Some require only that employers allow employees to use their regular breaks for this purpose; others go further and require employers to provide additional breaks as needed. Some state laws also require employers to provide an appropriate place for employees to express breast milk. You can find information on your state's requirements in "State Meal and Rest Break Laws," at the end of this chapter.

The federal law applies to all employers, but it includes an exception for employers with fewer than 50 employees, if allowing lactation breaks would impose an "undue hardship," meaning it would entail significant expense or difficulty, considering the employer's size, structure, and resources. Even if you believe your company fits within this exception, however, you still must follow your state's law on lactation breaks, if it has one. Before the health care reform law made lactation breaks mandatory, many employers voluntarily chose to allow them: Allowing nursing mothers to express breast milk at work allows employees to return to work sooner after having a baby, enhances employee loyalty to the company, and provides mothers and babies with the proven health benefits of breast-feeding.

Lactation Breaks

Our Company recognizes the value and importance of breast-feeding, and supports our employees' desire to breast-feed their infants. If you are breast-feeding your child, you may use your meal and rest breaks to express breast milk. If you need more time, please speak to

_____ .

How to Complete This Policy

In the blank, insert the position responsible for reviewing employee requests (for example, "the human resources department" or "your supervisor"). Because the federal health care reform act requires employers to provide reasonable break time for expressing breast milk, your company should grant any employee requests for a longer period.

Alternate Modifications to Tell Employees Where to Breast-Feed or Express Breast Milk

The federal health care law (and the laws of some states) requires employers to provide private space for lactation breaks. These modifications allow you to tell employees where they may take their breaks: in a separate space available solely for that purpose or in their own offices or other appropriate areas.

If You Have Dedicated Space for Expressing Breast Milk

Some larger companies with significant numbers of female employees have a private area dedicated to expressing breast milk. Typically, these lactation rooms contain a sink, some comfortable chairs, and a refrigerator where expressed milk can be stored. If employees actually breast-feed their infants on site, the room may also include child-friendly decorations and furnishings. If your company has a dedicated area, you may add the language below to the end of your policy.

Alternate Modification A

The Company is pleased to provide a private space for employees to express breast milk. We ask that you use this space only for its intended purpose. For the privacy and comfort of employees, only those who are breast-feeding or expressing breast milk may use this space.

If You Do Not Have Dedicated Space for Expressing Breast Milk

Employees who have private offices may feel comfortable breast-feeding or expressing breast milk there. You may have to provide some alterations—for example, a window shade or a locking door—for privacy. Employees who have more open workspaces will need different accommodations. Options might include allowing employees to use a vacant conference room, office, or even a large closet that can be made private and provides adequate space. The position you designate in the modification below can let employees know where they can breast-feed or express breast milk.

Alternate Modification B

Employees may express breast milk in their private offices, if they have one. If your office or workspace is not sufficiently private, or if you require additional fixtures to make your office private (such as a window shade or screen), please speak to _____ _____ .

6:5 Overtime

File Name: 06_Hours.rtf

Include This Policy?
- ☐ Yes
- ☐ No
- ☐ Use our existing policy
- ☐ Other _____

Alternate Modifications

Calculate Time Worked

Choose one: ☐ A ☐ B

Additional Clauses

Pay a Premium for Holiday Work

Insert?: ☐ Yes ☐ No

Choose Employees for Overtime

Insert?: ☐ Yes ☐ No

Related Policies

5:3 Exempt and Nonexempt
Employees

7:6 Pay Docking

Notes

_____
_____
_____
_____
_____
_____
_____
_____
_____
_____
_____
_____
_____
_____

6:5 Overtime

If you anticipate that any company employees will be asked to work overtime, you should adopt an overtime policy letting workers know, up front, that they will be expected to work overtime when necessary. This will help eliminate later complaints when managers actually have to ask employees to stay beyond their scheduled shifts. An overtime policy also protects the company from having to pay workers for unnecessary overtime or overtime work made necessary only by the employee's poor planning or faulty time management. Our sample policy requires workers to get advance authorization before working any overtime hours, which should prevent these abuses. The policy also explains how overtime is calculated, including which hours count toward the overtime threshold. Placing this information in the policy will save you the time it would otherwise take to explain the system to each worker who puts in extra time on the job.

Overtime

On occasion, we may ask employees to work beyond their regular scheduled hours. We expect employees to work a reasonable amount of overtime: This is a job requirement.

We will try to give employees advance notice when overtime work is necessary; however, it will not always be possible to notify workers in advance.

Exempt employees will not be paid for working beyond their regular scheduled hours. Nonexempt employees are entitled to payment for overtime, according to the rules set forth below (for information on which employees are exempt and which are nonexempt, see Section _____ of this Handbook):

- All overtime work must be approved in writing, in advance, by the employee's supervisor. Working overtime without permission violates Company policy and may result in disciplinary action.
- These rules apply to any type of work done after hours, including work done from home, work done using a Company-issued portable computing device (such as a laptop or smartphone), and work done using your own personal computer or portable device.
- For purposes of calculating how many hours an employee has worked in a day or week, our workweek begins at 12:01 a.m. on Monday and ends at midnight on Sunday. Our workday begins at 12:01 a.m. and ends at midnight each day.
- Nonexempt employees will be paid 1½ times their regular hourly rate of pay for every hour worked in excess of _____.

How to Complete This Policy

In the blank, insert the overtime standard—state or federal—that your company has to follow. Federal law requires employers to pay overtime to any nonexempt worker who works more than 40 hours in a seven-day week. However, a few states (including California) have a daily overtime standard, which requires employers to pay overtime to covered workers who put in more than a specified number of hours in a single workday. Check "State Overtime Rules" at the end of this chapter for information on your state's rules. Then complete the policy as follows: If federal law is more protective, or as protective, of workers as your state's law, insert "40 hours in a workweek" in the blank. If your state has a daily overtime standard, insert that standard in the blank. For example, California employers should insert "eight hours in a workday or 40 hours in a workweek."

CAUTION

California offers employees more extensive wage and hour protections than most other states. Workers in California are entitled to time-and-a-half for any hours worked beyond eight in a day or 40 in a week, as well as double time for hours worked beyond 12 in a day or for working more than eight hours on a seventh consecutive workday. (See "State Overtime Rules" at the end of this chapter for details.) And California law defines the categories of workers who are entitled to overtime more broadly than federal law. If your company does business in California, you should consult with an employment lawyer to make sure that your policies don't violate these rules.

Alternate Modifications to Calculate Time Worked

To Count Only Hours Spent Working as Time Worked

Most employers will want to pay overtime only when they are legally required to do so. Under federal law, paid hours that are not worked—such as vacation days, sick time, or holidays—do not count toward the overtime threshold of 40 hours per week. If your company will follow this federal standard, add the following bullet to the end of your policy.

Alternate Modification A

• Only time actually spent working counts as hours worked. Vacation time, sick days, holidays, or any other paid time during which an employee did not actually work will not count as hours worked.

To Count Paid Time Off as Time Worked

Although federal law does not require it, employers are free to count paid hours as hours worked, and some choose to do so. An employer might adopt this more generous policy to recognize the value of paid time off—which, after all, is supposed to be a true break from the job. The therapeutic value of paid days off diminishes if an employee has to work extra hours as a result.

If your company will treat some or all paid time off as hours worked, simply add the following bullet to the end of your policy In the blank, insert the types of paid time off that will count as hours worked, for example, paid vacation days or paid sick days. If all paid time off will count as hours worked, insert "all days off for which the employee is paid."

Alternate Modification B

- Hours worked means all time spent actually working, plus _____
  _____ .

Additional Clause to Pay a Premium for Holiday Work

Federal law does not require employers to pay extra for hours worked on a holiday, unless those hours push the employee's weekly total above 40 hours. Nonetheless, some employers want to reward their employees for working unpopular shifts. Any employer who has tried to staff shifts on Thanksgiving or New Year's Day knows that a little incentive helps fill the ranks.

If your company wants to pay employees more to work on holidays, add the following clause to the overtime policy. In the first blank, list the holidays for which employees will receive a premium (for example, New Year's Eve and New Year's Day). In the second blank, insert the premium that will be paid (such as two times the employee's regularly hourly wage).

Additional Clause

The Company will pay employees a premium for working on the following holidays: _____
_____
_____ .

Employees who agree to work on these days will receive _____
_____ .

Additional Clause to Choose Employees for Overtime

In certain industries and businesses, employees jump at the chance to earn the extra money that overtime work provides. Other companies might find that no one ever wants to work overtime. In either situation, you may want to adopt a policy that explains how employees are chosen for overtime work. Such a policy will assure employees in companies where overtime is popular that the company is doling out the opportunity to work overtime fairly. And, in companies where no one wants to work overtime, it will let workers know that they will have to put in their time when their turns come.

Additional Clause

Please let your supervisor know if you want to work overtime. Your supervisor will add your name to the overtime list. When overtime is available, it will be offered first to employees on the list, in the order in which their names appear.

If overtime work is necessary and no employees on the list are available, employees who are eligible to perform the work—that is, employees who do the same type of work during their regular work hours—will be asked to work overtime, in alphabetical order. Once an employee, on the list or off, has worked overtime, the next employee on the list or in alphabetical order will be asked to work overtime when it next becomes available, and so on.

CAUTION

New overtime rules are up in the air. On December 1, 2016, changes to the overtime rules were scheduled to go into effect, which would make many more white-collar employees eligible to earn overtime. Previously, office employees earning less than $455 a week were automatically eligible to earn overtime (that is, they were nonexempt employees). Employees earning more than $455 a week did not have to be paid overtime for working extra hours if they fit into one of the exemption categories (for example, because they were exempt as managers or as professional employees). Under the new rules, the wage cutoff was raised to $913 a week, or $47,476 a year. However, just days before these rules were to take effect, a federal court struck them down. It's not clear what will happen next; you can find legal updates at this book's online companion page (see Appendix A, "Creating Your Handbook," for details on accessing the page).

State Meal and Rest Break Laws

Note: Any state not listed in this chart does not have any applicable laws or regulations on rest and meal breaks for adults employed in the private sector. Many states also exclude professional, administrative, and executive employees from these rules.

Other exceptions may apply. For example, many states have special break rules for specific occupations or industries, which are beyond the scope of this chart. Check the statute or check with your state department of labor if you need more information. (See Appendix B for contact list.)

Alabama

Breast-feeding: No employment-specific laws. However, breast-feeding is allowed in any public or private location where the mother's presence is authorized.

Arkansas

Ark. Stat. Ann. § 11-5-116

Applies to: All employers.

Breast-feeding: Reasonable unpaid breaks to express breast milk; if possible, break time to run concurrently with other breaks.

California

Cal. Lab. Code §§ 512, 1030; Cal. Code Regs. tit. 8, §§ 11010-11170

Applies to: Employers in most industries.

Exceptions: Motion picture and other occupations. See wage orders, Cal. Code Regs. tit. 8, §§ 11010 to 11160, for additional exceptions.

Meal Break: 30 minutes, unpaid, after 5 hours, except employer and employee can agree to waive meal period if employee works 6 hours or less. Second 30-minute unpaid meal period when employee works more than 10 hours a day, except employer and employee can agree to waive the second meal period if the employee works 12 hours or less and took the first meal period. On-duty paid meal period permitted when nature of work prevents relief from all duties and parties agree in writing.

Rest Break: Paid 10-minute rest period for each 4 hours worked or major fraction thereof; as practicable, in the middle of the work period. Not required for employees whose total daily work time is less than 3½ hours.

Breast-feeding: Reasonable unpaid breaks to express breast milk; if possible, break time to run concurrently with other breaks.

Colorado

Colo. Code Regs. tit. 7 § 1103-1:7 and 1:8

Applies to: Retail and service, food and beverage, commercial support service, and health and medical industries.

Exceptions: Numerous exceptions are listed in the regulation.

Meal Break: 30 minutes, unpaid, after 5 hours of work; on-duty paid meal period permitted when nature of work prevents break from all duties.

Rest Break: Paid 10-minute rest period for each 4 hours or major fraction worked; if practical, in the middle of the work period.

Breast-feeding: Reasonable unpaid time to express breast milk for up to two years after child's birth.

Connecticut

Conn. Gen. Stat. Ann. §§ 31-51ii, 31-40w

Applies to: All employers, except as noted.

Exceptions: Employers who pay for rest breaks as described below, those with a written agreement providing other break rules, and those granted an exemption for reasons listed in statute.

Meal Break: 30 minutes, unpaid, after first 2 hours of work and before last 2 hours for employees who work 7½ or more consecutive hours.

Rest Break: As alternative to meal break, a total of 30 minutes paid in each 7½-hour work period.

Breast-feeding: Employee may use meal or rest breaks for breast-feeding or expressing breast milk.

Delaware

Del. Code Ann. tit. 19 § 707

Applies to: All employers, except as noted.

Exceptions: Employers with alternative written agreement and those granted exemptions specified in statute. Law does not apply to teachers.

Meal Break: 30 minutes, unpaid, after first 2 hours and before the last 2 hours, for employees who work 7½ consecutive hours or more.

Breast-feeding: Reasonable accommodations for limitations of a person related to pregnancy, childbirth, or a related condition may include break time and appropriate facilities for expressing breast milk.

State Meal and Rest Break Laws (continued)

District of Columbia

D.C. Code Ann. §§ 2-1402.82, 32-1231.01-32-1231.03

Applies to: All employers.

Breast-feeding: Reasonable unpaid time to express breast milk; runs concurrently with other paid or unpaid breaks provided by employer. Employer must make reasonable efforts to provide a private, sanitary location (other than a toilet stall) for expressing breast milk. Employer must provide reasonable accommodations to nursing mothers, unless it would cause an undue hardship.

Florida

Breast-feeding: No employment-specific laws. However, breast-feeding is allowed in any public or private location where the mother's presence is authorized.

Georgia

Ga. Code Ann. § 34-1-6

Applies to: All employers.

Breast-feeding: At employer's discretion, reasonable unpaid break time to express breast milk. Breast-feeding is allowed in any public or private location where the mother's presence is authorized.

Hawaii

Haw. Rev. Stat. §§ 378-2, 378-91 to 93

Applies to: All employers.

Breast-feeding: Reasonable unpaid break time to express breast milk for one year after child's birth.

Illinois

820 Ill. Comp. Stat. §§ 140/3, 260/10

Applies to: All employers.

Exceptions: Employees whose meal periods are established by collective bargaining agreement.

Employees who monitor individuals with developmental disabilities or mental illness, or both, and who are required to be on call during an entire 8-hour work period; these employees must be allowed to eat a meal while working.

Meal Break: 20 minutes, no later than 5 hours after the beginning of the shift, for employees who work 7½ or more continuous hours. Hotel room attendants are entitled to a 30-minute meal break if they work at least 7 hours.

Rest Break: In addition to meal break, hotel room attendants must receive two paid 15-minute rest breaks, if they work at least 7 hours.

Breast-feeding: Reasonable unpaid break time to breast-feed infant or express breast milk.

Indiana

Ind. Code § 22-2-14

Applies to: Employers with 25 or more employees.

Breast-feeding: Employer must make reasonable efforts to provide a private space, other than a restroom, for an employee to express breast milk during nonworking hours.

Kansas

Kan. Admin. Reg. 49-30-3

Applies to: Employees not covered under FLSA.

Meal Break: Not required, but if less than 30 minutes is given, break must be paid.

Breast-feeding: No employment-specific laws. However, breast-feeding is allowed in any public or private location where the mother's presence is authorized.

Kentucky

Ky. Rev. Stat. Ann. §§ 337.355, 337.365;

Ky. Admin. Regs. tit. 803, 1:065

Applies to: All employers, except as noted.

Exceptions: Written agreement providing different meal period; employers subject to Federal Railway Labor Act.

Meal Break: Reasonable off-duty period close to the middle of the shift; cannot be required to take it before the third or after the fifth hour of work. Coffee breaks and snack time do not count toward the meal break.

Rest Break: Paid 10-minute rest period for each 4-hour work period; rest period must be in addition to regularly scheduled meal period.

Breast-feeding: No employment-specific laws. However, breast-feeding is allowed in any public or private location where the mother's presence is authorized.

Maine

Me. Rev. Stat. Ann. tit. 26, § 601

Applies to: Most employers.

Exceptions: Small businesses with fewer than 3 employees on duty who are able to take frequent breaks during the workday; collective bargaining or other written agreement between employer and employee may provide for different breaks.

State Meal and Rest Break Laws (continued)

Meal and Rest Break: 30 minutes, unpaid, after 6 consecutive hours of work, except in cases of emergency.

Breast-feeding: Adequate unpaid time to express breast milk, or employee may use rest or meal time, for up to 3 years following childbirth.

Maryland

Md. Code Ann. Lab. & Empl. § 3-710

Applies to: Retail establishments with 50 or more retail employees.

Exceptions: Employees who work in an office or who work at a single location with 5 or fewer employees are not covered.

Meal Break: 30 minutes, unpaid, after 6 consecutive hours of work.

Rest Break: 15 minutes, unpaid, when working 4 to 6 consecutive hours. (This may be waived if the employee works less than 6 hours). Employees working 8 or more consecutive hours must receive a 15-minute unpaid break for every additional 4 consecutive hours after a meal break.

Breast-feeding: No employment-specific laws. However, breast-feeding is allowed in any public or private location where the mother's presence is authorized.

Massachusetts

Mass. Gen. Laws ch. 149, §§ 100, 101

Applies to: All employers, except as noted.

Exceptions: Excludes iron works, glass works, paper mills, letterpresses, print works, and bleaching or dyeing works. Attorney general may exempt businesses that require continuous operation if it won't affect worker safety. Collective bargaining agreement may also provide for different breaks.

Meal Break: 30 minutes, if work is for more than 6 hours.

Minnesota

Minn. Stat. Ann. §§ 177.253, 177.254, 181.939

Applies to: All employers.

Exceptions: Excludes certain agricultural and seasonal employees. A collective bargaining agreement may provide for different rest and meal breaks.

Meal Break: Sufficient unpaid time for employees who work 8 consecutive hours or more.

Rest Break: Paid adequate rest period within each 4 consecutive hours of work to utilize nearest convenient restroom.

Breast-feeding: Reasonable unpaid break time to express milk.

Mississippi

Miss. Ann. Code § 71-1-55

Breast-feeding: Employee may use meal or rest break for expressing breast milk.

Missouri

Breast-feeding: No employment-specific laws. However, breast-feeding is allowed in any public or private location where the mother's presence is authorized.

Montana

Breast-feeding: No employment-specific laws. However, breast-feeding is allowed in any public or private location where the mother's presence is authorized.

Nebraska

Neb. Rev. Stat. §§ 48-212, 48-1102

Applies to: Assembly plant, workshop, or mechanical establishment.

Exceptions: Other written agreement between employer and employees.

Meal Break: 30 minutes off premises for each 8-hour shift.

Breast-feeding: Employers with 15 or more employees must provide reasonable accommodation to nursing mothers, unless it would cause an undue hardship. Accommodation may include breaks and an appropriate location for breast-feeding or expressing breast milk.

Nevada

Nev. Rev. Stat. Ann. § 608.019

Applies to: Employers of two or more employees.

Exceptions: Employees covered by collective bargaining agreement; exemptions for business necessity.

Meal Break: 30 minutes for 8 continuous hours of work.

Rest Break: Paid 10-minute rest period for each 4 hours or major fraction worked; as practicable, in middle of the work period; not required for employees whose total daily work time is less than 3½ hours.

Breast-feeding: No employment-specific laws. However, breast-feeding is allowed in any public or private location where the mother's presence is authorized.

State Meal and Rest Break Laws (continued)

New Hampshire

N.H. Rev. Stat. Ann. § 275:30-a

Applies to: All employers.

Meal Break: 30 minutes after 5 consecutive hours, unless the employer allows the employee to eat while working and it is feasible for the employee to do so.

New Mexico

N.M. St. Ann. § 28-20-2

Breast-feeding: Flexible unpaid breaks to use breast pump in the workplace.

New York

N.Y. Lab. Law §§ 162, 206-c

Applies to: Factories, workshops, manufacturing facilities, mercantile (retail and wholesale) establishments.

Meal Break: Factory employees, 60 minutes between 11 a.m. and 2 p.m.; mercantile employees, 30 minutes between 11 a.m. and 2 p.m. If a shift starts before 11 a.m. and ends after 7 p.m., every employee gets an additional 20 minutes between 5 p.m. and 7 p.m. If a shift starts between 1 p.m. and 6 a.m., a factory employee gets 60 minutes, and a mercantile employee gets 45 minutes, in the middle of the shift. Labor commissioner may permit a shorter meal break; the permit must be in writing and posted conspicuously in the main entrance of the workplace.

Breast-feeding: Reasonable unpaid break time to express breast milk for up to three years after child's birth.

North Carolina

Breast-feeding: No employment-specific laws. However, breast-feeding is allowed in any public or private location where the mother's presence is authorized.

North Dakota

N.D. Admin. Code § 46-02-07-02

Applies to: Applicable when two or more employees are on duty.

Exceptions: Waiver by employee or other provision in collective bargaining agreement.

Meal Break: 30 minutes for each shift over 5 hours; unpaid if employee is completely relieved of duties.

Breast-feeding: No employment-specific laws. However, breast-feeding is allowed in any public or private location where the mother's presence is authorized.

Oklahoma

40 Ok. St. Ann. § 435

Breast-feeding: Reasonable unpaid breaks to breast-feed or express breast milk.

Oregon

Ore. Rev. Stat. 653.077; Or. Admin. R. §§ 839-020-0050, 839-020-0051

Applies to: All employers except as noted.

Exceptions: Agricultural workers and employees covered by a collective bargaining agreement.

Meal Break: 30 minutes for employees who work at least six hours, unpaid if relieved of all duties; paid time to eat if employee cannot be relieved of duty; a shorter paid break (but no less than 20 minutes), if employer can show that it is industry practice or custom. If shift of 7 hours or less, meal break must occur between hours 2 and 5; if shift longer than 7 hours, meal break must be between hours 3 and 6.

Rest Break: Paid 10-minute rest period for each 4 hours or major fraction worked; if practical, in the middle of the work period.

Rest period must be in addition to usual meal break and taken separately; can't be added to meal period or deducted from beginning or end of shift to reduce length of total work period.

Rest period is not required for certain solo adult employees serving the public, although they must be allowed to use restroom.

Breast-feeding: Employers with 25 or more employees must provide a 30-minute unpaid break for every 4 hours worked to express breast milk, for up to 18 months after child's birth.

Pennsylvania

43 P.S. § 1301.207

Applies to: Employers of seasonal farmworkers.

Meal Break: Seasonal farm workers are entitled to a 30-minute meal or rest break if they work at least 5 hours.

Breast-feeding: No employment-specific laws. However, breast-feeding is allowed in any public or private location where the mother's presence is authorized.

Rhode Island

R.I. Gen. Laws §§ 28-3-8, 28-3-14, 23-13-2.1, 28-5-7.4

Applies to: Employers with 5 or more employees.

State Meal and Rest Break Laws (continued)

Exceptions: Employers of health care facility or employers with fewer than 3 employees on any shift.

Meal Break: 20 minutes, unpaid, within a 6-hour shift or 30 minutes, unpaid, within an 8-hour shift.

Breast-feeding: Reasonable unpaid break time to breast-feed infant or express breast milk. Employers with 4 or more employees must provide reasonable accommodations to nursing mothers, which may include break time and private space for expressing breast milk, other than a restroom.

South Carolina

Breast-feeding: No employment-specific laws. However, breast-feeding is allowed in any public or private location where the mother's presence is authorized.

South Dakota

Breast-feeding: No employment-specific laws. However, breast-feeding is allowed in any public or private location where the mother's presence is authorized if the mother is in compliance with all other laws.

Tennessee

Tenn. Code Ann. §§ 50-2-103(h), 50-1-305

Applies to: Employers with 5 or more employees.

Meal Break: 30 minutes unpaid for employees scheduled to work 6 consecutive hours or more, unless workplace environment provides ample opportunity for appropriate meal break. Tipped employees who work in food or beverage service may waive right to meal break if employee requests waiver, knowingly and voluntarily, in writing, and employer consents. Employer may not coerce employee into waiving right to meal break. Employer must post waiver policy that includes a form stating the employee's right to a break, how long the waiver will last, and how the employee or employer may rescind the waiver.

Breast-feeding: Reasonable unpaid break time to express breast milk.

Texas

Breast-feeding: No employment-specific laws. However, breast-feeding is allowed in any public or private location where the mother's presence is authorized.

Vermont

Vt. Stat. Ann. tit. 21 § 304

Applies to: All employers.

Meal and Rest Break: Employees must be given reasonable opportunities to eat and use toilet facilities during work periods.

Breast-feeding: Reasonable time to express breast milk for up to three years after the child's birth. Breaks can be paid or unpaid.

Virginia

Breast-feeding: No employment-specific laws. However, breast-feeding is allowed in any public or private location where the mother's presence is authorized.

Washington

Wash. Admin. Code §§ 296-126-092, 286-131-020

Applies to: All employers except as noted.

Exceptions: Newspaper vendor or carrier, domestic or casual labor around private residence, sheltered workshop; separate provisions for agricultural labor.

Meal Break: 30-minute break, if work period is more than 5 consecutive hours, not less than 2 hours or more than 5 hours from beginning of shift. This time is paid if employee is on duty or is required to be at a site for employer's benefit. Employees who work 3 or more hours longer than regular workday are entitled to an additional half hour, before or during overtime.

Agricultural employees: 30 minutes if working more than 5 hours; additional 30 minutes if working 11 or more hours in a day.

Rest Break: Paid 10-minute rest break for each 4-hour work period, scheduled as near as possible to midpoint of each work period. Employee cannot be required to work more than 3 hours without a rest break. Scheduled rest breaks not required where nature of work allows employee to take intermittent rest breaks equivalent to required standard.

West Virginia

W. Va. Code § 21-3-10a

Applies to: All employers.

Meal Break: At least 20-minute break for each 6 consecutive hours worked, unless employees are allowed to take breaks as needed or to eat lunch while working.

Rest Break: Rest breaks of 20 minutes or less must be counted as paid work time.

State Meal and Rest Break Laws (continued)

Wisconsin

Wis. Admin. Code § DWD 274.02; Wis. Stat. Ann. § 103.935

Applies to: All employers; migrant workers.

Meal Break: For most workers, 30-minute meal period is recommended but not required. Meal period should be close to usual meal time or near middle of shift. Shifts of more than 6 hours without a meal break should be avoided. If employee is not free to leave the workplace or relieved of all duties for at least 30 minutes, meal period is considered paid time.

For migrant workers employed exclusively in agricultural labor, 30-minute meal period required after 6 continuous hours of work, unless the shift can be completed in an additional hour.

Rest Break: For migrant workers not employed exclusively in agricultural labor, rest period of at least 10 minutes within each 5 hours of continuous employment.

Breast-feeding: No employment-specific laws. However, breast-feeding is allowed in any public or private location where the mother's presence is authorized.

State Overtime Rules

This chart covers private-sector employment only. The overtime rules summarized are not applicable to all employers or all employees. Occupations that generally are not subject to overtime laws include health care and attendant care, emergency medical personnel, seasonal workers, agricultural labor, camp counselors, nonprofits exempt under the FLSA, salespeople working on a commission, transit drivers, baby-sitters, and other household workers, and many others. For more information, contact your state's department of labor and be sure to check its website, where most states have posted their overtime rules. (See Appendix B for contact details.)

Alabama

No state overtime rules that differ from FLSA.

Alaska

Alaska Stat. § 23.10.060 and following

Time and a half after x hours per DAY: 8

Time and a half after x hours per WEEK: 40

Employment overtime laws apply to: Employers of 4 or more employees; commerce or manufacturing businesses.

Notes: Voluntary flexible work hour plan of 10-hour day, 40-hour week, with premium pay after 10 hours is permitted.

Arizona

No state overtime rules that differ from FLSA.

Arkansas

Ark. Code Ann. §§ 11-4-211, 11-4-203

Time and a half after x hours per WEEK: 40

Employment overtime laws apply to: Employers of 4 or more employees.

Notes: Employees in retail and service establishments who spend up to 40% of their time on nonexempt work must be paid at least twice the state's minimum wage ($572 per week).

California

Cal. Lab. Code §§ 500-511; Cal. Lab. Code § 513; 860 Cal. Code Regs. tit. 8, §§ 11010 and following

Time and a half after x hours per DAY: Eight; after 12 hours, double time. Agricultural employees only: after 10 hours per day. (From 2019 to 2022, this will gradually decrease to 8 hours per day.)

Time and a half after x hours per WEEK: 40; on 7th day, time and a half for the first 8 hours; after 8 hours, double time. Agricultural employees only: after 60 hours per week. (From 2019 to 2022, this will gradually decrease to 40 hours per week.)

Notes: Employee may make written request to work make-up time for hours taken off for personal obligations. As long as total hours don't exceed 11 in a day or 40 in a week, employer won't owe daily overtime. Employer may not encourage or solicit employees to request make-up time. Employees may, by majority vote in a secret ballot election, opt for an alternative workweek of four 10-hour workdays, in which case the employer will not owe overtime.

Colorado

7 Colo. Code Regs. § 1103-1:4

Time and a half after x hours per DAY: 12 hours in one workday or 12 consecutive hours

Time and a half after x hours per WEEK: 40

Employment overtime laws apply to: Employees in retail and service, commercial support service, food and beverage, health & medical industries.

Connecticut

Conn. Gen. Stat. Ann. §§ 31-76b, 31-76c, Conn. Admin. Code § 31-62-E1

Time and a half after x hours per WEEK: 40. On 7th consecutive workday, time and a half for all hours worked.

Notes: In restaurants and hotels, time-and-a-half pay required for the 7th consecutive day of work or for hours that exceed 40 per week.

Delaware

No state overtime rules that differ from FLSA.

District of Columbia

D.C. Code Ann. § 32-1003(c); D.C. Mun. Regs. tit. 7, § 906

Time and a half after x hours per WEEK: 40

Notes: Employees must be paid one hour minimum wage for each day a split shift is worked, but not if the employee lives on the premises.

Florida

No state overtime rules that differ from FLSA.

Georgia

No state overtime rules that differ from FLSA.

State Overtime Rules (continued)

Hawaii

Haw. Rev. Stat. §§ 387-1; 387-3

Time and a half after x hours per WEEK: 40. Dairy, sugarcane, and seasonal agricultural work: 48 hours per week.

Notes: No employer shall employ any employee in split shifts unless all of the shifts within a period of twenty-four hours fall within a period of fourteen consecutive hours, except in case of extraordinary emergency.

Idaho

No state overtime rules that differ from FLSA.

Illinois

820 Ill. Comp. Stat. §§ 105/3(d), 105/4a

Time and a half after x hours per WEEK: 40

Employment overtime laws apply to: Employers of 4 or more employees.

Notes: Collective bargaining agreement ratified by Illinois Labor Relations Board may provide for different overtime provisions.

Indiana

Ind. Code Ann. § 22-2-2-4(k)

Time and a half after x hours per WEEK: 40.

Notes: Collective bargaining agreements ratified by the NLRB may have different overtime provisions. Domestic service work is not excluded from overtime laws.

Iowa

No state overtime rules that differ from FLSA.

Kansas

Kan. Stat. Ann. § 44-1204

Time and a half after x hours per WEEK: 46

Kentucky

*Ky. Rev. Stat. Ann. §§ 337.050, 337.285;
803 Ky. Admin. Regs. § 1:060*

Time and a half after x hours per WEEK: 40.

Louisiana

No state overtime rules that differ from FLSA.

Maine

Me. Rev. Stat. Ann. tit. 26, § 664(3)

Time and a half after x hours per WEEK: 40

Maryland

Md. Code Ann., [Lab. & Empl.] § 3-420

Time and a half after x hours per WEEK: 40; 48 hours for bowling alleys and residential employees caring for the sick, aged, intellectually disabled, or mentally ill in institutions other than hospitals; 60 hours for agricultural work that is exempt from the overtime provisions of the federal act.

Massachusetts

Mass. Gen. Laws ch. 151, § 1A

Time and a half after x hours per WEEK: 40. Time and a half for work on Sunday and certain holidays (for retail employees).

Employment overtime laws apply to: All employers for 40 hours a week; employers with more than 7 employees for Sunday and holiday overtime.

Michigan

Mich. Comp. Laws §§ 408.412 and 408.414a

Time and a half after x hours per WEEK: 40

Employment overtime laws apply to: Employers of 2 or more employees.

Minnesota

Minn. Stat. Ann. § 177.25

Time and a half after x hours per WEEK: 48

Mississippi

No state overtime rules that differ from FLSA.

Missouri

Mo. Rev. Stat. §§ 290.500 and 290.505

Time and a half after x hours per WEEK: 40; 52 hours for seasonal amusement or recreation businesses.

Montana

Mont. Code Ann. §§ 39-3-405 and 39-3-406

Time and a half after x hours per WEEK: 40; 48 hours for students working seasonal jobs at amusement or recreational areas.

Nebraska

No state overtime rules that differ from FLSA.

State Overtime Rules (continued)

Nevada

Nev. Rev. Stat. Ann. § 608.018

Time and a half after x hours per DAY: 8, if (1) employee receives health benefits from employer and employee's regular rate of pay is less than $1\frac{1}{2}$ times the minimum wage, or (2) employee does not receive health benefits from employer and employee's rate of pay is less than $12.375 per hour.

Time and a half after x hours per WEEK: 40

Notes: Employer and employee may agree to flextime schedule of four 10-hour days.

New Hampshire

N.H. Rev. Stat. Ann. § 279.21(VIII)

Time and a half after x hours per WEEK: 40

New Jersey

N.J. Stat. Ann. §§ 34.11-56a4 and 34.11-56a4.1

Time and a half after x hours per WEEK: 40

New Mexico

N.M. Stat. Ann. § 50-4-22(d)

Time and a half after x hours per WEEK: 40

New York

N.Y. Lab. Law §§ 160(3), 161; N.Y. Comp. Codes R. & Regs. tit. 12, § 142-2.2

Time and a half after x hours per WEEK: 40 for nonresidential workers; 44 for residential workers.

Notes: In some industries, employees must be given 24 consecutive hours off per week. See N.Y. Lab. Law § 161.

North Carolina

N.C. Gen. Stat. §§ 95-25.14, 95-25.4

Time and a half after x hours per WEEK: 40; 45 hours a week in seasonal amusement or recreational establishments.

North Dakota

N.D. Admin. Code § 46-02-07-02(4)

Time and a half after x hours per WEEK: 40; 50 hours per week, cabdrivers.

Ohio

Ohio Rev. Code Ann. § 4111.03

Time and a half after x hours per WEEK: 40

Employment overtime laws apply to: Employers who gross more than $150,000 a year.

Oklahoma

No state overtime rules that differ from FLSA.

Oregon

Or. Rev. Stat. §§ 652.020, 653.261, 653.265

Time and a half after x hours per WEEK: 40

Notes: Time and a half required after 10 hours a day in canneries, driers, packing plants, mills, factories, and manufacturing facilities.

Live-in domestic workers must receive time and a half for hours in excess of 44 per workweek.

Pennsylvania

43 Pa. Cons. Stat. Ann. § 333.104(c); 34 Pa. Code § 231.41

Time and a half after x hours per WEEK: 40

Rhode Island

R.I. Gen. Laws §§ 28-12-4.1 and following, 5-23-2(d)

Time and a half after x hours per WEEK: 40

Notes: Time and a half for Sunday and holiday work is required for most retail businesses (these hours are not included in calculating weekly overtime).

South Carolina

No state overtime rules.

South Dakota

No state overtime rules that differ from FLSA.

Tennessee

No state overtime rules.

Texas

No state overtime rules.

Utah

No state overtime rules.

Vermont

Vt. Stat. Ann. tit. 21, §§ 382, 384(b); Vt. Code R. § 24 090 003

Time and a half after x hours per WEEK: 40

Employment overtime laws apply to: Employers of 2 or more employees; doesn't apply to retail or service establishments, hotels, motels, or restaurants (among other industries).

State Overtime Rules (continued)

Virginia

No state overtime rules.

Washington

Wash. Rev. Code Ann. § 49.46.130

Time and a half after x hours per WEEK: 40

West Virginia

W. Va. Code §§ 21-5c-1(e), 21-5c-3

Time and a half after x hours per WEEK: 40

Employment overtime laws apply to: Employers of 6 or more employees at one location.

Wisconsin

Wis. Stat. Ann. §§ 103.01, 103.03; Wis. Admin. Code DWD §§ 274.01, 274.03, 274.04

Time and a half after x hours per WEEK: 40

Employment overtime laws apply to: Manufacturing, mechanical, or retail businesses; beauty parlors, laundries, restaurants, hotels; telephone, express, shipping, and transportation companies.

Wyoming

No state overtime rules that differ from FLSA.

Pay Policies

Let's face it. No matter how wonderful your company is to work for and no matter how much management encourages camaraderie, creativity, and teamwork on the job, employees don't show up every day for the fun of it. They work to get paid.

The basic exchange of the work relationship—labor for money—is easy enough to understand. But the laws regulating when, how, and how much employers must pay workers can get pretty complicated. One of the reasons for this complexity is that every level of government gets involved in legislating pay. The federal government has one set of rules, state governments have another, and some local or municipal governments also weigh in. Employers have to follow whichever law gives workers the most rights in any particular situation, which means they may have to piece together a complex quilt of laws from a variety of sources.

In this chapter, we'll show you how to put together compensation policies that tell workers what they need to know: when they will get paid, what kinds of work might entitle them to extra pay, and the reasons why money might have to be withheld from their paychecks.

7:1 Payday

File Name: 07_Pay Policies.rtf

Include This Policy?

☐ Yes

☐ No

☐ Use our existing policy

☐ Other _____

Alternate Modifications

None

Additional Clauses

Require Submission of Time Cards

Insert?: ☐ Yes ☐ No

Related Policies

None

Notes

_____
_____
_____
_____
_____
_____
_____
_____
_____
_____
_____
_____
_____
_____
_____
_____
_____
_____
_____
_____

7:1 Payday

The title pretty much says it all: Your payday policy should tell employees when they will get paid. It should also let employees know when they will get their paychecks if a payday falls on a holiday.

How often employers must pay employees is governed by state law (federal law doesn't require employers to follow any particular pay schedule). You can get information on your state's wage laws by contacting your state labor department. (See Appendix B for contact information.) For information on payday requirements, you can also check the U.S. Department of Labor's website, which provides a chart of state payday laws at www.dol.gov/whd/state/payday.htm.

Payday

Employees are paid _____ . You will receive your paycheck on _____ . If payday falls on a holiday, you will receive your paycheck on the last workday immediately before payday.

How to Complete This Policy

To complete this policy, you will need to determine how often and on what day of the week or month employees will be paid. Many states require employers to pay workers no less frequently than a certain interval—for example, weekly, biweekly, twice a month, or once a month. An employer may pay workers more often but may not make them wait longer to receive their paychecks than the law allows.

Some states, including Connecticut and New York, require employers to pay workers on a weekly basis. Some of these laws apply to only certain kinds of workers (for example, manual laborers). If your company does business in one of these states, it might adopt a two-part payday policy, one part for the workers who must be paid every week and the other for everyone else.

Other than the handful of states that require at least some workers to be paid weekly, state law usually allows employers to pay workers every other week. However, some states allow employers to pay workers less frequently, such as twice a month or even monthly.

Once you figure out how often employees must be paid—and how often the company wants to pay them, if you are considering more frequent paychecks—you can fill in the blanks in our sample policy. If your company does business in a state that requires weekly paychecks, insert "every week" in the first blank and insert the day of the week on which employees will be paid (usually Friday) in the second blank. For biweekly paychecks, insert "every other week" in the first blank and, again, insert the day of the week on which employees will be paid in the second blank. For paydays that fall twice a month, insert "twice a month" in the first blank and the dates of the month on which employees will be paid in the second blank (often the 1st and the 15th of each month). Finally, for monthly paychecks, insert "monthly" in the first blank and the date of the month on which employees will be paid in the second blank (usually the 1st of the month or the last day of the month).

Who Needs This Policy

Your state's law may require employers to give employees written notice of when they will be paid in certain circumstances. For example, Vermont requires workers to be paid weekly but allows employers to pay workers less frequently if they give their workers written notice of the pay schedule. If your company does business in such a state, adopting a written payday policy may not only be a good idea but may also be a legal requirement.

Even if state law doesn't require employers to put their pay schedule in writing, doing so is generally a good idea. Workers take an active interest in when they will be paid, for understandable reasons. Adopting a written policy can help you avoid having to answer a lot of anxious questions about when paychecks will arrive.

Reality Check: Pay Employees Before a Holiday

Our sample policy provides that paychecks will be distributed on the last working day before a payday, if the designated payday falls on a holiday. The purpose of this language is to make sure that your company meets your state's time limits: If your state requires workers to be paid every week or two, or provides (as a few do) that no more than a specified number of days may elapse between paychecks, your company has to hit that mark, no matter what the calendar says. If workers are paid late because the designated payday came on a holiday or weekend, your company will be in violation of the law.

Additional Clause to Require Submission of Time Cards

If your company requires workers to turn in a written or electronic record of hours worked each pay period, specify that in your payday policy. For example, some employers require workers to hand in time cards, time sheets, or other records. Below is an optional clause you can add to our sample policy if your company requires such records. Note that you may have to tinker with our wording if you use some other form of timekeeping. The blank space allows you to tell employees how many days in advance they must submit their time records. Most employers require workers to turn in their hours at least two or three days before payday.

Additional Clause

Employees must submit their hours, time cards, or time sheets to their supervisor [*number of*] days before payday.

7:2 Advances

Advances (loans made against an employee's coming paycheck) can be the bane of a payroll administrator's existence. They create additional record-keeping hassles and exceptions to the usual procedures. And there are some employees who are happy to take advantage of an employer's liberal policy by requesting frequent advances rather than balancing their personal budgets more carefully.

Because of these potential problems, many employers choose not to offer advances at all or to offer advances on a discretionary basis only, for situations that legitimately qualify as emergencies. Employers who allow advances often limit how often an employee can request them and how much money the employee can receive in advance of a paycheck. To allow you to choose the policy that best meets your company's needs, we offer alternative sample policies. Policy A prohibits advances; Policy B allows advances only at the company's discretion.

No law requires an employer to provide advances, or even to notify its employees of its policy on advances one way or the other. However, regardless of how your company decides to handle pay advances, adopting a policy setting out the rules will save time and help prevent misunderstandings. Some employees may assume that they can take an advance; if advance requests are routinely denied, these employees will be in for an unpleasant surprise. If your company does offer advances, you should let employees know how and when advances must be paid back. Your policy should also reserve the company's right not to grant an advance request.

Policy A

> ## No Advances
>
> Our Company does not allow employees to receive pay advances for any reason.

7:2   Advance Policy

File Name: 07_Pay Policies.rtf

Include This Policy?

☐ Yes

Choose one: ☐ A ☐ B

☐ No

☐ Use our existing policy

☐ Other _____

Alternate Modifications

Policy B only: Repayment of Advances

Choose one: ☐ A ☐ B

Additional Clauses

Allow Advances for Vacations

Insert?: ☐ Yes ☐ No

Related Policies

None

Notes

Policy B

Advance Policy

Please submit requests for pay advances to _____
_____ ; requests will be granted or
denied at the sole discretion of the Company.

If we grant your request for an advance, you may receive no more
than _____ .

How to Complete This Policy

Sample Policy B requires you to fill in the blanks to include the
person to whom advance requests must be submitted and the amount
of money an employee can receive in advance of a paycheck:

- **Who receives advance requests.** In this blank, designate
  someone with a substantial amount of authority, such as the
  Chief Financial Officer, President, or Director of Human
  Resources. You should designate the person who will ultimately
  decide whether advances will be granted, to minimize the paper
  shuffling needed to resolve the request. It doesn't hurt to choose
  someone whose gravitas will cut back on the number of frivolous
  advance requests.
- **How much money can be advanced.** In this blank, you can
  use either a dollar figure (such as $200, $500, or $1,000)
  or a percentage of the employee's pay (25% or 50% of the
  employee's regular earnings, for example). Make sure to set
  a reasonable limit, based on what workers generally earn.
  Otherwise, it could prove hard for the employee to pay back
  the advance.

Alternate Modifications for Repayment of Advances (Policy B Only)

To Set Time Limits for Repayment

Use this modification to let employees know when advances must
be paid back, if they will be expected to repay the company on
their own. (To require employees to repay advances through payroll
deductions, use Alternate Modification B, below.) Add the language
below to the end of Policy B. In the blank space, insert the time limit
for repayment. The time limit should be based, in part, on how large
an advance the company allows. If employees may take only limited
advances, 30 days should be sufficient. If the advance is substantial, it
might take workers more than a month to repay it—perhaps 60 days.

Alternate Modification A

All advances must be repaid within _____ days. Your request for an additional advance will be denied automatically if you have not yet repaid a previous advance.

To Allow Payroll Deductions to Pay Back Advances

Some employers adopt advance policies that allow them to deduct money from an employee's paycheck to repay an advance. These policies are eminently sensible; after all, it's much easier to get the money back if the employee never lays a hand on it. However, state laws may restrict an employer's right to withhold money to repay an advance.

Under federal law, an employer is allowed to deduct money from an employee's paycheck to repay an advance. Your state may require you to get the employee's written agreement to withhold the money, for example.

Contact your state labor department to find out your state's requirements. (You can find contact information in Appendix B.) If your company will take these deductions, with or without written consent, add the paragraph below to the end of Policy B. Fill in the blank with the number of days employees will have to repay advances. If written consent is required, use Form B (below) to obtain the employee's authorization for the deduction.

Alternate Modification B

All advances must be paid back, through payroll deductions, within _____ days. Your request for an additional advance will be denied automatically if you have not yet repaid a previous advance.

Additional Clause to Allow Advances for Vacations

Even employers who don't allow any advances may be willing to give early paychecks to employees who will be on vacation or on other paid leave when payday comes around. Although this is an advance of sorts, it's much easier for the employer to manage because the employee is simply getting paid a bit early, rather than borrowing money that will have to be paid back later. Your payroll administrator won't have to change the size of the employee's paychecks, just the timing.

If your company wants to allow these advances, you can add the following language to the end of either Policy A or Policy B, above.

Additional Clause

An employee who will be on vacation or other paid leave on payday may request an early paycheck. Please submit these requests to the payroll administrator. Although we cannot guarantee that every request will be granted, we will do our best to accommodate your request.

Form B: Payroll Deduction Authorization Form

If employees will be required to repay an advance through payroll deductions, ask them to sign the Payroll Deduction Authorization Form before they receive their money. (You can find this and all other forms at this book's online companion page; see Appendix A, "Creating Your Handbook," for information on accessing these materials.) The amount of the advance, how much the employee earns, and your state's law on payroll deductions will dictate how you fill in the blanks. Once you figure out how much the company is legally entitled to withhold from each paycheck, calculate how many paychecks it will take for the employee to repay the advance. Do this by dividing the total amount of the advance by the amount you can withhold from each paycheck. Then fill in the blanks accordingly.

Payroll Deduction Authorization Form

I have requested an advance from the Company. This advance is a loan, which I am fully obligated to repay. In consideration of the Company's decision to grant this request, I agree to repay the Company through payroll deductions. I hereby authorize the Company to withhold _____ from my paycheck in _____ equal installments to repay the advance. The total amount deducted from my pay shall be equal to the amount of the advance.

If my employment is terminated or I quit before this advance is repaid, I hereby authorize the Company to deduct the full amount I still owe the Company from my final paycheck, if allowed by law.

_____   _____

Employee's Signature   Date

_____

Employee's Name (Print)

7:3 Tip Credits

If employees earn tips from customers, their employer may be entitled to pay them a salary that is less than the minimum wage, as long as that salary plus the tips they actually earn add up to at least the minimum wage per hour worked. If your company follows this procedure (referred to as a "tip credit"), it is legally required to adopt a policy explaining the process to employees. Adopting a written policy also lets workers know what to expect, so they won't be surprised when they get that first paycheck.

Not all states allow employers to take a tip credit. Consult "State Minimum Wage Laws for Tipped and Regular Employees" at the end of this chapter to find out whether your state allows tip credits and how large the credit can be. The chart also indicates each state's minimum wage, how much employers must pay workers per hour if they take a tip credit, and which workers qualify for a tip credit.

Tip Credit

Employees who hold certain positions in our Company receive some of their compensation in the form of tips from customers. If you receive tips, the Company will pay you an hourly wage of at least _____ . However, if that wage plus the tips you actually earn during any pay period does not add up to at least the minimum wage for every hour you work, the Company will pay you the difference.

Who Needs This Policy

Only companies that employ workers who receive tips and pay those workers less than the minimum wage need this policy. In other words, an employer doesn't necessarily need this policy just because its workers receive tips: If a company pays its workers an hourly wage (before tips) that meets or exceeds the minimum wage, this policy is inapplicable. If you take a tip credit, use the Tip Credit Notice Form below to notify employees.

7:3 Tip Credit

File Name: 07_Pay Policies.rtf

Include This Policy?
- ☐ Yes
- ☐ No
- ☐ Use our existing policy
- ☐ Other _____

Alternate Modifications
None

Additional Clauses
None

Related Policies
None

Notes

Form C: Tip Credit Notice Form

Under federal law, employers are legally required to give notice to employees before taking a tip credit. This notice does not have to be in writing. For practical reasons, however, using a written notice is sensible. You'll have proof that you met your legal obligations, and employees will know exactly what to expect when payday comes around. Provide the Tip Credit Notice Form to employees and ask them to sign it to acknowledge receipt. (You can find this and all other forms at this book's online companion page; see Appendix A for information on accessing these materials.)

You must give employees additional information if you will both take a tip credit and require employees to contribute to a tip pool (addressed in the next policy). The form below provides information for both a tip credit and tip pool. If you do not have a tip pooling arrangement, simply delete the paragraph about tip pooling, just above the signature block. If you do not take a tip credit, you don't need to use this form.

You must complete the blanks on the form; the employee need only sign and date it. In the first blank, insert the hourly wage you will pay the employee. Under the FLSA, this amount must be at least $2.13; check the chart, "State Minimum Wage Laws for Tipped and Regular Employees," at the end of this chapter, for state requirements. In the second blank, insert the tip credit you will claim: This amount plus the hourly wage you pay the employee must equal at least the minimum wage. If you have a valid tip pooling arrangement, insert the amount (usually expressed as a percentage of tips earned) the employee will have to contribute to the pool in the final blank.

Tip Credit Notice Form

As a tipped employee, you will be subject to the Company's tip credit. Under the Fair Labor Standards Act, the Company is entitled to pay you a lower hourly wage, crediting a portion of the tips you receive to make up the difference. This form provides information on your wages and the tip credit:

- Your hourly wage (the amount of cash wage the Company will pay you per hour of work) is $_____ .

- The amount of your tips the Company will count as a tip credit per hour is $_____ . We will credit this amount of your tips per hour toward your wages.

- The Company may not claim a tip credit in excess of the tips you actually receive. In other words, if your tips are not sufficient to pay the tip credit amount noted above per hour, the Company must make up the difference.

- All tips you earn belong to you, unless you are required to contribute to a valid tip pool limited only to those employees who customarily and regularly receive their own tips.

- The tip credit will not apply to any employee who has not been notified of these rules.

You are required to contribute to a tip pooling arrangement, limited only to those employees who customarily and regularly receive their own tips. Your required contribution to the tip pool is $_____ . Other than this contribution, you have the right to retain all tips you receive. The tip credit will be taken only on the tips you actually receive (in other words, on the amount you receive from the tip pool after you make your contribution and the amount of tips you retain).

Please sign and date this form to acknowledge receipt.

_____   _____

Employee's Signature   Date

_____

Employee's Name (Print)

7:4   Tip Pooling

File Name: 07_Pay Policies.rtf

Include This Policy?
- ☐ Yes
- ☐ No
- ☐ Use our existing policy
- ☐ Other _____

Alternate Modifications

None

Additional Clauses

None

Related Policies

None

Notes

_____
_____
_____
_____
_____
_____
_____
_____
_____
_____
_____
_____
_____
_____
_____
_____
_____
_____
_____

7:4   Tip Pooling

Tip pooling (also known as "tipping out") is a source of much anxiety and frustration in the tipped workforce. Some employees—particularly those who have to deal most with the customers, such as wait staff or bell persons—deeply resent having to share their tips with employees who have less customer contact. Adopting a policy that explains exactly who is required to share how much of their tips can help ease this problem. If everyone knows ahead of time how the tip pool will work, there is less likelihood of confusion and resentment.

Tip Pooling

Employees in the following positions are required to pool tips:

_____

_____ .

If you hold one of these positions, you must contribute _____% of your tips to the pool at the end of each workday. The pool will be divided equally among all employees who worked that day and hold one of the positions listed above.

How to Complete This Policy

Which employees can participate in a tip pool? The rules depend on two things: whether your company takes a tip credit and (for now at least) where your company does business. If your company takes a tip credit, only employees who customarily and regularly receive tips, such as wait staff, bussers, bartenders, bellhops, and counter clerks may take part in the tip pool. Workers who do not receive tips of their own—such as dishwashers, cooks, chefs, and janitors—cannot be included in the pool.

If your company does not (or cannot, legally) take a tip credit, the rules about who can participate in the pool depend on how your federal court has interpreted the Department of Labor's rules. Some courts have found that employers who do not take a tip credit can require tipped employees to share their tips with employees who don't regularly receive them. Other courts have found that only tipped employees may be required to pool tips, whether or not the employer takes a credit.

You are always free to restrict the tip pool to tipped employees. If you decide to go this route, simply fill in the first blank with the titles of all positions that receive tips and will be required to contribute to the pool. Similarly, if you take a tip credit, you must restrict the tip pool to tipped employees—and can complete the policy the same way. However, if you don't take a tip credit and want non-tipped employees to share in the tip pool, you should raise this issue with the attorney who reviews your handbook.

The law also limits how much workers can be required to contribute to a pool. Only tips in excess of tips used for the tip credit may be taken for a pool. In other words, employees must be allowed to keep enough of their own tips to earn the minimum wage, when those tips are combined with the employees' hourly wage. To come up with a tip contribution amount, track employee tip amounts for a while to come up with an appropriate percentage. You can also check with a local trade organization to find out what percentage is usual in your industry. Remember, employees must receive at least the full minimum wage per hour once the pool is shared and divided.

CAUTION

Don't take a dip in the tip pool. All of the money in the tip pool must be shared among the workers who contribute to it, and only those workers. Employers cannot take any portion of the pooled tips for themselves under any circumstances. Tips belong to employees. If an employer violates this basic rule, the Department of Labor will find its tip pooling arrangement invalid, disallow any tip credit it takes, and require the employer to pay back the money it took from workers, plus interest and penalties.

Who Needs This Policy

Only companies that employ workers who receive tips and require those employees to share their tips with other workers need this policy.

7:5 Shift Premiums

File Name: 07_Pay Policies.rtf

Include This Policy?
- ☐ Yes
- ☐ No
- ☐ Use our existing policy
- ☐ Other _____

Alternate Modifications

None

Additional Clauses

None

Related Policies

For information and a policy on overtime, see Chapter 6. If employees will be allowed—or required—to put in overtime hours, use this policy to explain the rules.

Notes

_____
_____
_____
_____
_____
_____
_____
_____
_____
_____
_____
_____
_____
_____
_____
_____

7:5 Shift Premiums

A shift premium policy should tell employees whether they'll be paid extra for working certain shifts, if applicable.

Employers in industries that work in shifts often find it difficult to staff shifts that fall outside of the regular 9 a.m. to 5 p.m. workday. Some employers find that offering workers higher pay to work night shifts, swing shifts, or split shifts solves this problem. If your company offers a shift premium, you should adopt a policy explaining the premium in your handbook. After all, the incentive only works if employees know about it.

Shift Premiums

Employees who work the _____ shift will be paid a premium for each shift. This premium will be _____ .

How to Complete This Policy

In the first blank, insert the shifts for which your company pays a premium (for example, night shift, graveyard shift, or 3 p.m. to 11 p.m. shift). In the second blank, insert the premium amount. If all workers make the same wage, you can simply insert the dollar amount these shift workers will receive per hour. If workers earn varying rates, you can insert the dollar amount or percentage by which their pay will be increased for agreeing to work the tough-to-fill shift (for example, two dollars more per hour in addition to their regular hourly pay or an additional 20% of their regular hourly pay).

Some states, including California, require employers to pay their workers a certain premium for working a split shift: working one shift then coming back to work another shift after a relatively short break. Contact your state labor department (you can find contact details in Appendix B) to find out if your state imposes this type of requirement. If so, your company must pay split shift workers this premium, and you should set the premium in your policy to at least meet the minimum amount required by law.

7:6 Pay Docking

Pay docking refers to making deductions from an employee's salary for absences or as a penalty for violating work rules. Generally, employers must pay exempt employees on a salary basis. This means that the employees must receive their full salary for any week in which they perform any work, regardless of how many hours they work or how much work they get done. These rules are a general reflection of the fact that exempt employees are not, by definition, paid by the hour; instead, they must put in as many hours as it takes to get the job done.

There are some exceptions to this general rule, however. The overtime regulations include a longer list of situations when employers can withhold pay from exempt employees. Employers must adhere to this list very carefully: An employer that withholds pay improperly could inadvertently change its exempt employees to nonexempt employees, who are entitled to overtime pay.

The rules also create a "safe harbor" provision for employers who are trying to comply, which is where this policy comes in. Under the safe harbor provision, an employer won't be liable for violating the pay docking rules if it has a written policy prohibiting improper deductions, with a complaint mechanism, and it promptly reimburses any amounts that should not have been withheld.

Your pay docking policy should explain the circumstances under which exempt employees—those who are not entitled to earn overtime—can have their pay docked for missing work. It should also explain what employees can do if they believe their pay has been docked improperly.

7:6 Pay Docking

File Name: 07_Pay Policies.rtf

Include This Policy?

☐ Yes

☐ No

☐ Use our existing policy

☐ Other _____

Alternate Modifications

None

Additional Clauses

None

Related Policies

None

Notes

Docking the Pay of Exempt Employees

Our Company is legally required to pay exempt employees—those who are not entitled to earn overtime—on a salary basis. This means, among other things, that exempt employees must receive the same pay for each week in which they perform work, regardless of the quantity or quality of work performed, and regardless of how many hours they actually work, unless an exception applies. (For information on which employees are exempt, see Section _____ of this Handbook.)

Company policy prohibits docking the pay of an exempt employee—that is, paying the employee less than his or her full regular salary—except in the following circumstances:

- The employee takes at least one full day off for sickness or disability, in accordance with _____ .

- The employee takes at least one full day off for personal reasons other than sickness or disability (for example, for vacation).
- The employee serves an unpaid disciplinary suspension of at least one full day, imposed in good faith for violating a workplace conduct rule.
- The employee takes time off to serve on a jury, as a witness, or in the military; the employee receives money for jury fees, witness fees, or military pay; and the docked pay is an offset of the money received only.
- The employee starts or ends employment with our Company midweek (that is, the employee does not start work first thing Monday morning, or finish employment at the end of the workday on Friday).
- The employee violates a safety rule of major significance, and the amount docked is imposed as a penalty for that violation.
- The employee takes unpaid leave pursuant to the Family and Medical Leave Act.

If you are an exempt employee and you believe that pay has been improperly deducted from your salary in violation of these rules, please report it immediately using the Company's complaint policy. (See Section _____ of this Handbook.) Your complaint will be investigated and, if we find that your pay was improperly docked, you will be reimbursed for any amounts that should not have been withheld.

Who Needs This Policy

All companies that employ exempt employees *must* use this policy if they want the benefit of the safe harbor provision in the overtime rules.

How to Complete This Policy

In the first and third blanks, insert the appropriate section numbers for your Handbook's Employee Classification (see Chapter 5) and Complaint policies (see Chapter 20). In the second blank, insert the name of your company's plan or policy that provides paid time off for sickness or disability. For example, if your company offers paid sick leave, you should insert, "our sick leave policy." You may dock the employee's pay for this time only if you have a plan or policy that provides compensation for this time off.

RESOURCE

For more information on these rules. The Department of Labor has posted lots of resources on the overtime rules at its "Overtime Pay" page, www.dol.gov/whd/overtime_pay.htm.

7:7 Payroll Deductions

File Name: 07_Pay Policies.rtf

Include This Policy?
- ☐ Yes
- ☐ No
- ☐ Use our existing policy
- ☐ Other _____

Alternate Modifications

None

Additional Clauses

None

Related Policies

None

Notes

_____
_____
_____
_____
_____
_____
_____
_____
_____
_____
_____
_____
_____
_____
_____
_____
_____
_____
_____
_____

7:7 Payroll Deductions

Your payroll deduction policy should explain the mandatory deductions that will be taken from employees' paychecks, as well as the deductions an employee can request. Although all the information is usually right there on the pay stub, a policy can help clarify the reasons why deductions are taken (and why that paycheck is always so much smaller than the worker thinks it will be).

Payroll Deductions

Your paycheck reflects your total earnings for the pay period, as well as any mandatory or voluntary deductions from your paycheck. Mandatory deductions are deductions that we are legally required to take. Such deductions include federal income tax, Social Security tax (FICA), and any applicable state taxes. Voluntary deductions are deductions that you have authorized. Such deductions might include

_____
_____ .

   If you have any questions about your deductions, or wish to change your federal withholding form (Form W-4), contact _____
_____ .

How to Complete This Policy

In the space for voluntary deductions, list any contributions employees are allowed to make through payroll withholding, such as:

- insurance premiums
- flexible spending accounts
- contributions to pensions, 401(k)s, or other retirement accounts
- union dues
- charitable contributions, or
- contributions to credit unions or savings accounts.

   In the second blank, insert the name of the person or position that handles payroll matters. This might be the payroll administrator, human resources department, benefits coordinator, or whoever makes sure that paychecks go out on time or reports employee compensation to the IRS.

7:8   Wage Garnishments

Any employer can be required—by a court order, the IRS, or another government agency—to garnish an employee's wages. Most employers dislike these orders because wage garnishments are a payroll hassle. An employer who receives one will have to deduct the prescribed amount from the employee's wages, either for a limited amount of time (for example, when the employee owes a specified amount of money in unpaid taxes or student loans) or indefinitely (for example, for garnishments relating to child or spousal support), depending on the order.

No matter how much an employer dislikes having to deal with a wage garnishment order, the employee whose wages will be garnished likes it even less. Adopting a policy lets employees know that the company has no choice but to comply with these orders. Employees will know that there's not much point asking the employer to reduce, forgive, or postpone the garnishment; it's out of the company's hands. And hopefully, employees who are upset about a garnishment will take their complaints to the responsible person or agency, rather than to someone who can't change the situation (you).

Your wage garnishment policy should explain what a wage garnishment is and why an employee's wages might be garnished. It should also inform employees that the company must comply with orders to garnish wages.

Wage Garnishments

A wage garnishment is an order from a court or a government agency directing us to withhold a certain amount of money from an employee's paycheck and send it to a person or agency. Wages can be garnished to pay child support, spousal support or alimony, tax debts, outstanding student loans, or money owed as a result of a judgment in a civil lawsuit.

If we are instructed by a court or agency to garnish an employee's wages, the employee will be notified of the garnishment at once. Please note that we are legally required to comply with these orders. If you dispute or have concerns about the amount of a garnishment, you must contact the court or agency that issued the order.

7:8   Wage Garnishments
File Name: 07_Pay Policies.rtf

Include This Policy?
- ☐ Yes
- ☐ No
- ☐ Use our existing policy
- ☐ Other _____

Alternate Modifications
None

Additional Clauses
None

Related Policies
None

Notes

_____
_____
_____
_____
_____
_____
_____
_____
_____
_____
_____
_____
_____
_____
_____
_____
_____
_____
_____
_____

RESOURCE

Want more information on wage garnishments? The Department of Labor's website offers a helpful fact sheet on related federal law, including how much of an employee's wages can be garnished. You can download it at www.dol.gov/compliance/guide/garnish.htm.

7:9 Expense Reimbursement

Expenses often become a source of conflict between workers and management. Workers don't want to incur work-related expenses that the company refuses to pay. They want to know ahead of time what they will be reimbursed for, what they need to do to get reimbursed, and when they can expect repayment. Just as understandably, employers don't want to get hit with requests for reimbursement for extravagant, fraudulent, or unnecessary expenses. Employers also want some proof that the worker actually incurred the expenses claimed. An expense reimbursement policy can help you set things straight before your employees incur any expenses on behalf of the company.

Your expense reimbursement policy should tell employees which expenses will be reimbursed, how to get authorization to incur expenses, and the procedures for requesting reimbursement.

Expense Reimbursement

From time to time, employees may incur expenses on behalf of our Company. We will reimburse you for the actual work-related expenses you incur, as long as those expenses are reasonable. You must follow these procedures to get reimbursed:

- Get permission from your supervisor before incurring an expense.
- Spend the Company's money wisely. Make an effort to save money and use approved vendors if possible.
- Keep a receipt or some other proof of payment for every expense.
- Submit your receipts, along with an expense report, to your supervisor for approval within 30 days of incurring an expense.
- Your supervisor is responsible for submitting your expense report to _____

_____ .

If your report is approved, you will receive your reimbursement

_____ .

Remember that you are spending the Company's money when you pay for business-related expenses. We expect you to save money wherever possible. Your supervisor can assist you in deciding whether an expense is appropriate.

7:9   Expense Reimbursement

File Name: 07_Pay Policies.rtf

Include This Policy?
- ☐ Yes
- ☐ No
- ☐ Use our existing policy
- ☐ Other _____

Alternate Modifications
None

Additional Clauses
Require Employees to Use Particular Vendors
  Insert?:   ☐ Yes ☐ No
Include More Detail on Travel Expenses
  Insert?:   ☐ Yes ☐ No
Allow Mileage Reimbursement
  Insert?:   ☐ Yes ☐ No

Related Policies
None

Notes

_____
_____
_____
_____
_____
_____
_____
_____
_____
_____
_____
_____
_____
_____

> **Reality Check: An Expense by Any Other Name**
>
> Sometimes, state law dictates whether the employer or employee has to pay for a particular expense. For example, some states require employers to pay the cost of everything an employee needs in order to do the job, including uniforms and tools. Other states don't have such strict requirements; they allow employers to pass these costs on to their employees (or to refuse to reimburse these expenses, as the case may be). Contact your state labor department (you can find contact information in Appendix B) to find out what your state requires.

How to Complete This Policy

In the first blank, insert the position or department responsible for payroll matters (for example, the payroll department, the accounting department, or human resources). In the second blank, indicate when and how employees will receive their reimbursements (for example, "with your next paycheck" or "within 14 days").

Additional Clause to Require Employees to Use Particular Vendors

If your company has business accounts with particular vendors, such as messengers, caterers, or suppliers, you may want to modify our standard policy to require employees to do business with those vendors, if possible. This will save time and money: The company will know it's getting a good deal, and workers won't have to shop around. If you want to make this addition, insert the additional clause at the end of the list in our sample policy. Fill in the blank with the name of the position or department that handles payroll.

Additional Clause

- The Company maintains a list of preferred vendors for various work-related items and services. You must use these vendors, if possible. You can get a current copy of the list from _____ _____ .

Additional Clause to Include More Detail on Travel Expenses

The sample policy above is sufficient to handle very occasional employee travel. However, if the nature of your company's business requires employees to travel frequently, you may need a more detailed travel expense policy. Employees need to know what expenses will be reimbursed: Are they allowed to fly first class? To stay in a four-star hotel? You can modify the basic expense reimbursement policy above by simply adding this language at the end.

In the blank, insert the total amount employees will be paid per day for meals and other incidentals. To get an idea of how much other employers in the same field are offering as a per diem, contact a local industry organization or professional association. You can find out what the federal government pays per diem for travel at www.gsa.gov; select "Per Diem," then choose the state and city where your employees will travel. (Rates differ depending on the local cost of living.)

Additional Clause

Procedures for Travel Expenses

If employees are required to travel for work, the Company will reimburse you for your travel expenses, including:

- the cost of travel to and from the airport or train station, including parking expenses and tolls
- the cost of airline or train tickets—such tickets must be coach class, if possible
- the cost of an economy class rental car, if necessary
- a mileage reimbursement, for those employees who prefer to use their own cars for Company travel
- the cost of lodging (employees should select moderately priced lodging, if possible), and
- the cost of meals and other incidental expenses, up to a per diem of _____ per day.

You must request advance approval of all travel expenses from your supervisor and follow the procedures above to have your expenses reimbursed.

Additional Clause to Allow Mileage Reimbursement

If employees use their own cars for company business, you should modify our standard policy to include mileage reimbursement. Employees should also be required to have a valid driver's license and adequate auto insurance coverage.

To complete the additional clause, insert the rate of reimbursement in the first blank. Most employers pay a per-mile rate based on IRS standards (54 cents per mile in 2016). In the second blank, include the name of the department or position that handles payroll, which should be identical to what you inserted in the main Expense Reimbursement policy, above.

Additional Clause

Mileage Reimbursement

Employees who use their own vehicle for Company business will be reimbursed at the rate of _____. Employees are not entitled to separate reimbursement for gas, maintenance, insurance, or other vehicle-related expenses; the reimbursement rate above is intended to encompass all of these expenses.

Before using a personal vehicle for work-related purposes, employees must demonstrate that they have a valid driver's license and adequate insurance coverage.

The Company does not reimburse employees for their commute to and from the workplace.

To claim mileage reimbursement, you must follow these procedures:

- Keep a written record of your business-related travel, including the total mileage of each business trip, the date of travel, the location to which you traveled, and the purpose of your trip.
- If you anticipate having to travel an unusually long distance, get your supervisor's approval before making the trip.
- Submit your record to your supervisor for approval on the last day of the month.
- Your supervisor is responsible for submitting your record to

_____.

If your record is approved, you will receive your reimbursement payment with your next paycheck.

Form D: Expense Reimbursement Form

If employees will incur expenses, you should provide them with an expense form. A preprinted form will remind employees of what they have to submit along with their expense request—and streamline your paperwork. (You can find this and all other forms at this book's online companion page; see Appendix A for information on accessing the page.)

Expense Reimbursement Form

Date of Expense	Item or Service Purchased	Reason for Expense	Cost	Receipt Attached
_____	_____	_____	_____	☐ Yes ☐ No
_____	_____	_____	_____	☐ Yes ☐ No
_____	_____	_____	_____	☐ Yes ☐ No
_____	_____	_____	_____	☐ Yes ☐ No
_____	_____	_____	_____	☐ Yes ☐ No
_____	_____	_____	_____	☐ Yes ☐ No
_____	_____	_____	_____	☐ Yes ☐ No
_____	_____	_____	_____	☐ Yes ☐ No
_____	_____	_____	_____	☐ Yes ☐ No
_____	_____	_____	_____	☐ Yes ☐ No
_____	_____	_____	_____	☐ Yes ☐ No
_____	_____	_____	_____	☐ Yes ☐ No
_____	_____	_____	_____	☐ Yes ☐ No
_____	_____	_____	_____	☐ Yes ☐ No
_____	_____	_____	_____	☐ Yes ☐ No
_____	_____	_____	_____	☐ Yes ☐ No

Total: _____

_____   _____
Employee's Signature   Date Submitted

_____
Employee's Name (Print)

_____   _____
Supervisor's Signature   Date Approved

_____
Supervisor's Name (Print)

State Minimum Wage Laws for Tipped and Regular Employees

The chart below gives the basic state minimum wage laws. Depending on the occupation, the size of the employer's business, or the conditions of employment, the minimum wage may vary from the one listed here. Minimum wage rates in a number of states change from year to year; to be sure of your state's current minimum, contact your state department of labor or check its website, where most states have posted the minimum wage requirements. (See Appendix B for contact information.) Also, some local governments have enacted ordinances that set a higher minimum wage; contact your city or county government for more information.

"Maximum Tip Credit" is the highest amount of tips that an employer can subtract from the employee's hourly wage. The employee's total wages minus the tip credit cannot be less than the state minimum wage. If an employee's tips exceed the maximum tip credit, the employee gets to keep the extra amount.

"Minimum Cash Wage" is the lowest hourly wage that an employer can pay a tipped employee.

State and Statute	Notes	Basic Minimum Hourly Rate (*=tied to federal rate)	Maximum Tip Credit	Minimum Cash Wage for Tipped Employee	Minimum Tips to Qualify as a Tipped Employee (monthly unless noted otherwise)
United States 29 U.S.C. § 206; 29 U.S.C. § 203	This is the current federal minimum wage	$7.25	$5.12	$2.13	More than $30
Alabama	No minimum wage law				
Alaska Alaska Stat. § 23.10.065	Adjusts annually for inflation beginning in 2017, posted at www.labor.state.ak.us	$9.75	No tip credit	$9.75	N/A
Arizona Ariz. Rev. Stat. § 23-363	Adjusts annually for inflation, posted at http://www.ica.state.az.us/Labor/Labor_MinWag_main.aspx; does not apply to small businesses (those with gross revenue of less than $500,000 that are exempt from federal minimum wage laws)	$8.05	$3.00	$5.05	
Arkansas Ark. Code Ann. §§ 11-4-210 and 11-4-212	Applies to employers with 4 or more employees	$8.50	$5.87 (increases as minimum wage increases)	$2.63	Not specified

State Minimum Wage Laws for Tipped and Regular Employees (continued)

State and Statute	Notes	Basic Minimum Hourly Rate (*=tied to federal rate)	Maximum Tip Credit	Minimum Cash Wage for Tipped Employee	Minimum Tips to Qualify as a Tipped Employee (monthly unless noted otherwise)
California *Cal. Lab. Code § 1182.12*		$10 (Employers with 26 or more employees: minimum wage will increase to $10.50 on January 1, 2017, to $11 on January 1, 2018, and will continue to increase by $1 each following year until it reaches $15 in 2022. Employers with 25 or fewer employees: minimum wage will increase to $10.50 on January 1, 2018, $11 on January 1, 2019, and will increase by $1 each following year until it reaches $15 in 2023.)	No tip credit	$10 (Employers with 26 or more employees: minimum wage will increase to $10.50 on January 1, 2017, to $11 on January 1, 2018, and will continue to increase by $1 each following year until it reaches $15 in 2022. Employers with 25 or fewer employees: minimum wage will increase to $10.50 on January 1, 2018, $11 on January 1, 2019, and will increase by $1 each following year until it reaches $15 in 2023.)	N/A
Colorado *Colo. Const. Art. 18, § 15; 7 Colo. Code Regs. § 1103-1:3*	Adjusted annually for inflation, posted at www.coworkforce.com	$8.31	$3.02	$5.29	More than $30
Connecticut *Conn. Gen. Stat. Ann. §§ 31-58(j), 31-60; Conn. Admin. Code § 31-61-E2*		$10.10	36.8% for wait staff in hotel and restaurant industries; 18.5% for bartenders.	$6.38 for wait staff in hotel and restaurant industries; $8.23 for bartenders (increases as minimum wage increases)	$10 per week (full-time employees); $2 per day (part-time employees)
Delaware *Del. Code Ann. tit. 19, § 902(a)*		$8.25	$6.02	$2.23	More than $30
District of Columbia *D.C. Code Ann. § 32-1003*		$12.50 ($13.25 on January 1, 2018; $14.00 on January 1, 2019)	$9.17 (increases as minimum wage increases)	$3.33 ($3.89 on January 1, 2018; $4.45 on January 1, 2019)	Not specified

State Minimum Wage Laws for Tipped and Regular Employees (continued)

State and Statute	Notes	Basic Minimum Hourly Rate (*=tied to federal rate)	Maximum Tip Credit	Minimum Cash Wage for Tipped Employee	Minimum Tips to Qualify as a Tipped Employee (monthly unless noted otherwise)
Florida *Fla. Const., Art. X § 24; Fla. Stat. Ann. § 448.110*	Adjusted annually for inflation, posted at www.floridajobs.org	$8.10	$3.02	$5.08	More than $30
Georgia *Ga. Code Ann. § 34-4-3*	Applies to employers with 6 or more employees and more than $40,000 per year in sales	$5.15	Minimum wage does not apply to tipped employees	N/A	N/A
Hawaii *Haw. Rev. Stat. §§ 387-1 to 387-2*		$9.25 ($10.10 on January 1, 2018)	75¢ in 2016 and beyond, but only if the employee makes at least $7 more than minimum wage with tips	$8.50 (2017); $9.35 (2018)	More than $20
Idaho *Idaho Code §§ 44-1502; 44-1503*		$7.25	$3.90	$3.35	More than $30
Illinois *820 Ill. Comp. Stat. § 105/4; Ill. Admin. Code tit. 56, § 210.110*	Applies to employers with 4 or more employees	$8.25	40%	$4.95	At least $20
Indiana *Ind. Code Ann. § 22-2-2-4*	Applies to employers with 2 or more employees	$7.25*	$5.12	$2.13	Not specified
Iowa *Iowa Code 91D.1*	In first 90 calendar days of employment, minimum wage is $6.35	$7.25	40%	$4.35	At least $30
Kansas *Kan. Stat. Ann. § 44-1203*	Applies to employers not covered by the FLSA	$7.25	$5.12	$2.13	Not specified
Kentucky *Ky. Rev. Stat. Ann. § 337.275*		$7.25*	$5.12	$2.13	More than $30
Louisiana	No minimum wage law				
Maine *Me. Rev. Stat. Ann. tit. 26, §§ 663(8), 664*		$9 ($10 on January 1, 2018; $11 on January 1, 2019)	50%	$5 ($6 on January 1, 2018; $7 on January 1, 2019)	More than $30

State Minimum Wage Laws for Tipped and Regular Employees (continued)

State and Statute	Notes	Basic Minimum Hourly Rate (*=tied to federal rate)	Maximum Tip Credit	Minimum Cash Wage for Tipped Employee	Minimum Tips to Qualify as a Tipped Employee (monthly unless noted otherwise)
Maryland *Md. Code Ann., [Lab. & Empl.] §§ 3-413, 3-419*		$8.75 ($9.25 on July 1, 2017; $10.10 on July 1, 2018)	$5.12 (increases as minimum wage increases)	$3.63	More than $30
Massachusetts *Mass. Gen. Laws ch. 151, § 1; Mass. Regs. Code tit. 454, § 27.03*		$11	$7.25	$3.75	More than $20
Michigan *Mich. Comp. Laws §§ 408.412 to 408.424*	Applies to employers with 2 or more employees; excludes all employers subject to the FLSA, unless state minimum wage is higher than federal	$8.90 ($9.25 on January 1, 2018)	$5.52 (increases as minimum wage increases)	38% of the minimum wage, which is $3.38 in 2017	Not specified
Minnesota *Minn. Stat. Ann. § 177.24*	$7.75 for small employers (businesses with annual receipts of less than $625,000)	$9.50	No tip credit	$9.50	N/A
Mississippi	No minimum wage law				
Missouri *Mo. Rev. Stat. §§ 290.502, 290.512*	Doesn't apply to retail or service business with gross annual sales of less than $500,000	$7.65	50%	$3.83	Not specified
Montana *Mont. Code Ann. §§ 39-3-404, 39-3-409; Mont. Admin. R. 24.16.1508 & following*	Federal minimum wage for businesses with gross annual sales of more than $110,000. $4.00 for others. Adjusted annually. http://erd.dli.mt.gov/labor-standards/wage-and-hour-payment-act/minimum-wage-history	$8.15	No tip credit	$8.15	N/A
Nebraska *Neb. Rev. Stat. § 48-1203*	Applies to employers with 4 or more employees	$9	$6.87	$2.13	Not specified

	State Minimum Wage Laws for Tipped and Regular Employees (continued)				
State and Statute	Notes	Basic Minimum Hourly Rate (*=tied to federal rate)	Maximum Tip Credit	Minimum Cash Wage for Tipped Employee	Minimum Tips to Qualify as a Tipped Employee (monthly unless noted otherwise)
Nevada *Nev. Rev. Stat. Ann. §§ 608.100, 608.160, 608.250; Nev. Admin. Code 608.100; Nev. Const. Art. 15 § 16*	Adjusted annually, posted at labor.nv.gov	$7.25 if employer provides health benefits; $8.25 if no health benefits provided	No tip credit	$7.25 if employer provides health benefits; $8.25 if no health benefits provided	N/A
New Hampshire *N.H. Rev. Stat. Ann. § 279:21*		$7.25*	55%	45%	More than $30
New Jersey *N.J. Stat. Ann. § 34:11-56a4*		$8.44*	$6.31	$2.13 (suggested, not required)	Not specified
New Mexico *N.M. Stat. Ann.§ 50-4-22*		$7.50	$5.37	$2.13	More than $30
New York *N.Y. Lab. Law § 652*		$9	Depends on occupation	Depends on occupation	Depends on occupation
North Carolina *N.C. Gen. Stat. §§ 95-25.2(14), 95-25.3*		$7.25	$5.12	$2.13	More than $20
North Dakota *N.D. Cent. Code § 34-06-22; N.D. Admin. Code R. 46-02-07-01 to -03*		$7.25	33% of minimum wage	$4.86	More than $30
Ohio *Ohio Rev. Code Ann. § 4111.02; Ohio Const. art. II § 34a*	Same as federal minimum wage for employers with gross income under $299,000; adjusted annually, posted at www.com.ohio.gov/dico	$8.15	50%	$4.08	More than $30
Oklahoma *Okla. Stat. Ann. tit. 40, §§ 197.2, 197.4, 197.16*	Applies to employers with 10 or more full-time employees OR gross annual sales over $100,000 not otherwise subject to FLSA	$7.25	50% of minimum wage for tips, food, and lodging combined	$3.63	Not specified

State Minimum Wage Laws for Tipped and Regular Employees (continued)

State and Statute	Notes	Basic Minimum Hourly Rate (*=tied to federal rate)	Maximum Tip Credit	Minimum Cash Wage for Tipped Employee	Minimum Tips to Qualify as a Tipped Employee (monthly unless noted otherwise)
Oregon *Or. Rev. Stat. §§ 653.025, 653.035(3)*	Adjusted annually; posted at www.boli.state.or.us	$9.75 ($10.25 on July 1, 2017; $10.75 on July 1, 2018)	No tip credit	$9.75 ($10.25 on July 1, 2017; $10.75 on July 1, 2018)	N/A
Pennsylvania *43 Pa. Cons. Stat. Ann. §§ 333.103 and 333.104; 34 Pa. Code §§ 231.1 and 231.101*		$7.25*	$4.42	$2.83	More than $30
Rhode Island *R.I. Gen. Laws §§ 28-12-3 & 28-12-5*		$9.60	$5.71	$3.89	Not specified
South Carolina	No minimum wage law				
South Dakota *S.D. Codified Laws Ann. §§ 60-11-3 to -3.1*		$8.65	50%	$4.33	More than $35
Tennessee	No minimum wage law				
Texas *Tex. Lab. Code Ann. §§ 62.051 & 62.052*		$7.25	$5.12	$2.13	More than $20
Utah *Utah Code Ann. § 34-40-102; Utah Admin. R. 610-1*		$7.25	$5.12	$2.13	More than $30
Vermont *Vt. Stat. Ann. tit. 21, § 384(a); Vt. Code R. 24 090 003*	Applies to employers with 2 or more employees; adjusted annually, posted at www.vtlmi.info	$10 ($10.50 on January 1, 2018)	50% for employees of hotels, motels, restaurants, and tourist places	$5 (increases as minimum wage increases)	More than $120
Virginia *Va. Code Ann. §§ 40.1-28.9 and 28.10*	Applies to employees not covered by FLSA	$7.25	Tips actually received	Minimum wage less tips actually received	Not specified
Washington *Wash. Rev. Code Ann. § 49.46.020; Wash. Admin. Code § 296-126-022*	Adjusted annually; posted at www.lni.wa.gov	$11.00 ($11.50 on January 1, 2018; $12.00 on January 1, 2019)	No tip credit	$11.00 ($11.50 on January 1, 2018; $12.00 on January 1, 2019)	N/A

State Minimum Wage Laws for Tipped and Regular Employees (continued)					
State and Statute	Notes	Basic Minimum Hourly Rate (*=tied to federal rate)	Maximum Tip Credit	Minimum Cash Wage for Tipped Employee	Minimum Tips to Qualify as a Tipped Employee (monthly unless noted otherwise)
West Virginia *W.Va. Code §§ 21-5C-1, 21-5C-2, 21-5C-4*	Applies to employers with 6 or more employees at one location who are not covered by the FLSA	$8.75	70% of minimum wage	$2.62 (increases as minimum wage increases)	Not specified
Wisconsin *Wis. Admin. Code DWD § 272.03*		$7.25	$4.92	$2.33	Not specified
Wyoming *Wyo. Stat. § 27-4-202*		$5.15	$3.02	$2.13	More than $30

Employee Benefits

Most companies spend a significant amount of their workforce budgets on employee benefits. Indeed, about 40% of an average employee's compensation package goes toward benefits. Employers do this with good reason: Generous employee benefits can help entice high-quality workers, retain valuable employees, and improve labor relations. In addition, good benefits can actually help employees be more productive and effective in their jobs. For example, an employee with generous health insurance is less likely to miss work due to an untreated illness than an employee who's worried about high deductibles and copays.

Of course, your company can reap these rewards only if employees actually know about—and take advantage of—these benefit programs. Too often, employers pay for benefit programs that their employees don't even use, because the employees either don't know about the programs or don't understand them. The employee handbook is the ideal place to acquaint employees with their benefits.

The handbook is not, however, the ideal place to educate employees about every last detail of each benefit program. Unlike employee handbooks, benefit programs tend to change, even if only slightly, every year. If you put too much information in the handbook, you'll have to rewrite it every time your company needs to change and adjust the benefit programs. Or, if you leave out-of-date information in your handbook, you risk having employees rely on that information, unaware that the benefit no longer exists or may have changed significantly. This could damage employee relations and even leave your company vulnerable to a claim from the employee that it breached a contract (in the form of handbook language promising particular benefits).

CAUTION

If you have an electronic handbook, inform employees about their benefits through other means. A federal law commonly called ERISA requires that certain benefit information be given in writing to employees (see "Reality Check: Be Aware of ERISA," below, for more information about this law). This information must be provided in a particular format and style. Although employers are allowed to distribute this information electronically, they must follow strict rules in doing so. You should not use your handbook, electronic or paper, for this purpose. Talk to your attorney or benefits provider for more information.

As a result, most companies choose to describe their benefits quite generally in their employee handbooks and leave the details to separate handouts and brochures that can be distributed to employees whenever the need arises. The policies in this chapter follow that model. They allow you to toot your company's own horn and announce how wonderful the benefits are without binding your company to the details.

The benefits that employers provide usually fall into one of two groups: those that the employer provides voluntarily and those that are mandated by law. Voluntary benefit programs include dental insurance, on-site child care, life insurance, and retirement coverage (for example, a pension plan or a 401(k) plan). Legally mandated benefit programs include workers' compensation coverage and unemployment insurance. And somewhere in between is health insurance. Employers aren't required to provide it, but larger employers will have to pay a penalty if they don't (or even if they do, if employees still qualify for insurance subsidies, based on their income and the premium costs they have to bear under the employer's program).

To find out what sorts of benefits are mandated by law in your state, contact your state labor department. (See Appendix B for contact information.)

Your handbook should contain policies for every kind of benefit program you offer, regardless of whether the program is voluntary or legally mandated.

8:1 Employee Benefits: Introductory Statement

As explained above, you don't want to pack too many details into your benefits section, because you want to maintain flexibility. You should be able to change the benefits you provide at any time, and you want to avoid making promises in your handbook that you won't be able to keep.

This standard language maintains your company's flexibility to change benefits, explains the significance of official plan documents, and tells employees where to go for more information.

Employee Benefit Plans

As part of our commitment to our employees and their well-being, our Company provides employees with a variety of benefit plans, such as: _____

_____

_____

_____ .

Although we introduce you to those plans in this section, we cannot provide the details of each plan here. You should receive official plan documents for each of the benefit plans that we offer. Those documents (along with any updates we give you) should be your primary resource for information about your benefit plans. If you see any conflict between those documents and the information in this Handbook, you should rely on the official plan documents.

The benefits we provide are meant to help employees maintain a high quality of life, both professionally and personally. We sincerely hope that each employee will take full advantage of these benefits. If you have any questions about the benefits we offer, please talk to

_____ .

How to Complete This Policy

In addition to listing all of the benefits your company offers, you will have to choose someone to whom employees can go for more information about the various benefit plans. Try to pick someone in your company who is willing and able to get up to speed on these matters, such as an office manager or a human resources specialist. Don't simply instruct employees to call the customer service numbers at the various providers of your benefits plans. For employees to make

---

8:1   Employee Benefit Plans

File Name: 08_Employee Benefits.rtf

Include This Policy?
- ☐ Yes
- ☐ No
- ☐ Use our existing policy
- ☐ Other _____

Alternate Modifications
None

Additional Clauses
None

Related Policies
None

Notes

_____

_____

_____

_____

_____

_____

_____

_____

_____

_____

_____

_____

_____

_____

_____

_____

_____

the most of the benefits you offer—and for your company to get its money's worth from these programs—you need to have someone on site who can help employees wade through the often confusing maze of benefits rules.

Reality Check: Be Aware of ERISA

The word ERISA often strikes fear into the hearts of employers, because it is the acronym for one of the most dense and confusing federal laws on the books: The Employee Retirement Income Security Act.

Although it has the word "retirement" in its title, ERISA does not limit itself to retirement plans alone. In fact, the law governs the operation of virtually all employee benefit plans and most likely covers every benefit plan that your company offers its employees.

Among ERISA's many rules are those governing the information that employees must receive about their benefit plans. This information includes a summary plan description, notification of any changes to the plan, and information about how to appeal any adverse decisions made by the plan.

If you pay someone to administer a plan for you (for example, an insurance company provides health care coverage for your employees), that plan administrator will usually take care of complying with ERISA's requirements. Talk to your plan administrator and make sure that ERISA is being followed to the letter.

If you administer your own plan, however, that burden will fall on you. Unless you are incredibly sophisticated and experienced in ERISA matters, complying with ERISA is not something you can do on your own. Seek out professional help.

8:2 Domestic Partner Coverage

Some employers allow benefit coverage for domestic partners. Deciding whether to include domestic partner coverage is a complicated task—one that involves research into your state and local laws. Some localities require domestic partners to be covered; others prohibit it. Therefore, this is not something you can decide to do—or not do—based solely on your gut instinct or sense of morality. Make this decision only after consulting with your company's benefits administrator and/or lawyer.

The wording of your domestic partner policy will depend on many things, including state and local laws and the wording choices of your benefits administrator. The following is just an example of what such a policy might look like.

SAMPLE POLICY LANGUAGE

For those employees who are not married but who are in a committed relationship with another adult, we provide domestic partnership coverage.

To be eligible for benefits, the employee and the employee's partner must meet *all* of the following criteria:

- They must have lived together in an exclusive committed relationship for at least 12 months.
- They must be at least 18 years of age.
- They must live together in the same residence.
- They cannot be legally married to—or in a registered domestic partnership with—anyone else.
- They must not be related by blood more closely than would be allowed under the marriage laws of this state.
- They must complete and sign a Domestic Partnership Affidavit.

TIP

Domestic partnership still exists, even though same-sex marriage is legal. In 2015, the Supreme Court made same-sex marriage legal in every state. However, some states continue to recognize domestic partnerships, whether between same-sex or opposite-sex couples. In California, for example, a couple may register as domestic partners if at least one partner is collecting Social Security. Your lawyer and/or benefits administrator can help you determine whether you want to adopt (or retain) a domestic partner policy.

8:2 Domestic Partner Coverage

File Name: 08_Employee Benefits.rtf

Include This Policy?
- ☐ Yes
- ☐ No
- ☐ Use our existing policy
- ☐ Other _____

Alternate Modifications
None

Additional Clauses
None

Related Policies
None

Notes
_____
_____
_____
_____
_____
_____
_____
_____
_____
_____
_____
_____
_____
_____
_____
_____
_____
_____

8:3   Health Care Benefits

File Name: 08_Employee Benefits.rtf

Include This Policy?
- ☐ Yes
- ☐ No
- ☐ Use our existing policy
- ☐ Other _____

Alternate Modifications
None

Additional Clauses
None

Related Policies
None

Notes

_____
_____
_____
_____
_____
_____
_____
_____
_____
_____
_____
_____
_____
_____
_____
_____
_____
_____

8:3   Health Care Benefits

The health care coverage you offer to your employees is the flagship of your employee benefits program. No matter what other benefits you offer (tuition reimbursement, employee assistance programs, and the like), the most important one to your employees will be your health care program. Health care benefits include more than simply medical coverage. They also include any vision, dental, or similar benefits that you provide.

Because health care benefits have so many permutations and options, we cannot provide you with a standard policy to place in your handbook. We do, however, provide an example of a health care policy, with guidance on how to write your own.

SAMPLE POLICY LANGUAGE

Because your health is of great importance to us, we provide you with the following health care benefits: medical, dental, vision, and alternative care (including acupuncture and massage). If you have not already received detailed plan documents about each of these benefits, contact a representative in the Human Resources Department, who can provide you with all the information you need to start enjoying your health care benefits package right away.

Eligibility to receive health care benefits depends on your employee classification. (See Section ___ of this Handbook for information about employee classifications.) If you are a regular full-time employee, you are eligible to receive full health care benefits, and we will pay 100% of the cost of health care insurance premiums for you. You will be responsible for paying the premium for your spouse (or domestic partner) and any dependents you wish to be covered by our plan.

You and your covered family members become eligible for benefits 30 days after the day you start work.

As with all of the policies in this Handbook, our health care coverage may change at any time. For the most up-to-date information about your health care benefits, refer to the plan documents or contact the Human Resources Department.

What to Include in This Policy

When writing your health care benefits policy, it's important to keep in mind the advice we gave at the beginning of this chapter:
- Keep the information in the handbook general.
- Refer employees to official plan documents for details.

Obamacare

In 2010, Congress passed the Patient Protection and Affordable Care Act, typically referred to as the Affordable Care Act or simply as Obamacare. To say that the law has been controversial would be an understatement: It has been subject to legal and regulatory challenges, as well as delays. And, following the 2016 presidential election, the future of the law is very much uncertain; the information we provide here is accurate as we go to press, but check this book's companion page for updates. (Appendix A, "Creating Your Handbook," explains how to find the companion page.)

Much of the law is devoted to what health insurance must cover and how much it will cost. Unless you self-insure, however, these concerns will be addressed by your plan providers, not by you.

Larger employers must comply with the employer mandate, also referred to as play or pay. You are subject to the mandate if you have 50 or more full-time equivalent employees. To figure this out, add up your total employee hours and divide by the number of employees you have. If you come up with an average of 30 or more hours per week, you must comply with the mandate.

The mandate was delayed and then phased in. By 2016, all employers with 50 or more full-time equivalent employees must provide health insurance coverage to at least 95% of their eligible employees (those who work at least 30 hours per week) or pay a penalty. Even if you offer health coverage, you may have to pay a penalty if you have one or more employees enrolled in an insurance exchange plan. (This might happen if the employee's cost of participating in the plan exceeded a set percentage of the employee's income.)

Obamacare also includes other provisions that affect employers, from lactation break requirements to tax incentives to rules for wellness programs. Your lawyer or benefits administrator can help you sort through these issues, as well as the legal developments that unfold as a new administration takes office.

For details on Obamacare, visit www.healthcare.gov.

That being said, there are some details that you should include in your policy language. These details are not about the benefit itself but are about who is eligible for the benefit and who will pay for it. Include the following information in your medical benefits policy:

- the classification(s) of employees who are eligible for the benefit, often regular full-time employees (see Chapter 5 for policy language about employee classifications)

- the classification(s) of employees who are not eligible for the benefit, such as temporary employees or part-time employees
- the percentage of the premium that you will pay
- the percentage of the premium that the employee must pay, and
- whether family members will be covered (and who pays for that coverage).

> **CAUTION**
>
> **Does your plan cover spouses?** Since the Supreme Court's 2015 decision making gay marriage legal in every state, employers that offer insurance to employee spouses must make sure they are in compliance with the law. If you provide employee health care coverage through an insurer (as most employers do), your plan is almost certainly required to cover same-sex spouses on the same basis as opposite-sex spouses. (That is, you do not have to cover spouses, but you may not discriminate if you do.) Employers who self-insure (that is, they pay their own claims rather than going through an insurance company) should consult with a lawyer to make sure they are meeting their legal obligations.

8:4 State Disability Insurance

Some states require employers to withhold a portion of an employee's paycheck to pay for disability insurance. When employees suffer injuries off the job that prevent them from doing their work, they can receive disability benefits.

Even though money is taken out of their paychecks to pay for this benefit, many employees do not know about or understand it. This policy explains in general terms who is eligible for state disability benefits and alerts employees to the difference between disability coverage and workers' compensation.

State Disability Insurance

Sometimes, an employee suffers an illness or injury outside of the workplace that prevents the employee from working and earning income. If this happens to you, state disability insurance may provide you with a percentage of your salary while you are unable to work. This insurance is also available for the period of time when you are physically unable to work due to pregnancy and childbirth. All employees are eligible for this coverage and pay for it through deductions from their paychecks.

To find out more about state disability insurance, contact

_____ .

If you suffer from an illness or injury that is work related, then you may be eligible for workers' compensation insurance instead of state disability insurance. See the Workers' Compensation policy, below, or contact _____
for more information.

Who Needs This Policy

If your state requires you to withhold a percentage of your employees' wages to fund a state disability insurance program, you should have this policy in your handbook. Currently, only five states have these programs: California, Hawaii, New Jersey, New York, and Rhode Island.

8:4 State Disability Insurance

File Name: 08_Employee Benefits.rtf

Include This Policy?
- ☐ Yes
- ☐ No
- ☐ Use our existing policy
- ☐ Other _____

Alternate Modifications

None

Additional Clauses

None

Related Policies

8:6 Workers' Compensation

Notes

_____
_____
_____
_____
_____
_____
_____
_____
_____
_____
_____
_____
_____
_____
_____
_____
_____
_____
_____
_____

8:5 Disability Insurance

File Name: 08_Employee Benefits.rtf

Include This Policy?
- ☐ Yes
- ☐ No
- ☐ Use our existing policy
- ☐ Other _____

Alternate Modifications

None

Additional Clauses

None

Related Policies

None

Notes

_____
_____
_____
_____
_____
_____
_____
_____
_____
_____
_____
_____
_____
_____
_____
_____
_____
_____
_____
_____

8:5 Disability Insurance

In some instances, employees suffer a nonwork injury or illness that prevents them from working. Some employers provide long-term disability insurance, short-term disability insurance, or both to help employees in these circumstances. Short-term disability coverage can last anywhere from a few months to a couple of years, depending on the terms of your plan. Long-term coverage can last from a year or more to the employee's retirement age, again depending on the plan. If an employer has both types of coverage, the short-term policy typically kicks in first, with long-term benefits becoming available only after short-term coverage expires. As with health insurance benefits, it's best to keep your handbook description of disability benefits general. Leave the details to the plan documents that you distribute to your employees.

Disability Insurance

Sometimes, an employee suffers an injury or an illness outside of the workplace that prevents the employee from working. For eligible employees, this Company provides _____ disability coverage to protect them in these circumstances. This means they will receive a certain percentage of their salary while they are unable to work. To learn about the details of this coverage, including which employees are eligible, refer to the plan documents or contact _____ .

How to Complete This Policy

In the first space, indicate the type of disability insurance your company offers (short-term, long-term or both). In the second space, insert the position of the person who can explain these benefits to employees.

8:6 Workers' Compensation

Most employers must carry workers' compensation insurance to provide benefits to employees who suffer work-related injuries. This policy explains what workers' compensation insurance is, and it instructs employees to notify the company immediately if they are injured or become ill. This is a very important requirement, because it will encourage employees to address a work-related illness or injury as soon as it occurs rather than waiting until the injury or illness worsens. It can also help prevent harm to other employees.

Workers' Compensation Insurance

If you suffer from an illness or injury that is related to your work, you may be eligible for workers' compensation benefits. Workers' compensation will pay for medical care and lost wages resulting from job-related illnesses or injuries.

If you are injured or become ill through work, please inform your supervisor immediately regardless of how minor the injury or illness might be.

To find out more about workers' compensation coverage, contact

_____ .

Who Needs This Policy

All employers who are required by state law to provide workers' compensation coverage must have this policy in their handbooks. Contact your state labor department to find out about workers' compensation requirements in your state. (See Appendix B for contact information.)

Additional Clause to Refer to State Disability Insurance

If your state has a state disability insurance program (as discussed in Policy 8:4, above), you may want to add a sentence to your workers' compensation policy that refers to when an employee may be eligible for state disability insurance instead of workers' compensation. While workers' compensation covers work-related injuries and illnesses (for example, a construction worker who falls off a scaffolding while at work, breaks a leg, and is temporarily unable to work), it does not cover illnesses or injuries that are not related to an employee's work but that require the employee to miss work (for example, a construction worker who breaks a leg while on vacation skiing and is

---

8:6   Workers' Compensation Insurance

File Name: 08_Employee Benefits.rtf

Include This Policy?
- ☐ Yes
- ☐ No
- ☐ Use our existing policy
- ☐ Other _____

Alternate Modifications
None

Additional Clauses
Refer to State Disability Insurance
  Insert?:   ☐ Yes   ☐ No
Refer to Private Disability Insurance
  Insert?:   ☐ Yes   ☐ No

Related Policies
8:4   State Disability Insurance

Notes
_____
_____
_____
_____
_____
_____
_____
_____
_____
_____
_____
_____
_____
_____
_____
_____

temporarily unable to work). Below is an optional clause you can add to the end of our sample workers' compensation policy if your state has a state disability insurance program.

Additional Clause

> If you are unable to work because of an illness or injury that is not related to work, then you might be eligible for state disability insurance instead of workers' compensation. See the State Disability Insurance policy, above, or contact _____ _____ for more information.

Additional Clause to Refer to Disability Insurance

If your company provides disability coverage, it may be nice for you to include a clause in your workers' compensation policy alerting employees to this fact. This way, employees who have a nonwork injury or illness know where to look for the appropriate benefit.

Additional Clause

> If you are unable to work for an extended period because of a nonwork injury or illness, you might be eligible for disability insurance instead of workers' compensation. See the Disability Insurance policy in this handbook or contact _____ for more information.

8:7 Unemployment Insurance

Unemployment insurance is another state-mandated benefit. Depending on your state, unemployment insurance is funded through employer contributions, withholdings from employees' paychecks, or some combination of the two. Unemployment insurance pays benefits to employees who suddenly find themselves out of work.

The ins and outs of who is eligible for unemployment insurance can be rather complicated. As a result, this policy simply notifies employees that this benefit exists, and it instructs them on whom to contact for more information.

Unemployment Insurance

If your employment with our Company ends, you may be eligible for unemployment benefits. These benefits provide you with a percentage of your wages while you are unemployed and looking for work. To find out more, contact _____

_____ .

Who Needs This Policy

All employers who are required by state law to provide unemployment coverage should have this policy in their handbooks. Contact your state labor department to find out about requirements in your state. (See Appendix B for contact information.)

8:7 Unemployment Insurance

File Name: 08_Employee Benefits.rtf

Include This Policy?
- ☐ Yes
- ☐ No
- ☐ Use our existing policy
- ☐ Other _____

Alternate Modifications

None

Additional Clauses

None

Related Policies

None

Notes

8:8   Life Insurance

File Name: 08_Employee Benefits.rtf

Include This Policy?
- ☐ Yes
- ☐ No
- ☐ Use our existing policy
- ☐ Other _____

Alternate Modifications

None

Additional Clauses

None

Related Policies

None

Notes

_____
_____
_____
_____
_____
_____
_____
_____
_____
_____
_____
_____
_____
_____
_____
_____
_____
_____
_____
_____
_____
_____

8:8   Life Insurance

Employers are not required to carry life insurance coverage for their employees. Many do, however: It's a very popular benefit, especially for employees who have dependents or find it difficult to obtain this kind of coverage on their own. (Generally speaking, employees who receive group life insurance through their employer do not have to submit to a medical exam as they would if they were trying to get a policy on their own.)

If you choose to provide life insurance benefits, you will have to decide which employees to cover, the amount of coverage to offer, and the type of coverage. In addition, you can offer employees the option of purchasing coverage beyond what you provide. The permutations are endless, so it's wise to consult with a reputable vendor when designing your plan.

As with most of the benefit policies in this book, the life insurance policy is quite general, simply alerting employees to the benefit's existence and telling them where to go for more information.

Life Insurance

As an employee of this Company, you may be eligible to participate in our life insurance plan. Contact _____ to find out whether you are eligible and to learn more about the plan.

8:9 Education Reimbursement

Many companies recognize that encouraging employees to improve their skills and continue their education makes a lot of sense—both for the employees and for the company. Continuing education keeps employees professionally engaged, intellectually stimulated, and personally happy, and the company reaps the benefit of the employees' new knowledge and skills by staying competitive and on the cutting edge. (It may also qualify for a business tax deduction.)

If you have a reimbursement program that funds employee education in full or in part, let your employees know about it in your handbook.

Education Reimbursement

Our Company cares about the intellectual and professional growth of our employees. For this reason, we provide an education reimbursement program for [*state which classification of employees is eligible for this benefit*].

This policy applies to the following types of education:

- _____
- _____
- _____ , and
- _____ .

This policy reimburses the following types of education expenses:

- _____
- _____
- _____ , and
- _____ .

This policy reimburses your expenses at the following rate:

_____ .

Although we encourage employees to use this benefit, work must remain our employees' first priority. Employees must not allow their education efforts to interfere with their work. We reserve the right to end this benefit for employees who cannot keep up their job responsibilities while continuing their education.

To learn more about this policy, contact _____
_____ .

8:9   Education Reimbursement

File Name: 08_Employee Benefits.rtf

Include This Policy?
- ☐ Yes
- ☐ No
- ☐ Use our existing policy
- ☐ Other _____

Alternate Modifications
None

Additional Clauses
None

Related Policies
None

Notes

_____

_____

_____

_____

_____

_____

_____

_____

_____

_____

_____

_____

_____

_____

_____

_____

_____

_____

_____

_____

How to Complete This Policy

Most education reimbursement policies cover only permanent full-time employees, but you can apply your policy to whichever job classifications you like. Be sure to use the same terminology and criteria that you used in the employee classifications section of your handbook (see Chapter 5 for more information on this topic).

Once you describe who is eligible, you must explain exactly which types of education are covered. Do you cover courses taken at an accredited university only, or do you also cover community college courses and professional seminars and workshops? Do you cover only a certain number of hours per semester or as many hours as the employee chooses to take?

In addition, describe what types of expenses are covered. Do you reimburse tuition only or do you also reimburse the cost of books and materials?

Finally, explain how much you reimburse. Some companies will pay 100% of education expenses, while others pay only a portion. Still other companies tie their reimbursement to the grade the employee earns in the course (paying, for example, 100% for an "A," 75% for a "B," and so on).

Use of Company Property

In virtually every workplace, employees must use company equipment and property to do their jobs. This includes everything from the $3 stapler to the $3,000 computer to the $30,000 company car. Because you invest so much money in your equipment, it makes sense to say something about it in your handbook. There are a lot of issues to address, from personal use to proper maintenance and safety.

9:1 Company Property

File Name: 09_Company Property.rtf

Include This Policy?

☐ Yes

☐ No

☐ Use our existing policy

☐ Other _____

Alternate Modifications

None

Additional Clauses

None

Related Policies

For policies on personal use of the telephone and voicemail systems, see Chapter 14.

For policies on personal use of computers, software, and the Internet, see Chapter 15.

For policies on confidentiality and intellectual property, see Chapter 18.

Notes

_____

_____

_____

_____

_____

_____

_____

_____

_____

_____

_____

_____

_____

_____

9:1   General Use of Company Property

Regardless of the type of company property or equipment your employees use, you probably want them to take good care of it and use it only for company business. Anything less would affect your company's bottom line, as replacement and repair costs could pile up.

The following general use policy explains what constitutes proper use of company equipment, what you expect of employees when using company property, and why this matters in the first place.

Company Property

We have invested a great deal of money in the property and equipment that you use to perform your job. It is a senseless and avoidable drain on this Company's bottom line when people abuse Company property, misuse it, or wear it out prematurely by using it for personal business.

We ask all employees to take care of Company property and to report any problems to _____ .
If a piece of equipment or property is unsafe for use, please report it immediately.

Please use property only in the manner intended and as instructed.

We do not allow personal use of Company property unless specifically authorized in this Handbook.

Failure to use Company property appropriately, and failure to report problems or unsafe conditions, may result in disciplinary action, up to and including termination.

For information on use of the voicemail system, see Section _____ of this Handbook.

For information on use of computers, the Internet, and software, see Section _____ of this Handbook.

How to Complete This Policy

Choose an individual to whom employees can report problems. At some companies, this will simply be the employee's supervisor. Other companies designate one person to track and maintain company equipment.

9:2 Company Cars

If you provide cars for employees to drive, then you should explain the rules for their use in your handbook. This policy will need to address a variety of issues, from maintenance to personal use.

Company Cars

We have invested in Company vehicles so that our employees can use them on Company business in place of their own vehicles. This saves wear and tear on personal vehicles and eliminates the need for keeping track of mileage.

We need your help in keeping Company cars in good condition. Please keep them clean, and please remove any trash or personal items when you are finished using the vehicles.

Please immediately report any accidents, mechanical problems, or other problems to _____ _____ . We will try to have Company vehicles repaired or serviced as soon as possible.

Only authorized employees may use Company cars, and they may do so only on Company business.

You may not use Company vehicles while under the influence of drugs or alcohol or while otherwise impaired.

You may not text or talk on a cell phone while driving a Company vehicle.

You must have a valid driver's license to use Company cars, and we expect that you will drive in a safe and courteous manner. If you receive any tickets for parking violations or moving violations, you are responsible for taking care of them.

Violating this policy in any way may result in disciplinary action, up to and including termination.

Additional Clause for Employees With Assigned Cars

At some workplaces, the company car is not simply a vehicle that the employee checks out for a few hours while attending some event off site. In these workplaces (often in places where employees are salespeople who are almost constantly on the road), employees are assigned a company car on a more or less permanent basis. For as long as the employee works for the company, the employee has possession of the car and uses it for all business.

9:2 Company Cars

File Name: 09_Company Property.rtf

Include This Policy?
- ☐ Yes
- ☐ No
- ☐ Use our existing policy
- ☐ Other _____

Alternate Modifications
None

Additional Clauses
Employees With Assigned Cars
Insert?: ☐ Yes ☐ No

Related Policies
None

Notes
_____
_____
_____
_____
_____
_____
_____
_____
_____
_____
_____
_____
_____
_____
_____
_____
_____
_____
_____
_____

In such a situation, employers often make the employee responsible for maintaining the car. If you are in such a workplace, add the following paragraph to your policy.

Additional Clause

If you have been assigned a Company car, it is your responsibility to keep the car in good condition and repair. At a minimum, this means keeping the car clean, bringing it in for scheduled maintenance by an authorized service department, and checking and changing the oil on schedule. Periodically, we may inform you of other ways in which you must care for the car. We will, of course, reimburse you for any ordinary expenses associated with maintaining the vehicle.

9:3 Telephones

It's a good idea to let employees know that you expect them to use work phones for company business only, except in case of emergencies or quick calls. It isn't reasonable to prohibit all personal calls, as long as they are brief and infrequent; certainly you can allow an employee to tell a spouse or partner that he or she will be home late or to make sure that his or her kids made it home from school. But without a policy limiting personal calls, some employees may take advantage.

Telephone System

The Company's telephone system is for business use only. Employees are expected to keep personal calls to a minimum. If you must make or receive a personal call, please keep your conversation brief. Extensive personal use of Company phones is grounds for discipline.

See Section _____ of this Handbook for information on privacy and telephones.

9:3   Telephone System

File Name: 09_Company Property.rtf

Include This Policy?
- ☐ Yes
- ☐ No
- ☐ Use our existing policy
- ☐ Other _____

Alternate Modifications

None

Additional Clauses

None

Related Policies

For policies on personal use of the telephone and voicemail systems, see Chapter 14.

Notes

_____
_____
_____
_____
_____
_____
_____
_____
_____
_____
_____
_____
_____
_____
_____
_____
_____
_____

9:4   Return of Company Property

File Name: 09_Company Property.rtf

Include This Policy?

☐ Yes

☐ No

☐ Use our existing policy

☐ Other _____

Alternate Modifications

None

Additional Clauses

Garnish Final Paycheck

Insert?:   ☐ Yes   ☐ No

Related Policies

None

Notes

_____

_____

_____

_____

_____

_____

_____

_____

_____

_____

_____

_____

_____

_____

_____

_____

_____

_____

9:4   Return of Company Property

No employment relationship lasts forever, and when an employee leaves—whether through termination, layoff, or resignation—your company will want to get its property back.

Return of Company Property

When your employment with this Company ends, we expect you to return Company property, clean and in good repair. This includes this Employee Handbook, all manuals and guides, documents, phones, computers, equipment, keys, and tools.

We reserve the right to take any lawful action to recover or protect our property.

Additional Clause to Garnish Final Paycheck

Some states allow employers to garnish an employee's final paycheck to pay for lost, stolen, or damaged company property. Other states prohibit employers from doing this. To find out whether your state allows garnishment, contact your state labor department. (See Appendix B for contact information.)

If you live in a state that allows garnishment, consider adding the following paragraph to your policy.

Additional Clause

If you do not return a piece of property, we will withhold from your final paycheck the cost of replacing that piece of property. If you return a piece of property in disrepair, we will withhold from your final paycheck the cost of repair. We also reserve the right to take any other lawful action necessary to recover or protect our property.

Leave and Time Off

A little time off is a good thing, for employer and employee alike. Workers get a chance to have fun; deal with personal, civic, and family obligations; and recharge their batteries. Your company benefits, too: The business will be more productive if employees are healthy, rested, and focused on their jobs.

By now, offering at least some paid time off—for sickness and vacation—has become the nationwide standard. Also, an employer may be legally required to let employees take unpaid leave in certain circumstances. No matter what type of leave program your company decides to adopt, the policies in this chapter will help you set rules that are consistent, sensible, and easy to follow.

CONTENTS

10:1 Vacation

File Name: 10_Time Off.rtf

Include This Policy?
- [ ] Yes
- [ ] No
- [ ] Use our existing policy
- [ ] Other _____

Alternate Modifications

None

Additional Clauses

Cap Accrual of Vacation Time

   Insert?:   [ ] Yes   [ ] No

Pay Unused Vacation at Termination

   Insert?:   [ ] Yes   [ ] No

Related Policies

None

Notes

_____
_____
_____
_____
_____
_____
_____
_____
_____
_____
_____
_____
_____
_____
_____
_____
_____
_____
_____
_____

10:1 Vacation

Most employers offer paid vacation benefits to at least some of their employees, even though they aren't legally required to do so. Paid vacation has become standard business practice in this country. Employers who don't offer some paid days off for rest and relaxation will almost certainly have trouble attracting and retaining good employees.

Your vacation policy should explain who is eligible for vacation, how vacation time accrues, and how the employee can schedule time off.

Vacation

Our Company recognizes that our employees need to take time off occasionally to rest and relax, enjoy a vacation, or attend to personal matters. That's why we offer a paid vacation program.

Employees who _____
are eligible to participate in the paid vacation program.

Eligible employees accrue vacation time according to the following schedule:

Years of Employment	Vacation Accrual
_____	_____
_____	_____
_____	_____
_____	_____
_____	_____
_____	_____
_____	_____
_____	_____
_____	_____
_____	_____

Employees must schedule their vacations _____
in advance, with their supervisor. We will try to grant every employee's vacation request for the days off of their choice. Because we must have enough workers to meet our day-to-day needs, however, we might not be able to grant every vacation request, especially during holiday periods.

How to Complete This Policy

In the first blank space, indicate which employees will be eligible to participate in the vacation program (for example, "Employees who work at least 32 hours per week" or "Employees who have been with the company for at least three months"). Some employers limit these benefits to full-time employees or require employees to complete a waiting period before they can accrue or use vacation benefits. (For information and policies on these employee classifications, see Chapter 5.)

In the second blank, write in the schedule by which employees will accrue benefits. Many employers provide increases in benefits to employees who stay with the company over time. For example, a worker might accrue ten days of vacation during the first year or two of employment, then move up to 15 the next year, then 20. Once you figure out how many days of vacation employees will accrue, divide that number by 12 to figure out how many days of vacation they accrue each month. The sample accrual schedule below allows employees to accrue ten days of vacation during their first and second years of employment, 15 during their third and fourth years, and 20 during each year thereafter.

SAMPLE POLICY LANGUAGE

Years of Employment	Vacation Accrual
0–2	10 days per year, at the rate of $5/6$ of a day per month
2–4	15 days per year, at the rate of 1¼ days per month
4 or more	20 days per year, at the rate of $1^2/_3$ days per month

Of course, if your company provides the same number of vacation days to all employees, you can delete this schedule and replace it with your company's rule, such as "Eligible employees accrue 1 day of vacation per month."

In the third blank, insert how many days of notice your company requires employees to give (for example, "30 days").

Additional Clause to Cap Accrual of Vacation Time

Your company can encourage employees to use their vacation regularly—and avoid having employees out for weeks of collected vacation at a time—by capping how much vacation time employees can accrue. Employees who reach this limit won't earn any more vacation time until they take some vacation and bring themselves back down below the cap. To cap how much vacation time an employee can accrue, add this clause to your policy immediately after the accrual schedule. In the blank space, insert the cap: how many hours or days of vacation time an employee will be allowed to accrue.

Additional Clause

> Employees may not accrue more than _____ of vacation time. Once an employee's vacation balance reaches this limit, an employee may accrue more vacation only by taking some vacation time to bring the employee's balance back below the limit.

CAUTION

"Use it or lose it" policies are illegal in some states. An employer is legally entitled to cap how much vacation time an employee can accrue. However, some states forbid "use it or lose it" policies, by which an employee must forfeit accrued but unused vacation time over a certain limit or past a certain date. Because these states view earned vacation time as a form of compensation, which must be cashed out when the employee quits or is fired, a policy that takes vacation time away is seen as illegally failing to pay employees money that they have already earned. Although the difference may seem merely technical, an accrual cap is legal in these states, because it prohibits the employee from earning vacation time in the first place, rather than taking away vacation time after the employee has earned it. Contact your state labor department to find out about your state's rules. (See Appendix B for contact information.)

Additional Clause to Pay Unused Vacation at Termination

Some states require employers to cash out unused, accrued vacation time when an employee quits or is fired. You can find out your state's rule by checking "State Laws That Control Final Paychecks" at the end of Chapter 21. If your company does business in a state that requires employers to pay unused vacation, you might consider modifying the policy to inform employees that they will receive payment for unused vacation. To do so, simply add the clause below as the final paragraph of the policy.

Additional Clause

> Employees will be paid for any accrued and unused vacation when their employment terminates.

10:2 Holidays

Most companies offer their employees paid time off on certain holidays, such as New Year's Day, Independence Day, and Thanksgiving. Your holiday policy should tell employees which holidays the company observes and what happens when a holiday falls on a weekend.

Holidays

Our Company observes the following holidays each year:

_____

_____

_____

_____

_____

_____

_____

_____

_____

If a holiday falls on a weekend, the Company will inform you when the holiday will be observed. Ordinarily, holidays falling on a Saturday will be observed the preceding Friday; holidays falling on a Sunday will be observed the following Monday.

How to Complete This Policy

In the blank space, list the holidays that your company observes. The days you choose will, of course, depend on when your company is open. Most employers offer some combination of the following paid holidays: New Year's Day, Martin Luther King Jr. Day, President's Day, Good Friday, Memorial Day, Independence Day, Labor Day, Columbus Day, Veterans' Day, Thanksgiving, the Friday following Thanksgiving, Christmas Eve, Christmas Day, and New Year's Eve.

Additional Clause to Allow Floating Holidays

Some employees may not observe the religious holidays your company chooses to offer—for example, Christmas or Good Friday—and may wish to take a holiday on a day of significance to their own religion. Employers are legally obligated to accommodate their workers' religious practices, which in some cases may require an employer to give these workers time off for important religious holidays. Rather than

---

10:2 Holidays

File Name: 10_Time Off.rtf

Include This Policy?

☐ Yes

☐ No

☐ Use our existing policy

☐ Other _____

Alternate Modifications

None

Additional Clauses

Allow Floating Holidays

Insert?:   ☐ Yes   ☐ No

Related Policies

None

Notes

_____

_____

_____

_____

_____

_____

_____

_____

_____

_____

_____

_____

_____

_____

_____

_____

_____

requiring workers to come to management with these requests, your company can make floating holidays available to all workers, to allow them to participate in religious activities or attend to other personal matters.

Some employers offer only one or two floating holidays per year; others offer more floating holidays but trim the list of company-recognized holidays accordingly. If your company will offer floating holidays, add the clause below as the second paragraph of the policy, immediately after the list of holidays your company observes. In the blank, insert the number of floating holidays employees will be allowed to take each year.

Additional Clause

Eligible employees are also entitled to take _____ floating holidays each year. These holidays may be used to observe a religious holiday, to celebrate your birthday, or simply to take a day off for personal reasons. You must schedule your floating holidays with your supervisor in advance. If you do not use your floating holidays during the year, you may not carry them over to the next year.

10:3 Sick Leave

It's common practice for employers to provide paid sick days. In an increasing number of states and localities, it may also be the law. A number of cities now require employers that do business within the city limits to provide some paid sick time to their employees. And, following the groundbreaking example of Connecticut, which passed a law in 2011 requiring employers to offer some paid sick leave, California, Massachusetts, Oregon, Vermont, Washington, the District of Columbia, and Arizona have all passed laws requiring employers to provide some paid sick leave.

Even if your state or local government does not require you to offer paid sick time, it's a good idea. Paid sick days help workers who live paycheck to paycheck make ends meet, create fewer payroll hassles, and, perhaps most important, encourage sick workers to stay home rather than coming to work to infect the rest of the workforce or perform at a substandard level.

Your sick leave policy should explain who is eligible for leave, how much leave employees can take, and any notice requirements the company will impose.

Sick Leave

Our Company provides paid sick days to _____ . (For information on employee classifications, see Section _____ of this Handbook.) Eligible employees accrue _____ sick days per year at the rate of _____ per month. The Company will not pay employees for sick days that have accrued but have not been used when employment ends.

Employees should use sick leave when they are unable to work due to illness or injury. Please do not report to work if you are feeling too ill to do your job, you have a fever, or you have a contagious illness, such as influenza. By staying home and using paid sick leave, you are supporting your own health and preventing transmission of communicable illness to coworkers and customers. If your supervisor determines that you are not feeling well enough to work, you will be sent home.

You must report to your supervisor if you will need to take sick leave. We ask that employees call in as soon as they realize that they will be unable to work, before the regular start of their workday. You must report to your supervisor by phone each day you are out on leave.

Sick leave is not to be used as extra vacation time, personal days, or "mental health" days. Any employee who abuses sick leave may be subject to discipline.

10:3 Sick Leave

File Name: 10_Time Off.rtf

Include This Policy?
- ☐ Yes
- ☐ No
- ☐ Use our existing policy
- ☐ Other _____

Alternate Modifications

None

Additional Clauses

Limit Carryover or Cap Accrual of Sick Leave

Insert?: ☐ Yes ☐ No

If yes, choose one: ☐ A ☐ B

Cap Use of Sick Leave in One Year

Insert?: ☐ Yes ☐ No

Allow Other Uses for Sick Leave

Insert?: ☐ Yes ☐ No

Related Policies

None

Notes

_____
_____
_____
_____
_____
_____
_____
_____
_____
_____
_____
_____
_____

How to Complete This Policy

In the first blank, indicate who is eligible for paid sick leave. Some employers provide sick days only to certain employees. Your company might cover only full-time employees, only full-time employees and part-time employees who work at least a minimum number of hours per week, or only employees who have been employed for at least a certain period of time. (See Chapter 5 for more information and policies on these employee classifications.)

In the third and fourth blanks, indicate the rate at which sick leave will accrue. For example, many employers provide that employees will accrue 12 paid sick days per year, at a rate of one per month. Others allow employees to accrue six or ten sick days per year, at a rate of the appropriate fraction of a day per month.

  CAUTION

Check the latest federal, state, and local requirements for sick leave. As we go to press, federal law doesn't require employers to offer paid sick leave. As noted above, however, a growing number of state and local governments do. Paid sick leave is a hot trend in statehouses across the country, so make sure to check for new legal developments in the area where you do business before adopting your policy. Applicable law may determine how you complete your policy (for example, who is eligible for sick leave and how the benefit accrues). The lawyer who reviews your handbook can make sure your policy complies with the latest requirements.

Additional Clause to Limit Carryover or Cap Accrual of Sick Leave

The policy above is silent on the issue of carryover: whether employees can simply keep accruing unused sick leave month after month, year after year. However, many employers either set a cap on how much sick leave an employee can accrue or don't allow employees to carry over sick leave from one year to the next at all. The problem with a flat "no carryover" policy is that an employee might get sick at the beginning of the year, before enough sick leave hours have accrued to cover the absence. And policies that zero out sick leave at the end of the year tend to encourage employees to take that leave before it disappears, whether they're sick or not, resulting in numerous cases of the "holiday flu."

Another problem with "no carryover" policies is that they might be illegal. Currently, all of the states that require employers to provide paid sick leave also require employers to let employees carry over a set amount of accrued sick leave at the end of the year. For all of these reasons, employers interested in restricting carryover should consider a limit rather than a cap.

A different option for limiting a pile-up of sick leave is to cap how many hours or days of sick leave an employee can accrue. For example, once an employee has accrued ten unused sick days, that employee accrues no more sick leave until some of the accrued time is used. If your state or local government requires you to provide paid sick leave, you'll need to make sure you can legally place a cap on accrual. For example, Washington recently passed a law requiring paid sick leave, and—unlike the laws in other states that currently require paid sick leave—it does not explicitly allow employers to cap accrual. However, it does allow employers to limit carryover of sick leave from one year to the next.

To limit carryover of sick leave from year to year, use Additional Clause A, below. To limit sick leave accrual, use Additional Clause B, instead. In the blank space, insert the maximum number of sick days or hours that an employee may carry over or accrue, respectively. In either case, insert the additional clause at the end of the policy.

Additional Clause A: Limit Carryover of Sick Leave

> Employees may carry over no more than _____ of paid sick leave from one calendar year to the next.

Additional Clause B: Cap Accrual of Sick Leave

> Employees may accrue a maximum of _____ of paid sick leave. Once an employee has reached this limit, no more sick leave will accrue until the employee uses sick leave to reduce the accrued total below the maximum.

Additional Clause to Cap Use of Sick Leave in One Year

Some states that require employers to provide paid sick leave also allow employers to put a limit on how much sick leave employees may use in one year. This limit might be less than the total hours an employee accrues during the year. In California, for example, employers may cap the total amount of paid sick leave an employee accrues at 48 hours or six days. However, employers are legally entitled to limit the total amount of paid sick leave an employee may use in one year to 24 hours or three days.

If you wish to cap the amount of leave employees can use in a year (and your state and local government allow you to do so), insert the following clause at the end of the policy; in the blank space, insert the total annual sick leave employees will be allowed to take.

Additional Clause

Employees may use no more than _____ of paid sick leave in a calendar year.

Additional Clause to Allow Other Uses for Sick Leave

Our policy indicates that employees can use sick leave when they are too injured or ill to work. However, many employers make sick leave available for other purposes. For example, employees might be allowed to use sick leave to go to appointments with a doctor or dentist, to care for a sick family member, or to take a family member for medical care. Some state laws require employers to make sick leave available for employees to care for a sick family member or for other reasons. Contact your state labor department to find out your state's rules; Appendix B provides contact information.

If your state requires employers to make sick leave available for additional purposes, or if your company wants to allow employees to use sick leave for additional reasons, add this clause immediately after the first sentence in the second paragraph of our sample policy. In the blank, indicate the additional uses of sick leave the company offers (for example, "care for a sick family member" or "attend necessary medical and dental appointments").

Additional Clause

Employees may also use sick leave to _____
_____
_____
_____
_____ .

10:4 Paid Time Off

Rather than adopting separate policies on vacation, sick leave, floating holidays, or other types of leave, many employers now adopt a single policy to give employees a certain number of paid days off per year, which the employees can use as they wish. Using a unified paid time off ("PTO") policy can benefit your company by reducing paperwork and record-keeping hassles and reducing the oversight management needs to exercise over employees, particularly regarding their use of sick leave. Because employees are entitled to take PTO for any reason, no one will have to make sure they are really sick—and they won't feel compelled to prove it ("(cough), I really caught a bad cold (sniffle)").

However, adopting a unified PTO policy can have significant drawbacks in some states. Because PTO is legally considered vacation time and sick leave, any state laws that regulate these issues apply to an employee's entire allotment of PTO. For example, some states require employers to pay an employee for accrued, unused vacation time when the employee quits or is fired. In these states, an employer that has a PTO policy will have to pay out the entire unused allotment of PTO. If your company does business in one of these states, management should think twice—and perhaps consult with a lawyer—before adopting a PTO policy. If your state requires employers to provide paid sick leave, your PTO policy will also have to comply with those provisions.

If your company adopts a PTO policy, remember that the policy takes the place of vacation, sick leave, and floating holiday policies. You should adopt one or the other, not both. Your PTO policy should explain which employees are eligible for PTO, how many days of PTO will be granted per year, and any procedures employees must follow to take PTO.

10:4 Paid Time Off

File Name: 10_Time Off.rtf

Include This Policy?
- ☐ Yes
- ☐ No
- ☐ Use our existing policy
- ☐ Other _____

Alternate Modifications
None

Additional Clauses
Cap Accrual of PTO
   Insert?:   ☐ Yes   ☐ No
Pay Unused PTO at Termination
   Insert?:   ☐ Yes   ☐ No

Related Policies
None

Notes

_____
_____
_____
_____
_____
_____
_____
_____
_____
_____
_____
_____
_____
_____
_____
_____
_____

Paid Time Off

Instead of offering separate vacation, sick leave, and personal days or floating holidays, our Company offers a paid time off ("PTO") program that combines all of these benefits. We believe this program will give employees the flexibility to manage their time off as they see fit. Employees may use PTO for sickness, for vacation, to attend a child's school activities, to care for elderly or ill family members, to take care of personal errands or business, or simply to take a day off work.

You are eligible to participate in the PTO program if you _____ _____ . (For information on employee classifications, see Section _____ of this Handbook.)

PTO accrues according to the following schedule:

Years of Employment	PTO Accrual
_____	_____
_____	_____
_____	_____
_____	_____
_____	_____
_____	_____
_____	_____
_____	_____
_____	_____

Employees must schedule time off in advance with their supervisors. We will try to grant every employee's PTO request for the days off they choose. Because we must have enough workers to meet our day-to-day needs, however, we might not be able to grant every PTO request, especially during holiday periods.

If circumstances, such as a medical or family emergency, prevent advance scheduling, you must inform your supervisor as soon as possible that you are taking paid time off.

Because PTO encompasses vacation and sick leave, employees must manage their PTO responsibly to ensure that they have time available for emergencies, such as personal or family illness. An employee who needs time off but has no accrued PTO may be eligible to take unpaid leave.

How to Complete This Policy

In the first blank, indicate which employees will be eligible to participate in the PTO program. Some employers limit these benefits to full-time employees or full-time employees and part-time employees who work a minimum number of hours per week, or institute a waiting period before employees may accrue or use benefits. (For information and policies on these employee classifications, see Chapter 5.)

In the second blank, write in the schedule by which employees will accrue benefits. Many employers provide higher benefits to employees who have been with the company longer. For example, a worker might accrue 20 days of PTO during the first year or two of employment, then move up to 25, then 30. Once you figure out how many days of PTO employees will accrue, divide that number by 12 to figure out how many days of PTO employees accrue each month. The sample accrual schedule below allows employees to accrue 20 days of PTO during their first year of employment, 25 during their second year, and 30 during each year thereafter.

SAMPLE POLICY LANGUAGE

Years of Employment	PTO Accrual
0–1	20 days per year, at the rate of $1^2/_3$ days per month
1–2	25 days per year, at the rate of $2^1/_{12}$ days per month
2 or more	30 days per year, at the rate of 2½ days per month

If your company provides the same number of PTO days or hours to all employees, you can delete this schedule and replace it with your company's rule. For example, "Eligible employees accrue 24 PTO days per year, at the rate of two days per month."

Additional Clause to Cap Accrual of PTO

Some employers place an upper limit on the amount of PTO an employee can accrue. An employee who reaches this limit does not accrue any more PTO until he or she takes some time off. Imposing this type of cap can prevent employees from going months, or even years, without taking enough time off to prevent burnout. It can also help the company guard against having an employee gone for months at a time. If you wish to place a cap on PTO accrual, add this clause to the policy. In the blank, insert the maximum number of PTO days or hours an employee can accrue.

Additional Clause

Employees may not accrue more than _____ of PTO. Once an employee's PTO balance reaches this limit, an employee may accrue more PTO only by taking some PTO to bring the employee's balance back below the limit.

Additional Clause to Pay Unused PTO at Termination

In those states that require employers to cash out unused accrued vacation time when an employee quits or is fired (see Policy 10:1, above), employers will generally have to pay an employee for unused, accrued PTO on termination. If your company does business in one of these states, consider modifying the policy to inform employees that they will receive payment for unused PTO. To do so, simply add the clause below as the final paragraph of the policy.

 SEE AN EXPERT

If your state requires employers to cash out vacation pay, you might be better off with separate policies on vacation, sick leave, and perhaps floating holidays. Talk to a local lawyer who knows about your state's employment laws to determine the best choice for your company.

Additional Clause

Employees will be paid for any accrued and unused PTO when their employment ends.

10:5 Family and Medical Leave

Working people have always had a tough time balancing the demands of a job with personal and family needs. Today, with large numbers of women in the workforce and many workers having to care for young children and aging parents, the stresses created by this juggling act have become more acute than ever.

In response to this problem, Congress passed the Family and Medical Leave Act ("FMLA"). The FMLA requires employers who have at least 50 employees to allow eligible workers to take up to 12 weeks of unpaid leave per year in the following circumstances:

- to bond with a new child (through birth, adoption, or foster care)
- to care for a family member who is suffering from a serious health condition
- for the employee's own serious health condition, or
- for a qualifying exigency arising out of a family member's active duty or call to active duty in the military.

Employees also have the right to take up to 26 weeks of leave in a single 12-month period to care for a family member who incurred or aggravated a serious injury or illness on active duty, for which the family member is undergoing treatment or recuperation, in outpatient status, or is on the temporary disability retired list. This provision also covers veterans suffering from a serious, service-related illness or injury, as long as the veteran was a member of the Armed Forces, Guard, or Reserves in the past five years.

Many states have passed laws similar to the FMLA, and some of these laws apply to employers with fewer than 50 employees. Some state laws require employers to provide leave for a wider variety of circumstances than the FMLA. For example, some states include time off to care for a seriously ill domestic partner, to take a child or parent to necessary medical and dental appointments, or to donate bone marrow. And some of these laws provide for more than 12 weeks of leave per year. You can find information on these laws in "State Family and Medical Leave Laws" at the end of this chapter.

A company that is covered by both the FMLA and a state family and medical leave law must follow whichever law gives its employees more rights and protections in a given situation: the state law, the FMLA, or both. Because of these potential overlaps between federal and state law, an employer might find itself in one of four situations, any of which may require it to have a different family and medical leave policy:

10:5 Family and Medical Leave

File Name: 10_Time Off.rtf

Include This Policy?
- ☐ Yes
    - *Choose one:* ☐ A ☐ B
- ☐ No
- ☐ Use our existing policy
- ☐ Other _____

Alternate Modifications
None

Additional Clauses
Policy A only: Continue Health Insurance
   Insert?:   ☐ Yes ☐ No
Policy A only: Limit Leave Available to Spouses
   Insert?:   ☐ Yes ☐ No
Policy A only: Allow Employees to Supplement Workers' Compensation or Disability Benefits
   Insert?:   ☐ Yes ☐ No

Related Policies
None

Notes

_____
_____
_____
_____
_____
_____
_____
_____
_____
_____
_____

1. The employer has fewer than 50 employees and either does not do business in a state with a family and medical leave law or does not have to comply with the state's law because the employer is too small. These employers are free to offer family and medical leave but are not legally required to do so.

2. The employer has fewer than 50 employees and does business in a state with a family and medical leave law that applies to it. These employers must comply with their state's law but not with the FMLA.

3. The employer has at least 50 employees but does not do business in a state with a family and medical leave law. These employers comply with the FMLA only.

4. The employer has at least 50 employees and does business in a state with a family and medical leave law. These employers must comply with both the FMLA and their state's law.

Because of the intricacies of state family and medical leave laws—and the sometimes complicated ways they interact with the FMLA—we cannot address the needs of employers who find themselves in the second or fourth groups here. If the chart at the end of this chapter indicates that your company has to follow a state family and medical leave law, either alone or in conjunction with the FMLA, consult with a lawyer who can help you work out a family and medical leave policy that meets your state's requirements.

We offer two alternate policies below. The first is for employers who have to comply with the FMLA only (third group). The second is for smaller employers—those who, because they have fewer than 50 employees, do not have to comply with the FMLA (first group)—who wish to adopt a family and medical leave policy.

Alternate Policy A: For Employers Who Must Comply With the FMLA Only

Family and Medical Leave

Employees who have worked for our Company for at least 12 months, have worked at least 1,250 hours during the previous year, and work within 75 miles of at least 50 Company employees, are eligible to take family and medical leave.

Reasons for Leave

12-Week Entitlement

Eligible employees may take up to 12 weeks of unpaid leave in a 12-month period for these purposes:

- for the employee's own serious health condition
- to care for a spouse, child, or parent who has a serious health condition
- to bond with a newborn, newly adopted child, or recently placed foster child, or
- to handle a qualifying exigency relating to a spouse's, child's, or parent's deployment to a foreign country on active duty or call to active duty in the Armed Forces, National Guard, or Reserves.

A serious health condition is an illness, injury, impairment, or physical or mental condition that involves either inpatient care or continuing treatment by a health care practitioner for a condition that prevents the employee or family member from performing the functions of the job, participating in school, or performing other daily activities. Incapacity relating to pregnancy, prenatal care, or childbirth is a serious health condition. If you have questions about what qualifies as a serious health condition, contact _____ .

Qualifying exigencies include issues arising out of a family member's short-notice deployment; attending military events and activities; arranging for alternative child care; making financial and legal arrangements; attending counseling sessions; attending post-deployment activities; and visiting the family member while on short-term, temporary rest leave. Other activities and events may also qualify; if you have questions about qualifying exigencies, contact

_____ .

26-Week Entitlement

Employees may be eligible for additional leave if their child, parent, spouse, or next of kin (1) is a current member of the Armed Forces, including the National Guard or Reserves, (2) suffers or aggravates a serious illness or injury in the line of duty on active duty, and (3) is undergoing treatment, recuperation, or therapy; is in outpatient status; or is on the temporary disability retired list. This leave is also available for family members of veterans suffering from a serious, service-related illness or injury, if the veteran was a member of the Armed Forces, National Guard, or Reserves within five years of needing care.

Employees in this situation may take up to 26 weeks of leave in a single 12-month period to care for the family member. This leave is not in addition to the 12 weeks of leave available for reasons addressed above. Employees eligible for this type of leave are entitled to 26 total weeks of leave in a 12-month period, for all reasons.

Leave Available

Eligible employees may take up to 12 weeks of unpaid leave in a 12-month period for any of the purposes listed under "12-Week Entitlement," above. This 12-month period begins _____ .

A parent who takes leave to care for a newborn, newly adopted child, or recently placed foster child must complete this leave within a year after the birth, adoption, or placement.

Eligible employees may take up to 26 weeks of unpaid leave to care for a family member who suffers a serious injury or illness, as described under "26-Week Entitlement," above. This 12-month period begins on the first day of leave.

Notice Requirements

Employees are required to give notice at least 30 days in advance if their need for leave is foreseeable. If you fail to do so, we may delay your leave. If you can't give 30-days' notice, you must give notice as soon as is practicable under the circumstances and must generally comply with our usual procedures. We may ask you to explain why you were unable to give 30-days' notice.

When you give notice, you must provide enough information for us to determine whether the leave qualifies as FMLA leave. If you have already taken FMLA leave for the same reason, you must refer either to the reason or to the need for FMLA leave when you give notice.

Reinstatement

When you return from leave, you have the right to return to your former position or an equivalent position.

However, you have no greater right to reinstatement than you would have had if you had not been on leave. If your position is eliminated for reasons unrelated to your leave, for example, you have no right to reinstatement.

The Company may not be obligated to reinstate you if you are a key employee—that is, you are among the highest paid 10% of our workforce and holding your job open would cause the Company substantial economic harm. If the Company classifies you as a key employee, you will be notified soon after you request leave.

Use of Paid Leave

An employee who has accrued paid time off _____ _____ use these benefits to receive pay for all or a portion of family and medical leave, as long as the reason for leave is covered by the applicable type of time off. To use paid leave, you must comply with the usual requirements for using that type of leave (for example, notice or scheduling requirements). If you do not, you may not be allowed to use paid leave, but will still be entitled to take unpaid FMLA leave if you are eligible.

If an employee takes paid sick, vacation, or PTO leave, workers' compensation leave, disability leave, or other leave for a reason that qualifies for family and medical leave, the Company may designate that time off as family and medical leave and count it against the employee's entitlement.

Certification

The Company may ask employees to provide a certification regarding the need for leave. If you take leave for your own or a family member's serious health condition, or to care for a family member who suffers or aggravates a serious injury or illness in military service, a health care practitioner must complete part of this form. For qualifying exigency leave, you must complete the form. We will provide you with the certification form you must submit.

The Company has the right to seek a second opinion (and perhaps, a third opinion), and periodic recertifications. We may also ask you to provide other types of documentation, such as a copy of active duty orders or proof of a family relationship to the person whom you will be caring for.

The Company may also ask you to provide a fitness-for-duty report from your doctor before you return to work after taking leave for your own serious health condition.

Intermittent Leave

Employees may take leave all at one time or intermittently—that is, a few hours or days at a time—for all types of leave listed above except leave to care for a new child. In the case of leave for your own serious health condition, to care for a family member with a serious health condition, or to care for a family member who suffers or aggravates a serious injury or illness in military service, intermittent leave is available only if it is medically necessary.

If you need intermittent leave for scheduled medical treatment, you must make a reasonable effort to schedule your leave so it doesn't unduly disrupt the Company's operations. We may temporarily assign you to a different position with equivalent pay and benefits to accommodate the intermittent schedule.

The Company will consider requests for intermittent leave to care for a new child on a case-by-case basis.

How to Complete This Policy

In the first two blanks, insert the position of the person who handles FMLA requests at your company. In the third blank space, indicate what method your company will use to measure the 12-month period during which employees are entitled to 12 weeks of leave. (For the 26-week leave provision, the 12-month period always begins on the first day of leave, as the policy states.) There are four methods from which you can choose:

- the calendar year (insert "January 1")
- a fiscal year or a year that starts on an employee's anniversary date (insert the date your fiscal year begins or "the date when the employee started work")
- a year that begins on the date the employee first takes FMLA leave (insert "the date an employee first takes FMLA leave"), or
- a year measured backward from the date the employee uses any FMLA leave (insert "one year before an employee takes FMLA leave").

In the fourth blank, insert either "may" or "must." The FMLA allows employers to require employees to use paid time off—such as vacation leave or personal days—during any FMLA leave, and also paid sick days during an FMLA leave for the employee's own serious health condition. This prevents employees from taking 12 weeks of unpaid leave and then tacking on available vacation or sick days. If you choose this option, insert "must." Even if an employer does not require employees to use paid time off, the FMLA always gives employees this option. So, if your company doesn't require your employees to use paid time off, insert "may."

Additional Clause to Continue Health Insurance (Policy A Only)

The FMLA requires employers who provide group health insurance to continue that benefit while employees are on leave. Employers must continue to pay whatever portion of the premium the employer would pay if the employee were not on leave. However, if the employee does not return from leave, the employer can require the employee to pay back the employer unless the employee doesn't return for reasons beyond the employee's control (for example, a serious health condition that does not improve sufficiently to allow the employee to return to the job).

If your company offers health insurance, add the following clause to the policy, immediately after the "Notice Requirements" section.

Additional Clause

> **Health Insurance During Leave**
>
> Your health insurance benefits will continue during leave. You will be responsible for paying any portion of the premium that you ordinarily pay while you are working, and you must make arrangements to make these payments while you are out. Employees who choose not to return from family and medical leave may be required to reimburse the Company for any premiums paid on the employee's behalf during the leave.

Additional Clause to Limit Leave Available to Spouses Who Work for the Same Company

The FMLA allows—but does not require—employers to limit the total leave available to spouses who work for the same company. This limit doesn't apply to all types of leave, however. Spouses may be limited to 12 combined weeks of FMLA leave to care for a newborn, newly adopted child, or recently placed foster child, and to care for a parent with a serious health condition. Spouses who are eligible for 26 weeks of leave to care for a family member who is seriously injured in military service may be limited to a combined total of 26 weeks of leave for this, to care for a newborn, newly adopted child, or recently placed foster child, and to care for a parent with a serious health condition. If a spouse needs leave for a different reason (for example, for his or her own serious health condition), that isn't included in the combined 12-week limit.

Note that this limit applies only to married spouses (including same-sex spouses), not to unmarried couples.

If you want to limit the leave available to spouses, add the following clause to your policy at the end of the "Leave Available" section.

Additional Clause

> If you and your spouse both work for our Company, the two of you will be entitled to a combined total of 12 weeks of leave to care for a newborn, newly adopted child, or recently placed foster child, and to care for a parent with a serious health condition. If you both qualify for the leave described under "26-Week Entitlement," above, you will be entitled to a combined total of 26 weeks of leave for this purpose, to care for a newborn, newly adopted child, or recently placed foster child, and to care for a parent with a serious health condition.

Additional Clause to Allow Employees to Take Paid Leave to Supplement Workers' Compensation or Disability Benefits

Employees are allowed to use accrued paid leave to get compensation while they are out on FMLA leave. But what about employees who are receiving some wage replacement from workers' compensation or disability insurance, but are not receiving their full pay? The FMLA allows the employer and employee to agree that the employee may supplement those benefits with paid leave, up to the employee's usual pay. If you wish to allow this type of supplement, add this clause to the end of the "Use of Paid Leave" section.

Additional Clause

If you are receiving workers' compensation or disability benefits while on FMLA leave, you may not use accrued paid leave for all of the hours you miss; this would result in you receiving more than your usual pay. However, you may use accrued paid leave—as long as you are otherwise eligible—to supplement your benefits, so you receive your usual pay while on leave. For example, if you are receiving 60% of your usual compensation through disability insurance, you may use paid leave to be paid for the other 40%.

CAUTION

Include the Department of Labor's notice in your handbook. The Department of Labor has created a poster and notice, "Employee Rights Under the Family and Medical Leave Act." Employers who are covered by the FMLA must include this information in the employee handbook or other written materials on leave, or distribute a copy to new employees when they are hired. You should include this notice immediately following your FMLA policy in the handbook. You can download a copy at www.dol.gov/whd/regs/compliance/posters/fmlaen.pdf.

**Alternate Policy B: For Employers Who Don't
Have to Comply With the FMLA**

Family and Medical Leave

Because of our small size, our Company is not required to comply
with the federal Family and Medical Leave Act (FMLA). However, we
recognize that our employees may occasionally need to take unpaid
leave to care for a new child, to care for a seriously ill family member,
to handle an employee's own medical issues, or to handle issues relating
to a family member's military service, possibly including caring for a
family member who is injured while serving in the military.

If you anticipate that you might need time off to deal with family
and medical issues, please talk to your supervisor. We can't guarantee
that we'll grant every request, but we will seriously consider every
request on a case-by-case basis. Among other things, we may consider
our staffing needs, your position at the Company, the reason why you
need leave, and how long you expect your leave to last.

RESOURCE

Want more information on the FMLA? You can find it in *The
Essential Guide to Family & Medical Leave*, by Lisa Guerin and Deborah C.
England (Nolo), which includes information on eligibility, reasons for leave,
notice requirements, reinstatement rights, record-keeping obligations,
and much more. It also provides detailed information on state family and
medical leave laws and explains what to do when these and other laws—
such as the Americans with Disabilities Act or workers' compensation
statutes—overlap with the FMLA.

10:6 Leave for Children's School Activities

File Name: 10_Time Off.rtf

Include This Policy?
- ☐ Yes
- ☐ No
- ☐ Use our existing policy
- ☐ Other _____

Alternate Modifications
None

Additional Clauses
Add Minimum or Maximum Increments
Insert?: ☐ Yes ☐ No

Related Policies
None

Notes

_____
_____
_____
_____
_____
_____
_____
_____
_____
_____
_____
_____
_____
_____
_____
_____
_____
_____

10:6 Leave for Children's School Activities

Some states require certain employers to allow employees to take some time off to attend parent-teacher conferences and other school activities for their children. (To find out whether your state requires this type of leave, check the "State Family and Medical Leave Laws" chart at the end of this chapter.) Even in states that don't require this type of time off, employers may choose to allow it anyway: It's one more way companies can help their workers balance work with the demands of raising a family.

A school activities policy should tell employees what types of leave are covered, how much time off they can take, and how to request time off.

Time Off for School Activities

Employees whose children have not yet graduated from high school may take up to _____ of leave for school activities each year. You may use this time to _____ .

You must request time off for school activities at least _____ in advance. School activities leave is generally unpaid; however, you [may *or* must] use accrued vacation leave to be paid for this time off.

How to Complete This Policy

In the first blank, insert how many hours employees may take off per year for school activities. If your state requires you to offer this time off, insert the appropriate number of hours from the "State Family and Medical Leave Laws" chart at the end of this chapter. In the second blank, insert the activities for which employees may take leave. In the third blank, insert how many days notice employees must provide before taking leave (a typical notice period is seven days). Finally, you'll have to choose whether to allow or require employees to use accrued paid leave during this time off.

Additional Clause to Add Minimum or Maximum Increments

Some state laws allow you to limit the amount of time an employee may take at once or in a month, or allow you to require employees to take at least a certain amount of leave at once (for example, two hours). If your company does business in one of these states, or if your company is offering school activities leave voluntarily and would like to set such limits, add all or part of the following clause as the second sentence of your policy. In the blanks, insert the maximum and/or minimum increments of leave your company allows.

Additional Clause

You may take no more than _____ of leave per _____ .
You must take at least _____ of leave at a time.

CAUTION

If your state combines school activities leave with other types of time off, you will have to modify this policy. The laws of Massachusetts and Vermont, for example, allow employees to take a combined total of 24 hours of leave per year for school activities and for certain other reasons (to take a family member for a routine medical or dental appointment, for example). If your company operates in a state with a combined leave law, you should change this policy to reflect all types of allowed leave. You'll probably also want to change the title of the policy. Start by reviewing the requirements set out in the "State Family and Medical Leave Laws" chart at the end of this chapter, and make sure to have your policy reviewed by a lawyer.

10:7 Bereavement Leave

File Name: 10_Time Off.rtf

Include This Policy?
- ☐ Yes
- ☐ No
- ☐ Use our existing policy
- ☐ Other _____

Alternate Modifications
None

Additional Clauses
None

Related Policies
None

Notes
_____
_____
_____
_____
_____
_____
_____
_____
_____
_____
_____
_____
_____
_____
_____
_____
_____
_____
_____
_____

10:7 Bereavement Leave

Many employers offer their employees a few days off when a family member dies. These policies recognize that an employee who has experienced the death of a loved one will likely have both practical and personal issues that require attention. Some employers choose to let their employees take sick or vacation leave for this purpose. By offering bereavement leave, however, an employer communicates sensitivity and concern for its employees' well-being.

CAUTION

Your state may require bereavement leave. In 2014, Oregon became the first state to require some employers to give employees time off for a death in the family. Other states have considered similar laws. Before adopting a bereavement policy, make sure it complies with any applicable state or local laws. The lawyer who reviews your handbook can help you with this issue.

Your bereavement policy should explain who is eligible for leave, how many days of leave will be granted, and whether the leave will be paid or unpaid.

Bereavement Leave

If you suffer the death of an immediate family member, you are entitled to take up to _____ days off work. This leave will be _____ .

Immediate family members include _____
_____
_____
_____
_____ .

The Company will consider, on a case-by-case basis, requests for bereavement leave for the death of someone who does not qualify as an immediate family member under this policy.

How to Complete This Policy

In the first blank, insert the number of days employees can take off for bereavement leave. Many employers offer three days, although your company may choose to offer more or fewer.

In the second blank, indicate whether bereavement leave will be paid or unpaid.

In the third blank, list those who qualify as immediate family members. Some employers limit bereavement leave, particularly if it is paid, to parents, children, siblings, and spouses. A number of employers also make bereavement leave available to those who have lost their domestic partners, grandparents, aunts, uncles, or in-laws. You can also include any family member who lives with the employee.

10:8 Military Leave

File Name: 10_Time Off.rtf

Include This Policy?

☐ Yes

☐ No

☐ Use our existing policy

☐ Other _____

Alternate Modifications

None

Additional Clauses

Paid Time Off

Insert?: ☐ Yes ☐ No

Health Benefits

Insert?: ☐ Yes ☐ No

Related Policies

None

Notes

_____

_____

_____

_____

_____

_____

_____

_____

_____

_____

_____

_____

_____

_____

_____

_____

_____

10:8 Military Leave

The federal Uniformed Services Employment and Reemployment Rights Act of 1994 ("USERRA") requires all employers, regardless of size, to reinstate employees who take time off work to serve in the U.S. Armed Forces. USERRA protects employees who give proper notice before taking leave, spend no more than five years on leave, are released or discharged from service under honorable conditions, and report back or apply for reinstatement within specified time limits (which depend on the length of the employee's service). When employees return from military leave, the employer must reinstate them to the same position they would have held had they been continuously employed throughout their leave, as long as they are otherwise qualified for the job. This includes any pay raises, promotions, or additional job responsibilities they would have received had they never taken a leave.

Almost every state has a law prohibiting discrimination against those in the state's militia or National Guard, and many of these laws also require employers to grant leave for certain types of military service. These state laws are summarized in "State Laws on Military Leave" at the end of this chapter.

Your policy on military leave should include an explanation of eligibility and notice requirements and a description of employees' reinstatement rights when their military service ends.

How to Complete This Policy

In the blank, indicate whether military leave will be paid or unpaid. USERRA requires employers to offer only unpaid leave; however, employers are free to offer paid leave if they wish. Because some military commitments can be lengthy, many employers who offer paid leave do so only for a limited number of days—two or three weeks, for example. If your company will offer a limited amount of paid leave, insert "paid for _____ days and unpaid after that," replacing the blank with the number of days for which you will provide pay.

Military Leave

Our Company supports those who serve in the armed forces to protect our country. In keeping with this commitment, and in accordance with state and federal law, employees who must be absent from work for military service are entitled to take a military leave of absence. This leave will be _____ .

When an employee's military leave ends, that employee will be reinstated to the position he or she would have held if continuously employed, as long as the employee meets the requirements of federal and state law.

Employees who are called to military service must tell their supervisors as soon as possible that they will need to take military leave. An employee whose military service has ended must return to work or inform the Company that he or she wants to be reinstated in accordance with these guidelines:

- For a leave of 30 or fewer days, the employee must report back to work on the first regularly scheduled workday after completing military service, allowing for travel time.
- For a leave of 31 to 180 days, the employee must request reinstatement within 14 days after military service ends.
- For a leave of 181 days or more, the employee must request reinstatement within 90 days after military service ends.

Additional Clause for Employers Who Offer Paid Time Off

If your company, like most employers, offers any type of paid time off—such as vacation and/or personal days—you should modify this policy to allow employees to use this paid time during their military leaves, unless your company has chosen to pay employees for all military leaves. If your company offers paid time off and has decided that military leave will be unpaid or paid only for a limited number of days, add this sentence to the end of the first paragraph.

Additional Clause

During this unpaid leave, employees are entitled to use applicable paid time off (vacation time or personal days).

Additional Clause for Employers Who Offer Health Benefits

If your company makes health insurance available to employees as a benefit (see Chapter 8), you should modify this policy to inform workers of the circumstances in which these benefits will continue during their military leave. USERRA requires employers to continue to offer health insurance to employees on leave for military service. Employees who return to work after an absence of 30 or fewer days are entitled to insurance continuation at the same cost, if any, paid by employees not on leave. Employees who are absent for more than 30 days must be offered the chance to continue their coverage, but they can be required to pay the full premium. If your company offers health insurance, modify the policy by adding the following clause to the end of the second paragraph.

Additional Clause

The Company will continue your health insurance benefits during your leave, under these circumstances:

- If you are absent for 30 or fewer days, you will be treated as any employee not on leave. The Company will continue to pay its share of the insurance premium, and you must continue to pay your usual share (if any).
- If your leave lasts longer than 30 days, you will have to pay the entire premium to continue your benefits.

RESOURCE

For more information on USERRA and military leave, see *The Essential Guide to Federal Employment Laws*, by Lisa Guerin and Sachi Barreiro (Nolo). You'll also find lots of helpful materials at the Department of Labor's website (www.dol.gov) and at the website of Employer Support of the Guard and Reserve (www.esgr.mil).

10:9 Time Off to Vote

Most states prohibit employers from firing or disciplining employees for taking some time off work to cast their ballots, especially if their work schedules or commute make it difficult to vote outside of work hours. Some states require employers to pay employees for this time, and some states allow employers to require advanced notice or proof that the employee voted. These state laws are summarized in "State Laws on Taking Time Off to Vote" at the end of this chapter.

Your policy on voting leave should state how many hours employees can take off to vote, whether employees will be paid for these hours, and what notice or other requirements employees must meet to qualify for voting leave.

Voting

Our Company encourages employees to exercise their right to vote. If your work schedule and the location of your polling place will make it difficult for you to get to the polls before they close, you are entitled to take up to _____ hours off work, at the beginning or end of your shift, to cast your ballot. This time will be _____ .

Employees who will need to take time off work to vote must inform their supervisors at least _____ day(s) in advance. Employees are expected to work with their supervisors to ensure that their absence doesn't negatively impact Company operations.

How to Complete This Policy

There are three spaces for you to fill in, based on your state's legal requirements and your company's preferences. In the first space, insert the number of hours employees can take off work in order to vote. Consult the chart at the end of this chapter to find out what your state requires; most states that mandate time off to vote require employers to provide two hours, although a few require more. If your state doesn't impose a requirement, your company can decide how many hours to allow.

In the second space, indicate whether this time off will be paid or unpaid. As you can see from the chart, some states require paid leave. If your company does business in one of these states, insert "paid" in the blank. If your state does not require employers to pay employees for the time they take off work to vote, the company can choose either.

10:9 Voting

File Name: 10_Time Off.rtf

Include This Policy?

☐ Yes

☐ No

☐ Use our existing policy

☐ Other _____

Alternate Modifications

None

Additional Clauses

Require Proof of Voting

Insert?:   ☐ Yes   ☐ No

Related Policies

None

Notes

In the final space, insert the number of days' notice employees will have to give before taking time off to vote. The chart indicates whether your state requires employees to give notice. If your company does business in a state with a notice requirement, simply insert the number of days your state mandates (some states require only one day's notice). If your state has no rules about notice, your company can decide for itself how much notice to require, if any.

Additional Clause to Require Proof of Voting

A few states allow employers to require employees to supply proof that they actually voted in order to claim leave time. If your company does business in one of these states, you can modify our policy to require such proof.

Your state may require employees to supply a certain type of proof, such as a receipt or a state elections form. The sample addition, below, gives supervisors the authority to tell employees what types of proof are acceptable.

To inform employees of this proof requirement, simply add the following clause to the end of the policy.

Additional Clause

Employees who take time off to vote must supply their supervisor with proof that they actually voted. Your supervisor can tell you what types of proof of voting are acceptable.

10:10 Jury Duty

Almost every state prohibits employers from firing or disciplining employees for jury service. Generally, employers must allow employees to take time off for this purpose; some states also require employers to provide at least some pay for this time off. Check "State Laws on Jury Duty" at the end of this chapter to find out what your state requires.

Your policy on jury duty should let employees know whether jury service will be paid or unpaid, explain any notice requirements for employees called to jury duty, and clearly state that employees will not face discipline or retaliation for serving on a jury.

Jury Duty

If you are called for jury duty, you are entitled to take time off, as necessary, to fulfill your jury obligations. This leave will be _____ . No employee will face discipline or retaliation for jury service.

You must immediately inform your supervisor when you receive your jury duty summons. If you are chosen to sit on a jury, you must inform your supervisor how long the trial is expected to last. You must also check in with your supervisor periodically during your jury service, so the Company knows when to expect you back at work.

How to Complete This Policy

In the blank, indicate whether leave to serve on a jury will be paid or unpaid. (Check "State Laws on Jury Duty" to find out whether your state requires paid leave for any employees.) Even if your state doesn't require paid leave, employers are free to provide it.

You will see that some states require paid leave only for full-time employees. If your company does business in one of these states, you can limit the policy accordingly by filling in the blank as follows: "paid for full-time employees only; part-time employees will not be paid for time taken off for jury service." If your state requires employers to pay only a certain number of days of jury duty leave, you can modify your policy to reflect this limit by using the Additional Clause to Limit Number of Paid Days of Leave, below.

10:10 Jury Duty

File Name: 10_Time Off.rtf

Include This Policy?
- ☐ Yes
- ☐ No
- ☐ Use our existing policy
- ☐ Other _____

Alternate Modifications
None

Additional Clauses
Limit Number of Paid Days of Leave
Insert?: ☐ Yes ☐ No
Require Employees to Report Back to Work
Insert?: ☐ Yes ☐ No

Related Policies
None

Notes

_____
_____
_____
_____
_____
_____
_____
_____
_____
_____
_____
_____
_____
_____
_____
_____

Additional Clause to Limit Number of Paid Days of Leave

Some states that require paid leave for jury duty allow employers to pay for only a certain number of days off. If your company does business in one of these states, or if your company offers paid leave even though your state law doesn't require it, you may want to limit how much paid leave an employee can take. If so, replace the second sentence of the standard policy with the sentence below. In the blank, indicate how many days of paid leave your company will offer.

Additional Clause

You will be paid for up to _____ days of jury service; if your service extends beyond this period, the remainder of your leave will be unpaid.

Reality Check: Juror Fees Don't Pay the Bills

Many states pay jurors a fixed amount per day for serving on a jury. However, these stipends are usually meager. In some states, employees probably give their children a larger allowance than the court will pay for serving on a jury. In light of this sad state of affairs, many employers voluntarily take on the responsibility of paying their employees for time spent on jury duty.

But what if an employee gets called for the next "trial of the century" and is out of work for months? That's where the modification to limit how much paid leave the company will provide comes in. If your company chooses to compensate employees for jury duty, you can use this modification to put some outside limit on the obligation. Employers commonly adopt a policy limiting paid jury duty leave to ten to 20 workdays per year.

Additional Clause to Require Employees to Report Back to Work

Some employers require employees to call in on any day when jury service ends before the end of the workday, so that the employee can be asked to report back to work for the remainder of the day, if desired. To impose this requirement, add the sentence below to the end of the standard policy. If your company offers unpaid leave for jury duty, remember that employees are entitled to be paid for any time they actually spend working.

Additional Clause

> On any day when your jury service ends before the end of your usual workday, you must check in with your supervisor to find out whether you need to return to work for that day.

State Family and Medical Leave Laws

Arkansas

Ark. Code Ann. §§ 9-9-105, 11-3-205

Employers Covered: For adoption leave: employers that allow workers to take leave for the birth of a child; for leave to donate organs and bone marrow: all employers.

Eligible Employees: For adoption leave: all employees; for leave to donate organs or bone marrow: employees who are not eligible for FMLA leave.

Family Medical Leave: Employees must be given the same leave as allowed for childbirth to adopt a child no older than 18 (does not apply to stepparent or foster parent adoptions). Employees may take up to 90 days of unpaid leave to donate organs or bone marrow.

California

Cal. Govt. Code §§ 12945 and 12945.2; Cal. Lab. Code §§ 230 and following; Cal. Unemp. Ins. Code §§ 3300 and following; Cal. Lab. Code §§ 245.5, 246 and 246.5

Employers Covered: For pregnancy leave: employers with 5 or more employees; for domestic violence leave and school activity leave: employers with 25 or more employees; for family medical leave: employers with 50 or more employees; for paid family and disability leave: employers whose employees contribute to state temporary disability insurance ("SDI") fund; for paid sick leave: all employers.

Eligible Employees: For pregnancy, domestic violence, or school activity leave: all employees; for family medical leave: employees with more than 12 months of service with the employer, and who have at least 1,250 hours of service with the employer during the previous 12-month period; for paid family and disability leave benefits program: employees who contribute to SDI fund; for paid sick leave: employees who have worked at least 30 days within a year for the same employer.

Family Medical Leave: Up to 4 months for disability related to pregnancy (in addition to 12 weeks under state family leave law). Up to 12 weeks of leave per year to care for seriously ill family member, for employee's own serious illness, or to bond with new child. Employees who contribute to SDI fund may receive paid family leave benefits for up to 6 weeks of leave per year to care for a seriously ill family member (including a registered domestic partner) or bond with a new child; up to 52 weeks of leave paid by state fund for own short-term disability.

School Activities: 40 hours per year, but not more than 8 hours per calendar month, to enroll a child in a school or with a licensed child care provider or to participate in activities related to the school or licensed child care provider.

Domestic Violence: Reasonable time for issues dealing with domestic violence, stalking, or sexual assault, including health, counseling, and safety measures. Family member or domestic partner of a victim of a felony may take leave to attend judicial proceedings related to the crime.

Paid Sick Leave: One hour of sick leave for every 30 hours worked; however, employers may cap use of sick leave at 24 hours per year. Employees may use sick leave for their own illnesses, to care for an ill family member, or to deal with the effects of domestic violence.

Colorado

Colo. Rev. Stat. §§ 19-5-211; 24-34-402.7

Employers Covered: For adoption leave: all employers who offer leave for birth of a child; for domestic violence leave and school activities leave: employers with 50 or more employees.

Eligible Employees: For adoption leave and school activities leave: all employees; for domestic violence leave: employees with one year of service.

Family Medical Leave: Employee must be given same leave for adoption as allowed for childbirth (doesn't apply to stepparent adoption).

School Activities: 18 hours per year, no more than 6 hours per month, to attend parent-teacher conferences and meetings relating to special education, truancy, attendance, discipline, drop-out prevention, or response to intervention.

Domestic Violence: Up to 3 days in any 12-month period to seek restraining order, obtain medical care or counseling, relocate, or seek legal assistance for victim of domestic violence, sexual assault, or stalking.

Connecticut

Conn. Gen. Stat. Ann. §§ 31-51kk to 31-51qq; 46a-60

Employers Covered: For pregnancy leave: employers with 3 or more employees; for family medical or serious health leave: employers with 75 or more employees; for paid sick leave: service industry employers with at least 50 employees.

Eligible Employees: For pregnancy leave and paid sick leave: all employees; for family medical or serious health condition leave: employees with one year and at least 1,000 hours of service in last 12 months.

State Family and Medical Leave Laws (continued)

Family Medical Leave: Reasonable amount of pregnancy leave required. 16 weeks per any 24-month period for childbirth, adoption, employee's serious health condition, care for family member with serious health condition, or bone marrow or organ donation, or a qualifying exigency arising out of a family member's active duty in the military. 26 weeks per 12-month period for each family member who is also a current member of the armed forces and is undergoing medical treatment.

Paid Sick Leave: One hour of paid sick leave for every 40 hours worked, up to 40 hours accrued per year, for the employee's own medical needs or to care for an ill family member.

District of Columbia

D.C. Code Ann. §§ 32-501 and following; 32-1202, 32-131.01 and following

Employers Covered: Leave other than paid sick leave: employers with 20 or more employees; paid sick leave: all employers.

Eligible Employees: Leave other than paid sick leave: employees who have worked at company for at least one year and at least 1,000 hours during the previous 12 months; paid sick leave: all employees accrue sick leave upon hire and may use sick leave after 90 days of employment.

Family Medical Leave: 16 weeks per any 24-month period for childbirth, adoption, foster care, placement of a child with the employee for whom the employee permanently assumes and discharges parental responsibility, or care for family member with serious health condition. Additional 16 weeks per any 24-month period for employee's serious health condition.

School Activities: Up to 24 hours of unpaid leave per year (all employees, all employers).

Domestic Violence: Leave described under "Paid Sick Leave" may also be used for employee or family member who is a victim of stalking, domestic violence, or abuse to get medical attention, get services, seek counseling, relocate, take legal action, or take steps to enhance health and safety.

Paid Sick Leave: Paid sick leave for the employee's own illness or to care for a family member. Amount of paid leave depends on employer size: employers with 100 or more employees must provide at least one hour of paid leave for every 37 hours worked, up to seven days of leave per year; employers with 25 to 99 employees must provide at least one hour of paid leave for every 43 hours worked, up to five days of leave per year; employers with fewer than 25 employees must provide at least one hour of paid leave for every 87 hours worked, up to three days of leave per year.

Florida

Fla. Stat. § 741.313

Employers Covered: Employers with at least 50 employees.

Eligible Employees: Employees with at least 3 months of employment.

Domestic Violence: Up to 3 days in any 12-month period if employee or family/household member is victim of domestic violence, with or without pay at discretion of employer.

Hawaii

Haw. Rev. Stat. §§ 398-1 to 398-11; 378-1, 378-71 to 378-74

Employers Covered: For childbirth, adoption, and serious health condition leave: employers with 100 or more employees; for pregnancy leave, temporary disability, and domestic violence leave: all employers; for bone marrow leave: employers with 50 or more employees.

Eligible Employees: For childbirth, adoption, and serious health condition leave: employees with 6 months of service; for pregnancy, domestic violence, and temporary disability leave: all employees.

Family Medical Leave: 4 weeks per calendar year for childbirth, adoption, or care for family member with serious health condition; "reasonable period" of pregnancy/maternity leave required by discrimination statute and case law; up to 7 days' unpaid leave for bone marrow donors and up to 30 days' unpaid leave for organ donors. Up to 26 weeks of temporary disability leave paid by state insurance program.

Domestic Violence: Employer with 50 or more employees must allow up to 30 days' unpaid leave per year for employee who is a victim of domestic or sexual violence or if employee's minor child is a victim. Employer with 49 or fewer employees must allow up to 5 days' leave.

Illinois

820 Ill. Comp. Stat. §§ 147/1 and following; 180/1 and following

Employers Covered: For school activities leave, employers with 50 or more employees. For domestic violence leave, all employers.

Eligible Employees: For school activities leave: employees who have worked at least half time for 6 months; for domestic violence leave: all employees.

School Activities: Eight hours per year (no more than 4 hours per day); required only if employee has no paid leave available.

State Family and Medical Leave Laws (continued)

Domestic Violence: If employer has at least 50 employees, up to 12 weeks' unpaid leave per 12-month period for employee who is a victim of domestic violence or sexual assault or for employee with a family or household member who is a victim. If employer has at least 15 but not more than 49 employees, up to 8 weeks' unpaid leave during any 12-month period. If employer has fourteen or fewer employees, up to 4 weeks' unpaid leave during any 12-month period.

Iowa

Iowa Code § 216.6

Employers Covered: Employers with 4 or more employees.

Eligible Employees: All employees.

Family Medical Leave: Up to 8 weeks for disability due to pregnancy, childbirth, or related conditions.

Kentucky

Ky. Rev. Stat. Ann. § 337.015

Employers Covered: All employers.

Eligible Employees: All employees.

Family Medical Leave: Up to 6 weeks for adoption of a child under 7 years old.

Louisiana

La. Rev. Stat. Ann. §§ 23:341 to 23:342; 23:1015 and following; 40:1299.124

Employers Covered: For pregnancy/maternity leave: employers with 25 or more employees; for leave to donate bone marrow: employers with 20 or more employees; for school activities leave: all employers.

Eligible Employees: For pregnancy/maternity or school activities leave: all employees; for leave to donate bone marrow: employees who work 20 or more hours per week.

Family Medical Leave: "Reasonable period of time" for pregnancy disability and childbirth, not to exceed 6 weeks for normal pregnancy and 4 months for more disabling pregnancies; up to 40 hours' paid leave per year to donate bone marrow.

School Activities: 16 hours per year.

Maine

Me. Rev. Stat. Ann. tit. 26, §§ 843 and following

Employers Covered: For domestic violence leave: all employers; for family medical leave: employers with 15 or more employees at one location.

Eligible Employees: All employees for domestic violence leave; employees with at least one year of service for family medical leave.

Family Medical Leave: 10 weeks in any two-year period for childbirth, adoption (for child 16 or younger), employee's serious health condition, care for family member with serious health condition, or death or serious health condition of family member suffered while on active military duty.

Domestic Violence: "Reasonable and necessary" leave for employee who is victim of domestic violence, sexual assault, or stalking, or whose parent, spouse, or child is a victim, to prepare for and attend court, for medical treatment, and for other necessary services.

Maryland

Md. Code Ann., [Lab. & Empl.] §§ 3-801, 3-802, 3-803

Employers Covered: For adoption leave: employers with 15 or more employees; for family military leave: employers with at least 50 employees.

Eligible Employees: All employees for adoption leave; employees who have worked at least 12 months, and at least 1,250 hours in the last 12 months, for military family leave.

Family Medical Leave: Employee must be given same leave for adoption as allowed for childbirth. Employee must be allowed to take off the day immediate family member leaves for or returns from active military duty outside the United States.

Massachusetts

Mass. Gen. Laws ch. 149, §§ 52D, 105D, 148C; ch. 151B, § 1(5)

Employers Covered: For maternity and adoption leave: employers with 6 or more employees; for school activities leave: employers with 50 or more employees; for domestic violence leave: employers with 50 or more employees; for paid sick leave: all employers.

Eligible Employees: For maternity and adoption leave: employees who have completed the employer's probationary period, or if there is no probationary period, employees who have completed 3 months of service as full-time employees; for paid sick leave: all employees accrue sick leave upon hire and may use sick leave after 90 days of employment; for all other leave: employees who are eligible under FMLA.

Family Medical Leave: Eight weeks total for childbirth/ maternity or adoption of child younger than 18 (younger than 23 if disabled); additional 24 hours total per year (combined

State Family and Medical Leave Laws (continued)

with school activities leave) to accompany minor child or relative age 60 or older to medical and dental appointments.

School Activities: 24 hours per year total (combined with family medical leave for medical and dental appointments).

Domestic Violence: 15 days of unpaid leave in 12-month period if employee, or family member of employee, is a victim of abusive behavior, to seek medical attention or counseling, obtain a protective order from a court, attend child custody proceedings, and other related purposes. Employee may also use leave described under "Paid Sick Leave" for these purposes.

Paid Sick Leave: One hour of sick leave for every hour worked, although employers may cap annual accrual at 40 hours per week. Employers with 11 or more employees must provide paid time off; employers with 10 or fewer employees may provide unpaid time off. Employees may use leave for their own illnesses or to care for an ill family member.

Minnesota

Minn. Stat. Ann. §§ 181.940 and following

Employers Covered: For childbirth/maternity and adoption leave: employers with 21 or more employees at one site; for bone marrow donation: employers with 20 or more employees; for school activities: employers with 2 or more employees.

Eligible Employees: For maternity leave: employees who have worked at least half time for one year; for bone marrow donation: employees who work at least 20 hours per week; for school activities: employees who have worked at least one year.

Family Medical Leave: 12 weeks for childbirth/maternity or adoption; up to 40 hours paid leave per year to donate bone marrow; parent can use accrued sick leave to care for sick or injured child. Up to ten days if family member is killed or injured in active military service (all employers).

School Activities: 16 hours in 12-month period; includes activities related to child care, preschool, or special education.

Domestic Violence: Employee may use sick leave for reasonable time off to receive assistance because of sexual assault, domestic violence, or stalking.

Montana

Mont. Code Ann. §§ 49-2-310, 49-2-311

Employers Covered: All employers.

Eligible Employees: All employees.

Family Medical Leave: Reasonable leave of absence for pregnancy disability and childbirth.

Nebraska

Neb. Rev. Stat. § 48-234

Employers Covered: Employers that allow workers to take leave for the birth of a child.

Eligible Employees: All employees.

Family Medical Leave: Employee must be given same leave as allowed for childbirth to adopt a child, unless child is over 8 (or over 18 for special needs child); does not apply to stepparent or foster parent adoptions.

Nevada

Nev. Rev. Stat. Ann. §§ 392.920, 613.335, 392.4577

Employers Covered: All employers.

Eligible Employees: All employees.

Family Medical Leave: Same sick or disability leave policies that apply to other medical conditions must be extended to pregnancy, miscarriage, and childbirth.

School Activities: Employers may not fire or threaten to fire a parent, guardian, or custodian for attending a school conference or responding to a child's emergency. Employers with 50 or more employees must provide parent with a child in public school 4 hours of leave per school year, which must be taken in increments of at least 1 hour, to attend parent-teacher conferences, attend school-related activities during regular school hours, attend school-sponsored events, or volunteer or be involved at the school.

New Hampshire

N.H. Rev. Stat. Ann. § 354-A:7(VI)

Employers Covered: Employers with 6 or more employees.

Eligible Employees: All employees.

Family Medical Leave: Temporary disability leave for pregnancy/childbirth or related medical condition.

New Jersey

N.J. Stat. Ann. §§ 34:11B-1 and following; 34-11C and following; 43:21-1 and following

Employers Covered: Employers with 50 or more employees; for paid family and temporary disability leave, employers subject to the New Jersey Unemployment Compensation Law; for domestic violence leave, employees with 25 or more employees.

Eligible Employees: Employees who have worked for at least one year and at least 1,000 hours in previous 12 months; for paid family and temporary disability leave benefits program:

State Family and Medical Leave Laws (continued)

employees who worked 20 calendar weeks in covered New Jersey employment; or earned at least 1,000 times New Jersey minimum wage during 52 weeks preceding leave.

Family Medical Leave: 12 weeks (or 24 weeks reduced leave schedule) in any 24-month period for pregnancy/maternity, childbirth, adoption, or care for family member with serious health condition. Employees may receive paid family leave benefits for up to 6 weeks of leave per year to care for a seriously ill family member (including a registered domestic partner) or bond with a new child. Employee may receive temporary disability benefits while the employee is unable to work, up to 26 weeks.

Domestic Violence: 20 unpaid days in one 12-month period for employee who is (or whose family member is) a victim of domestic violence or a sexually violent offense.

New Mexico

N.M. Stat. Ann. §§ 50-4A-1 and following

Employers Covered: All employers.

Eligible Employees: All employees.

Domestic Violence: Employer must provide intermittent paid or unpaid leave time for up to fourteen days in any calendar year, taken by an employee for up to eight hours in one day, to obtain or attempt to obtain an order of protection or other judicial relief from domestic abuse or to meet with law enforcement officials, to consult with attorneys or district attorneys' victim advocates, or to attend court proceedings related to the domestic abuse of an employee or an employee's family member.

New York

N.Y. Lab. Law §§ 201-c; 202-a

Employers Covered: Employers that allow workers to take leave for the birth of a child must allow adoption leave; employers with 20 or more employees at one site must allow leave to donate bone marrow; employers with at least one employee for 30 days are covered by the state's temporary disability program 4 weeks later; for paid family leave, all employers.

Eligible Employees: All employees are eligible for adoption leave; employees who work at least 20 hours per week are eligible for leave to donate bone marrow; employees who have worked for a covered employer for at least 4 consecutive weeks are eligible for temporary disability benefits. For paid family leave, employees are eligible once they have worked for their employer for 26 weeks.

Family Medical Leave: Employees must be given same leave as allowed for childbirth to adopt a child of preschool age or younger, or no older than 18 if disabled; up to 24 hours' leave to donate bone marrow. Temporary disability insurance benefits available for up to 26 weeks while employee is unable to work. Beginning in January of 2018, employee may take paid leave to care for a family member with a serious health condition, to bond with a new child, or for qualifying exigency arising out of a family member's call to active duty in the military. Employee can receive 50% of average wages for up to 8 weeks in 2018, which will gradually increase to 67% of average wages for up to 12 weeks by 2021. Leave is paid by the state, not the employer.

North Carolina

N.C. Gen. Stat. §§ 95-28.3, 50B-5.5

Employers Covered: All employers.

Eligible Employees: All employees.

School Activities: Parents and guardians of school-aged children must be given up to 4 hours of leave per year.

Domestic Violence: Reasonable time off from work to obtain or attempt to obtain relief from domestic violence and sexual assault.

Oregon

Ore. Rev. Stat. §§ 659A.029, 659A.150 and following, 659A.312, 659A.270 and following; S.B. 454, 78th Leg. Assem., Reg. Sess. (Or. 2015)

Employers Covered: For childbirth, adoption, and serious health condition leave: employers with 25 or more employees; for domestic violence leave: employers with 6 or more employees; for leave to donate bone marrow: all employers; for paid sick leave: all employers.

Eligible Employees: For childbirth, adoption, or serious health condition: employees who have worked 25 or more hours per week for at least 180 days (except parental leave, which only requires that the employee has worked 180 days); for leave to donate bone marrow: employees who work an average of 20 or more hours per week; for domestic violence leave: all employees; for paid sick leave: all employees accrue sick leave upon hire and may use leave after 90 days of employment.

Family Medical Leave: 12 weeks per year for pregnancy disability; additional 12 weeks per year for parental leave, serious health condition, care for family member with serious health condition, deal with the death of a family

State Family and Medical Leave Laws (continued)

member, or care for child who has an illness, injury, or condition that requires home care; employee who takes 12 weeks of parental leave may take an additional 12 weeks to care for a sick child. Up to 40 hours or amount of accrued paid leave (whichever is less) to donate bone marrow.

Domestic Violence: Reasonable leave for employee who is victim of domestic violence, harassment, sexual assault, or stalking, or whose minor child is a victim, to seek legal treatment, medical services, counseling, or to relocate/secure existing home.

Paid Sick Leave: One hour of sick leave for every 30 hours worked, although employers may cap use at 40 hours per year. Employers with 10 or more employees (or 6 or more employees in Portland) must provide paid time off; employers with 9 or fewer employees (or 5 or fewer employees in Portland) may provide unpaid time off. Employees may use leave for their own illnesses, to care for an ill family member, to deal with domestic violence issues, or for any purpose described under the "Family Medical Leave" section.

Rhode Island
R.I. Gen. Laws §§ 28-48-1 and following; 28-41-34 through 28-41-42

Employers Covered: For family medical leave: employers with 50 or more employees.

Eligible Employees: For family medical leave: employees who have worked an average of 30 or more hours a week for at least 12 consecutive months; for school activities leave: all employees; for temporary disability and temporary caregiver leave: all employees who meet the earning requirements.

Family Medical Leave: 13 weeks in any two calendar years for childbirth, adoption of child up to 16 years old, employee's serious health condition, or care for family member with serious health condition. While temporarily unable to work due to disability (including pregnancy), employees can collect benefits from state insurance fund for up to 30 weeks. Four weeks of benefits are available as temporary caregiver insurance (to bond with a new child or care for a family member with a serious health condition); this time plus temporary disability time may not exceed 30 total weeks.

School Activities: Up to 10 hours a year.

South Carolina
S.C. Code Ann. § 44-43-80

Employers Covered: Employers with 20 or more workers at one site in South Carolina.

Eligible Employees: Employees who work an average of at least 20 hours per week.

Family Medical Leave: Employers may—but are not required to—allow employees to take up to 40 hours paid leave per year to donate bone marrow.

Tennessee
Tenn. Code Ann. § 4-21-408

Employers Covered: Employers with 100 or more employees.

Eligible Employees: Employees who have worked 12 consecutive months as full-time employees.

Family Medical Leave: Up to 4 months of unpaid leave for pregnancy, childbirth, nursing, and adoption; employee must give 3 months' notice unless a medical emergency requires the leave to begin sooner; these laws must be included in employee handbook.

Vermont
Vt. Stat. Ann. tit. 21, §§ 471 and following

Employers Covered: For childbirth and adoption leave: employers with 10 or more employees; for family medical and school activities leave: employers with 15 or more employees; for paid sick leave: all employers.

Eligible Employees: Employees who have worked an average of 30 or more hours per week for at least one year. For paid sick leave, employees who have worked for a covered employer for an average of 18 hours per week for at least 20 weeks.

Family Medical Leave: 12 weeks per year for pregnancy, childbirth, adoption of child age 16 or younger, employee's serious health condition, or care for family member with a serious health condition; combined with school activities leave, additional 4 hours of unpaid leave in a 30-day period (up to 24 hours per year) to take a family member to a medical, dental, or professional well-care appointment or respond to a family member's medical emergency.

School Activities: Combined with leave to take family members to appointments, 4 hours' total unpaid leave in a 30-day period (up to 24 hours per year) to participate in child's school activities.

Paid Sick Leave: Employee accrues one hour of paid sick leave for every 52 hours worked. For 2017 and 2018, employer may limit accrual to 24 hours of sick leave per year. For 2019, employer may limit accrual to 40 hours per year. Employers with 5 or fewer employees do not need to comply with the law until 2018.

State Family and Medical Leave Laws (continued)

Washington

Wash. Rev. Code Ann. §§ 49.78.010 and following, 49.12.265 and following, 49.12.350 and following, 49.76.010 and following, 49.86.005 and following

Employers Covered: All employers must provide domestic violence leave; employers with 8 or more employees must provide pregnancy disability leave; employers with 50 or more employees must provide leave to care for newborn, adopted, or foster child, or family member with serious health condition.

Eligible Employees: All employees who accrue paid sick leave may use it to care for sick family members (including state registered domestic partners); employees who have worked at least 1,250 hours in the previous year are eligible for parental leave to care for newborn, adopted, or foster child, or leave to care for a family member with serious health condition.

Family Medical Leave: In addition to any leave available under federal FMLA and state law, employee may take leave for the period of time when she is temporarily disabled due to pregnancy or childbirth; employers with 50 or more employees must allow up to 12 weeks during any 12-month period for the birth or placement of a child, employee's serious health condition, or care for a family member with a serious health condition; all employees can use paid sick leave to care for a sick family member.

Domestic Violence: Reasonable leave from work, with or without pay, for employee who is victim of domestic violence, sexual assault, or stalking, or whose family member is a victim, to prepare for and attend court, for medical treatment, and for other necessary services.

Wisconsin

Wis. Stat. Ann. § 103.10

Employers Covered: Employers with 50 or more employees.

Eligible Employees: Employees who have worked for at least one year and have worked 1,000 hours in the preceding 12 months.

Family Medical Leave: 6 weeks per 12-month period for pregnancy/maternity, childbirth, or adoption; additional 2 weeks per 12-month period to care for family member (including domestic partner) with a serious health condition; additional 2 weeks per 12-month period to care for the employee's own serious health condition.

State Laws on Military Leave

Alabama
Ala. Code §§ 31-12-1 to 31-12-4

Alabama National Guard members called to active duty for at least 30 consecutive days or for federally funded duty for service other than training have the same leave and reinstatement rights and benefits guaranteed under USERRA (doesn't apply to normal annual training, weekend drills, and required schools).

Alaska
Alaska Stat. § 26.05.075

Employees called to active service in the state militia are entitled to unlimited unpaid leave and reinstatement to their former or a comparable position, with the pay, seniority, and benefits the employee would have had if not absent for service. Employee must return to work on next workday, after time required for travel. Disabled employee must request reemployment within 30 days of release; if disability leaves the employee unable to do the job, employee must be offered a position with similar pay and benefits.

Arizona
Ariz. Rev. Stat. §§ 26-167, 26-168

Members of the National Guard, Arizona National Guard, and U.S. armed forces reserves called to training or active duty have the same leave and reinstatement rights and benefits guaranteed under USERRA. Members of the National Guard called for active duty or to attend camps, formations, maneuvers, or drills are entitled to unlimited unpaid leave and reinstatement to their former or a higher position with the same seniority and vacation benefits. Employer may not dissuade employees from enlisting in state or national military forces by threatening economic reprisal.

Arkansas
Ark. Code Ann. § 12-62-413

Employees called to active state duty as a member of the armed forces (which includes the National Guard, militia, and reserves) of Arkansas or any other state have the same leave and reinstatement rights and benefits guaranteed under USERRA.

California
Cal. Mil. & Vet. Code §§ 394, 394.5, 395.06

Members of the California National Guard called to active duty are entitled to unlimited unpaid leave and reinstatement to their former position or to a position of similar seniority, status, and pay without loss of retirement or other benefits. Full-time employees must be reinstated, unless the employer's circumstances have so changed as to make reinstatement impossible or unreasonable. Part-time employees must be reinstated if an open position exists. Reinstated employees cannot be terminated without cause for one year. Full-time employees must apply for reinstatement within 40 days of discharge, while part-time employees must apply for reinstatement within 5 days of discharge.

Employees in the U.S. armed forces reserves, National Guard, or Naval Militia are entitled to 17 days' unpaid leave per year for military training, drills, encampment, naval cruises, special exercises, or similar activities. Employer may not terminate employee or limit any benefits or seniority because of a temporary disability resulting from duty in the National Guard or Naval Militia (up to 52 weeks). Employer cannot discriminate against employee because of membership in the military services.

Colorado
Colo. Rev. Stat. §§ 28-3-609, 28-3-610.5

Employees who are members of Colorado National Guard or U.S. armed forces reserves are entitled to 15 days' unpaid leave per year for training and reinstatement to their former or a similar position with the same status, pay, and seniority. Employees called to active state service in the Colorado National Guard are entitled to unlimited unpaid leave and reinstatement to their former or comparable position, with the pay, seniority, and benefits the employee would have had if not absent for service.

Connecticut
Conn. Gen. Stat. Ann. §§ 27-33a, 27-34a

Members of the Connecticut National Guard ordered into active state service by the governor are entitled to the same rights and benefits guaranteed under USERRA, except those pertaining to life insurance. Employees who are members of the state armed forces (state organized militia, naval militia, Marine Corps branch of the naval militia, or National Guard) are entitled to take leave to perform ordered military duty, including meetings or drills, that take place during regular work hours, without loss or reduction of vacation or holiday benefits. Employer may not discriminate in terms of promotion or continued employment.

State Laws on Military Leave (continued)

Delaware

Del. Code Ann. tit. 20, § 905

National Guard members who are called to state active duty shall be entitled to the same rights, privileges, and protections as they would have had if called for military training under federal law protecting reservists and National Guard members.

Florida

Fla. Stat. Ann. §§ 250.481, 250.482, 627.6692(5)

Discrimination against members of the reserves is prohibited. Employees who are called to active duty in the Florida National Guard, or into active duty by the laws of any other state, may not be penalized for absence from work. Upon return from service, employee is entitled to reinstatement with full benefits unless employer's circumstances have changed to make reinstatement impossible or unreasonable or impose an undue hardship. Employee cannot be terminated without cause for one year after reinstatement. If a member of the National Guard or Reserves is receiving COBRA benefits and is called to active duty, the period of time when that service-member is covered by TRICARE (military health benefits) won't count against his or her COBRA entitlement.

Georgia

Ga. Code Ann. § 38-2-280

Discrimination against members of the U.S. military reserves or state militia is prohibited. Employees called to active duty in the U.S. uniformed services, the Georgia National Guard, or the national guard of any other state, are entitled to unlimited unpaid leave for active service and up to 6 months' leave in any 4-year period for service school or annual training. Employee is entitled to reinstatement with full benefits unless employer's circumstances have changed to make reinstatement impossible or unreasonable. Employee must apply for reinstatement within 90 days of discharge or within 10 days of completing school or training.

Hawaii

Haw. Rev. Stat. § 121-43

Members of the National Guard are entitled to unlimited unpaid leave while performing ordered National Guard service and while going to and returning from service, and reinstatement to the same or a position comparable in seniority, status, and pay. If an employee is not qualified for his or her former position because of a disability sustained during service but is qualified for another position, the employee is entitled to the position that is most similar to his or her former position, unless employer's circumstances have changed to make reinstatement impossible or unreasonable. Employee cannot be terminated without cause for one year after reinstatement. Employer cannot discriminate against employee because of any obligation as a member of the National Guard.

Idaho

Idaho Code §§ 46-224, 46-225, 46-407

Members of Idaho National Guard or national guard of another state ordered to active duty by their state's governor may take up to one year of unpaid leave and are entitled to reinstatement to former position or a comparable position with like seniority, status, and pay. If an employee is not qualified for his or her former position because of a disability sustained during service but is qualified for another position, the employee is entitled to the position that is most similar to his or her former position in seniority, status, and pay. Employee must apply for reinstatement within 30 days of release. Returning employees may not be fired without cause for one year. Members of the National Guard and U.S. armed forces reserves may take up to 15 days' leave per year for training without affecting the employee's right to receive normal vacation, sick leave, bonus, advancement, and other advantages of employment. Employee must give 90 days' notice of training dates.

Illinois

20 Ill. Comp. Stat. §§ 1805/30.15, 1805/30.20; 330 Ill. Comp. Stat. § 60/4

Members of the National Guard called to active state duty by order of the governor are entitled to leave and reinstatement with the same increases in status, seniority, and wages that were earned during the employee's military duty by employees in like positions, or to a position of like seniority, status, and pay, unless employer's circumstances have changed so that reinstatement would be unreasonable or impossible or impose an undue hardship. If employee is no longer qualified for the position because of a disability acquired during service but is qualified for any other position, then the employee is entitled to the position that will provide like seniority, status, and pay. If reasonably possible, employee must give advance notice of military service. Members of the National Guard must submit request for reemployment the day after finishing duty if duty lasted less than 31 days, within 14 days if duty lasted longer than 30 days, or within 90 days if duty lasted longer than 180 days. Members of the U.S. uniformed services must submit request for reemployment within 90 days. Employee can't be discharged without cause for one year. Employees who quit their jobs to enter military service are entitled to restoration after receiving an honorable discharge.

Indiana

Ind. Code Ann. §§ 10-17-4-1 to 10-17-4-5

Members of U.S. armed forces reserves may take up to 15 days' unpaid (or paid at employer's discretion) leave per year for training. Employee must provide evidence of dates of departure and return, and proof of completion of the training upon return. Leave does not affect vacation, sick leave, bonus, or promotion rights. Employee must be reinstated to former or a similar position with no loss of seniority or benefits. It's a misdemeanor for an employer to knowingly or intentionally refuse to allow an employee who is a member of the Indiana National Guard or the reserves, or who is retired from the military, to attend assembly for drills, instruction, encampments, maneuvers, or exercises.

Iowa

Iowa Code § 29A.43

Members of the U.S. armed forces reserves, National Guard, state military forces, or Civil Air Patrol called into temporary duty are entitled to reinstatement to former or a similar position. Leave does not affect vacation, sick leave, bonuses, or other benefits. Employee must provide evidence of satisfactory completion of duty and of qualifications to perform the job's duties. Employers may not discriminate against these employees or discharge them due to their military affiliations.

Kansas

Kan. Stat. Ann. §§ 48-517, 48-222

Employees called into active duty by the state of Kansas, or any other state, are entitled to unlimited leave and reinstatement to the same position or a comparable position with like seniority, status, and pay. Reemployment not required if employer's circumstances have changed so as to make reemployment impossible/unreasonable or if reemployment would impose undue hardship on employer. Reinstated employees may not be discharged without cause for one year. Members of the Kansas National Guard are entitled to 5 to 10 days' leave each year to attend annual muster and camp of instruction. Employer's failure to allow

employee to attend or punishing employee who attends is a misdemeanor.

Kentucky

Ky. Rev. Stat. Ann. §§ 38.238, 38.460

Members of National Guard are entitled to unlimited unpaid leave for active duty or training and reinstatement to former position with no loss of seniority or benefits. Employer may not in any way discriminate against employee or use threats to prevent employee from enlisting in the Kentucky National Guard or active militia.

Louisiana

La. Rev. Stat. Ann. §§ 29:38, 29:38.1

Employees called into active duty in National Guard, state militia, or any branch of the state military forces of Louisiana or any other state are entitled to reinstatement to same or comparable position with same seniority, status, benefits, and pay. If employee is not qualified for former position because of disability sustained during active duty, but is otherwise qualified to perform another position, employer or successor shall employ person in other or comparable position with like seniority, status, benefits, and pay provided the employment does not pose a direct threat or significant risk to the health and safety of the individual or others that cannot be eliminated by reasonable accommodation. Employees on leave are entitled to the benefits offered to employees who take leave for other reasons. Employee must report to work within 72 hours of release or recovery from service-related injury or illness and cannot be fired, except for cause, for one year after reinstatement. Employer cannot discriminate against employee because of any obligation as a member of the state National Guard or U.S. reserves.

Maine

Me. Rev. Stat. Ann. tit. 37-B, § 342; tit. 26, §§ 811 to 813

Employer may not discriminate against employee for membership or service in National Guard or United States armed forces reserves. Employees in the National Guard or reserves are entitled to military leave in response to state or federal military orders. Upon completion of service, employees must be reinstated, at the same pay, seniority, benefits, and status, and must receive all other employment advantages as if they had been continuously employed. For the first 30 days of an employee's military leave, the employer must continue the employee's health, dental, and

State Laws on Military Leave (continued)

life insurance at no additional cost to the employee. After 30 days, the employee may continue these benefits at his or her own expense (paying the employer's group rates).

Maryland

Md. Code Ann. [Public Safety] § 13-705

Members of the state National Guard and Maryland Defense Force ordered to military duty have the same leave and re-instatement rights and benefits guaranteed under USERRA. Maryland employers with 15 or more employees must allow employees who have been employed for at least 90 days to take at least 15 days off each year to respond to an emergency mission of the Maryland Wing of the Civil Air Patrol. Employees must give as much notice as possible of their need for this leave. After arriving at the emergency location, employees must notify their employer and estimate how long the mission will take. Employees are entitled to reinstatement upon their return from this type of leave. Employers may not penalize employees for exercising their rights under this law, nor may they retaliate against employees who complain that an employer has violated the law.

Massachusetts

Mass. Gen. Laws ch. 151B, § 4; ch 33 § 13

Employers may not discriminate against employees and applicants based on their membership in, application to perform, or obligation to perform military service, including service in the National Guard. Employees who are members of the armed forces are entitled to the same rights and protections granted under USERRA.

Michigan

Mich. Comp. Laws §§ 32.271 to 32.274

Employees who are called to active duty in the U.S. uniformed services, the National Guard, or the military or naval forces of Michigan or any other state, are entitled to take unpaid leave, and to be reinstated when their service has ended. Employees are also entitled to take time off to attend military encampment, drills, or instruction. Employers may not discriminate against employees based on their military service, nor may an employer use threats to prevent employees from enlisting.

Minnesota

Minn. Stat. Ann. § 192.34

Employer may not discharge employee, interfere with military service, or dissuade employee from enlisting by threatening employee's job. Applies to employees who are members of the U.S., Minnesota, or any other state military or naval forces.

Mississippi

Miss. Code Ann. §§ 33-1-15, 33-1-19, 33-1-21

Employers may not discriminate against employees or applicants based on their current membership in the reserves of the U.S. armed forces or their former member-ship in the U.S. armed forces. Employers may not threaten employees to dissuade them from enlisting.

Members of the U.S. armed forces reserves or U.S. military veterans may take time off for state or federal military training or duty, with reinstatement to their former position (or a similar position) once their leave is over. Employees must provide evidence that they have completed their training.

Missouri

Mo. Rev. Stat. § 41.730

Employer may not discharge employee, interfere with employee's military service, or use threats to dissuade employee from enlisting in the state organized militia.

Montana

Mont. Code Ann. §§ 10-1-1005, 10-1-1006, 10-1-1007

Employees who are ordered to federally funded military service are entitled to all rights available under USERRA. Members of the Montana National Guard, or the national guard of any other state, who are called to active state duty during a state-declared disaster or emergency are entitled to leave for duration of service. Leave may not be deducted from sick leave, vacation, or other leave, although employee may voluntarily use that leave. Returning employee is entitled to reinstatement to same or similar position with the same senior-ity, status, pay, health insurance, pension, and other benefits, provided that the employee told the employer of membership in the military at the time of hire, or if the employee enlisted during employment, at the time of enlistment. Employer may not in any way discriminate against employee or dissuade employee from enlisting in the state organized militia.

Nebraska

Neb. Rev. Stat. § 55-161

Employees who are called into active duty in the Nebraska National Guard, or the national guard of any other state, have the same leave and reinstatement rights and benefits guaranteed under USERRA.

State Laws on Military Leave (continued)

Nevada

Nev. Rev. Stat. Ann. §§ 412.139, 412.606

Employers may not discriminate against members of the Nevada National Guard and may not discharge any employee because he or she assembles for training, participates in field training, is called to active duty, or otherwise meets as required for ceremonies, maneuvers, and other military duties.

New Hampshire

N.H. Rev. Stat. Ann. §§ 110-B:65, 110-C:1

Members of the state National Guard or militia called to active duty by the governor have the same leave and reinstatement rights and benefits guaranteed under USERRA. Employer may not discriminate against employee because of connection or service with state National Guard or militia; may not dissuade employee from enlisting by threatening job.

New Jersey

N.J. Stat. Ann. § 38:23C-20

An employee is entitled to take unpaid leave for active service in the U.S. or state military services. Upon return, employee must be reinstated to the same or a similar position, unless employer's circumstances have changed to make reinstatement impossible or unreasonable. If same or similar position is not possible, employer shall restore such person to any available position, if requested by such person, for which the person is capable and qualified to perform the duties. Employee must apply for reinstatement within 90 days of release from service. Employee may not be fired without cause for one year after returning from service. Employee is also entitled to take up to 3 months' leave in 4-year period for annual training or assemblies relating to military service, or to attend service schools conducted by the U.S. armed forces. Employee must apply for reinstatement within 10 days.

New Mexico

N.M. Stat. Ann. §§ 28-15-1, 28-15-2, 20-4-6

Members of the U.S. armed forces, National Guard, or organized reserve may take unpaid leave for service (or for up to 1 year of hospitalization after discharge). Employee who is still qualified must be reinstated in former or similar position with like status, seniority, and pay unless employer's circumstances have changed to make reinstatement impossible or unreasonable. Employee may not be fired without cause for one year after returning from service. Employee must request reinstatement within 90 days. Employer may

not discriminate against or discharge employee because of membership in the National Guard; may not prevent employee from performing military service.

New York

N.Y. Mil. Law §§ 317, 318

Members of the U.S. armed forces or organized militia are entitled to unpaid leave for active service; reserve drills or annual training; service school; or initial full-time or active duty training. Returning employee is entitled to reinstatement to previous position, or to one with the same seniority, status, and pay, unless the employer's circumstances have changed and reemployment is impossible or unreasonable. Employee must apply for reinstatement within 90 days of discharge from active service, 10 days of completing school, reserve drills, or annual training, or 60 days of completing initial full-time or active duty training. Employee may not be discharged without cause for one year after reinstatement. Employers may not discriminate against persons subject to state or federal military duty.

North Carolina

N.C. Gen. Stat. §§ 127A-201, 127A-202, 127A-202.1, 127B-14

Members of the North Carolina National Guard, or the national guard of any other state, who are called to active state duty by a state governor are entitled to take unpaid leave. Unless the employer's circumstances now make it unreasonable, returning employee must be restored to previous position or one of comparable seniority, status, and salary; if no longer qualified, employee must be placed in another position with appropriate seniority, status, and salary. Employee must apply for reinstatement, in writing, within 5 days of release from duty or hospitalization continuing after release. Employer may not discriminate against or discharge an employee because of membership in the national guard of any state or discharge an employee called up for emergency military service.

North Dakota

N.D.C.C. §§ 37-29-01, 37-29-03

Employers may not terminate, demote, or otherwise discriminate against volunteer members of the North Dakota National Guard or North Dakota air national guard, or volunteer civilian members of the civil air patrol. The employer must allow such employees to be absent or tardy from work for up to 20 days in a calendar year

State Laws on Military Leave (continued)

because they are responding to a disaster or national emergency (20-day limit does not apply to involuntarily activated members of the North Dakota National Guard). An employee who needs this leave must make a reasonable effort to notify the employer. Upon request, the employee must also provide written verification of the dates and times of service.

Ohio

Ohio Rev. Code Ann. § 5903.02

Employees who are members of the Ohio organized militia or National Guard called for active duty or training; members of the commissioned public health service corps; or any other uniformed service called up in time of war or emergency have the same leave and reinstatement rights and benefits guaranteed under USERRA.

Oklahoma

Okla. Stat. Ann. tit. 44, §§ 71, 208.1

Employees in the Oklahoma National Guard who are ordered to state active duty or full-time National Guard duty have the same reinstatement rights and other benefits guaranteed by USERRA. Members of the state National Guard must be allowed to take time off to attend state National Guard drills, instruction, encampment, maneuvers, ceremonies, exercises, or other duties.

Oregon

Ore. Rev. Stat. §§ 659A.082, 659A.086

Members of Oregon or other states' organized militias called into active state service or state active duty may take unpaid leave for term of service. Returning employee is entitled to reinstatement with no loss of seniority or benefits including sick leave, vacation, or service credits under a pension plan. Employee must return to work within 7 calendar days of release from service.

Pennsylvania

51 Pa. Cons. Stat. Ann. §§ 7302 to 7309

Employees who enlist or are drafted during a time of war or emergency called by the president or governor, along with reservists or members of Pennsylvania National Guard called into active duty, are entitled to unpaid military leave. Leave expires 90 days after enlistment/draft period, 90 days after military duty for reservists, 30 days after state duty for Pennsylvania National Guard members. Returning employee must be reinstated to same or similar position with same status, seniority, and pay. If no longer qualified due to disability sustained during military duty, employer must restore to position with like seniority, status, and pay unless employer or successor's circumstances have changed so as to make it impossible or unreasonable to do so. Employers may not discharge or discriminate against any employee because of membership or service in the military. Employees called to active duty are entitled to 30 days' health insurance continuation benefits at no cost.

Rhode Island

R.I. Gen. Laws §§ 30-11-2 to 30-11-9; 30-21-1

Members of state military forces and the National Guard of Rhode Island or any other state who are called to active duty have the same leave and reinstatement rights and benefits guaranteed under USERRA. Members of the National Guard or U.S. armed forces reserves are entitled to unpaid leave for training and are entitled to reinstatement with the same status, pay, and seniority. Employees in the U.S. armed forces are entitled to reinstatement to the same position or a position with similar seniority, status, and pay unless the employer's circumstances make reinstatement impossible or unreasonable. Employee must request reinstatement within 40 days. Employer may not discriminate against or discharge employee because of membership in the state military forces or U.S. reserves, interfere with employee's military service, or dissuade employee from enlisting by threatening employee's job.

South Carolina

S.C. Code Ann. §§ 25-1-2310 to 25-1-2340

Members of the South Carolina National Guard or State Guard, or the national or state guard of any state, who are called to active duty by a state governor are entitled to unpaid leave for service. Upon honorable discharge from service, the employee must be reinstated to the same position or a position with similar seniority, status, and pay. Employee must apply for reinstatement in writing, within 5 days of release from service or related hospitalization. Employer has no duty to reinstate if the employer's circumstances make reinstatement unreasonable.

South Dakota

S.D. Codified Laws Ann. § 33A-2-9

Members of the South Dakota National Guard ordered to active duty by governor or president have the same leave and reinstatement rights and benefits guaranteed under USERRA.

State Laws on Military Leave (continued)

Tennessee

Tenn. Code Ann. § 58-1-604

Employer may not terminate or refuse to hire an employee because of Tennessee National Guard membership or because employee is absent for a required drill, including annual field training.

Texas

Tex. Govt. Code Ann. § 437.204

Members of the Texas military forces or the military forces of any other state have the right to be reinstated following a call to active duty or training. Employees are entitled to be reinstated to the same position they held before leaving, with no loss of time, efficiency rating, vacation time, or other benefits. An employee must give notice of his or her intent to return to work as soon as practicable after release from duty.

Utah

Utah Code Ann. § 39-1-36

Members of U.S. armed forces reserves who are called to active duty, active duty for training, inactive duty training, or state active duty may take up to 5 years of unpaid leave. Upon return, employee is entitled to reinstatement to previous employment with same seniority, status, pay, and vacation rights. Employer may not discriminate against an employee based on membership in armed forces reserves.

Vermont

Vt. Stat. Ann. tit. 21, § 491, Vt. Stat. Ann. tit. 20, § 608

Employees who are members of U.S. armed forces reserves, an organized unit of the National Guard of Vermont or any other state, or the ready reserves are entitled to 15 days per year of unpaid leave for military drills, training, or other temporary duty under military authority. Returning employee must be reinstated to former position with the same status, pay, and seniority, including any seniority that accrued during the leave of absence. Employer may not discriminate against an employee who is a member or an applicant for membership in the National Guard of Vermont or any other state. Members of the National Guard of Vermont or any other state ordered to state active duty by the governor have the right to take unpaid leave from civilian employment, and cannot be required to exhaust their vacation or other accrued leave.

Virginia

Va. Code Ann. §§ 44-93.2 to 44-93.4

Members of the Virginia National Guard, Virginia Defense Force, or the national guard of another state, called to active duty by the governor are entitled to take unpaid leave and may not be required to use vacation or any other accrued leave (unless employee wishes). Returning employee whose absence does not exceed five years must be reinstated to previous position or one with same seniority, status, and pay; if position no longer exists, then to a comparable position unless employer's circumstances would make reemployment unreasonable. Employee must apply for reinstatement, in writing, within (a) 14 days of release from service or related hospitalization if service length did not exceed 180 days, or (b) 90 days of release from service or related hospitalization if service length exceeded 180 days. Employer cannot discriminate against employees because of membership in state military service.

Washington

Wash. Rev. Code Ann. §§ 73.16.032 to 73.16.035

Employees in Washington who are members of the armed forces or the national guard of any state are entitled to take leave when called to active duty for training, inactive duty training, full-time national guard duty, or state active duty. Employees are entitled to be reinstated, following their military duty, to the position they previously held or one with like seniority, status, and pay. The time limit for requesting reinstatement depends on the length of the employee's military leave.

Employers may not discriminate against employees based on their membership in any branch of the uniformed services.

West Virginia

W.Va. Code § 15-1F-8

Employees who are members of the organized militia in active state service have the same leave and reinstatement rights and benefits guaranteed under USERRA.

Wisconsin

Wis. Stat. Ann. §§ 111.321, 321.64, 321.65

Employees who enlist, are inducted, or are ordered to serve in the U.S. armed forces for 90 days or more, or civilian employees who are asked to perform national defense work during an officially proclaimed emergency, may take leave

State Laws on Military Leave (continued)

for military service and/or training. Employees who are called to state active duty in the Wisconsin National Guard or the national guard of any other state, or called to active service with the state laboratory of hygiene during a public health emergency, are also entitled to take military leave.

Upon completion of military leave, employees are entitled to reinstatement to their prior position or to one with equivalent seniority, status, and pay. A reinstated employee may not be discharged without cause for up to one year.

Employers may not discriminate against employees based on their military service.

Wyoming

Wyo. Stat. §§ 19-11-103, 19-11-104, 19-11-107, 19-11-111

Employees of the armed forces or national guard of any state who report for active duty, training, or a qualifying physical exam may take up to 5 years' leave of absence.

Employee must give advance notice of service. Employee may use vacation or any other accrued leave but is not required to do so. Returning employee is entitled to reemployment with the same seniority, rights, and benefits, plus any additional seniority and benefits that employee would have earned if there had been no absence, unless employer's circumstances have changed so that reemployment is impossible or unreasonable or would impose an undue hardship. Time limits set forth governing written application for reinstatement based on length of uniformed service. Employee is entitled to complete any training program that would have been available to employee's former position during period of absence. Employee may not be terminated without cause for one year after returning to work. Employer cannot discriminate against applicant or member of the uniformed services.

State Laws on Taking Time Off to Vote

Note: The states of Connecticut, Delaware, Florida, Idaho, Indiana, Louisiana, Maine, Michigan, Mississippi, Montana, New Hampshire, New Jersey, North Carolina, Oregon, Pennsylvania, Rhode Island, South Carolina, Vermont, Virginia, Washington, and the District of Columbia are not listed in this chart because they do not have laws or regulations on time off to vote that govern private employers. Check with your state department of labor if you need more information. (See Appendix B for contact list.)

Alabama

Ala. Code § 17-1-5

Time off work for voting: Necessary time up to one hour. The employer may decide when hours may be taken.

Time off not required if: Employee has 2 nonwork hours before polls open or one nonwork hour after polls are open.

Time off is paid: No.

Employee must request leave in advance: "Reasonable notice."

Alaska

Alaska Stat. § 15.56.100

Time off work for voting: Not specified.

Time off not required if: Employee has 2 consecutive non-work hours at beginning or end of shift when polls are open.

Time off is paid: Yes.

Arizona

Ariz. Rev. Stat. § 16-402

Time off work for voting: As much time as will add up to 3 hours when combined with nonwork time. Employer may decide when hours are taken.

Time off not required if: Employee has 3 consecutive non-work hours at beginning or end of shift when polls are open.

Time off is paid: Yes.

Employee must request leave in advance: Prior to the day of the election.

Arkansas

Ark. Code Ann. § 7-1-102

Time off work for voting: Employer must schedule employees' work schedules on election days to enable employees to vote.

Time off is paid: No.

California

Cal. Elec. Code § 14000

Time off work for voting: Up to 2 hours at beginning or end of shift, whichever gives employee most time to vote and takes least time off work.

Time off not required if: Employee has sufficient time to vote during nonwork time.

Time off is paid: Yes (up to 2 hours).

Employee must request leave in advance: 2 working days before election.

Colorado

Colo. Rev. Stat. § 1-7-102

Time off work for voting: Up to 2 hours. Employer may decide when hours are taken, but employer must permit employee to take time at beginning or end of shift, if employee requests it.

Time off not required if: Employee has 3 nonwork hours when polls are open.

Time off is paid: Yes (up to 2 hours).

Employee must request leave in advance: Prior to election day.

Georgia

Ga. Code Ann. § 21-2-404

Time off work for voting: Up to 2 hours. Employer may decide when hours are taken.

Time off not required if: Employee has 2 nonwork hours at beginning or end of shift when polls are open.

Time off is paid: No.

Employee must request leave in advance: "Reasonable notice."

Hawaii

Haw. Rev. Stat. § 11-95

Time off work for voting: 2 consecutive hours excluding meal or rest breaks. Employer may not change employee's regular work schedule.

Time off not required if: Employee has 2 consecutive nonwork hours when polls are open.

Time off is paid: Yes.

Employee required to show proof of voting: Only if employer is verifying whether employee voted when they took time off to vote. A voter's receipt is proof of voting by the employee. If employer verifies that employee did not vote, hours off may be deducted from pay.

Illinois

10 Ill. Comp. Stat. §§ 5/7-42, 5/17-15

Time off work for voting: 2 hours. Employer may decide when hours are taken except that employer must permit a 2-hour absence during working hours if employee's working hours begin less than 2 hours after opening of polls and end less than 2 hours before closing of polls.

Time off is paid: Yes.

Employee must request leave in advance: Prior to the day of election. One day in advance (for general or state election). Employer must give consent (for primary).

Iowa

Iowa Code § 49.109

Time off work for voting: As much time as will add up to 3 hours when combined with nonwork time. Employer may decide when hours are taken.

Time off not required if: Employee has 3 consecutive nonwork hours when polls are open.

Time off is paid: Yes.

Employee must request leave in advance: In writing "prior to the date of the election."

Kansas

Kan. Stat. Ann. § 25-418

Time off work for voting: Up to 2 hours or as much time as will add up to 2 hours when combined with nonwork time. Employer may decide when hours are taken, but it may not be during a regular meal break.

Time off not required if: Employee has 2 consecutive nonwork hours when polls are open.

Time off is paid: Yes.

Kentucky

Ky. Const. § 148; Ky. Rev. Stat. Ann. § 118.035

Time off work for voting: "Reasonable time," but not less than 4 hours. Employer may decide when hours are taken.

Time off is paid: No.

Employee must request leave in advance: One day before election.

Employee required to show proof of voting: No proof specified, but employee who takes time off and does not vote may be subject to disciplinary action.

Maryland

Md. Code Ann. [Elec. Law] § 10-315

Time off work for voting: 2 hours.

Time off not required if: Employee has 2 consecutive nonwork hours when polls are open.

Time off is paid: Yes.

Employee required to show proof of voting: Yes; also includes attempting to vote. Must use state board of elections form.

Massachusetts

Mass. Gen. Laws ch. 149, § 178

Time off work for voting: First 2 hours that polls are open. (Applies to workers in manufacturing, mechanical, or retail industries.)

Time off is paid: No.

Employee must request leave in advance: Must apply for leave of absence (no time specified).

Minnesota

Minn. Stat. Ann. § 204C.04

Time off work for voting: May be absent for the time necessary to appear at the employee's polling place, cast a ballot, and return to work.

Time off is paid: Yes.

Missouri

Mo. Rev. Stat. § 115.639

Time off work for voting: 3 hours. Employer may decide when hours are taken.

Time off not required if: Employee has 3 consecutive nonwork hours when polls are open.

Time off is paid: Yes (if employee votes).

Employee must request leave in advance: "Prior to the day of election."

Employee required to show proof of voting: None specified, but pay contingent on employee actually voting.

State Laws on Taking Time Off to Vote (continued)

Nebraska

Neb. Rev. Stat. § 32-922

Time off work for voting: As much time as will add up to 2 consecutive hours when combined with nonwork time. Employer may decide when hours are taken.

Time off not required if: Employee has 2 consecutive nonwork hours when polls are open.

Time off is paid: Yes.

Employee must request leave in advance: Prior to or on election day.

Nevada

Nev. Rev. Stat. Ann. § 293.463

Time off work for voting: If it is impracticable to vote before or after work: Employee who works 2 miles or less from polling place may take 1 hour; 2 to 10 miles, 2 hours; more than 10 miles, 3 hours. Employer will decide when hours are taken.

Time off not required if: Employee has sufficient nonwork time when polls are open.

Time off is paid: Yes.

Employee must request leave in advance: Prior to election day.

New Mexico

N.M. Stat. Ann. § 1-12-42

Time off work for voting: 2 hours. (Includes Indian nation, tribal, and pueblo elections.) Employer may decide when hours are taken.

Time off not required if: Employee's workday begins more than 2 hours after polls open or ends more than 3 hours before polls close.

Time off is paid: Yes.

New York

N.Y. Elec. Law § 3-110

Time off work for voting: As many hours at beginning or end of shift as will give employee enough time to vote when combined with nonwork time. Employer may decide when hours are taken.

Time off not required if: Employee has 4 consecutive nonwork hours at beginning or end of shift when polls are open.

Time off is paid: Yes (up to 2 hours).

Employee must request leave in advance: Not more than 10 or less than 2 working days before election.

North Dakota

N.D. Cent. Code § 16.1-01-02.1

Time off work for voting: Employers are encouraged to give employees time off to vote when regular work schedule conflicts with times polls are open.

Time off is paid: No.

Ohio

Ohio Rev. Code Ann. § 3599.06

Time off work for voting: "Reasonable time."

Time off is paid: Yes.

Oklahoma

Okla. Stat. Ann. tit. 26, § 7-101

Time off work for voting: 2 hours, unless employee lives so far from polling place that more time is needed. Employer may decide when hours are taken or may change employee's schedule to give employee nonwork time to vote.

Time off not required if: Employee's workday begins at least 3 hours after polls open or ends at least 3 hours before polls close.

Time off is paid: Yes.

Employee must request leave in advance: One day before election, either orally or in writing.

Employee required to show proof of voting: Yes.

South Dakota

S.D. Codified Laws Ann. § 12-3-5

Time off work for voting: 2 consecutive hours. Employer may decide when hours are taken.

Time off not required if: Employee has 2 consecutive nonwork hours when polls are open.

Time off is paid: Yes.

Tennessee

Tenn. Code Ann. § 2-1-106

Time off work for voting: "Reasonable time" up to 3 hours during the time polls are open. Employer may decide when hours are taken.

Time off not required if: Employee's workday begins at least 3 hours after polls open or ends at least 3 hours before polls close.

State Laws on Taking Time Off to Vote (continued)

Time off is paid: Yes.

Employee must request leave in advance: Before noon on the day before the election.

Texas
Tex. Elec. Code Ann. § 276.004

Time off work for voting: Employer may not refuse to allow employee to take time off to vote, but no time limit specified.

Time off not required if: Employee has 2 consecutive nonwork hours when polls are open.

Time off is paid: Yes.

Utah
Utah Code Ann. § 20A-3-103

Time off work for voting: 2 hours at beginning or end of shift. Employer may decide when hours are taken.

Time off not required if: Employee has at least 3 nonwork hours when polls are open.

Time off is paid: Yes.

Employee must request leave in advance: "Before election day."

West Virginia
W.Va. Code § 3-1-42

Time off work for voting: Up to 3 hours. (Employers in health, transportation, communication, production, and processing facilities may change employee's schedule so that time off doesn't impair essential operations but must allow employee sufficient and convenient time to vote.)

Time off not required if: Employee has at least 3 nonwork hours when polls are open.

Time off is paid: Yes (if employee votes).

Employee must request leave in advance: Written request at least 3 days before election.

Employee required to show proof of voting: None specified, but time off will be deducted from pay if employee does not vote.

Wisconsin
Wis. Stat. Ann. § 6.76

Time off work for voting: Up to 3 consecutive hours. Employer may decide when hours are taken.

Time off is paid: No.

Employee must request leave in advance: "Before election day."

Wyoming
Wyo. Stat. § 22-2-111

Time off work for voting: One hour, other than a meal break. Employer may decide when the hour is taken.

Time off not required if: Employee has at least 3 consecutive nonwork hours when polls are open.

Time off is paid: Yes (if employee votes).

Employee required to show proof of voting: None specified, but pay contingent on employee voting.

State Laws on Jury Duty

Alabama

Ala. Code §§ 12-16-8 to 12-16-8.1

Paid leave: Full-time employees are entitled to usual pay.

Notice employee must give: Must show supervisor jury summons the next working day; must return to work the next scheduled hour after discharge from jury duty.

Employer penalty for firing or penalizing employee: Liable for actual and punitive damages.

Alaska

Alaska Stat. § 09.20.037

Unpaid leave: Yes.

Additional employee protections: Employee may not be threatened, coerced, or penalized.

Employer penalty for firing or penalizing employee: Liable for lost wages and damages; may be required to reinstate the fired employee.

Arizona

Ariz. Rev. Stat. § 21-236

Unpaid leave: Yes.

Additional employee protections: Employee may not lose vacation rights, seniority, or precedence. Employer may not require employee to use annual, sick, or vacation hours.

Employer penalty for firing or penalizing employee: Class 3 misdemeanor, punishable by a fine of up to $500 or up to 30 days' imprisonment.

Note: Employers with 5 or fewer full-time employees: Court must postpone an employee's jury service if another employee is already serving as a juror.

Arkansas

Ark. Code Ann. § 16-31-106

Unpaid leave: Yes.

Additional employee protections: Absence may not affect sick leave and vacation rights.

Notice employee must give: Reasonable notice.

Employer penalty for firing or penalizing employee: Class A misdemeanor, punishable by a fine of up to $2,500.

California

Cal. Lab. Code §§ 230, 230.1

Unpaid leave: Employee may use vacation, personal leave, or comp time.

Notice employee must give: Reasonable notice.

Employer penalty for firing or penalizing employee: Employer must reinstate employee with back pay and lost wages and benefits. Willful violation is a misdemeanor.

Colorado

Colo. Rev. Stat. §§ 13-71-126, 13-71-133 to 13-71-134, 18-1.3-501

Paid leave: All employees (including part-time and temporary who were scheduled to work for the 3 months preceding jury service): regular wages up to $50 per day for first 3 days of jury duty. Must pay within 30 days of jury service.

Additional employee protections: Employer may not make any demands on employee that will interfere with effective performance of jury duty.

Employer penalty for firing or penalizing employee: Class 2 misdemeanor, punishable by a fine of $250 to $1,000 or 3 to 12 months' imprisonment, or both. May be liable to employee for triple damages and attorneys' fees.

Connecticut

Conn. Gen. Stat. Ann. §§ 51-247 and 51-247a

Paid leave: Full-time employees: regular wages for the first 5 days of jury duty; after 5 days, state pays up to $50 per day.

Additional employee protections: Once employee serves 8 hours of jury duty, employer may not require employee to work more hours on the same day.

Employer penalty for firing or penalizing employee: Criminal contempt: punishable by a fine of up to $500 or up to 30 days' imprisonment, or both. Liable for up to 10 weeks' lost wages for discharging employee. If employer fails to pay the employee as required, may be liable for treble damages and attorneys' fees.

Delaware

Del. Code Ann. tit. 10, §§ 4514, 4515

Unpaid leave: State pays $20 per diem for travel, parking, other out-of-pocket expenses. State pays certain other expenses if jury is sequestered.

Employer penalty for firing or penalizing employee: Criminal contempt: punishable by a fine of up to $500 or up to 6 months' imprisonment, or both. Liable to discharged employee for lost wages and attorneys' fees and may be required to reinstate the fired employee.

State Laws on Jury Duty (continued)

District of Columbia

D.C. Code Ann. §§ 11-1913, 15-718

Paid leave: Full-time employees: regular wages for the first 5 days of jury duty, less jury fee from state. State attendance fee: $30, if not paid full regular wages by employer. State travel allowance: $2 per day.

Employer penalty for firing or penalizing employee: Criminal contempt: punishable by a fine of up to $300 or up to 30 days' imprisonment, or both, for a first offense; up to $5,000 or up to 180 days' imprisonment, or both, for any subsequent offense. Liable to discharged employee for lost wages and attorneys' fees and may be required to reinstate the fired employee.

Florida

Fla. Stat. Ann. §§ 40.24, 40.271

Unpaid leave: Yes. State pays $15 per day for first three days of service if juror does not receive regular wages those days. State pays $30 per day for the fourth and subsequent days.

Additional employee protections: Employee may not be threatened with dismissal.

Employer penalty for firing or penalizing employee: Threatening employee is contempt of court. May be liable to discharged employee for compensatory and punitive damages and attorneys' fees.

Georgia

Ga. Code Ann. § 34-1-3

Paid leave: According to Opinion of the Attorney General Number 89-55, issued in 1989, employers must pay an employee's wages while on jury duty, minus any funds the employee receives for jury service.

Additional employee protections: Employee may not be discharged, penalized, or threatened with discharge or penalty for responding to a subpoena or making a required court appearance.

Notice employee must give: Reasonable notice.

Employer penalty for firing or penalizing employee: Liable for actual damages and reasonable attorneys' fees.

Hawaii

Haw. Rev. Stat. § 612-25

Unpaid leave: Yes.

Employer penalty for firing or penalizing employee: Petty misdemeanor: punishable by a fine of up to $1,000 or up to 30 days' imprisonment. May be liable to discharged employee for up to 6 weeks' lost wages, reasonable attorneys' fees, and may be required to reinstate the fired employee.

Idaho

Idaho Code § 2-218

Unpaid leave: Yes.

Employer penalty for firing or penalizing employee: Criminal contempt: punishable by a fine of up to $300. Liable to discharged employee for triple lost wages and reasonable attorneys' fees. May be ordered to reinstate the fired employee.

Illinois

705 Ill. Comp. Stat. § 310/10.1

Unpaid leave: Yes.

Additional employee protections: A regular night shift employee may not be required to work if serving on a jury during the day. May not lose any seniority or benefits.

Notice employee must give: Must give employer a copy of the summons within 10 days of issuance.

Employer penalty for firing or penalizing employee: Employer will be charged with civil or criminal contempt, or both; liable to employee for lost wages and benefits; may be ordered to reinstate employee.

Indiana

Ind. Code Ann. §§ 34-28-4-1, 35-44-3-11

Unpaid leave: Yes.

Additional employee protections: Employee may not be deprived of benefits or threatened with the loss of them.

Employer penalty for firing or penalizing employee: Class B misdemeanor: punishable by up to 180 days' imprisonment; may also be fined up to $1,000. Liable to discharged employee for lost wages and attorneys' fees and may be required to reinstate the fired employee.

Iowa

Iowa Code § 607A.45

Unpaid leave: Yes.

Additional employee protections: Employer may not threaten or coerce employee based on jury notice or jury duty.

Employer penalty for firing or penalizing employee: Contempt of court. Liable to discharged employee for up to 6 weeks' lost wages and attorneys' fees and may be required to reinstate the fired employee.

State Laws on Jury Duty (continued)

Kansas

Kan. Stat. Ann. § 43-173

Unpaid leave: Yes.

Additional employee protections: Employee may not lose seniority or benefits. (Basic and additional protections apply to permanent employees only.)

Employer penalty for firing or penalizing employee: Liable for lost wages and benefits, damages, and attorneys' fees and may be required to reinstate the fired employee.

Kentucky

Ky. Rev. Stat. Ann. §§ 29A.160, 29A.990

Unpaid leave: Yes.

Additional employee protections: Employer may not threaten or coerce employee based on jury notice or jury duty.

Employer penalty for firing or penalizing employee: Class B misdemeanor: punishable by up to 89 days' imprisonment or fine of up to $250, or both. Liable to discharged employee for lost wages and attorneys' fees. Must reinstate employee with full seniority and benefits.

Louisiana

La. Rev. Stat. Ann. § 23:965

Paid leave: Regular employee entitled to one day full compensation for jury service. May not lose any sick, vacation, or personal leave or other benefit.

Additional employee protections: Employer may not create any policy or rule that would discharge employee for jury service.

Notice employee must give: Reasonable notice.

Employer penalty for firing or penalizing employee: For each discharged employee: fine of $100 to $1,000; must reinstate employee with full benefits. For not granting paid leave: fine of $100 to $500; must pay full day's lost wages.

Maine

Me. Rev. Stat. Ann. tit. 14, § 1218

Unpaid leave: Yes.

Additional employee protections: Employee may not lose or be threatened with loss of employment or health insurance coverage.

Employer penalty for firing or penalizing employee: Class E crime: punishable by up to 6 months in the county jail or a fine of up to $1,000. Liable for up to 6 weeks' lost wages,

benefits, and attorneys' fees. Employer may be ordered to reinstate the employee.

Maryland

Md. Code Ann., [Cts. & Jud. Proc.] §§ 8-501, 8-502

Unpaid leave: Yes.

Additional employee protections: Employer cannot threaten or coerce an employee. An employee may not be required to use annual, sick, or vacation leave. An employee who spends at least 4 hours on jury service (including travel time) may not be required to work a shift that begins on or after 5 p.m. that day or before 3 a.m. the following day.

Employer penalty for firing or penalizing employee: Employer penalty for violating these provisions is a fine up to $1,000.

Massachusetts

Mass. Gen. Laws ch. 234A, §§ 48 and following

Paid leave: All employees (including part-time and temporary who were scheduled to work for the 3 months preceding jury service): regular wages for first 3 days of jury duty. If paid leave is an "extreme financial hardship" for employer, state will pay. After first 3 days, state will pay $50 per day.

Michigan

Mich. Comp. Laws § 600.1348

Unpaid leave: Yes.

Additional employee protections: Employee may not be threatened or disciplined; may not be required to work in addition to jury service, if extra hours would mean working overtime or beyond normal quitting time.

Employer penalty for firing or penalizing employee: Misdemeanor, punishable by a fine of up to $500 or up to 90 days' imprisonment, or both. Employer may also be punished for contempt of court, with a fine of up to $7,500 or up to 93 days' imprisonment, or both.

Minnesota

Minn. Stat. Ann. § 593.50

Unpaid leave: Yes.

Additional employee protections: Employer may not threaten or coerce employee.

Employer penalty for firing or penalizing employee: Criminal contempt: punishable by a fine of up to $700 or up to 6 months' imprisonment, or both. Also liable to

State Laws on Jury Duty (continued)

employee for up to 6 weeks' lost wages and attorneys' fees and may be required to reinstate the fired employee.

Mississippi

Miss. Code Ann. §§ 13-5-23, 13-5-35

Unpaid leave: Yes.

Additional employee protections: Employee may not be intimidated or threatened. Employee may not be required to use annual, sick, or vacation leave for jury service.

Notice employee must give: Reasonable notice is required.

Employer penalty for firing or penalizing employee: If found guilty of interference with the administration of justice: at least one month in the county jail or up to 2 years in the state penitentiary, or a fine of up to $500, or both. May also be found guilty of contempt of court, punishable by a fine of up to $1,000 or up to 6 months' imprisonment, or both.

Note: Employers with 5 or fewer full-time employees: Court must postpone an employee's jury service if another employee is already serving as a juror.

Missouri

Mo. Rev. Stat. § 494.460

Unpaid leave: Yes.

Additional employee protections: Employer may not take or threaten to take any adverse action. Employee may not be required to use annual, sick, vacation, or personal leave.

Employer penalty for firing or penalizing employee: Employer may be liable for lost wages, damages, and attorneys' fees and may be required to reinstate the fired employee.

Montana

Mont. Admin. R. 24.16.2520

Paid leave: No paid leave laws regarding private employers.

Nebraska

Neb. Rev. Stat. § 25-1640

Paid leave: Normal wages minus any compensation (other than expenses) from the court.

Additional employee protections: Employee may not lose pay, sick leave, or vacation or be penalized in any way; may not be required to work evening or night shift.

Notice employee must give: Reasonable notice.

Employer penalty for firing or penalizing employee: Class IV misdemeanor, punishable by a fine of up to $500.

Nevada

Nev. Rev. Stat. Ann. §§ 6.190, 193.140

Unpaid leave: Yes.

Additional employee protections: Employer may not recommend or threaten termination; may not dissuade or attempt to dissuade employee from serving as a juror, and cannot require the employee to work within 8 hours before jury duty or if employee's duty lasts four hours or more (including travel time to and from the court), between 5 p.m. that day and 3 a.m. the next day. Cannot be required to take paid leave.

Notice employee must give: At least three days' notice.

Employer penalty for firing or penalizing employee: Terminating or threatening to terminate is a gross misdemeanor, punishable by a fine of up to $2,000 or up to 364 days' imprisonment, or both; in addition, employer may be liable for lost wages, damages equal to lost wages, and punitive damages to $50,000 and must reinstate employee. Dissuading or attempting to dissuade is a misdemeanor, punishable by a fine of up to $1,000 or up to 6 months in the county jail, or both.

New Hampshire

N.H. Rev. Stat. Ann. § 500-A:14

Unpaid leave: Yes.

Additional employee protections: Employer cannot threaten or coerce employee.

Employer penalty for firing or penalizing employee: Employer may be found guilty of contempt of court; also liable to employee for lost wages and attorneys' fees and may be required to reinstate the fired employee.

New Jersey

N.J. Stat. Ann. § 2B:20-17

Unpaid leave: Yes.

Additional employee protections: Employer cannot threaten or coerce employee.

Employer penalty for firing or penalizing employee: Employer may be found guilty of a disorderly persons offense, punishable by a fine of up to $1,000 or up to 6 months' imprisonment, or both. May also be liable to employee for economic damages and attorneys' fees and may be ordered to reinstate the fired employee.

State Laws on Jury Duty (continued)

New Mexico

N.M. Stat. Ann. §§ 38-5-18 to 38-5-19

Unpaid leave: Yes.

Additional employee protections: Employer cannot threaten or coerce employee. An employee may not be required to use annual, sick, or vacation leave.

Employer penalty for firing or penalizing employee: Petty misdemeanor, punishable by a fine of up to $500 or up to 6 months in the county jail, or both.

New York

N.Y. Jud. Ct. Acts Law § 519

Unpaid leave: Yes.

Paid leave: Employers with more than 10 employees must pay first $40 of wages for the first 3 days of jury duty.

Notice employee must give: Must notify employer prior to beginning jury duty.

Employer penalty for firing or penalizing employee: May be found guilty of criminal contempt of court, punishable by a fine of up to $1,000 or up to 30 days in the county jail, or both.

North Carolina

N.C. Gen. Stat. § 9-32

Unpaid leave: Yes.

Additional employee protections: Employee may not be demoted.

Employer penalty for firing or penalizing employee: Liable to discharged employee for reasonable damages; must reinstate employee to former position.

North Dakota

N.D. Cent. Code § 27-09.1-17

Unpaid leave: Yes.

Additional employee protections: Employee may not be laid off, penalized, or coerced because of jury duty, responding to a summons or subpoena, serving as a witness, or testifying in court.

Employer penalty for firing or penalizing employee: Class B misdemeanor, punishable by a fine of up to $1,500 or up to 30 days' imprisonment, or both. Liable to employee for up to 6 weeks' lost wages and attorneys' fees, and may be required to reinstate the fired employee.

Ohio

Ohio Rev. Code Ann. §§ 2313.19, 2313.99

Unpaid leave: Yes.

Additional employee protections: An employee may not be required to use annual, sick, or vacation leave.

Notice employee must give: Reasonable notice. Absence must be for actual jury service.

Employer penalty for firing or penalizing employee: May be found guilty of contempt of court, punishable by a fine of up to $250 or 30 days' imprisonment, or both, for first offense.

Oklahoma

Okla. Stat. Ann. tit. 38, §§ 34, 35

Unpaid leave: Yes.

Additional employee protections: Employee can't be subject to any adverse employment action, and can't be required to use annual, sick, or vacation leave.

Notice employee must give: Reasonable notice.

Employer penalty for firing or penalizing employee: Misdemeanor, punishable by a fine of up to $5,000. Liable to discharged employee for actual and exemplary damages; actual damages include past and future lost wages, mental anguish, and costs of finding suitable employment.

Oregon

Or. Rev. Stat. § 10.090

Unpaid leave: Yes (or according to employer's policy).

Additional employee protections: Employee may not be threatened, intimidated, or coerced, and can't be required to use annual, sick, or vacation leave.

Employer penalty for firing or penalizing employee: Court may order reinstatement with or without back pay, and a $720 civil penalty.

Pennsylvania

42 Pa. Cons. Stat. Ann. § 4563; 18 Pa. Cons. Stat. Ann. § 4957

Unpaid leave: Yes (applies to retail or service industry employers with 15 or more employees and to manufacturers with 40 or more employees).

Additional employee protections: Employee may not be threatened or coerced, or lose seniority or benefits. (Any employee who would not be eligible for unpaid leave will be automatically excused from jury duty.)

Employer penalty for firing or penalizing employee: Liable to employee for lost benefits, wages, and attorneys' fees; may be required to reinstate the fired employee.

Rhode Island

R.I. Gen. Laws § 9-9-28

Unpaid leave: Yes.

Additional employee protections: Employee may not lose wage increases, promotions, length of service, or other benefit.

Employer penalty for firing or penalizing employee: Misdemeanor punishable by a fine of up to $1,000 or up to one year's imprisonment, or both.

South Carolina

S.C. Code Ann. § 41-1-70

Unpaid leave: Yes.

Employer penalty for firing or penalizing employee: For discharging employee, liable for one year's salary; for demoting employee, liable for one year's difference between former and lower salary.

South Dakota

S.D. Codified Laws Ann. §§ 16-13-41.1, 16-13-41.2

Unpaid leave: Yes.

Additional employee protections: Employee may not lose job status, pay, or seniority.

Employer penalty for firing or penalizing employee: Class 2 misdemeanor, punishable by a fine of up to $500 or up to 30 days in the county jail, or both.

Tennessee

Tenn. Code Ann. § 22-4-106

Paid leave: Regular wages minus jury fees, as long as the employer has at least 5 employees, and the employee is not a temporary worker who has been employed for less than 6 months.

Additional employee protections: Employer may not demote, suspend, or discriminate against employee. Night shift employees are excused from shift work during and for the night before the first day of jury service.

Notice employee must give: Employee must show summons to supervisor the next work day after receiving it.

Employer penalty for firing or penalizing employee: Employees are entitled to reinstatement and reimbursement

for lost wages and work benefits. Violating employee rights or any provisions of this law is a Class A misdemeanor, punishable by up to 11 months, 29 days' imprisonment or a fine up to $2,500, or both. Liable to employee for lost wages and benefits and must reinstate employee.

Texas

Tex. Civ. Prac. & Rem. Code Ann. §§ 122.001, 122.002

Unpaid leave: Yes.

Notice employee must give: Employee must notify employer of intent to return after completion of jury service.

Employer penalty for firing or penalizing employee: Liable to employee for not less than one year's nor more than 5 years' compensation and attorneys' fees. Must reinstate employee.

Note: Only applies to permanent employees.

Utah

Utah Code Ann. § 78B-1-116

Unpaid leave: Yes.

Additional employee protections: Employer may not threaten or coerce employee or take any adverse employment action against employee. Employee may not be requested or required to use annual or sick leave or vacation.

Employer penalty for firing or penalizing employee: May be found guilty of criminal contempt, punishable by a fine of up to $500 or up to 6 months' imprisonment, or both. Liable to employee for up to 6 weeks' lost wages and attorneys' fees and may be required to reinstate the fired employee.

Vermont

Vt. Stat. Ann. tit. 21, § 499

Unpaid leave: Yes.

Additional employee protections: Employee may not be penalized or lose any benefit available to other employees; may not lose seniority, vacation credit, or any fringe benefits.

Employer penalty for firing or penalizing employee: Fine of up to $200.

Virginia

Va. Code Ann. § 18.2-465.1

Unpaid leave: Yes.

State Laws on Jury Duty (continued)

Additional employee protections: Employee may not be subject to any adverse personnel action and may not be forced to use sick leave or vacation. Employee who has appeared for 4 or more hours cannot be required to start a shift after 5 p.m. that day or before 3 a.m. the next morning.

Notice employee must give: Reasonable notice.

Employer penalty for firing or penalizing employee: Class 3 misdemeanor, punishable by a fine of up to $500.

Washington

Wash. Rev. Code Ann. § 2.36.165

Unpaid leave: Yes.

Additional employee protections: Employee may not be threatened, coerced, harassed, or denied promotion.

Employer penalty for firing or penalizing employee: Intentional violation is a misdemeanor, punishable by a fine of up to $1,000 or up to 90 days' imprisonment, or both; also liable to employee for damages and attorneys' fees and may be required to reinstate the fired employee.

West Virginia

W.Va. Code § 52-3-1

Unpaid leave: Yes.

Additional employee protections: Employee may not be threatened or discriminated against; regular pay cannot be cut.

Employer penalty for firing or penalizing employee: May be found guilty of civil contempt, punishable by a fine of $100 to $500. May be required to reinstate the fired employee. May be liable for back pay and for attorneys' fees.

Wisconsin

Wis. Stat. Ann. § 756.255

Unpaid leave: Yes.

Additional employee protections: Employee may not lose seniority or pay raises; may not be disciplined.

Employer penalty for firing or penalizing employee: Fine of up to $200. May be required to reinstate the fired employee with back pay.

Wyoming

Wyo. Stat. § 1-11-401

Unpaid leave: Yes.

Additional employee protections: Employee may not be threatened, intimidated, or coerced.

Employer penalty for firing or penalizing employee: Liable to employee for up to $1,000 damages for each violation, costs, and attorneys' fees. May be required to reinstate the fired employee with no loss of seniority.

Performance

A company is only as good as its employees or, more to the point, as its employees' performance. It makes sense, then, for you to say something about performance in the employee handbook. Employees need to see, in writing, that the company expects a certain level of performance from them and that it will accept no less. They also need to understand that how they perform affects everyone else at the company.

Of course, with all of the people doing all of the various jobs within your company, it's hard for one handbook policy to tell each employee what is expected. That is the stuff of performance evaluations. The policies in this chapter will let you establish a benchmark of excellence for employees to strive for, then refer employees to the performance evaluation system (if there is one) for more details.

11:1 Job Performance Expectations

Although it should be self-evident that employees should perform well, a job performance expectation policy can be a useful reminder. It also warns employees that if they don't perform well, your company may discipline or even terminate them. This policy lets employees know that the company takes their performance seriously and that it expects them to do so, too. It also points out to employees that their performance doesn't just affect company management but has an impact on their coworkers as well. As the fortunes of the company go, so go the fortunes of the employees.

Your Job Performance

Each and every employee contributes to the success or failure of our Company. If one employee allows his or her performance to slip, then all of us suffer. We expect everyone to perform to the highest level possible.

Poor job performance can lead to discipline, up to and including termination.

Additional Clause to Specify Performance Standards

Depending on the products or services your company provides, you may want to give more information about the type of performance you expect from your employees. For example, a software company might want to encourage innovation and "thinking outside the box," while a manufacturer might want to stress adherence to workplace rules.

If you would like to say more about your expectations, insert an additional paragraph after the first paragraph of the standard policy, above. Although we can't give you a standard modification to use, below is an example of what you might write.

SAMPLE POLICY LANGUAGE

We believe our connection to our customers is of the utmost importance to our success. Therefore, every employee at Better Bread Bakery, from the accountant on up to the head baker, must make customer service a top priority. Excellent performance includes excellent customer service.

11:2 Job Performance Reviews

Rather than rely on casual feedback to keep their employees' performance on track, many companies have structured performance evaluation systems by which supervisors formally evaluate each employee's performance every so often (usually every six months or year).

If your company has such a system, then you should mention it in the handbook. To keep your flexibility, however, the following standard policy doesn't give a detailed description of how the system works. It simply alerts employees to the fact that there is a system for performance appraisal, and it states that the company requires employees to participate in it. You can give employees the details in other forms of communication, such as memoranda and company meetings.

Performance Reviews

Because our employees' performance is vital to our success, we conduct periodic reviews of individual employee performance. We hope that, through these reviews, our employees will learn what we expect of them, and we will learn what they expect of us.

We require all employees to participate in the review process. Failure to participate could lead to discipline, up to and including termination.

To learn more about our performance review system, contact

_____ .

11:2 Performance Reviews

File Name: 11_Performance.rtf

Include This Policy?
☐ Yes
☐ No
☐ Use our existing policy
☐ Other _____

Alternate Modifications
None

Additional Clauses
None

Related Policies
None

Notes

_____
_____
_____
_____
_____
_____
_____
_____
_____
_____
_____
_____
_____
_____
_____
_____
_____
_____
_____

Workplace Behavior

The workplace behavior section of a handbook is something of a grab bag of policies that define the minimum standards of conduct your company expects from its employees. Other sections of the handbook give more details about the various rules that employees must follow, but this section is where you set out the basics of how employees must behave while at work. It's also where you set out your company's discipline policy, if there is one.

CONTENTS

12:1 Please Act Professionally

File Name: 12_Work Behavior.rtf

Include This Policy?
- ☐ Yes
- ☐ No
- ☐ Use our existing policy
- ☐ Other _____

Alternate Modifications
None

Additional Clauses
Treatment of Customers
Insert?:   ☐ Yes   ☐ No

Related Policies
None

Notes

_____
_____
_____
_____
_____
_____
_____
_____
_____
_____
_____
_____
_____
_____
_____
_____
_____
_____

12:1 Professional Conduct

Although you may not have articulated it before, your company probably expects something more than mere work product from its employees. After all, they come into the workplace every day and interact with other employees, clients, and vendors. How they conduct themselves during these interactions is important to the smooth operation—indeed, to the success—of your business.

The following policy on professional conduct tells employees that you expect them to behave in a professional manner. It provides an explanation of professional conduct and informs employees that acting unprofessionally can be grounds for discipline.

Please Act Professionally

People who work together have an impact on each other's performance, productivity, and personal satisfaction in their jobs. In addition, how our employees act toward customers and vendors will influence whether those relationships are successful for our Company.

Because your conduct affects many more people than just yourself, we expect you to act in a professional and courteous manner toward coworkers, customers, vendors, and any member of the public while representing the Company or conducting Company business.

Although it is impossible to give an exhaustive list of everything that professional conduct means, it does, at a minimum, include the following:

- following all of the rules in this Handbook that apply to you
- refraining from rude, offensive, or outrageous behavior toward coworkers, customers, and vendors
- treating coworkers, customers, and vendors with patience, respect, and consideration, and
- being courteous and helpful to your coworkers and the public.

Individuals who act unprofessionally will face discipline, up to and including termination.

CAUTION

Don't prohibit employees from criticizing your company. Not long ago, it was common for employee handbooks to prohibit employees from criticizing or being disrespectful of the company or its managers. However, in the last few years, the National Labor Relations Board (NLRB)—the federal agency that enforces laws regarding unions and workplace organizing—has cracked down on employer policies that might constrain workers from speaking to each other (and complaining publicly) about the terms and conditions of their employment. Among other things, the NLRB has found that policies requiring employees to be respectful, avoid denigrating, and even avoid slandering the Company are illegal, because employees might interpret them to ban protected conversations, including criticism and protest, about company policies. Although you can ask employees to be respectful of coworkers, customers, and the public, asking them not to criticize the company itself or their managers is currently a no-no.

Who Needs This Policy

A professional conduct policy can do no harm to a business, and it might do a lot of good. It encourages employees to "play nice," and it gives additional leeway in disciplining employees who behave unpleasantly without violating a specific rule or letting their performance or productivity drop.

Employee Conduct Outside of Work

The professional conduct policy in this chapter does not police employee conduct outside of work. Some companies believe that how employees act at all times—including during their private time—reflects on the company. Or maybe they prefer to employ only people with certain beliefs, so they allow employees' conduct outside of work to have an impact on their decisions about employees.

If your company is concerned about your employees' conduct outside of work, tread carefully and consult with a lawyer. Many states have laws that protect employees from the prying eyes of their employer when they are not at work. These include laws protecting employees' right to privacy and laws prohibiting discrimination based on political activities, legal off-duty conduct, or marital or family status.

Additional Clause Regarding Treatment of Customers

If employees have a great deal of contact with customers, you might want to add something to your professional conduct policy to emphasize how employees should treat customers. Does your company take the approach that "the customer is always right"? Does your company expect employees to do whatever it takes to make customers happy? Or are there limits to what your company expects employees to do for customers?

If you would like to include specific information about customer relations in this policy, add the following paragraph at the end of the sample policy (and complete it as appropriate for your company).

Additional Clause

The success of this Company depends in great part on the loyalty and goodwill of our customers. As a result, we expect our employees to behave in the following manner when interacting with customers:

- to treat all customers with courtesy and respect
- to always be helpful and cheerful toward customers
- to _____
  _____
- to _____
  _____, and
- to _____
  _____ .

12:2 Punctuality and Attendance

You may think it goes without saying that your company expects employees to show up to work consistently and on time. In these days of flexible schedules and telecommuting, however, prudent employers who care about punctuality and attendance specifically demand it. Otherwise, employees may think that it doesn't really matter what time they show up, as long as they get their work done. This policy makes it clear that it does matter, and that your company will discipline employees who take a lax attitude. It also sets out a process that employees can follow if they are unable to be at work or if they are going to be late.

Punctuality and Attendance

You are important to the effective operation of this business. When you are not here at expected times or on expected days, someone else must do your job or delay doing his or her own job while waiting for you to arrive. If you work with customers or vendors, they may grow frustrated if they can't reach you during your scheduled work times.

As a result, we expect you to keep regular attendance and to be on time and ready to work at the beginning of each scheduled workday. (In Section _____ of this Handbook, you can find a description of this Company's work hours, timekeeping, and scheduling policies.)

Of course, things will sometimes happen that will prevent you from showing up to work on time. For example, you may be delayed by weather, a sick child, or car trouble. If you are going to be more than _____ minutes late, please call _____ _____ . If you cannot reach this person, please _____ . Please give this notice as far in advance as possible.

If you must miss a full day of work for reasons other than vacation, sick leave, or other approved leave (such as leave to serve on a jury or for a death in a family), you must notify

_____

as far in advance as possible. If you cannot reach this person, _____ . (You can find information about this Company's vacation and leave policies in Handbook Section _____ .)

If you are late for work or fail to appear without calling in as required by this policy or by other policies in this Handbook, you will face disciplinary action, up to and including termination.

12:2 Punctuality and Attendance

File Name: 12_Work Behavior.rtf

Include This Policy?
- ☐ Yes
- ☐ No
- ☐ Use our existing policy
- ☐ Other _____

Alternate Modifications

None

Additional Clauses

None

Related Policies

None

Notes

_____
_____
_____
_____
_____
_____
_____
_____
_____
_____
_____
_____
_____
_____
_____
_____
_____
_____
_____
_____

How to Complete This Policy

To complete the policy you must decide three things:

- How much leeway will you give employees in terms of punctuality? That is, how many minutes late must they be before you require them to call in? This is something that you must decide based on the needs of your business. Typical periods range from 15 minutes to two hours.
- Whom do employees have to call if they are going to be late or miss work? Typically, this person is the employee's supervisor, but in some businesses this person might be the human resources manager, office manager, or whoever will be responsible for making sure the employee's duties are covered while the employee is out of the office.
- What should employees do if they can't reach the designated person? You might instruct employees to simply leave a voicemail for the individual, or you might require them to leave a message for that person with someone who holds a position that is always staffed, such as the office receptionist.

12:3 Dress, Grooming, and Personal Hygiene

Workplace dress standards vary. Some employers ask only that their employees be clean and neat. Other employers have more specific policies. For example, some companies require a certain mode of dress or a uniform.

We provide three alternate policies below; choose the one that fits your business best.

Policy A requires a clean and neat appearance from employees. It is very general and nonspecific. This allows you flexibility to set standards department by department, if you wish, through memos and instructions from supervisors. It also informs employees that your company will accommodate the needs of people with disabilities or people with specific religious or ethnic practices.

Policy B requires employees to wear a uniform. Most states have rules regarding who must pay for a work uniform: the employer or the employee. States also have rules as to who must pay for cleaning and repairing the uniform. If you require your employees to wear uniforms, be sure to check out your state's laws on these issues. Once you do so, you can add that information to the policy. For more information, contact your state labor department. (See Appendix B for contact information.)

Policy C requires employees to dress professionally, in addition to maintaining a neat and clean appearance.

Alternate Policy A: Clean and Neat Appearance

> **Employee Appearance and Dress**
>
> Please dress appropriately for your position and job duties, and please make sure you are neat and clean at all times.
>
> If you have any questions about the proper attire for your position, please contact _____
>
> _____ .
>
> We will try to reasonably accommodate an employee's special dress or grooming needs that are the result of religion, ethnicity, race, or disability.

12:3 Employee Appearance and Dress

File Name: 12_Work Behavior.rtf

Include This Policy?
- ☐ Yes
  - *Choose one:* ☐ A ☐ B ☐ C
- ☐ No
- ☐ Use our existing policy
- ☐ Other _____

Alternate Modifications
None

Additional Clauses
Policy C only: Allow Casual Dress on Fridays
  Insert?: ☐ Yes ☐ No
Safety Concerns
  Insert?: ☐ Yes ☐ No
Body Piercings and Tattoos
  Insert?: ☐ Yes ☐ No

Related Policies
None

Notes

Alternate Policy B: Uniforms

Employees must wear a uniform during work hours. Please make sure you are neat and clean at all times, and please keep your uniform clean and in good condition.

If you have any questions about your uniform or about our appearance standards, please contact _____

_____ .

Alternate Policy C: Professional Dress

We believe that a professional image enhances our work product and makes us more competitive in the marketplace. In part, we convey that image through the appearance of our employees. We ask all employees to wear attire that is professional and appropriate. We also ask our employees to maintain a neat and clean appearance at all times.

Who Needs This Policy

Whether you need this policy will depend on your company culture and image and on the amount of contact employees have with outsiders. The more formal or professional the culture and the more employees interact with people outside the company, the more you will need a policy governing dress and appearance.

Additional Clause to Allow Casual Dress on Fridays

Many employers allow professional employees to dress casually on Fridays. For some, this means that employees still have to dress up but that they can forgo the suit and tie. For others, it means T-shirts and blue jeans.

If you require professional dress during the week but would like to relax the rules on Fridays, add the following paragraph to Policy C. In the first blank, list the types of clothing you find acceptable on casual Fridays—such as slacks, collared shirts, jeans, dress shorts, and sandals. In the second blank, list clothing you do not find acceptable, even on Fridays—for example, T-shirts, tank tops, short or athletic shorts, or clothing that is torn or see-through.

Additional Clause

Although we require professional attire Monday through Thursday, we celebrate Fridays here by allowing employees to dress casually. Acceptable casual clothing includes _____

_____

_____ .

Unacceptable casual clothing includes _____

_____

_____ .

Even on Fridays, however, we ask employees to use good judgment and to maintain a neat and clean appearance.

Additional Clause Regarding Safety Issues

In some workplaces, employees cannot wear certain clothing or wear their hair in a certain style because of safety concerns. For example, most food service companies require employees to wear hair nets, and many companies in the manufacturing industry prohibit loose-fitting clothes and jewelry, which could get caught in machinery.

If there are health and safety reasons for dress and grooming standards, you should detail those either in the health and safety chapter of the handbook or through memos and instructions from supervisors. In this policy, you can simply refer employees to those rules by adding the following paragraph to your policy.

Additional Clause

We place specific restrictions on the dress and appearance of some employees for safety reasons. To learn about those restrictions, refer to _____

_____ .

Additional Clause Regarding Body Piercings and Tattoos

Personal expression doesn't stop with the clothes an employee chooses to wear. An increasing number of workers are also expressing themselves through the images they tattoo on their bodies and the jewelry they pierce into their skin. If such things are contrary to the look or image that you want your employees to convey, then you might want to add a clause to your dress code mandating that such forms of expression be covered while the employee is at work.

To keep your mandate on the right side of the law, be sure that you apply it in the same way to everyone, regardless of race, gender, religion, or other protected characteristic. For example, don't forbid women from having visible tattoos while allowing men to do so.

One somewhat tricky area of the law arises when an employee claims that the tattoo or piercing is a form of religious expression. If this happens, consult with an attorney before enforcing the policy.

The clause below requires employees to cover tattoos and remove piercings. It tells employees to talk to someone within the company if they have religious reasons for the tattoo or piercing.

Additional Clause

> Tattoos and body piercings are contrary to the image of this Company. Employees must cover their tattoos and cover or remove body piercings while on the worksite or while conducting company business. Employees who have religious reasons for their tattoos or piercings should consult with _____ for guidance about following this policy.

Reality Check: Avoid Discriminatory Dress Codes

For the most part, the law will allow your company to govern how employees appear at work. Be careful, however, that you don't bump up against antidiscrimination laws when demanding certain modes of dress or appearance. Particular areas to watch out for include the following:

- **Sexual harassment.** If you require employees of a certain gender to dress in a sexually provocative way (for example, requiring female employees to wear tight, low-cut tops or short skirts), you may be accused of harassing those employees or of encouraging other people to harass them.
- **Sex discrimination.** Demanding different modes of dress for female and male employees leaves your company vulnerable to claims of gender discrimination. In addition, some states specifically prohibit employers from requiring female employees to wear skirts.
- **Race discrimination.** Some grooming policies disproportionately affect members of one race. For example, requiring that all men be clean-shaven can have a negative impact on African American men, some of whom have a physical sensitivity to shaving.
- **Religious discrimination.** Some religions impose certain dress and grooming requirements on their members. For example, traditional Sikhs may not cut their hair; some Muslim women may wear the hijab (headscarf). If your company's grooming or dress policies force people to violate the tenets of their religion, the company could open itself up to claims of religious discrimination.

Although it's good to watch out for these issues, antidiscrimination laws do not mean that you can't require certain modes of dress; they just mean you must have a really good reason for doing so. If your company has a good reason for wanting to impose a grooming or dress standard that might raise discrimination issues, consult a lawyer for help.

12:4 Pranks and Practical Jokes

File Name: 12_Work Behavior.rtf

Include This Policy?
☐ Yes
☐ No
☐ Use our existing policy
☐ Other _____

Alternate Modifications
None

Additional Clauses
None

Related Policies
None

Notes

_____
_____
_____
_____
_____
_____
_____
_____
_____
_____
_____
_____
_____
_____
_____
_____
_____
_____

12:4 Pranks and Practical Jokes

Most employers understand that employees who enjoy their work tend to be better and more productive performers. In some workplaces, however, employees carry enjoyment too far by playing pranks and practical jokes on each other. Although this may seem harmless at first blush, pranks and practical jokes can lead to real trouble.

For example, some pranks that employees think are harmless have racial or sexual undertones. For the victim of the prank, this may feel more like harassment or discrimination than innocent fun, which can lead to legal trouble.

Even if the prank or joke doesn't cross the legal line, it may have the effect of disrupting the workplace and lowering the morale of the individual who was on the receiving end of the so-called humor.

This policy prohibits all pranks and practical jokes. It warns employees that they might face disciplinary action if they engage in such behavior.

Pranks and Practical Jokes

Although we want our employees to enjoy their jobs and have fun working together, we cannot allow employees to play practical jokes or pranks on each other. At best, these actions disrupt the workplace and dampen the morale of some; at worst, they can endanger employees and lead to complaints of discrimination, harassment, or assault.

If you have any questions about this policy, contact _____ _____ .

Employees who play pranks or practical jokes will face disciplinary action, up to and including termination.

Who Needs This Policy

Although this type of conduct occurs in all types of workplaces—from corporate law firms to longshoring operations—it does tend to be more prevalent in male-dominated and blue-collar industries. If you operate a business in these industries, or if your company has had problems with pranks and practical jokes in the past, you should consider having a policy explicitly prohibiting such activity.

On the other hand, if your employees do not tend to engage in such behavior, you can probably forgo this policy. Your policies regarding professional conduct, discrimination, and harassment should help you deal with any situations that arise.

12:5 Threatening, Abusive, or Vulgar Language

Despite the old playground taunt, words can hurt you. They can lead to harassment and discrimination lawsuits, lower the morale and productivity of employees, and destroy the congenial atmosphere of the workplace.

In addition, employee violence is often preceded by threatening and abusive language. If an employee says something threatening or abusive, don't treat the situation lightly simply because the incident involves only words. Not only could your company be held legally liable if the employee later becomes violent (under a theory of law called "negligent retention"), but you or an employee could be injured or worse. Having a policy against this sort of language is a good first step in protecting a workplace from potential violence, and it can lay the groundwork for nipping a bad situation in the bud.

Threatening, Abusive, or Vulgar Language

Threatening, abusive, or vulgar language has no place in our workplace. It destroys morale and relationships, and it impedes the effective and efficient operation of our business.

As a result, we will not tolerate threatening, abusive, or vulgar language from employees while they are at work, conducting Company business, or attending Company-related business or social functions.

If you have any questions about this policy, contact _____ _____ .

Employees who violate this policy will face disciplinary action, up to and including termination.

12:6 Horseplay

File Name: 12_Work Behavior.rtf

Include This Policy?
- ☐ Yes
- ☐ No
- ☐ Use our existing policy
- ☐ Other _____

Alternate Modifications

None

Additional Clauses

None

Related Policies

None

Notes

_____

_____

_____

_____

_____

_____

_____

_____

_____

_____

_____

_____

_____

_____

_____

_____

_____

_____

_____

_____

12:6 Horseplay

Horseplay is boisterous physical interaction that disrupts the ordinary operation of a workplace. It usually begins innocently enough, arising from employees' more juvenile and playful impulses. Initially, it does not involve malice, ill will, or anger; it's just a matter of employees goofing off.

That being said, such aggressive playful conduct can often get out of hand, and what started out as innocent, yet loud, fun can turn into a fight or a brawl. Depending on the circumstances, it can also turn into discrimination, harassment, or assault. It's also a safety hazard.

Because horseplay is disruptive and can often lead to trouble, many employers ban it outright.

Horseplay

Although we want our employees to have fun while they work, we don't allow employees to engage in horseplay: fun that has gotten physical, boisterous, and out of control. Horseplay disrupts the work environment and can get out of hand, leading to fighting, hurt feelings, safety hazards, or worse.

Employees who engage in horseplay will face disciplinary action, up to and including termination.

12:7 Fighting

Fights among employees not only injure the people involved but also damage collegiality among workers, disrupt the workplace, and can lead to more violence, physical and emotional injuries, and lawsuits. This policy prohibits fighting among employees and promises disciplinary action to those who engage in it. Verbal fighting can be just as damaging as physical fighting and is therefore encompassed by this policy.

Fighting

Verbal or physical fighting among employees is absolutely prohibited. Employees shall not engage in, provoke, or encourage a fight. Those who violate this policy will be disciplined, up to and including termination.

12:7 Fighting

File Name: 12_Work Behavior.rtf

Include This Policy?
- ☐ Yes
- ☐ No
- ☐ Use our existing policy
- ☐ Other _____

Alternate Modifications
None

Additional Clauses
None

Related Policies
None

Notes
_____
_____
_____
_____
_____
_____
_____
_____
_____
_____
_____
_____
_____
_____
_____
_____
_____
_____
_____
_____

12:8 Sleeping on the Job

File Name: 12_Work Behavior.rtf
- ☐ Yes
- ☐ No
- ☐ Use our existing policy
- ☐ Other _____

Alternate Modifications
None

Additional Clauses
Allow Employees to Sleep Sometimes
Insert?: ☐ Yes ☐ No
Emphasize the Safety Hazard of Sleeping
Insert?: ☐ Yes ☐ No

Related Policies
None

Notes
_____
_____
_____
_____
_____
_____
_____
_____
_____
_____
_____
_____
_____
_____
_____
_____

12:8 Sleeping on the Job

Depending on the type of business, employees who sleep on the job can create anything from a nuisance to a safety hazard. Most employers ban sleeping on the worksite outright, but some employers who schedule employees for exceptionally long shifts (for example, 24 hours) will expressly allow employees to sleep during designated times.

The following policy prohibits sleeping entirely and is designed for a business in which sleeping employees do not pose a safety hazard. If you would like to allow employees to sleep at designated times, or if you would like to emphasize the unsafe nature of sleeping, see the optional additional clauses that follow.

Sleeping on the Job

When our employees arrive at work, we expect them to be physically prepared to work through their day. Employees who sleep on the job dampen morale and productivity and deprive us of their work and companionship.

As a result, we do not allow any employees to sleep while at work. Employees who feel sick or unable to finish the day because of weariness should talk to _____ about using sick leave to take the rest of the day off. (See Section _____ of this Handbook for information about our sick leave policy.)

Additional Clause to Allow Employees to Sleep Sometimes

If you would like to allow your employees to sleep at certain times, add the following clause at the end of the sample policy.

Additional Clause

We make an exception to this policy for certain employees who _____ .

To find out if you fit within this exception, contact _____
_____ .

Additional Clause to Emphasize the Safety Hazard of Sleeping

If employees who sleep on the job pose a safety risk (either to themselves or to others), add the following paragraph between the first and second paragraphs of the sample policy. In the blank, insert a description—either by job department or job title—of which employees pose a safety hazard when they sleep.

Additional Clause

For certain employees, sleeping on the job creates a safety hazard. Employees who work in _____

_____

_____

create unacceptable risks to their own safety and the safety of others when they fail to be attentive and alert while working. For these employees, sleeping on the job violates both this policy and our safety policies. (See Section _____ of this Handbook for information about our safety program.)

12:9 Insubordination

File Name: 12_Work Behavior.rtf

Include This Policy?

☐ Yes

☐ No

☐ Use our existing policy

☐ Other _____

Alternate Modifications

None

Additional Clauses

None

Related Policies

None

Notes

_____

_____

_____

_____

_____

_____

_____

_____

_____

_____

_____

_____

_____

_____

_____

_____

_____

_____

12:9 Insubordination

An insubordinate employee is one who refuses to follow orders or instructions. Insubordination is a particularly destructive force in the workplace because it interferes with one of an employer's most basic rights: to operate the business as it sees fit. This means telling employees what jobs need to be done and how. It also means directing and controlling a company's business and culture.

Of course, not every instance of an employee refusing to follow an order constitutes insubordination. Under federal law and the laws of most states, employees have a right to refuse to work in unsafe conditions. They also have a right to refuse to do anything illegal.

The policy below prohibits insubordination while explaining how employees may disobey orders acceptably if necessary.

CAUTION

Criticism is not insubordination. The National Labor Relations Board (NLRB), the federal agency that enforces labor laws, has found that employers may not penalize employees for coming together to discuss the terms and conditions of employment. This includes online discussions (such as in a Facebook post), as well as comments that your company might find distasteful or worse. Some employers might consider it insubordinate for an employee to criticize a supervisor online, for example, but the comments might be protected if other employees join in and plan to bring the situation to the attention of the company or otherwise take action to stop it. The safest course is to limit insubordination to the refusal to follow orders or obey instructions without a good reason.

Insubordination

Insubordination occurs when an employee willfully and unreasonably refuses to obey the lawful orders or follow the lawful instructions given by a supervisor. Insubordinate employees will face discipline, up to and including termination.

If you believe you have been asked to do something illegal or to work in unsafe conditions, please raise the issue with your supervisor. You may also report your concerns using the complaint procedure described in Section _____ of this Handbook.

12:10 Personal Cell Phones at Work

Most of your employees probably have personal cell phones that they bring to work. Apparently, the main thing employees do with their phones at work—based on surveys—is bother each other. These workplace annoyances result from loud ring tones, inappropriate personal conversations, interruptions to meetings and presentations, and rudeness to coworkers or customers while talking on the phone.

Some companies respond to these concerns by simply banning personal cell phones at work. For most employers, however, an outright ban is overkill. Allowing personal cell phones gives employees a chance to touch base with family members and friends while on breaks or at lunch, or to receive emergency messages during the day, all without using company phones. Most companies can achieve the results they want—fewer interruptions and less time wasted—while allowing employees to have their cell phones at work by simply prohibiting employees from using cell phones (or allowing them to ring) at certain times, in particular locations, or for excessive amounts of time. The policy below contains basic cell phone etiquette for the workplace that most companies will want to adopt.

Personal Cell Phones at Work

Although our Company allows employees to bring their personal cell phones to work, we expect employees to keep personal conversations to a minimum. While occasional, brief personal phone calls are acceptable, frequent or lengthy personal calls can affect productivity and disturb others. For this reason, we generally expect employees to make and receive personal phone calls during breaks only.

Employees must turn off the ringers on their cell phones while away from their cell phones. If you share workspace with others, you must turn off the ringer on your phone while at work.

Employees must turn off their cell phones or leave their phones elsewhere while in meetings, presentations, or trainings. Employees must also turn off their cell phones or leave their phones elsewhere while meeting with clients or serving customers.

It is inappropriate to interrupt a face-to-face conversation with a coworker in order to take a personal phone call.

Remember, others can hear your cell phone conversations. Try to talk quietly, and save intimate discussions for another time.

Employees who violate this policy will be subject to discipline, up to and including termination.

12:10 Personal Cell Phones at Work

File Name: 12_Work Behavior.rtf

Include This Policy?
- ☐ Yes
- ☐ No
- ☐ Use our existing policy
- ☐ Other _____

Alternate Modifications
None

Additional Clauses
None

Related Policies
13:7   Cell Phones and Driving

Notes
_____
_____
_____
_____
_____
_____
_____
_____
_____
_____
_____
_____
_____
_____
_____
_____
_____

12:11 Progressive Discipline

File Name: 12_Work Behavior.rtf

Include This Policy?
☐ Yes
☐ No
☐ Use our existing policy
☐ Other _____

Alternate Modifications
None

Additional Clauses
None

Related Policies
None

Notes

_____
_____
_____
_____
_____
_____
_____
_____
_____
_____
_____
_____
_____
_____
_____
_____
_____

12:11 Progressive Discipline

In a progressive discipline system, employers use a range of disciplinary actions and counseling sessions to motivate employees to improve their conduct. In such a system, the goal of the discipline is not punitive, but communicative. A progressive discipline system can be a valuable tool in improving employee performance and productivity. It can also protect a company from lawsuits by ensuring that the company is fair to employees and by forcing it to document employee misconduct and the company's response.

If you have a progressive discipline system at your workplace, you should explain it to employees in general terms in the handbook.

Progressive discipline systems vary greatly from workplace to workplace. As a result, we cannot provide standard policy language. An example of what a progressive discipline policy might look like is provided below.

As you'll see, our sample policy explicitly reserves the employer's right to fire at will and to deviate from the disciplinary steps laid out in the policy. A significant legal hazard of adopting a progressive discipline policy is that it can tie an employer's hands. This can lead, in turn, to an erosion of an employer's at-will employment policy. After all, if you promise to follow a particular process every time an employee commits misconduct, you are agreeing that employees have the right to rely on that process. Rather than having the right to end the employment relationship at will, your company will instead have the obligation to follow the procedures laid out in your disciplinary policy. To avoid this outcome, make sure your discipline policy preserves employment at will and keeps the company's disciplinary options open.

SAMPLE POLICY LANGUAGE

Any employee conduct that violates company rules or that, in the opinion of the Company, interferes with or adversely affects our business is sufficient grounds for disciplinary action.

Disciplinary action can range from coaching to immediate discharge. Our general policy is to take disciplinary steps in the following order:

- coaching
- verbal warnings
- written warning(s), and
- termination.

However, we reserve the right to alter the order described above, to skip disciplinary steps, to eliminate disciplinary steps, or to create new and/or additional disciplinary steps.

In choosing the appropriate disciplinary action, we may consider any number of factors, including:

- the seriousness of your conduct
- your history of misconduct
- your employment record
- your length of employment with this Company
- the strength of the evidence against you
- your ability to correct the conduct
- your attitude about the conduct
- actions we have taken for similar conduct by other employees
- how your conduct affects this Company, its customers, and your coworkers, and
- any other circumstances related to the nature of the misconduct, to your employment with this Company, and to the effect of the misconduct on the business of this Company.

We will give those considerations whatever weight we deem appropriate. Depending on the circumstances, we may give some considerations more weight than other considerations, or no weight at all.

Some conduct may result in immediate termination. Here are some examples:

- theft of company property
- excessive tardiness or absenteeism
- arguing or fighting with customers or coworkers
- brandishing a weapon at work
- threatening the physical safety of customers, coworkers, managers, or supervisors
- physically or verbally assaulting someone at work
- any illegal conduct at work
- using or possessing alcohol or illegal drugs at work
- working under the influence of alcohol or illegal drugs
- failing to carry out reasonable job assignments
- insubordination
- making false statements on a job application
- violating Company rules and regulations, and
- discrimination and harassment.

Of course, it is impossible to compile an exhaustive list of the types of conduct that will result in immediate termination. Those listed above are merely illustrations.

You should remember that your employment is at the mutual consent of you and this Company. This policy does not change this fact. This means that you or this Company can terminate our employment relationship at will, at any time, with or without cause, and with or without advance notice.

As a result, this Company reserves its right to terminate your employment at any time, for any lawful reason, including reasons not listed above. You also have the right to end your employment at any time.

Reality Check: Follow Your Disciplinary Policy

If a company puts a written progressive discipline policy in the handbook, it must follow the policy, even when it doesn't want to. From an employee relations standpoint, a company's failure to follow its own policies will only make the company's personnel decisions look arbitrary and unfair. In addition, a company might have trouble convincing employees to follow rules when it fails to do so itself.

From a legal standpoint, a company's failure to follow its own progressive discipline policy leaves the company vulnerable to lawsuits. Even if there is a good reason for firing someone, the company will have trouble proving it if it didn't follow the policy. In addition, some courts might view a written policy as a type of contract between the company and its employees. In such a situation, the court might view failure to follow the policy as a breach of contract.

RESOURCE

Want more information on employee discipline? See *The Employee Performance Handbook*, by Margie Mader-Clark and Lisa Guerin (Nolo). It includes all of the information, tools, and strategies you need to design a progressive discipline system, figure out whether a particular situation calls for discipline, deal with employee emotions during disciplinary meetings, document your decisions, and much more.

Health and Safety

Workplace safety is of paramount concern to savvy employers. And for good reason: Dangerous situations, accidents, violence, or breaches of security can have disastrous workplace consequences, including lost productivity, raised insurance premiums, stolen or damaged equipment, employee injuries, or even deaths.

What's more, the government regulates workplace safety issues very heavily. Both federal and state laws require employers to provide a workplace free of hazards that could cause serious harm to their employees. These laws also require employers to investigate and report workplace accidents, provide employees with safety training for their jobs, and keep records on workplace safety. Depending on the type of business an employer runs, virtually every aspect of its operations may be subject to detailed safety rules.

Although no employer can guarantee an accident-free workplace, policies that promote workplace safety are a good start.

13:1 Safety Policy

File Name: 13_Health Safety.rtf

Include This Policy?
☐ Yes
☐ No
☐ Use our existing policy
☐ Other _____

Alternate Modifications
None

Additional Clauses
Give Specific Safety Instructions
Insert?: ☐ Yes ☐ No

Related Policies
Chapter 12 provides policies on workplace behavior—including horseplay, fighting, and professional conduct.

Notes

_____
_____
_____
_____
_____
_____
_____
_____
_____
_____
_____
_____
_____
_____
_____
_____
_____

13:1 Workplace Safety

A basic safety policy is a must for every employer, in every type of business. Federal and state laws require employers to keep their workplace free of hazards, investigate accidents quickly, and keep proper safety records. An employer cannot meet these legal requirements unless its employees follow safe work habits and report workplace accidents and injuries.

Your workplace safety policy should tell employees that safety is a top concern for your company, let employees know about safety rules, and explain how to report accidents or injuries.

CAUTION

Some states require particular policy language. The federal law that regulates health and safety on the job is called the Occupational Safety and Health Act, or OSHA (29 U.S.C. §§ 651 and following). In addition, almost half of the states have adopted their own workplace safety laws that are at least as strict as OSHA. Although OSHA doesn't require employers to adopt a written workplace safety policy, some of these state laws do. For example, California employers must adopt a written "injury and illness prevention program." To find out what your state requires, contact your state labor department (see Appendix B for contact information) or consult with an experienced employment attorney.

Safety Policy

Our Company takes employee safety very seriously. In order to provide a safe workplace for everyone, every employee must follow our safety rules:

- Horseplay, roughhousing, and other physical acts that may endanger employees or cause accidents are prohibited.
- Employees must follow their supervisors' safety instructions.
- Employees in certain positions may be required to wear protective equipment, such as hair nets, hard hats, safety glasses, work boots, ear plugs, or masks. Your supervisor will let you know if your position requires protective gear.
- Employees in certain positions may be prohibited from wearing dangling jewelry or apparel, or may be required to pull back or cover their hair, for safety purposes. Your supervisor will tell you if you fall into one of these categories.
- All equipment and machinery must be used properly. This means all guards, restraints, and other safety devices must be used at all times. Do not use equipment for other than its intended purpose.
- All employees must immediately report any workplace condition that they believe to be unsafe to their supervisor. The Company will look into the matter promptly.
- All employees must immediately report any workplace accident or injury to _____
  _____ .

Additional Clause to Give Specific Safety Instructions

Every type of industry has its own unique safety hazards. Our basic standard policy can be modified to include safety rules particular to your company. For example, you might want to include rules on the proper use of certain types of equipment and machinery; proper techniques for physical labor, such as lifting and carrying heavy objects; or ergonomic rules for those who operate computers or cash registers or perform other types of repetitive motions. If so, simply add these rules to the end of the policy.

Of course, the specific rules you adopt will depend on what your company's employees do and the resources you have available to assist them; we can't provide standard policy language that will work for everyone. Here is an example of policy language that provides ergonomics information for employees who use computers.

SAMPLE POLICY LANGUAGE

Most of our Company's employees work at computers, some for nearly the full workday. We recognize that proper equipment, furnishings, and body positioning can help employees avoid discomfort or injury while working at computers. To help employees work comfortably and efficiently, without putting unnecessary stress and strain on their bodies, our Company has an ergonomics program.

When you begin working at our Company, a trained member of the ergonomics team will assess your workstation. You will be provided the equipment necessary to work comfortably. Your equipment and furnishings (for example, chair height, position of keyboard and mouse, monitor height and tilt, and so on) will be adjusted to fit your physical requirements. You will also receive training and handouts on avoiding computer-related injuries. If you have any special ergonomics needs, please raise them at this time.

If at any time you have ergonomics questions or concerns, you would like to request special equipment, or you would like a reassessment of your workspace, feel free to contact a member of the ergonomics team.

13:2 Workplace Security

A workplace security policy explains what measures the company expects employees to take to keep its premises and property safe from intruders. Clearly, what you include in the policy will depend on the nature of your workplace: An office building in a bustling metropolis will have different security concerns from a farming operation. However, any security policy should include rules on securing the premises (locking up, closing gates, shutting off machinery, or securing tools, for example), rules on after-hours access to the workplace, and rules on workplace visitors.

Workplace Security

It is every employee's responsibility to help keep our workplace secure from unauthorized intruders. Every employee must comply with these security precautions.

When you leave work for the day, please do all of the following:

_____

_____

_____ .

After-hours access to the workplace is limited to those employees who need to work late. If you are going to be working past our usual closing time, please let your supervisor know.

Employees are allowed to have an occasional visitor in the workplace, but workplace visits should be the exception rather than the rule. If you are anticipating a visitor, please let _____

_____ know. When your visitor arrives, you will be notified.

How to Complete This Policy

In the first blank space, list all of the things employees are expected to do before they leave for the day. For example, the policy might tell employees to shut off their computers, turn off equipment, turn off lights, close and lock office windows, store and secure tools, lock and garage company vehicles, or lock any area that won't be used any more that day.

In the second blank space, list the position of the person who will greet visitors to your company. This might be a receptionist, security guard, or front desk attendant.

If you have additional security rules, you can add them at the end of the policy.

13:2 Workplace Security

File Name: 13_Health Safety.rtf

Include This Policy?

☐ Yes

☐ No

☐ Use our existing policy

☐ Other _____

Alternate Modifications

None

Additional Clauses

Require Escorts for Visitors

Insert?:   ☐ Yes   ☐ No

Require Badges for Visitors

Insert?:   ☐ Yes   ☐ No

Instructions for Employees Who Are the Last to Leave the Workplace

Insert?:   ☐ Yes   ☐ No

Related Policies

None

Notes

_____

_____

_____

_____

_____

_____

_____

_____

_____

_____

_____

_____

_____

_____

_____

_____

Additional Clause to Require Escorts or Badges for Visitors

Our sample policy allows employees to have visitors but asks them to keep visitors to a minimum. Some businesses, particularly large companies and companies that have industrial operations, put more restrictions on visitors in the workplace. Visitors might be required to wear a badge or other identification, or the employee who invited the visitor might be required to accompany the visitor at all times on company premises and escort the visitor to and from the entrance. If you wish to adopt either of these policies, simply add one or both of the modifications below at the end of the policy, after the paragraph on visitors.

Additional Clause

> Visitors must wear an identification badge at all times when they are in our workplace. Visitors can get a badge at _____
>
> _____ .
>
> They must return the badge when they leave Company premises.

Additional Clause

> Do not leave your visitor unattended in the workplace. If you have a visitor, you must accompany your visitor at all times. This includes escorting your visitor to and from the entrance to our Company.

Additional Clause to Give Instructions to Employees Who Are the Last to Leave the Workplace

In many companies, supervisors, managers, or the owner are always the last to leave the workplace. And some workplaces (such as 24-hour convenience stores or factories that operate round the clock) never close. However, if employees at your company are sometimes the last ones at work, you should modify this policy to let them know how to secure the premises. Insert the sample modification, below, filling in the blanks to tell employees what is expected of them. For example, the policy might direct employees to lock the building or security gates, set an alarm, make sure all windows are closed and locked, or turn off all equipment and lights.

Additional Clause

If you are the last to leave the workplace for the evening, you are responsible for doing all of the following: _____

_____

_____

_____ .

If you have questions about any of these responsibilities, please talk to your supervisor.

13:3 What to Do in an Emergency

File Name: 13_Health Safety.rtf

Include This Policy?

☐ Yes

☐ No

☐ Use our existing policy

☐ Other _____

Alternate Modifications

None

Alternate Modifications

None

Additional Clauses

Location of Emergency Supplies

Insert?:   ☐ Yes   ☐ No

Related Policies

None

Notes

_____

_____

_____

_____

_____

_____

_____

_____

_____

_____

_____

_____

_____

_____

_____

_____

13:3 What to Do in an Emergency

Every business should have a written policy letting employees know what to do in case of emergency. Employees should be familiar with evacuation routes and procedures to ensure their safety should disaster strike. Employees should also be told where to congregate once they have left the workplace. This will help management—and rescue workers—figure out whether anyone is missing and may need assistance getting out of the workplace.

In this policy, you can describe evacuation plans, the location of emergency equipment (such as first aid supplies or fire extinguishers) kept on site, and where employees should go if they are forced to leave the workplace.

What to Do in an Emergency

In case of an emergency, such as a fire, earthquake, or accident, your first priority should be your own safety. In the event of an emergency causing serious injuries, IMMEDIATELY DIAL 9-1-1 to alert police and rescue workers of the situation.

If you hear a fire alarm or in case of an emergency that requires evacuation, please proceed quickly and calmly to the emergency exits. The Company will hold periodic drills to familiarize everyone with the routes they should take. Remember that every second may count. Don't return to the workplace to retrieve personal belongings or work-related items. Once you have exited the building, head toward the _____ _____.

(For our Company's policy on workplace violence, see Section _____ of this Handbook.)

Reality Check: Fire Drills Are Not Just for Kids

All of us probably remember the fire drills of grade school, but when was the last time your company held a fire drill? Emergency drills are vitally important for every business. They help workers learn emergency evacuation procedures, so they'll know what to do if a real disaster strikes. Of course, these drills disrupt business and may take 15 or 20 minutes to conduct. But if that advance planning later saves lives or prevents serious injuries, the inconvenience will seem a very small price to pay.

Additional Clause to Include Location of Emergency Supplies

Many businesses keep a store of emergency supplies in the workplace. If your company takes this very sensible precaution, modify the policy to let employees know where the supplies are kept. You can add the modification below, filling in the blanks to indicate the location of the supplies. If your company keeps additional types of supplies that are not listed below, add them on at the end.

Additional Clause

Our Company keeps emergency supplies on hand. First aid kits are located _____ .

Fire extinguishers can be found _____ .

Earthquake preparedness kits are kept _____ .

We also keep a supply of flashlights in _____ .

13:4 Smoking

File Name: 13_Health Safety.rtf

Include This Policy?

☐ Yes

Choose one: ☐ A ☐ B

☐ No

☐ Use our existing policy

☐ Other _____

Alternate Modifications

None

Additional Clauses

Regulate E-Cigarettes (Vaping)

Insert?: ☐ Yes ☐ No

Regulate When Employees May Smoke

Insert?: ☐ Yes ☐ No

Help Employees Quit Smoking

Insert?: ☐ Yes ☐ No

If yes, choose one: ☐ A ☐ B

Prohibit Discrimination Against Smokers

Insert?: ☐ Yes ☐ No

Related Policies

None

Notes

_____

_____

_____

_____

_____

_____

_____

_____

_____

_____

_____

13:4 Smoking

Smoking can be a divisive workplace issue. Smokers want the freedom to enjoy a cigarette without having to stand outside in the cold; nonsmokers want to work comfortably, without smoke irritating their eyes and throats, and without the increased health risks attributable to secondhand smoke. It is the employer's unfortunate job to balance these interests.

There are a few legal guidelines that can help. In all states, employers may ban smoking in the workplace. If your company wants to prohibit employees from lighting up, it can do so. However, if your company wants to allow smoking or allow it in certain areas, you will have to check your state and local laws to find out exactly what is allowed. These laws are summarized in "State Laws on Smoking in the Workplace" at the end of this chapter. Some states require employers to ban smoking, at least in certain kinds of businesses. For example, California bans smoking in the workplace, public or private. And other states prohibit smoking in certain kinds of business establishments, such as hospitals or restaurants. You will also need to check local laws.

Because of these variations, we offer you two sample policies to choose from. Policy A bans smoking altogether; Policy B allows smoking in designated areas.

Policy A

Smoking Is Prohibited

For the health, comfort, and safety of our employees, smoking is not allowed on Company property.

Policy B

Smoking Policy

To accommodate employees who smoke as well as those who do not, the Company has created smoking and nonsmoking areas. Smoking is allowed only in _____

_____ .

The Company has posted signs designating smoking and nonsmoking areas. Employees who smoke are required to observe these signs and to smoke in designated areas only.

Reality Check: Special Rules for Smoking Areas

States that allow smoking on the job often impose strict rules to prevent smoke from spreading to the rest of the workplace. Some require that any workplace smoking area have a separate ventilation system, so the smoky air does not recirculate to the rest of the office. Others require physical barriers—such as walls or partitions—to separate smoking and nonsmoking areas.

Even if your state does not impose these requirements, however, it's a good idea to keep smoking areas separate from the rest of the workplace. Nonsmokers who are physically troubled by smoke can complain to the Occupational Safety and Health Administration (OSHA) and may even have a legal claim under the Americans with Disabilities Act (ADA). There's no need to invite this kind of problem: If your company allows smoking, keep the air clean for nonsmokers by designating a smoking area that won't allow smoke to enter the rest of the workplace.

Who Needs This Policy

This is one of the few policies that is mandatory, at least in some states. If your company plans to allow smoking anywhere in the workplace, certain states require employers to adopt a written smoking policy. In states that require a smoking policy, the rules vary as to what the policy must include. Check "State Laws on Smoking in the Workplace" at the end of this chapter to see what your state requires.

Additional Clause to Include E-Cigarettes ("Vaping")

Electronic cigarettes (e-cigarettes) are small, battery-operated devices that allow users to inhale a vapor containing nicotine. Referred to as "vaping" rather than "smoking," use of these devices in the workplace can be controversial. On the one hand, some experts claim that use of e-cigarettes can help smokers quit or cut way back, which has a number of health benefits. On the other hand, e-cigarettes contain nicotine and other potentially harmful chemicals, and the vapor they release can be bothersome to other employees.

Every year, more states and local governments regulate e-cigarettes. Some simply include them in workplace smoking bans. In California, for example, employees may not smoke or vape in the workplace, period. Some states and local governments don't regulate use of e-cigarettes. And some are in between, perhaps limiting their purchase or use by minors but not by adults. (You can find a frequently updated list of state and local laws on e-cigarettes at the website of Americans for Nonsmokers' Rights, www.no-smoke.org.)

If your state requires you—or your Company would like—to include e-cigarettes in your smoking policy, add this additional clause to either Policy A or Policy B.

Additional Clause

> This policy also applies to electronic cigarettes (e-cigarettes) as well as traditional tobacco cigarettes and other smoking products.

Additional Clause to Regulate When Employees May Smoke

"Smoking breaks" are a major source of workplace tension. Nonsmokers wonder why their smoking coworkers feel they have a right to take ten minutes off every hour or so to light up, and employers notice the lost work time (and resulting lost productivity). To combat this problem, some employers add language to their smoking policies reminding employees that they may smoke during scheduled or authorized breaks only. The modification below can be added to Policy A. You should add it to Policy B only if employees are required to smoke somewhere other than their workspaces (otherwise, they can smoke while working and need not take a break).

Additional Clause

> You may smoke during meal or rest breaks only. Employees may not take "smoking breaks" in addition to the regular breaks provided to every employee under our policies.
>
> (For our Company's policy on work and rest breaks, see Section _____ of this Handbook.)

Additional Clause to Help Employees Quit Smoking

It's no secret that employees who smoke tend to cost employers more money, on average, than nonsmokers. Smokers tend to have higher rates of absenteeism and higher health care costs. At the same time, we all know that smoking is a tough habit to give up, especially for those who try to quit on their own, without any support or encouragement.

Some employers offer to help their employees quit smoking by referring employees to, or paying for, smoking cessation programs. If your company offers health insurance to employees and your provider offers such a program, you can refer employees to that program by adding Additional Clause A, below, to the end of the policy. If not, your company may want to offer financial and other support to employees who want to enroll in such a program. Add Additional Clause B, below, to the end of your policy to do so.

Additional Clause A

Our Company encourages those who wish to quit smoking. Our health insurance provider offers a program to help employees stop smoking. If you are interested in this program, ask _____ _____ for more details. Or you can contact our insurance carrier directly.

(For information on health insurance, see Section _____ of this Handbook.)

Additional Clause B

Our Company encourages those who wish to quit smoking. If you are interested in getting help to stop smoking, the _____ _____ can direct you to local smoking cessation programs. If you complete one of the programs on the Company's approved list, we will pay the cost of your participation.

Additional Clause to Prohibit Discrimination Against Smokers

Many states prohibit employment discrimination against smokers. Some of these laws apply only to smoking, while others protect any lawful activity in which the employee chooses to engage outside of work hours. Either way, in these states, employers may not make employment decisions based on the fact that an employee or applicant smokes. Check "State Laws on Smoking in the Workplace" at the end of this chapter to see whether your company needs to comply with this type of law.

If your state prohibits this kind of discrimination, you might want to add the following modification to the smoking policy to let employees know that your company will comply with the law.

Additional Clause

We recognize that smoking tobacco products is legal and that employees have the right to smoke outside of work hours. Our Company will not discriminate against any applicant or employee based on that person's choice to smoke.

13:5 Violence

Violence in the workplace is a frightening topic. The media reports stories about former employees, disgruntled clients or customers, or abusive spouses storming into a business and injuring or killing all who cross their paths. Of course, no policy can eliminate the risk that your company might face a violent incident. But a commonsense policy to prohibit violence—and to let employees know what to do if they fear or experience a violent incident—can go a long way toward making the workplace safer.

Violence Is Prohibited

We will not tolerate violence in the workplace. Violence includes physical altercations, coercion, pushing or shoving, horseplay, intimidation, stalking, and threats of violence. Any comments about violence will be taken seriously, and may result in your termination. Please do not joke or make offhand remarks about violence.

Who Needs This Policy

Including an antiviolence policy in your handbook provides several benefits. First, it lets employees know that the company will take all violent incidents seriously and defines violence in a way that includes jokes about violence, roughhousing, or threats. This puts employees on notice that violence is no laughing matter. It should also minimize instances in which an employee alleged to have acted violently comes up with excuses like "I didn't mean it" or "I was only joking."

Second, it tells employees what to do if a violent incident occurs: to take steps to protect themselves and their coworkers immediately by calling emergency personnel if necessary, and to report less serious incidents to company management. If managers aren't made aware of escalating aggressions in the workplace, they won't be able to intervene while the problem is still brewing. Encouraging employees to come forward will go a long way toward helping prevent more serious incidents.

And, third, it lays down the law on weapons in the workplace. (See "Alternate Modifications Regarding Weapons," below.)

13:5 Violence Is Prohibited

File Name: 13_Health Safety.rtf

Include This Policy?
- ☐ Yes
- ☐ No
- ☐ Use our existing policy
- ☐ Other _____

Alternate Modifications

Weapons Policy
Choose one: ☐ A ☐ B

What to Do in Case of Violence
Choose one: ☐ A ☐ B

Additional Clauses

None

Related Policies

None

Notes

_____
_____
_____
_____
_____
_____
_____
_____
_____
_____
_____
_____
_____
_____
_____

Alternate Modifications Regarding Weapons

You will need to add policy language to address weapons in the workplace. We present two options below. Alternate Modification A prohibits weapons except for items required for work, and employees must get authorization even in this situation. Alternate Modification B is for companies that have at least a few employees who must carry weapons.

To Prohibit Weapons

Use this modification to prohibit all weapons in the workplace, except for items required for work. In any workplace, an employee might have to use an item that could be considered a weapon (such as a knife). Therefore, this modification allows employees to carry and use such items, if they are authorized to do so by their supervisor. Companies that do not require or allow employees to use weapons generally should use this modification.

Alternate Modification A

> ## No Weapons
>
> No weapons are allowed in our workplace. Weapons include firearms, knives, brass knuckles, martial arts equipment, clubs or bats, and explosives. If your work requires you to use an item that might qualify as a weapon, you must receive authorization from your supervisor to bring that item to work or use it in the workplace. Any employee found with an unauthorized weapon in the workplace will be subject to discipline, up to and including termination.

To Allow Weapons for Certain Employees

Some companies may require their employees to carry weapons. For example, a company that provides security services may require employees to carry a gun or nightstick. If a significant number of employees will need to carry weapons regularly, use this modification to specify who is authorized to do so and under what circumstances. In the blank space, list the positions for which workers are required to carry weapons; don't list the names of individual workers, as this will require you to update the policy every time you have a personnel change.

Alternate Modification B

> ### Weapons in the Workplace
>
> Weapons are generally not allowed in our workplace. Weapons include firearms, knives, brass knuckles, martial arts equipment, clubs or bats, and explosives.
>
> However, some of our employees are required to carry weapons in order to perform their jobs. Weapons may be required in the following positions: _____
>
> _____ .
>
> If you hold one of these positions, ask your supervisor whether you will be required to carry a weapon. If your job requires you to carry a weapon, you must receive authorization from your supervisor to do so. You may be required to complete training courses, pass a safety test, and/or get a license in order to be authorized to carry a weapon.

CAUTION

Employees may have a legal right to keep guns in a company-owned parking lot. Although employers are free to prohibit guns and other weapons in their actual workplace, the company parking lot may be a different story. Almost half of the states have passed laws giving employees the right to keep a gun in their car, even if that car is parked on your property. State laws might require that the gun to be locked in the trunk or glove box, or might impose other restrictions or limits. If you are considering a parking lot weapons ban, you'll need to check with a lawyer to make sure you are within your legal rights.

Alternate Modifications on What to Do in Case of Violence

Some companies employ their own security personnel or do business in a building that has its own security force. If this is true for your company, you may want to ask employees to contact these security people—who are already on site and are familiar with the layout of the workplace—first in the event of a violent incident. You can use Alternate Modification A, below, to accomplish this; in the first blank, insert the telephone number of the internal security personnel.

If your workplace does not have private security, you should tell employees to dial 9-1-1 when confronted with violence. You can use Alternate Modification B, below, to accomplish this.

In either modification, fill in the second blank with the person to whom employees should report violence that does not require an immediate response.

Alternate Modification A

What to Do in Case of Violence

If you observe an incident or threat of violence that is immediate and serious, call security personnel at _____ .
If you are unable to reach someone at this number, IMMEDIATELY DIAL 9-1-1 and report the incident to the police.

If the incident or threat does not appear to require immediate police intervention, please contact _____
and report it as soon as possible, using the Company's complaint procedure. All complaints will be investigated and appropriate action will be taken. You will not face retaliation for making a complaint.

Alternate Modification B

What to Do in Case of Violence

If you observe an incident or threat of violence that is immediate and serious, IMMEDIATELY DIAL 9-1-1 and report it to the police.

If the incident or threat does not appear to require immediate police intervention, please contact _____
_____ and report it as soon as possible, using the Company's complaint procedure. All complaints will be investigated and appropriate action will be taken. You will not face retaliation for making a complaint.

Reality Check: Stress Can Lead to Violence

Problems outside the workplace—such as money troubles, relationship problems, and drug or alcohol addictions—can lead to violence on the job. Many violent workplace incidents stem from domestic violence, for example. Your company can take great strides toward minimizing the chances of a violent incident—and improving the lives of its employees—by adopting an Employee Assistance Program (EAP).

EAPs can help employees with a variety of problems inside and outside the workplace. Common offerings include therapy for individuals or couples; help kicking a drug, alcohol, or smoking habit; advice on exercise and nutrition; anger management classes; assistance with estate planning; and debt management counseling. Talk to your company's insurance carrier for more information about EAPs. Many insurers offer EAP services as part of an overall mental health benefit.

RESOURCE

For information on federal and state health and safety laws, go to the website of the Occupational Safety and Health Administration, the federal agency that administers workplace health and safety rules, at www.osha.gov. You'll find a number of helpful publications describing employers' legal obligations, as well as a list of state health and safety agencies.

RESOURCE

For information on preventing and investigating workplace violence, see *The Essential Guide to Workplace Investigations*, by Lisa Guerin (Nolo). This step-by-step guide includes detailed information on investigating common workplace problems, including violence.

13:6 Domestic Violence

File Name: 13_Health Safety.rtf

Include This Policy?
- ☐ Yes
- ☐ No
- ☐ Use our existing policy
- ☐ Other _____

Alternate Modifications

None

Additional Clauses

None

Related Policies

10:5 Family and Medical Leave (some states require employers to offer domestic violence leave)

Notes

_____
_____
_____
_____
_____
_____
_____
_____
_____
_____
_____
_____
_____
_____
_____
_____
_____
_____

13:6 Domestic Violence

Intimate partner violence—violence perpetrated against a former or current spouse or lover—accounts for a significant portion of workplace violence. When employees are targeted for stalking, threats, and violent acts, their productivity, attendance, and general health suffer. And sometimes, these incidents go beyond the intended victim to harm other employees as well.

Domestic violence often follows an escalating cycle in which pressure, threats, and coercion lead up to acts of physical violence. A partner who comes to the victim's workplace intending to cause harm has probably already made threats and committed other acts of violence or property damage. By encouraging employees to come forward and let the company know when they fear an abusive partner, your company can take steps to protect its employees and prevent that violence from coming to work.

Your domestic violence policy should explain how employees can convey concerns about a violent partner and how the company will handle such reports.

Domestic Violence

If you have been threatened or are concerned about violence or abuse by a current or former spouse, intimate partner, or other family member, we encourage you to report it to _____ _____ . We will keep this information as confidential as possible. The Company will not discriminate against employees who are victims of domestic violence.

Once you make a report, the Company will decide what steps to take for your safety and the safety of other employees. The Company may ask you to provide copies of any restraining orders or other legal papers you have filed against the abuser, as well as a picture of the abuser, for security purposes.

We understand that domestic violence can affect performance and attendance. If you need time off to ensure your own safety, appear in court, or handle other matters relating to domestic violence, please let us know.

How to Complete This Policy

Our sample policy leaves you space to designate the department or position that will receive reports of domestic violence (typically, the human resources department). The person who takes these reports should be prepared to provide employees with information about local domestic violence resources, such as shelters, hotlines, and legal clinics.

Reality Check: State Law May Allow Your Company to Get a Restraining Order

Victims of domestic violence sometimes get a restraining order (sometimes referred to as a "stayaway" order), prohibiting the abuser from going to certain locations—such as the victim's home, school, or workplace—and/or from getting within a certain distance of the victim. The purpose of these orders is to allow police to step in before violence has occurred: Once the abuser gets too close to the victim, he or she has violated the law and can be arrested before doing any physical harm.

If an employee has gotten a restraining order to keep the abuser away from the workplace, you must get a copy of it and make sure those who let the public into your workplace—security personnel, a doorman, or a receptionist, for example—know not to let the abuser enter. If the employee hasn't gotten a restraining order, you can encourage him or her to do so and to name your company as a place the abuser must avoid.

In some states, your company can get its own restraining order to keep the abuser away from the workplace. This allows your company to protect itself if, for example, the employee is reluctant to take legal action (for example, because he or she is afraid of confronting the abuser), or the employee's restraining order does not prohibit the abuser from entering the workplace. To find out whether your state allows these orders, go to the website of Legal Momentum, www.legalmomentum.org/employment-and-victims-violence, select "State Law Guides," then "Workplace Restraining Orders."

13:7 Cell Phones and Driving

File Name: 13_Health Safety.rtf

Include This Policy?
- ☐ Yes
- ☐ No
- ☐ Use our existing policy
- ☐ Other _____

Alternate Modifications
None

Alternate Modifications
None

Additional Clauses
Allow Hands-Free Devices

Insert?: ☐ Yes ☐ No

Related Policies
None

Notes
_____
_____
_____
_____
_____
_____
_____
_____
_____
_____
_____
_____
_____
_____
_____

13:7 Cell Phones and Driving

Studies show that drivers who are distracted cause more accidents, and that cell phones, smartphones, and other forms of wireless technology are increasingly to blame for our lack of attention to the road. As a result of this research, a growing number of states have passed laws that limit the use of cell phones while driving and require drivers who wish to talk on the phone to use a "hands-free" device. And many employers, recognizing that they could be held legally responsible for accidents their employees cause while working or driving a company vehicle, have adopted policies that do the same.

Our sample policy tells employees not to use cell phones or other wireless devices while driving, and explains what to do if they receive a call on the road.

Don't Use a Cell Phone While Driving

We know that our employees may use their cell phones or other wireless devices, whether these devices belong to the employee or are issued by the Company, for work-related matters.

Employees are prohibited from using cell phones or wireless devices for work-related matters while driving, however. We are concerned for your safety and for the safety of other drivers and pedestrians, and using a cell phone or wireless device while driving can lead to accidents.

If you must make a work-related call or send or read a text while driving, you must wait until you can pull over safely and stop the car before calling or texting. If you receive a work-related call while driving, you must ask the caller to wait while you pull over safely and stop the car. If you are unable to pull over safely, you must tell the caller that you will have to call back when it is safe to do so.

Who Needs This Policy

We advise all employers to adopt this policy. This is an important safety issue for employers whose employees might conduct business while driving, whether they travel for business, drive as part of their jobs (for example, making sales or deliveries), or must have frequent contact with clients, customers, vendors, or coworkers. Whenever an employee causes an accident while doing business—even if the employee is making work-related calls on the weekend in his or her own car—the employer could be held liable. And one way to avoid liability is to show—through this policy, among other things—that the company prohibited employees from using cell phones while driving.

Additional Clause to Allow or Provide Hands-Free Devices

If you wish to allow employees to use a hands-free device to talk on the phone while driving, you may add the language below as the last paragraph of the policy. If your company issues cell phones to employees for work-related calls, you should probably also issue hands-free equipment to allow them to use the phones in accordance with this modification. To do so, simply add a sentence at the end of the modification as follows: "The Company will provide hands-free equipment to all employees who have been issued company cell phones and/or wireless devices."

Before you add this language, make sure your state and locality allow the use of hands-free equipment to use a cell phone while driving.

Additional Clause

Employees may use hands-free equipment to make or answer calls while driving without violating this policy. However, safety must always be your first priority. We expect you to keep these calls brief. If, because of weather or traffic conditions or for any other reason, you are unable to concentrate fully on the road, you must either end the conversation or pull over and safely park your vehicle before resuming your call.

State Laws on Smoking in the Workplace

Note: These rules typically don't apply to some types of businesses, such as those that primarily sell or research tobacco products, theatrical productions, hotel rooms, private clubs, private conventions, and workplaces that are private residences (except to provide medical care or to care for children). For a complete list of exceptions in your state, refer to the listed statutes or contact your state department of labor or state or local health department.

Alabama

Ala. Code §§ 22-15A-3, 22-15A-5, and 22-15A-6

Workplaces where laws apply: Enclosed places of employment with five or more employees.

Exceptions: Common work areas if a majority of the workers who work in that area agree that a smoking area will be designated.

Where smoking prohibited: Employer may prohibit smoking in all or part of workplace. Individual employee may designate his or her own work area as a nonsmoking area. No smoking in common work areas unless majority of workers in that area agree to designate it as a smoking area.

Where smoking permitted: Majority of workers in an area may decide to designate common work area as smoking area, unless employer prohibits.

Smoking area requirements: Ventilated or separated to minimize toxic effects of smoke.

Accommodations for nonsmokers: Employers must provide signs to post if an employee designates his or her own work area as nonsmoking.

Employer smoking policy: Written policy must meet minimum requirements and be communicated to all employees.

Alaska

Alaska Stat. §§ 18.35.300, 18.35.310, and 18.35.320

Workplaces where laws apply: Any private place of business that posts signs regulating smoking; restaurants serving at least 50; grocery stores.

Exceptions: (1) A portion of a place or vehicle that is designated as a smoking section under § 18.35.320; (2) a limousine for hire or taxicab, if the driver consents and the driver ascertains that all passengers consent to smoking in the vehicle.

Where smoking prohibited: Throughout workplace except in designated smoking area. Employer may designate entire site nonsmoking. A smoking section may not be designated under § 18.35.320 for students on the grounds of or in an elementary or secondary school, indoors or outdoors.

Where smoking permitted: Designated smoking area.

Smoking area requirements: Ventilated or separated to protect nonsmokers from active by-products of smoke.

Accommodations for nonsmokers: Reasonable accommodations to protect the health of nonsmokers.

Arizona

Ariz. Rev. Stat. § 36-601.01

Workplace where laws apply: Any enclosed workplace.

Where smoking prohibited: Entire enclosed workplace. Employer may permit smoking outside so long as people entering or leaving the building will not be subject to breathing tobacco smoke and the smoke does not enter the building.

Employer smoking policy: The prohibitions on smoking shall be communicated to all employees and to each prospective employee upon application for employment.

Protection from discrimination: No employer may discharge or retaliate against an employee for exercising rights under this law.

Arkansas

Ark. Code Ann. §§ 20-27-1804 and 20-27-1805, Ark. Admin. Code §§ 016.24.3-I to 016.24.3-X

Workplace where laws apply: Any enclosed workplace.

Exceptions: Nonpublic workplaces with fewer than 3 employees; restaurants and bars that prohibit minors; designated areas within or outside of long-term care facilities.

Where smoking prohibited: Entire enclosed workplace.

Smoking area requirements: When smoking is permitted in restaurant or bar, employer must post signs that meet certain size and placement criteria and say: "HEALTH WARNING. THIS IS A SMOKING AREA. OCCUPANTS WILL BE EXPOSED TO SECONDHAND SMOKE. IT IS UNLAWFUL FOR ANYONE UNDER 21 YEARS OF AGE TO ENTER OR WORK IN ANY PART OF THE ESTABLISHMENT AT ALL TIMES."

Employer smoking policy: The prohibitions on smoking shall be communicated to each prospective employee upon application for employment.

Protection from discrimination: No employer may discharge or retaliate against an employee for making a complaint under this law or furnishing information about a violation to an enforcement authority.

State Laws on Smoking in the Workplace (continued)

California

Cal. Lab. Code §§ 96, 98.6, 6404.5

Workplaces where laws apply: Any enclosed indoor workplace.

Exceptions: Truck cabs if no nonsmoking employees are present.

Where smoking prohibited: Employer may not knowingly or intentionally permit smoking in any enclosed workplace; must take reasonable steps to prevent nonemployees from smoking. May designate entire site nonsmoking.

Protection from discrimination: Employer may not discriminate, retaliate, or take any adverse action against employee (or applicant) for engaging in lawful activity during nonwork hours away from the employer's premises. Employee may recover a penalty of up to $10,000 for violation by employer.

Colorado

Colo. Rev. Stat. §§ 25-14-204 to 25-14-206; 24-34-402.5

Workplaces where laws apply: Any indoor workplace (includes tobacco and marijuana smoke).

Exceptions: Places of employment not open to the public, under the control of the employer, and with 3 or fewer employees.

Where smoking is prohibited: The common areas of retirement facilities, publicly owned housing facilities, and, except as specified in Section 25-14-205(1)(k), nursing homes, but not including any resident's private residential quarters or areas of assisted living facilities specified in Section 25-14-205(1)(k).

Accommodations for nonsmokers: Exempted employers must designate a smoke-free area if requested by an employee.

Protection from discrimination: Employee may not be fired for lawful conduct offsite during nonwork hours.

Connecticut

Conn. Gen. Stat. Ann. §§ 31-40q, 31-40s

Workplaces where laws apply: Enclosed facilities.

Where smoking prohibited: Employers with 5 or more employees must prohibit smoking, except in designated smoking rooms. Employer may prohibit smoking throughout the workplace.

Smoking area requirements: Employers with fewer than 5 employees: Existing physical barriers and ventilation systems. Employers with 5 or more employees: Air must be exhausted directly outside with a fan and cannot recirculate to other areas of the building; room must be in a nonwork area where no employee is required to enter.

Accommodations for nonsmokers: Employers with fewer than 5 employees: Employer must provide one or more clearly designated work areas for nonsmoking employees. Employers with 5 or more employees: If there are smoking rooms, employer must provide sufficient nonsmoking break rooms.

Accommodations for smokers: Each smoking room designated by an employer shall be in a nonwork area for the use of employees only; air from the smoking room shall be exhausted directly to the outside by an exhaust fan, and no air from such room shall be recirculated to other parts of the building.

Protection from discrimination: Employer may not require employee to refrain from smoking as a condition of employment.

Delaware

Del. Code Ann. tit. 16, §§ 2902 to 2907

Workplaces where laws apply: Indoor areas.

Where smoking prohibited: Any indoor enclosed area where the general public is permitted or may be invited.

Protection from discrimination: Employer may not discriminate against or retaliate against employee who files a complaint or testifies in a proceeding about violation of workplace smoking laws.

District of Columbia

D.C. Code Ann. §§ 7-1701 to 7-1703.03

Workplaces where laws apply: Any public or private workplace.

Where smoking prohibited: Throughout the workplace, except for designated smoking area.

Where smoking permitted: Designated smoking area.

Smoking area requirements: Physical barrier or separate room.

Accommodations for smokers: Employer required to provide smoking area.

Employer smoking policy: Must have written policy that designates a smoking area; must notify each employee orally and post policy within 3 weeks after adopting it.

Protection from discrimination: Employee may not be fired or discriminated against in hiring, wages, benefits, or terms of employment because of being a smoker.

State Laws on Smoking in the Workplace (continued)

Florida

Fla. Stat. Ann. §§ 386.201 to 386.209

Workplaces where laws apply: All enclosed indoor workplaces (more than 50% covered and surrounded by physical barriers).

Exceptions: Stand-alone bars.

Where smoking prohibited: Smoking is prohibited throughout the workplace.

Smoking area requirements: A customs smoking room in an airport in-transit lounge may not be designated in any common area; must be enclosed by physical barriers that are impenetrable by secondhand tobacco smoke, and exhaust tobacco smoke directly to the outside, and comply with the signage requirements.

Employer smoking policy: Employer must develop and enforce a policy prohibiting smoking in the workplace. May post "No Smoking" signs to increase awareness.

Georgia

Ga. Code Ann. §§ 31-12A-1 to 31-12A-13

Workplace where laws apply: Any enclosed workplace.

Exceptions: Common work areas, conference rooms, meetings rooms, and private offices in private places of employment that are open to the public by appointment only.

Where smoking prohibited: Entire indoor workplace except for designated smoking area. Employer may designate the entire workplace nonsmoking.

Where smoking permitted: Any designated smoking area.

Smoking area requirements: Smoking area must be in a nonwork area where no employee is required to enter (except to perform custodial and maintenance work when the smoking area is unoccupied). Must have ventilation system that exhausts air outdoors; have no air recirculating to nonsmoking areas; and be only for employee use.

Employer smoking policy: Smoking prohibition must be communicated to all employees and applicants.

Hawaii

Haw. Rev. Stat. §§ 328J-1 to J-17

Workplaces where laws apply: Any enclosed area.

Where smoking prohibited: Entire enclosed workplace and within a "presumptively reasonable" distance of 20 feet from any entrance, exit, or ventilation intake.

Protection from discrimination: Employer may not discharge, refuse to hire, or retaliate against employee or applicant for attempting to prosecute a violation of this law.

Idaho

Idaho Code §§ 39-5501 and following

Workplaces where laws apply: Enclosed indoor area used by the general public, including restaurants, businesses, retail stores, and grocery stores.

Where smoking prohibited: Everywhere except designated smoking area. Only employers with five or fewer employees may designate smoking areas.

Where smoking permitted: Employer or proprietor designates. May prohibit smoking throughout enclosed place of employment.

Smoking area requirements: Must not be accessible to minors, must be separated from the rest of the building by a floor to ceiling partition; must not be the sole entrance to the workplace or restroom, and must be located in an area where no employee is required to enter as part of the employee's work responsibilities. Must post "Warning: Smoking Permitted" signs.

Protection from discrimination: Employer may not discharge or discriminate against employee because employee has made a complaint or has given information to the Department of Health and Welfare or the Department of Labor for violation of this law.

Illinois

410 Ill. Comp. Stat. §§ 82/1 and following; 820 Ill. Comp. Stat. § 55/5

Workplaces where laws apply: Any enclosed indoor workplace.

Where smoking prohibited: Entire workplace and within 15 feet of entrance, exit, or ventilation intake of workplace.

Protection from discrimination: Employee may not be discriminated against for asserting rights under the clean indoor air laws. May not be refused a job, fired, or discriminated against in terms of compensation or benefits because of using lawful products outside of work. Different insurance rates or coverage for smokers are not discriminatory if:

- difference is based on cost to employer, and
- employees are given a notice of carriers' rates.

Indiana

Ind. Code Ann. §§ 7.1-5-12-4, 22-5-4-1

State Laws on Smoking in the Workplace (continued)

Workplaces where laws apply: All places of employment.

Where smoking prohibited: All places of employment.

Employer smoking policy: Employer must inform employees that smoking is prohibited.

Protection from discrimination: Employer may not require prospective employee to refrain from using tobacco products outside of work in order to be hired or discriminate against employee who uses them in terms of wages, benefits, or conditions of employment.

Iowa

Iowa Code §§ 142D.1 to 142D.9.

Workplaces where laws apply: All enclosed indoor areas.

Exceptions: State fairgrounds; designated smoking areas of National Guard and correctional facilities.

Where smoking prohibited: All enclosed indoor areas.

Where smoking permitted: Outdoor areas not otherwise prohibited by law, unless employer chooses to prohibit smoking there. Such areas must be marked with signs.

Protection from discrimination: An employer shall not discharge, refuse to employ, or in any manner retaliate against an employee, applicant for employment, or customer because that employee, applicant, or customer exercises any rights under this law, registers a complaint, or attempts to prosecute a violation of the law.

Kansas

Kan. Stat. Ann. §§ 21-6109 to 21-6116

Workplaces where laws apply: Any enclosed workplace.

Where smoking prohibited: Any enclosed workplace.

Employer smoking policy: Written policy must prohibit smoking without exception in all areas of the place of employment. Policy shall be communicated to all current employees within one week of its adoption and to all new employees upon hiring. Written policy available upon request.

Protection from discrimination: Employer may not discharge, refuse to hire, or take other adverse action against an employee or applicant in retaliation for reporting or attempting to prosecute a violation of the smoking laws.

Kentucky

Ky. Rev. Stat. Ann. § 344.040

Protection from discrimination: As long as employee complies with workplace smoking policy, employer may not: discharge employee or discriminate in terms of wages, benefits, or conditions of employment because of being a smoker or nonsmoker; require employee to refrain from using tobacco products outside of work as a condition of employment. A difference in employee contribution rates for smokers and nonsmokers in relation to an employer-sponsored health plan is a lawful practice, as well as the offering of incentives or benefits offered to employees who participate in a smoking cessation program.

Louisiana

La. Rev. Stat. Ann. §§ 40:1291.1 to 40:1291-23, 23:966

Workplaces where laws apply: Any enclosed workplace.

Exceptions: Bars, outdoor patios.

Where smoking prohibited: Any enclosed workplace.

Where smoking permitted: Outdoors, unless employer posts signs prohibiting smoking in the outdoor area.

Protection from discrimination: Employer may not:
- require prospective employee to refrain from using tobacco products outside of work as a condition of employment, or
- discriminate against smokers or nonsmokers regarding termination, layoffs, wages, benefits, or other terms of employment.

Maine

Me. Rev. Stat. Ann. tit. 22, § 1580-A; tit. 26, § 597

Workplaces where laws apply: Structurally enclosed business facilities.

Where smoking prohibited: Employer may prohibit throughout entire workplace.

Where smoking permitted: Designated smoking area, meaning an outdoor area where smoking is permitted, which must be at least 20 feet from entryways, vents, and doorways.

Employer smoking policy: Written policy concerning smoking and nonsmoking rules. State bureau of health will assist employees and employers with creating policy.

Protection from discrimination: Employer may not discriminate or retaliate against employee for assisting with enforcement of workplace smoking laws. As long as employee follows workplace smoking policy, employer may not: discriminate in wages, benefits, or terms of employment because of use of tobacco products outside of work; require employee to refrain from tobacco use as a condition of employment.

State Laws on Smoking in the Workplace (continued)

Maryland

Md. Code Ann. [Health-Gen.] §§ 24-501 and following; Md. Regs. Code §§ 09.12.23.01 to 09.12.23.04

Workplaces where laws apply: Any indoor work area.

Where smoking prohibited: Entire indoor workplace. Employer must post "No smoking" notice at each entrance.

Protection from discrimination: Employer may not discharge or discriminate against an employee because that employee has made a complaint or charge against the employer under this law or has testified or is about to testify in a proceeding regarding this law.

Massachusetts

Mass. Gen. Laws ch. 270, § 22

Workplaces where laws apply: Any enclosed workplace.

Where smoking prohibited: Where employees work in an enclosed workspace.

Protection from discrimination: An individual, person, entity or organization subject to the smoking prohibitions of this section shall not discriminate or retaliate in any manner against a person for making a complaint of a violation of this section or furnishing information concerning a violation, to a person, entity or organization or to an enforcement authority.

Michigan

Mich. Stat. 333.12601 to 333.12616

Workplaces where laws apply: Places of employment.

Where smoking prohibited: In places of employment (enclosed indoor areas that contain at least one workspace for at least one employee).

Protection from discrimination: Employer may not take retaliatory or adverse action against employee or applicant for exercising rights under smoking laws.

Minnesota

Minn. Stat. Ann. §§ 144.411 to 144.417, 181.938

Protection from discrimination: Enclosed indoor workplace.

Where smoking prohibited: Entire indoor workplace.

Protection from discrimination: Employer may not discipline, discharge, or refuse to hire employee for use of lawful consumable products, including tobacco, during nonwork hours, unless not using tobacco is a bona fide occupational qualification related to the job's duties or is necessary to avoid a conflict of interest. Employer cannot discharge, refuse

to hire, penalize, discriminate against, or in any manner retaliate against an employee or applicant because the individual exercises any right to a smoke-free environment.

Mississippi

Miss. Code Ann. § 71-7-33

Protection from discrimination: Employer may not make it a condition of employment for prospective or current employee to abstain from smoking during nonwork hours, as long as employee complies with laws or policies that regulate workplace smoking.

Missouri

Mo. Rev. Stat. §§ 191.765 to 191.771, 290.145

Workplaces where laws apply: Enclosed indoor workplaces.

Exceptions: Bars or restaurants seating fewer than 50 people, bowling alleys and billiard parlors, and stadiums seating more than 15,000 people.

Where smoking prohibited: Entire workplace except for designated smoking area.

Where smoking permitted: Employer may designate smoking area (may not be more than 30% of workplace).

Smoking area requirements: Existing physical barriers and ventilation systems that isolate area.

Protection from discrimination: Employer may not refuse to hire, discharge, or in any way discriminate against employee for lawful use of tobacco offsite during nonwork hours, unless use interferes with employee's or coworkers' performance or employer's business operations.

Montana

Mont. Code Ann. §§ 50-40-104; 39-2-313

Workplaces where laws apply: Any enclosed indoor workplace.

Where smoking prohibited: Entire workplace.

Protection from discrimination: Employer may not discharge, refuse to hire, or discriminate against employee in regard to compensation, promotion, benefits, or terms of employment because of lawful tobacco use offsite during nonwork hours. Use that affects job performance, other workers' safety, or conflicts with a genuine job requirement is not protected. It is not discrimination to have different insurance rates or coverage for smokers if:

- difference is based on cost to employer, and
- employees are given a written statement of carriers' rates.

State Laws on Smoking in the Workplace (continued)

Nebraska

Neb. Rev. Stat. §§ 71-5716 to 71-5734

Workplaces where laws apply: Any enclosed indoor workplace.

Where smoking prohibited: Entire workplace.

Nevada

Nev. Rev. Stat. Ann. §§ 202.2483, 613.333

Workplaces where laws apply: Indoor workplaces.

Exceptions: Bars, brothels, strip clubs, areas in casinos where minors are prohibited from loitering, enclosed areas within bars that minors are prohibited from entering.

Protection from discrimination: Employer may not fail or refuse to hire, discharge, or discriminate in terms of compensation, benefits, or conditions of employment because of employee's lawful use of any product offsite during nonwork hours, unless use adversely affects job performance or the safety of other employees. Employer may not retaliate against employee or applicant for exercising rights under smoking laws.

New Hampshire

N.H. Rev. Stat. Ann. §§ 155:64 to 155.77; 275:37-a

Workplaces where laws apply: Enclosed workplaces where 4 or more people work.

Where smoking prohibited: Throughout the workplace except for designated smoking area. If smoking area cannot be effectively segregated, smoking will be totally prohibited. Employer may declare entire workplace nonsmoking.

Where smoking permitted: Designated smoking area, but no smoking area is permitted in certain workplaces, including restaurants, cocktail lounges, or grocery stores.

Smoking area requirements: Must be effectively segregated, which means procedures for accurately and fairly determining preference have been followed; the size and location of no-smoking and smoking-permitted areas are designed, designated, or juxtaposed so that smoke does not cause harm or unreasonably intrude into the area occupied by persons who are not smoking; and in buildings with existing ventilation systems, smoking areas are near exhaust vents.

Accommodations for nonsmokers: Special consideration for employees with medically proven conditions adversely affected by smoke, as documented by an occupational physician.

Employer smoking policy: Written policy outlining either smoking prohibition or areas where smoking permitted. Policy must be handed out or posted; employees must receive policy orientation. If there is a designated smoking area, must be written training procedures for:

- enforcing smoking policy
- handling complaints and violations, and
- accommodating employees with medical conditions.

Protection from discrimination: Employer may not require employee or applicant to refrain from using tobacco products outside of work as a condition of employment, as long as employee complies with workplace smoking policy. Employer may not retaliate or discriminate against any employee who exercises rights under smoking laws; however, laws do not give employee right to refuse to perform normal duties, even if duties require entering a smoking area.

New Jersey

N.J. Stat. Ann. §§ 26:3D-56 to 26:3D-61; 34:6B-1

Workplaces where laws apply: Any indoor workplace.

Where smoking prohibited: Entire workplace.

Protection from discrimination: Employer may not discharge or discriminate in terms of hiring, compensation, benefits, or conditions of employment because employee does or does not smoke, unless smoking or not smoking relates to work and job responsibilities.

New Mexico

N.M. Stat. Ann. §§ 24-16-4, 24-16-12, 50-11-3

Workplaces where laws apply: Indoor workplaces.

Exceptions: Workplaces with fewer than two employees that are not commonly accessible to the public, except for bars and restaurants. However, employer must provide smoke-free workplace if employee requests it.

Employer smoking policy: Employer must have a written smoking policy.

Protection from discrimination: Employer may not: refuse to hire, discharge, or disadvantage an employee with respect to compensation, terms, conditions, or privileges of employment because the individual is a smoker or nonsmoker; or require that an employee abstain from tobacco products during nonwork hours. Employer may restrict smoking if it relates to a genuine occupational requirement or if it materially threatens a legitimate conflict of interest policy.

State Laws on Smoking in the Workplace (continued)

New York

N.Y. Pub. Health Law §§ 1399-n to 1399-x; N.Y. Lab. Law § 201-d(2b),(6)

Workplaces where laws apply: Indoor workspaces.

Where smoking prohibited: Smoking is prohibited throughout the workplace, in copy machine and common equipment areas, and in company vehicles.

Employer smoking policy: Must post "No Smoking" signs; must make good-faith effort to ensure that employees do not smoke.

Protection from discrimination: Employee may not be discharged, refused employment, or discriminated against in terms of compensation or benefits because of lawful use of products offsite during nonwork hours when not using employer's equipment or property. It is not discrimination to offer insurance with different rates or coverage for smokers if:
- difference is based on cost to employer, and
- employees are given a written statement of carriers' rates.

North Carolina

N.C. Gen. Stat. §§ 95-28.2, 130A-491, 130A-492, 130A-496

Workplaces where laws apply: Discrimination laws apply to employers with 3 or more employees. Restaurants and bars must comply with smoking laws.

Where smoking prohibited: Enclosed areas of restaurants and bars.

Protection from discrimination: Employer may not discharge, refuse to hire, or discriminate in regard to compensation, benefits, or terms of employment because of employee's use of lawful products offsite during nonwork hours. Use that affects employees' job performance or other workers' safety or conflicts with a genuine job requirement is not protected. It is not discrimination to offer insurance with different rates or coverage for smokers if:
- difference is based on cost to employer
- employees are given written notice of carriers' rates, and
- employer makes equal contribution for all employees.

North Dakota

N.D. Cent. Code §§ 14-02.4-03, 23-12-09 and 23-12-10

Workplace where laws apply: Any enclosed workplace. Smoking includes the use of e-cigarettes and other oral smoking devices.

Exceptions: Outdoor areas of employment, except within 20 feet of areas where smoking is prohibited.

Where smoking prohibited: Entire indoor workplace.

Protection from discrimination: Employer cannot discharge, refuse to hire, or retaliate against employee or applicant for exercising rights related to this law. Employer may not refuse to hire, discharge, or discriminate with regard to training, apprenticeship, tenure, promotion, compensation, benefits, or conditions of employment because of employee's lawful activity offsite during nonwork hours, unless it is in direct conflict with employer's essential business-related interests.

Ohio

Ohio Rev. Code Ann. §§ 3794.01 to 3794.09, Ohio Admin. Code §§ 3701-52-01 to 3710-52-09

Workplace where laws apply: Any enclosed workplace.

Exceptions: Family-owned, family-operated business in which all employees are related to the employer and the area is not open to the public, as long as the smoke will not migrate to nonsmoking areas.

Where smoking prohibited: Entire indoor workplace and outside immediately adjacent to entrances or exits to the building. Employer may designate the entire workplace nonsmoking.

Where smoking permitted: Outdoors, including outdoor patios that are physically separate from enclosed areas, as long as windows and doors prevent migration of the smoke into enclosed areas.

Smoking area requirements: Employer must ensure that tobacco smoke does not enter enclosed areas through entrances, windows, ventilation systems, or other means.

Protection from discrimination: Employer may not discharge, refuse to hire, or in any manner retaliate against any individual for exercising any right, including reporting a violation of the law.

Oklahoma

Okla. Stat. Ann. tit. 40, §§ 500 to 503; Okla. Admin. Code §§ 310:355-5-1 and following

Workplace where laws apply: Any indoor workplace.

Exceptions: Family-owned, family-operated business in which all employees are related to the employer or where all the employees are smokers, and there is only occasional public access.

State Laws on Smoking in the Workplace (continued)

Where smoking prohibited: Throughout workplace except in designated smoking area. Employer may designate entire site nonsmoking. All buildings owned by an educational facility.

Where smoking permitted: Designated smoking area.

Smoking area requirements: Smoking area must be in a nonwork area where no employee is required to enter (except to perform custodial and maintenance work when the smoking area is unoccupied). Must: have ventilation systems that exhaust air outdoors at least 15 feet from entrances, exits, or air intake; be fully enclosed; have no air recirculating to nonsmoking areas; and be under negative air pressure so that no smoke can drift or circulate into a nonsmoking area.

Protection from discrimination: Employer may not:

- discharge or disadvantage employee in terms of compensation, benefits, or conditions of employment because of being a nonsmoker or smoking during nonwork hours, or
- require that employee abstain from using tobacco products during nonwork hours as a condition of employment.

Employer may restrict nonwork smoking if it relates to a genuine occupational requirement.

Oregon

Or. Rev. Stat. §§ 433.835 to 433.875, 659A.315

Workplaces where laws apply: All enclosed areas used by employees.

Where smoking prohibited: In all enclosed workplace and outdoor spaces within 10 feet of a building exit, entrance, open window, or vent intake serving an enclosed area.

Protection from discrimination: Employer may not require that employee refrain from lawful use of tobacco products during nonwork hours as a condition of employment, unless there is a genuine occupational requirement.

Pennsylvania

35 Pa. Cons. Stat. Ann. §§ 637.2 to 637.11

Workplaces where laws apply: All indoor workplaces.

Where smoking prohibited: All indoor workplaces.

Where smoking permitted: Outdoor areas, if employer permits. May make entire workplace smoke free.

Smoking area requirements: Must have a "Smoking Permitted" sign.

Protection from discrimination: An employer may not discharge an employee, refuse to hire an applicant for employment, or retaliate against an employee because the individual exercises a right to a smoke-free environment.

Rhode Island

R.I. Gen. Laws §§ 23-20.10-1 to 23-20.10-14

Workplaces where laws apply: All enclosed facilities within places of employment.

Where smoking prohibited: All enclosed facilities within places of employment. Required signs must be posted.

Where smoking permitted: Employer may designate outdoor area.

Smoking area requirements: Must be physically separate from enclosed workspace, to prevent smoke from getting into the workplace.

Employer smoking policy: Smoking policy must be communicated to all employees and applicants.

Protection from discrimination: Employers cannot prohibit the use of tobacco outside of work, and cannot discriminate in compensation, terms, or benefits for tobacco use outside of work, or retaliate against an employee for reporting or attempting to prosecute a violation of the law.

South Carolina

S.C. Code Ann. § 41-1-85

Protection from discrimination: Employer may not take personnel actions, including hiring, discharge, demotion, or promotion, based on use of tobacco outside the workplace.

South Dakota

S.D. Codified Laws Ann. §§ 34-46-13 to 34-46-19, 60-4-11

Workplaces where laws apply: Any enclosed space under the control of a private or public employer.

Where smoking prohibited: The entire workplace.

Protection from discrimination: Employer may not discharge employee because of using tobacco products offsite during nonwork hours, unless not smoking is a genuine occupational requirement or smoking ban is necessary to avoid conflict of interest. It is not discrimination to have insurance policies with different rates or coverage for smokers.

State Laws on Smoking in the Workplace (continued)

Tennessee

Tenn. Code Ann. § 39-17-1801 to 39-17-1812, 50-1-304(e); Tenn. Comp. R. & Regs. §§ 0800-06-01-.01 to 0800-06-01-.08

Workplaces where laws apply: All enclosed workplaces.

Exceptions: Age-restricted venues; businesses with 3 or fewer employees (smoking permitted in area not accessible to the public).

Where smoking is prohibited: All enclosed workplaces.

Where smoking is permitted: Nonenclosed spaces, including outdoor patios.

Employer smoking policy: Prohibition must be communicated to all current employees and all prospective employees upon application for employment.

Protection from discrimination: Employee may not be fired for use of a lawful product during nonwork hours as long as employee observes workplace policy when at work.

Utah

Utah Code Ann. §§ 26-38-2 and 26-38-3; Utah Admin. Code §§ R392-510-1 to R392-510-14

Workplaces where laws apply: All enclosed indoor workplaces unless owner operated with no employees and not open to the public.

Where smoking prohibited: Entire workplace; within 25 feet of any entranceway, exit, open window, or air intake of a building where smoking is prohibited. Employer can choose to prohibit smoking outdoors.

Smoking area requirements: Any enclosed area where smoking is permitted must be designed and operated to prevent exposure of persons outside the area to tobacco smoke generated in the area.

Employer smoking policy: An employer shall establish a policy to prohibit employee smoking within 25 feet of any entranceway, exit, open window, or air intake of a building where smoking is prohibited.

Protection from discrimination: An employer may not discriminate or take any adverse action against an employee or applicant because that person has sought enforcement of the provisions of this law or the smoking policy of the workplace or otherwise protests the smoking of others.

Vermont

Vt. Stat. Ann. tit. 18, §§ 1421, 1427

Workplaces where laws apply: All enclosed structures where employees perform services.

Where smoking prohibited: Entire enclosed structure.

Protection from discrimination: Employer may not discharge, discipline, or otherwise discriminate against employee who assists in enforcement of workplace smoking laws.

Virginia

Va. Code Ann. § 15.2-2820 to 15.2-2833

Where smoking prohibited: Educational, healthcare, and recreational facilities and retail establishments: must designate reasonable no-smoking areas. Restaurants: entire establishment.

Where smoking permitted: Restaurants: outdoor areas; areas that are structurally separate from no-smoking areas. Educational, healthcare, recreational facilities, and retail establishments: everywhere except designated no-smoking areas.

Smoking area requirements: Restaurants: must be structurally separate and separately vented from no-smoking area. At least one public entrance to restaurant must be into no-smoking area.

Washington

Wash. Rev. Code §§ 70.160.011 to 70.160.900

Workplaces where laws apply: Any enclosed workplace.

Exceptions: Outdoor structures, gazebos, and lean-tos provided for smokers that are at least 25 feet from entrances and exits.

Where smoking prohibited: Any area that employees are required to pass through or within 25 feet of an entrance or exit.

West Virginia

W.Va. Code § 21-3-19

Protection from discrimination: Employer may not refuse to hire, discharge, or penalize an employee with respect to compensation, conditions of employment, or other benefits for using tobacco products offsite during nonwork hours. It is not discrimination to have insurance policies with different rates or coverage for smokers if:

- difference is based on cost to employer, and
- employees are given a notice of carriers' rates.

State Laws on Smoking in the Workplace (continued)

Wisconsin

Wis. Stat. Ann. §§ 101.123; 111.35

Workplaces where laws apply: All places of employment, which covers any enclosed place employees normally frequent in the course of employment, including offices, work areas, elevators, employee lounges, restrooms, conference and meeting rooms, classrooms, hallways, stairways, lobbies, common areas, vehicles, and employee cafeterias.

Where smoking prohibited: All places of employment.

Protection from discrimination: Employer may not discriminate against employee who uses or does not use lawful products offsite during nonwork hours. Use that impairs employee's ability to perform job, creates a conflict of interest, or conflicts with a genuine occupational requirement is not protected. It is not discrimination to have insurance policies with different coverage and rates for smokers and nonsmokers if:

- difference is based on cost to employer, and
- each employee is given a written statement of carriers' rates.

Wyoming

Wyo. Stat. § 27-9-105(a)(iv)

Protection from discrimination: Employer may not make use or nonuse of tobacco products outside of work a condition of employment unless nonuse is a genuine occupational qualification. May not discriminate regarding compensation, benefits, or terms of employment because of use or nonuse of tobacco products outside of work. It is not discrimination to offer insurance policies with different rates and coverage for smokers and nonsmokers if:

- difference reflects actual cost to employer, and
- employees are given written notice of carriers' rates.

Employee Privacy

Sensibly, many companies are not inclined to monitor their employees' every move in the workplace. Most employers cannot afford to spend the time or money it would take to monitor every phone call or bathroom break, nor do they especially want to. There is rarely a need for extensive worker surveillance in most types of businesses. Moreover, keeping such close track of workers can breed resentment and anxiety.

On the other hand, some companies may, one day, have to take a closer look at what their employees are up to. If management learns or suspects that an employee has brought a weapon to work or stolen company property, for example, the company will have to investigate. This means that company officials may need to conduct a search or keep closer tabs on employees.

The policies in this chapter protect an employer's ability to search or monitor employees by telling them that their workspaces and workplace communications are not private. They also reserve the employer's right to search or inspect at any time. If company officials conduct searches without policies like these in place, the company will be open to lawsuits by angry employees claiming that their right to privacy was violated.

This chapter also includes a policy on cameras and camera phones in the workplace. These days, with technology making recording devices smaller and more affordable, it isn't only employers that can violate employees' privacy: Their coworkers can also get in on the act. This policy prohibits employees from taking pictures of coworkers, company property, and potentially valuable trade secrets.

Striking a Balance: How Privacy Laws Work

In many areas of employment law, the rules are fairly simple: The federal government or state legislature passes laws setting out the rights of employees and employers, and then everyone has to do what the law says. Once you enter the realm of privacy law, however, things get a bit more confusing. Although there are a few clear-cut rules, questions of privacy in the workplace are generally resolved on a case-by-case basis. Judges examine the reasons both sides acted as they did: why the employee expected privacy and why the employer searched or monitored. Judges then decide whose side of the argument seems more reasonable, in what is aptly called a "balancing test."

Clearly, an employer's goal is to tip the scales in its favor. Employers can do this by exercising restraint, never searching or monitoring employees without good reason. At the same time, an employer shouldn't give its employees reason to believe that their communications or workspaces are private. Adopting the policies in this chapter can help manage employees' expectations of how much privacy they are entitled to in the workplace, thereby taking some of the weight away from the employees' side of this balancing test scale. A written policy makes it much harder for employees to later argue that they had a reasonable expectation of privacy at work.

14:1 Workplace Privacy

Workplace searches are controversial and carry with them an element of legal risk. The reasons are obvious: Employees feel a sense of ownership toward their personal workspaces and actually do own their personal possessions. Most employees assume that no one can snoop into these areas without their permission. Searching calls up images of police and prison, not the enlightened American workplace. For these reasons, many companies neither want to nor do conduct workplace searches.

However, there may come a time when even the most reluctant employer has to poke around in a desk or locker. For example, if management learns that an employee has brought a gun or a pornography collection to work or has stolen company property, company officials will need to find out what's going on. And, unless the employee volunteers the contraband, there may be a need to search.

Policy A will put employees on notice that company officials may search in these worst-case scenarios. An employer doesn't have to start conducting random searches or doing a "locker check" every morning if it adopts this policy; it simply reserves the company's rights should the unfortunate need to search arise.

Policy B is a more aggressive policy. It is probably more than most employers need. However, if your company deals in small, valuable items—such as jewelry or electronic components—or handles large amounts of cash, you may want to warn employees that the company reserves its right to find out what they are carrying out of the workplace.

Alternate Policy A

Company Property Is Subject to Search

Employees do not have a right to privacy in their workspaces or in any other property belonging to the Company. The Company reserves the right to search Company property at any time, without warning, to ensure compliance with our policies, including those that cover employee safety, workplace violence, harassment, theft, drug and alcohol use, and possession of prohibited items. Company property includes, but is not limited to, lockers, desks, file cabinets, storage areas, and workspaces. If you use a lock on any item of Company property (a locker or file cabinet, for example), you must give a copy of the key or combination to _____ .

14:1 Search Policy
File Name: 14_Privacy.rtf

Include This Policy?
☐ Yes
  Choose one: ☐ A ☐ B
☐ No
☐ Use our existing policy
☐ Other _____

Alternate Modifications
  None

Additional Clauses
  None

Related Policies
  Chapter 15 provides policies on employee email and Internet use.

Notes

Alternate Policy B

Company and Personal Property Are Subject to Search

Employees do not have a right to privacy in their workspaces, any other Company property, or any personal property they bring to the workplace. The Company reserves the right to search Company premises at any time, without warning, to ensure compliance with our policies, including those that cover employee safety, workplace violence, harassment, theft, drug and alcohol use, and possession of prohibited items. The Company may search Company property, including but not limited to lockers, desks, file cabinets, storage areas, and workspaces. If you use a lock on any item of Company property (a locker or file cabinet, for example), you must give a copy of the key or combination to _____ .

The Company may also search personal property brought onto Company premises, including but not limited to toolboxes, briefcases, backpacks, purses, and bags.

CAUTION

For policies allowing more intrusive searches or surveillance, talk to a lawyer. Some employers want to adopt a search policy that allows them to search an employee's pockets, clothing, or body before the employee leaves work. Because we all have a strong expectation of privacy of our own bodies (and the clothing we wear on them), an employer will need a carefully drafted search policy before undertaking this type of search. (Your company will also need an *extremely* compelling reason to conduct the search, one that would arise only in a rare and unusual situation.) Similarly, some employers want to install security devices—such as hidden cameras or one-way mirrors—to keep an eye on customers and employees. These surveillance devices are highly controversial, and a growing number of states have adopted specific rules that limit an employer's right to use them. If your company wants to adopt a policy allowing surveillance or intrusive searches, talk to an employment lawyer in your state.

14:2 Telephone Monitoring

If your company will monitor employees' telephone calls, you must adopt a policy to let employees know about it. Federal law allows employers to monitor employee phone calls "in the ordinary course of business" (for example, to keep tabs on customer service). However, some states require the consent of one or both parties to the conversation for monitoring to be legal. By adopting a policy and requiring employees to consent, in writing, to monitoring, your company will be protected from lawsuits claiming invasion of privacy.

Your telephone policy should let employees know whether the company plans to monitor calls on work telephones and under what circumstances.

Telephone Monitoring

The Company reserves the right to monitor calls made from or received on Company telephones. Therefore, no employee should expect that conversations made on Company telephones will be private.

Additional Clause to Designate Nonmonitored Phones

If your company chooses to monitor employee phone calls, it may want to designate specified phones that are not monitored for employees to use for personal calls. By doing this, an employer can avoid employee claims of invasion of privacy by giving them an opportunity to make personal calls that won't be overheard. Employees who fail to use the designated phones have no cause for complaint if their personal calls from nondesignated work phones are monitored.

To insert this additional clause, simply add this language to the end of your telephone policy.

Additional Clause

The Company has designated telephones that employees may use for personal calls. Calls made from these phones will not be monitored. Employees may make personal calls during their breaks; if you must make a personal call during your work hours, you are expected to keep the conversation brief.

Telephones for personal calls are located _____

_____ .

14:2 Telephone Monitoring

File Name: 14_Privacy.rtf

Include This Policy?
- ☐ Yes
- ☐ No
- ☐ Use our existing policy
- ☐ Other _____

Alternate Modifications
None

Additional Clauses
Designate Nonmonitored Phones
Insert?:   ☐ Yes   ☐ No

Related Policies
Policy 9:3 covers employee use of company phones.

Notes

_____
_____
_____
_____
_____
_____
_____
_____
_____
_____
_____
_____
_____
_____
_____
_____
_____
_____

Reality Check: How to Monitor Telephone Calls

If your company plans to monitor employee phone calls, it must make sure not to violate the privacy of the employee or the person on the other end of the line. Although the law of telephonic monitoring is still in flux, a few clear guidelines have emerged:

- **Make a monitoring announcement.** We've all called a bank, utility company, or other institution and heard that "calls may be monitored for quality assurance." The purpose of this message is simple: to tell the person outside the company that their call may be recorded or overheard. Your company policy will let employees know what to expect, but the company must also tell the other party to the phone call that the conversation may be monitored. In fact, some states allow eavesdropping only if all parties to the call consent. A monitoring announcement lets everyone on the line know that they may have a silent partner.

- **If the call is personal, get off the line.** Federal law allows monitoring for clear business purposes. However, courts have held that employers no longer have a business purpose to monitor once they realize that they are listening in on a private conversation. Whoever is listening in should stop monitoring as soon as he or she finds out that a call is personal.

- **Choose monitors carefully.** The people who actually listen to employee phone calls must be discreet and professional. Even if an employer has a solid business reason for monitoring calls, it will be on shaky legal ground if its monitors blab what they overhear to all who care to listen. Choose monitors who can keep their mouths shut, and use as few monitors as possible.

Form E: Telephone Monitoring Policy Acknowledgment

If your company decides to adopt a policy allowing it to monitor employee telephone calls, you should ask employees to sign a form acknowledging that they have read the policy and understand that their calls can be monitored.

Using an acknowledgment form helps ensure that employees actually read the policy and take steps to keep their personal calls private (for example, by making them on designated phones, on personal cell phones, or outside of work altogether). Employees who sign the form will have a very tough time arguing that their privacy was violated because they didn't know that their telephone calls could be monitored.

How to Complete This Form

Our form assumes that you have designated phones that will not be monitored for employees to use for personal calls. If you do not have such phones and you have not adopted the additional clause on designated phones in your policy, you should delete the last paragraph of the form, immediately before the signature and date lines.

If you have designated phones that will not be monitored, complete the policy by inserting the location of these phones; use the same language you used in the policy.

You can find this and all other forms (and policies) at this book's online companion page (see Appendix A for information on accessing these materials).

Telephone Monitoring Policy Acknowledgment

My signature on this form indicates that I have read the Company's telephone monitoring policy and I agree to abide by its terms. I understand that telephone calls I make or receive on Company phones are not private, and that the Company may monitor these calls at any time.

    I also understand that I may make or receive personal calls on the telephones located _____

_____ ,

and that these calls will not be monitored. I agree to abide by the Company's policy regarding personal calls.

_____   _____

Signature   Date

_____

Print Name

14:3 Cameras and Camera Phones

Today, even the most basic cell phones come with recording devices, such as cameras or video capability. While these can be great features outside of the workplace, they pose considerable challenges on the job. Employers have become increasingly concerned about employees violating their coworkers' privacy by photographing them surreptitiously at work. And employers who have visible trade secrets to protect—whether in the form of documents, devices, processes, or personnel—are understandably worried that employees might use these small recording devices to steal or transmit confidential information.

We have provided two sample policies below. Policy A allows employees to have recording devices, including cell phones with recording capabilities, in the workplace, but prohibits employees from bringing them into certain areas of the workplace. If you adopt this policy, you must complete it by listing the areas where employees may not bring their camera phones and other recording devices (for example, company restrooms, changing areas, research facilities, and so on).

Policy A also includes some commonsense rules for employees who take photographs or make recordings at work. For example, the policy clarifies that employees may not photograph or record confidential information, may not violate the privacy of others, and so on.

Policy B prohibits cameras and cell phones with recording capabilities outright. This policy might make more sense for a company that has valuable trade secrets to protect, such as a high-tech engineering company, research and development company, or manufacturing company that closely guards its production process. As you can see, this policy allows employees to ask their supervisors for permission to bring a cell phone with recording capabilities to work if their personal situation requires it. If you adopt this policy, you will have to insert the place where employees can leave their recording devices while at work (for example, with the receptionist or office manager).

⚠ CAUTION

Banning cameras may violate the National Labor Relations Act (NLRA). The National Labor Relations Board (NLRB) has struck down an employer policy prohibiting employees from taking photographs or recordings at work, finding that such a ban unduly restricts employee rights to document their working conditions, such as safety hazards. In that case, the NLRB said that the employer (a fast food restaurant) could not show that a total ban was justified. Would the NLRB rule differently

14:3 Cameras and Camera Phones

File Name: 14_Privacy.rtf

Include This Policy?
- ☐ Yes
    - *Choose one:* ☐ A ☐ B
- ☐ No
- ☐ Use our existing policy
- ☐ Other _____

Alternate Modifications
None

Alternate Modifications
None

Additional Clauses
None

Related Policies
None

Notes

_____
_____
_____
_____
_____
_____
_____
_____
_____
_____
_____
_____
_____
_____
_____
_____

if the employer had strong privacy concerns or valuable trade secrets to protect? It's up in the air for now. If you are considering a complete ban on workplace cameras (or on employee use of them at work), you should talk to an attorney.

Alternate Policy A

Camera Phones and Other Recording Devices

Employees may not bring cameras, video and audio recording devices, or digital devices (such as cell phones, MP3 players, or PDAs) that have recording capability, to any of the following areas:_____

_____ .

Guidelines for Camera and Recording Device Use

Employees who use cameras, camera phones, or other digital devices to capture photos, audio, or video on Company property or at Company events must follow these rules:

1. Employees may record or take pictures of other employees, customers, clients, or visitors only with their permission. If you intend to publicize the pictures or other recordings—for example, by posting them on the Internet, using them in a Company newsletter, or submitting them to a photography contest—you must disclose this to the subjects.

2. Employees may not record or take pictures of Company trade secrets or other confidential information. This includes, but is not limited to, [*list the most common types of trade secrets your company has, such as "customer lists," "pricing information," "recipes," "design plans," "software code," and so on*].

3. Employees may not take or use pictures or recordings to harass others. All Company policies—including the Company's policies on harassment, discrimination, and threats—apply to workplace photographs and recordings.

4. If you have any questions about whether it's appropriate to record or take a photograph at work or use a workplace photograph or recording in a particular way, please ask your supervisor.

Alternate Policy B

Camera Phones and Other Recording Devices

The use of cameras, video and audio recording devices, or digital devices (such as cell phones, MP3 players, or PDAs) that have recording capability can cause violations of privacy and breaches of confidentiality.

For that reason, we do not allow cameras, video or audio recording equipment, or cell phones or other digital devices that have these capabilities, on Company property. If you have such a device with you, you may either leave it in your car or _____ _____ .

If you believe that your personal circumstances require you to have your cell phone at work, and your cell phone has a camera or other recording capability, please talk to your supervisor.

Computers, Email, and the Internet

Computers can be an employer's best friend or worst nightmare. On the one hand, computers can improve efficiency, allow employees to communicate with one another across great distances, and provide access to the vast ocean of information that is the World Wide Web. On the other hand, computers also give employees the opportunity to spend their days sending harassing or threatening email, downloading pornographic images or pirated software, and shopping online.

So how does a savvy employer get the benefits without the downside? By adopting comprehensive policies that govern how employees may use computer equipment, including email, Internet access, and software. In this chapter, we show you how to create policies that tell employees how the company expects them to use its computer equipment and that will allow management to read email and monitor Internet traffic, to make sure that employees follow the rules. We also provide policy language dealing with something employees might do on their own computers that could have a significant impact on the company: blogging, social networking, and other online posts.

15:1 Email
File Name: 15_Computers.rtf

Include This Policy?
- ☐ Yes
- ☐ No
- ☐ Use our existing policy
- ☐ Other _____

Additional Clauses
Monitoring
   Insert?:   ☐ Yes   ☐ No
Email Rules and Style
   Insert?:   ☐ Yes   ☐ No

Related Policies
Chapter 14 explains privacy issues in detail.

Notes

_____
_____
_____
_____
_____
_____
_____
_____
_____
_____
_____
_____
_____
_____
_____
_____
_____

15:1 Email

Any company that makes electronic communications equipment available to employees is asking for trouble if it doesn't have a policy explaining the company's rules for email use and allowing the company to monitor messages sent on that equipment. Even an employer that has never read employee email and doesn't plan to set up a regular system of monitoring should protect its right to do so. If your company is ever faced with a problem involving employee email—an employee who sends sexually explicit images, proselytizes other employees to join a religious group, transmits trade secrets to a competitor, or gets involved in a "flame war" with a client, for example—a company official will have to read the messages involved to figure out what to do. If your company doesn't have a policy warning employees that the company can read their messages at any time, an employee might sue for violation of privacy.

Your email policy should tell employees what the company considers proper use of its email system, reserve the company's right to read employee email at any time, and establish a schedule for purging the email system.

CAUTION
Make sure employees know that their computer use is not private. Perhaps the most important goal of computer policies is to reserve the company's right to monitor employee communications when necessary. The policies must tell employees that they should not expect their email or Internet use to be private.

Email

Use of the Email System

The email system is intended for official Company business. Although you may use the email system occasionally for personal messages, you may do so during nonwork hours only.

Email Is Not Private

Email messages, including attachments, sent and received on Company equipment are the property of the Company. We reserve the right to access, monitor, read, and/or copy email messages at any time, for any reason. You should not expect privacy for any email you send using Company equipment, including messages that you consider to be personal or label with a designation such as "Personal" or "Private."

All Conduct Rules Apply to Email

All of our policies and rules of conduct apply to employee use of the email system. This means, for example, that you may not use the email system to send harassing or discriminatory messages, including messages with explicit sexual content or pornographic images; to send threatening messages; or to reveal company trade secrets.

Email Security

To avoid email viruses and other threats, employees should not open email attachments or click on links in email from people and businesses they don't recognize, particularly if the email appears to have been forwarded multiple times or has a nonexistent or peculiar subject heading. Even if you know the sender, do not open an email attachment or click a link that has a strange name or is not referenced in the body of the email. It may have been transmitted automatically, without the sender's knowledge.

If you believe your computer has been infected by a virus, worm, or other security threat to the Company's system, you must inform the IT department immediately.

Employees may not share their email passwords with anyone, including coworkers or family members. Revealing passwords to the Company's email system could allow an outsider to access the Company's network.

Retaining and Deleting Email Messages

Because email messages are electronic records, certain messages must be retained for compliance purposes. Please refer to our record-keeping policy for guidance on which records must be kept, and for how long. If you have any questions about whether and how to retain a particular email message, please ask your manager.

Because of the large volume of emails our Company sends and receives each day, we discourage employees from storing large numbers of email messages that are not subject to the retention rules explained above. Please make a regular practice of deleting email messages once you have read and/or responded to them. If you need to save a particular message, you may print out a paper copy, archive the email, or save it on your hard drive or disk. The Company will purge email messages that have not been archived after _____ days.

The Company may have occasion to suspend our usual rules about deleting email messages (for example, if the company is involved in a lawsuit requiring it to preserve evidence). If this happens, employees will be notified of the procedures to follow to save email messages. Failing to comply with such a notice could subject the company to serious legal consequences, and will result in discipline, up to and including termination.

Violations

Any employee who violates this policy can be subject to discipline, up to and including termination.

How to Complete This Policy

Many email policies provide that messages will be purged every 60 to 90 days. (For more on the importance of purging email, see "Reality Check: Don't Fight the Urge to Purge Email," below.) Select a time period that makes sense for your company, given its rate of email traffic, the capacities of the system, and how quickly employees read (and respond to) their email.

Reality Check: Don't Fight the Urge to Purge Email

There are two very good reasons to purge your company's email system by deleting older messages regularly. First, if employees don't delete messages, the company will eventually have a storage problem on its hands. Many employees simply don't get around to deleting old messages, no matter what the company's policy asks them to do. If your company has a lot of email traffic, the system's capacity to store information will be overwhelmed unless it is cleaned out periodically.

Second, purging emails can reduce your company's legal liability and its legal obligations if it faces a lawsuit. In many kinds of business lawsuits, including lawsuits brought by employees, customers, or other businesses, email becomes evidence. Realizing this, lawyers who sue businesses routinely ask for months, or even years, of the company's email messages in "discovery," the legal process by which parties to a lawsuit gather documents and information from each other and from third parties. Although courts often put limits on what companies have to hand over (for example, they may require a company to disclose only emails on a certain subject matter or emails for a limited time period), businesses that don't purge regularly can spend a lot of time trying to pull together the requested documents.

Once the company learns that it is (or might soon be) facing a lawsuit, however, the rules change. The company has a legal duty to preserve all evidence that might be relevant to the case. If this happens at your company, you'll have to override your usual purge rules and make sure you hang on to every relevant document.

CAUTION

Banning personal use of email is legally risky. Some employers don't want employees using the company email system for personal messages under any circumstances. Although such a policy might seem reasonable, it's fraught with legal risk. Because these bans are often violated, they are seldom enforced. Inconsistent enforcement can lead to legal claims (for retaliation or discrimination, for example) by employees who believe they were unfairly singled out for discipline. And, the NLRB has recently found that employers may not prohibit employees from using the company email system, during nonwork hours, to discuss the terms and conditions of their employment, unless such a ban is necessary to maintain productivity or discipline. For these reasons, you should talk to an attorney if you are considering banning personal use of the company's email system.

Additional Clause on Monitoring

Your email policy absolutely must inform employees that their messages are not private and must reserve the company's right to monitor and read messages at any time, as our policy does.

If the company has monitoring software it plans to use, or if someone will be assigned to read employee email on a regular basis, you should add language to the policy to let employees know. After all, the purpose of an email policy is not only to allow the company to read those problematic messages after they've been sent, but also to deter employees from sending them in the first place. Telling employees that their messages will be monitored and/or read will almost certainly help accomplish this second goal.

Whether your company should regularly monitor employee email is a tough issue to sort through. Doing so will force employees to take the email policy seriously and thereby make them less likely to send messages that are harassing, threatening, or otherwise in violation of your policy. It's just human nature: We aren't as quick to break the rules if we think we will get caught.

But there are some serious downsides as well, with employee dissatisfaction topping the list. Employees don't want to feel like the company doesn't trust them or plans to check up on their every keystroke. Monitoring also costs time and money: The company will have to invest in monitoring software and assign someone the task of actually reviewing or reading messages. And some employers just find monitoring distasteful. They don't want to be cast in the role of Big Brother.

Ultimately, the company's philosophy, workforce, and needs will determine whether the benefits of monitoring outweigh the disadvantages. If your company has no immediate plans to monitor or read employee email, you need not add monitoring language. The provision on privacy that's already in the policy is sufficient.

However, if your company plans to regularly monitor messages, you should add that information to your policy at the end of the "Email Is Not Private" provision. The exact language of your policy will depend on how you will monitor. Here are some sample policy provisions to consider:

SAMPLE POLICY LANGUAGE FOR MONITORING THAT FLAGS KEYWORDS

In addition, the Company's software automatically searches the messages you send for questionable content, including sexual or racial comments, threats, trade secrets, competitive information, and curse words. Any message deemed questionable will be forwarded to, and read by, Company management.

SAMPLE POLICY LANGUAGE FOR RANDOM MONITORING

In addition, the Company will select and read employee messages at random to ensure that employees are in compliance with this policy.

SAMPLE POLICY LANGUAGE FOR "KEYLOGGER" MONITORING

In addition, the Company's monitoring software automatically creates a copy of every message you draft, even if you never send it. Company personnel will regularly read these copies to make sure that no employee violates this policy.

Additional Clause on Email Rules and Style

You can include as much—or as little—in the policy about appropriate use of the email system as you wish. However, you should tell employees that their email messages are subject to the same rules (no harassment, no threats, and so on) that apply to their workplace behavior in general. You can make a general statement to this effect or go into more detail, listing the types of misconduct to which email is particularly susceptible.

Some employers include email-writing guidelines in their policies. Because email is seen as an informal medium, some workers send out even work-related messages sprinkled with emoticons (smiley faces or other symbols) and exclamation points, written in all lower- or uppercase letters, or filled with acronyms or usages peculiar to the online world. What's worse, some workers send out email without considering its content or style, then later regret having expressed anger too hastily or sent a message that doesn't look professional.

The standard email policy provided includes a general statement about proper email use. If your company is concerned about usage and "netiquette" problems, however, you can include more explicit instructions on the proper use of email.

Additional Clause

Guidelines for Email Writing

1. Always spell-check or proofread your business email messages. Email is official Company correspondence. Spelling errors in email are all too common, and they look sloppy and unprofessional.

2. Use lowercase and capital letters in the same way that you would in a letter. Using all capital letters is the email equivalent of shouting at someone; it can also be hard on the eyes. Failing to use capital letters at all (to begin a sentence or a formal noun) can confuse your reader and seem overly cute. Unless you are writing poetry, use standard capitalization.

3. Remember your audience. Although email encourages informal communication, that might not be the most appropriate style to use if you are addressing the CEO of an important customer. And, remember that your email can be forwarded to unintended recipients, some of whom may not appreciate joking comments or informalities.

4. Don't use email for confidential matters. Again, remember the unintended recipient. Your email might be forwarded to someone you didn't anticipate or might be sitting on a printer for all to see. If you need to have a confidential discussion, do it in person or over the phone.

5. Send messages sparingly. There is rarely a need to copy everyone in the Company on an email. Carefully consider who really needs to see the message, and address it accordingly.

6. Don't leave the subject line blank. Always include a brief description so readers will know what your email is about at a glance. This makes it easier for all of us to manage our email, and makes it more likely that you will receive a response to your message.

7. Don't overuse the "urgent" tag. Mark a message as urgent only if it is truly important and must be answered right away.

15:2 Using the Internet

If your company offers employees Internet access, you should have a policy telling them what uses of the Internet the company considers appropriate. Without such a policy, an employer runs the practical risk that its employees will spend work time surfing the Web, shopping online, exchanging instant messages with friends both near and far, and perhaps unwittingly downloading viruses that will crash the company's computer system. An employer also runs the legal risk that employees will use its Internet access to engage in illegal behavior, such as pirating software or viewing pornographic images that create a hostile work environment (and therefore a potential sexual harassment problem).

Your Internet policy should describe proper uses of the Internet and tell employees which sites are off limits. If your company uses software that makes a record of sites an employee visits, you should include that information in your policy as well.

15:2 Using the Internet

File Name: 15_Computers.rtf

Include This Policy?
- ☐ Yes
- ☐ No
- ☐ Use our existing policy
- ☐ Other _____

Alternate Modifications

Privacy of Internet Use
Choose one: ☐ A ☐ B

Personal Email Accounts
Choose one: ☐ A ☐ B

Additional Clauses

None

Related Policies

None

Notes

Using the Internet

Personal Use of the Internet

Our network and Internet access are for official Company business. Employees may access the Internet for personal use only outside of work hours and only in accordance with the other terms of this policy. An employee who engages in excessive Internet use, even during nonwork hours, may be subject to discipline.

Prohibited Uses of the Internet

Employees may not, at any time, access the Internet using Company equipment for any of the following purposes:

- to view websites that offer pornography, gambling, or violent imagery, or are otherwise inappropriate in the workplace
- to operate an outside business, online auction, or other sales site; solicit money for personal purposes; or otherwise act for personal financial gain or profit
- to download or copy software, games, text, photos, or any other works in violation of copyright, trademark, or other laws
- to stream, run, or download any non-company-licensed software program without the express consent of the IT department
- to stream, run, or download music, video, games, widgets, or any form of multimedia, from the Internet, or
- to read, open, or download any file from the Internet without first screening that file for viruses using the company's virus detection software.

If you believe that your job may require you to do something that would otherwise be forbidden by this policy, ask your manager how to proceed.

No Personal Posts Using Company Equipment

Employees may not use the Company's equipment to transmit their personal opinions by, for example, posting a comment to a blog or social networking page or contributing to an online forum. Even if you don't identify yourself as a Company employee, your use of Company equipment could cause your opinion to be mistaken for the Company's view.

How to Complete This Policy

This policy leaves you a space to designate someone authorized to approve software downloads. The purpose of this provision is to keep the company out of trouble for unauthorized use of copyrighted software, otherwise known as software "piracy." If someone in your company has to approve downloads ahead of time, that person will help prevent employees from unwittingly violating someone else's copyright or license.

For companies with computer specialists or dedicated technical help, simply fill in the position of the appropriate person (for example, the systems operator). If yours is a smaller company, don't worry; you don't need to have a highly paid technical army on staff to enforce this provision. If an employee oversees your company's computer system, that person should be able to figure out which software can be downloaded freely (and which can't). If your company uses an outside consultant to provide technical support, you can simply name a company official, who can pass questions on to the consultant and let employees know what to do. In either case, name the position to which employees should bring their questions (for example, "the IT director").

Alternate Modifications on Privacy of Internet Use

As you did in your email policy, you must inform employees that their Internet use is not private. Even if you don't currently monitor employee Internet use, you may one day have to do so (if, for example, an employee is accused of viewing pornography online). We offer you two modifications, of which you should choose one. Alternate Modification A is for employers who want to reserve the right to monitor employee Internet activity. Alternate Modification B is for employers who are already monitoring. Insert either modification at the end of the policy.

Alternate Modification A

Internet Use Is Not Private

We reserve the right to monitor employee use of the Internet at any time. You should not expect that your use of the Internet—including but not limited to the sites you visit, the amount of time you spend online, and the communications you have—will be private.

Alternate Modification B

> ### Internet Use Is Not Private
>
> Our Company uses monitoring software that, among other things, tracks the sites an employee visits and how much time is spent at a particular site. You should not expect that your use of the Internet—including but not limited to the sites you visit, the amount of time you spend online, and the communications you have—will be private.

Alternate Modification on Personal Web-Based Email

Although most companies have policies that address use of the company's email system (such as Policy 15:1), many companies have no policy regarding employees' accessing their personal email accounts from work. At first blush, it might seem like overkill to limit an employee's ability to check a personal email account from work. After all, if the company doesn't want employees to send a lot of personal messages on its own system, shouldn't it allow them to access their own accounts, at least during breaks and lunch?

Unfortunately, it's not that simple. Personal email accounts, such as those available from Gmail, Hotmail, Yahoo!, and Comcast, are Web based. When an employee accesses this type of account from work, messages sent and received bypass the employer's security system. This means bad things—such as viruses, Trojan horses, and spyware—can get in, and good things—like trade secrets—can get out, and the company will never know about it.

Even employees with the best intentions can create huge problems for a company via their personal email accounts. Take, for example, the common practice of employees sending work-related documents or messages to their personal email address. Most employees who do this are simply trying to make it easier to work from home; some are trying to get around an employer system that allows them to save only a limited number of messages by keeping those messages in their personal account. And still other employees automatically forward messages they receive at work to their personal account, to make sure they can access their email while traveling for business.

But these practices can prove very harmful. Those work documents and messages are stored not on the company's servers but on the Internet, where they could be accessed by people outside the company. What if the employee's ISP automatically scans messages to send targeted advertising? What if someone hacks into the ISP's server? What if the employee's laptop is stolen, with a saved password that allows the thief easy access to the employee's Web-based account? This is especially problematic if the forwarded information is something the employer has an obligation to keep private, such as medical records, customer information, or company trade secrets.

Allowing employees to transact business using their personal email accounts also means that some of the company's business records are no longer under its control. The company might not even know about key negotiations, discussions, and deals that are carried out on personal email. It won't have access to those records if it needs to recreate contract talks, review an employee's personnel file, or respond to a subpoena.

For all of these reasons, all companies should prohibit employees from using their personal email accounts to transact company business, as both of our modifications do, below. Companies that are concerned enough about the security risks that they have decided to ban employee access to personal email accounts from work should use Alternate Modification A. Alternate Modification B allows employees to access their accounts, but imposes some limits. In either case, insert the modification at the end of the policy.

Alternate Modification A

Don't Use Personal Email Accounts for Work

Employees may not use their own personal email accounts to transact Company business. This includes storing work-related documents and email messages in your personal email account, sending work to your personal email account, engaging in work-related communications (with customers, clients, or coworkers, for example) using your personal email account, or "bouncing" messages from your Company email to your personal email when you are out of the office.

Although employees may find these practices convenient, they can create significant security problems, expose confidential Company information, and compromise the Company's record-keeping obligations. If you work off site (for example, at home or on business travel), please contact the IT department to find out how to safely transmit and protect Company information.

No Access to Personal Email

Accessing your personal email account from work creates security risks for the Company's computer system and network. Therefore, employees may not use Company equipment to access their personal email accounts.

Alternate Modification B

Don't Use Personal Email Accounts for Work

Employees may not use their own personal email accounts to transact Company business. This includes storing work-related documents and email messages in your personal email account, sending work to your personal email account, engaging in work-related communications (with customers, clients, or coworkers, for example) using your personal email account, or "bouncing" messages from your Company email to your personal email when you are out of the office.

Although employees may find these practices convenient, they can create significant security problems, expose confidential Company information, and compromise the Company's record-keeping obligations. If you work off site (for example, at home or on business travel), please contact the IT department to find out how to safely transmit and protect Company information.

Rules for Accessing Personal Email

Accessing your personal email account from work creates security risks for the Company's computer system and network. To help control these risks, you must follow these rules when using Company equipment to access your personal email:

- You may access your personal email account during nonwork hours only.
- Do not open any personal email messages from an unknown sender. Personal email is subject only to the security controls imposed by your provider, which may be less strict than the Company's. If a personal message contains a virus or other malware, it could infect the Company's network.
- Before you open any attachment, you must scan it for viruses using the Company's antivirus software.
- You may not transact Company business using your personal email account, nor may you transmit any Company documents using your personal email account.

Form F: Email and Internet Policy Acknowledgment Form

If your company adopts an email and/or Internet policy that allows the company to monitor, you should ask employees to sign a form acknowledging that they have read the policy and agree to abide by its terms. (You can find this and all other forms at this book's online companion page; see Appendix A for information on accessing these materials.)

Currently, at least one state (Delaware) requires employers to get a signed acknowledgment form from their employees before monitoring their employees' Internet or email use. (Employers who don't get a signed form must give daily electronic notice that they are monitoring for every day an employee accesses the employer's email or Internet access system.) Other states are considering legislation that would impose a similar requirement. If your company does business in a state with this type of law, you must use this acknowledgment form.

Even if your state doesn't require an employee's signed acknowledgment, however, it's a good idea to use this form. Having to sign a form draws an employee's attention to the policy, which not only makes the employee more likely to comply with the policy but also takes away the employee's ability to argue, later, that he or she was unaware of it.

How to Complete This Form

You will have to modify this form depending on whether you have adopted an email policy, an Internet policy, or both. For example, if you've adopted an email policy but have chosen not to adopt a policy that allows the company to monitor Internet traffic, be sure to modify the form to delete the language referring to Internet monitoring. If, on the other hand, you have adopted a policy to monitor Internet traffic but not email use, you will need to modify the form to delete the language referring to email policies. Online, you'll find three different versions of this form from which you can choose, depending on your company's policies.

Email and Internet Policy Acknowledgment

My signature on this form indicates that I have read the Company's email and Internet policies and I agree to abide by their terms. I understand that any email messages I send or receive using Company equipment are not private, and that the Company may access, monitor, read, and/or copy those messages at any time, for any reason. I also understand that the Company reserves the right to monitor my Internet use, and that such monitoring may occur at any time, for any reason.

_____   _____
Signature   Date

_____
Print Name

BYOD, CYOD, or COPE?

Just a couple of years ago, a big trend in workplace technology was BYOD (bring your own device): allowing employees to use their own mobile devices for both business and pleasure. Previously, BYOD was almost nonexistent. Companies were advised to ban employees from using their own devices (which were then primarily phones and personal digital assistants, or PDAs) for work. Companies issued work phones or corporate BlackBerrys to employees who needed them, and that was that.

But employees love their personal devices, especially their iPhones. Companies reported increased demands by employees to use the devices they like and feel comfortable with for work purposes, rather than having to double up on their devices and phone numbers and abandon their favorite apps and platforms.

Today, some employers are thinking twice or even abandoning BYOD programs. Personal devices don't all have the features companies need to protect their confidential information, access business communications and documents from employer equipment, and adequately enforce company policies. If an employee loses a BYO device, can the company wipe it remotely (and without destroying the employee's photo collection, text history, and contact list)? If the employee is accused of using a BYO personal device to harass a coworker, how will a court weigh the competing privacy rights if the company wants to inspect the employee's phone?

A lot of the legal issues and practical effects associated with BYOD are still emerging, as are the mobile management solutions that allow companies to protect their data. As a result, many companies have turned instead to CYOD (choose your own device) and COPE (company-owned, personally enabled) policies, in which the company provides the device and the employee has the ability to use it for both business and pleasure. These solutions solve the problems of device choice and duplication, while giving the company more control over its data and intellectual property.

Because there is such variety in the types of policies you might adopt here, and because the law is still developing in this area, employers that want a BYOD, CYOD, or COPE policy should ask a lawyer to draft it for them.

15:3 Software Use

File Name: 15_Computers.rtf

Include This Policy?
- [ ] Yes
- [ ] No
- [ ] Use our existing policy
- [ ] Other _____

Alternate Modifications

None

Additional Clauses

None

Related Policies

None

Notes

_____
_____
_____
_____
_____
_____
_____
_____
_____
_____
_____
_____
_____
_____
_____
_____
_____
_____
_____

15:3 Software Use

The purpose of a software policy is to prevent employees from using company software in violation of its licensing agreements and to make sure that employees don't download pirated software from the Internet. If employees violate the terms of a software license agreement that the company is party to, the company will be on the hook. Illegal software copying and use is so common that many employees don't even know it's illegal. An employee might think it's perfectly fine to make a copy of company software to install on a home computer as long as that computer is used for work, for example. But software licenses typically authorize only a single user, at a single computer. Adopting a software use policy will let employees know the rules.

This policy also tells employees that the company will conduct periodic audits of its computer equipment to monitor compliance with the software policy. This language lets employees know that the company is serious about enforcing the policy. It also puts employees on notice that the company reserves the right to inspect their computers.

Software Use

It is our Company's policy to use licensed software only in accordance with the terms of its license agreement. Violating a license agreement is not only unethical: It is also illegal and can subject the Company to criminal prosecution and substantial monetary penalties.

To help us adhere to this policy, employees may not do any of the following without permission from _____

_____ :

- copy any Company software program, for any reason
- install a Company software program on a home computer
- install a personal software program (that is, software owned by the employee) on any Company computer, or
- download any software program from the Internet to a Company computer.

The Company may audit Company-owned computers at any time to ensure compliance with this policy.

How to Complete This Policy

We've left you a space to designate someone authorized to approve any deviations from the policy. Choose the same person or position that you designated to approve software downloads in your Internet Policy, above.

15:4 Online Posting

Chances are very good that many of your company's employees are posting personal content on the Internet. They may be posting at their own blog or website, or they may be posting at social networking or community sites: uploading photos to a Facebook page, adding comments to other websites, sending out Tweets, or exchanging parenting advice or recipes in a chat room.

Some employers are understandably wary about trying to "crack down" on personal posts. After all, personal posts are often a creative outlet, a way for friends and people with similar interests to stay in touch, a place to share opinions and be part of a larger community. They are, in a word, personal, and few employers really want to snoop through their employees' personal writings. What's more, some employers have found that an employee who likes the company and has a popular blog can actually boost the company's reputation.

Unfortunately, however, not all employees like their jobs. An employee post that reveals company trade secrets, slams a company product that's about to be released, or threatens or harasses other employees can also be an unmitigated disaster for the company.

As an employer, you have the right to control what employees do with the time and equipment you pay for, generally speaking. But when employees use their own computers to express their own opinions on their own time, your rights are much more limited. For example, many states have laws that prohibit employers from taking action against employees for legal activities they pursue in their off-duty hours. And, state law may prohibit employers from taking action against an employee based on his or her political views. In addition to these state rules, federal law prohibits employers from taking action against employees for communicating with each other about the terms and conditions of their employment, or about forming a union. All of these topics might conceivably be covered in an employee's personal post.

If you decide to adopt a personal posting policy, you should explain that employees may not make personal posts during work time or using work equipment, and lay down some general ground rules on content relating to the company.

If your company sells its products on sites that allow users to comment or review the products (like Amazon), appears on online review sites (such as Yelp), or is discussed in user boards, blogs, and/ or social networking sites, you also need to make sure that employees always identify themselves—and their relationship to the company— if they post content or reviews of your company's products. The Federal Trade Commission (FTC), the federal government agency

15:4 Personal Blogs and Posts
File Name: 15_Computers.rtf

Include This Policy?
☐ Yes
☐ No
☐ Use our existing policy
☐ Other _____

Alternate Modifications
None

Additional Clauses
None

Related Policies
None

Notes

that regulates deceptive advertising and other consumer protection matters, recently issued regulations governing endorsements and testimonials about products, including statements that appear online. The purpose of these rules is to make sure consumers fully understand the relationship between the person making the endorsement and the product, so they can make informed decisions about how much weight to give the endorser's statement.

The FTC has said that an employment relationship is the type of connection that a consumer would want to know about in evaluating product endorsements. So, your policy must tell employees that if they post reviews or other types of statements about company products, they must be up front about their relationship to the company.

CAUTION

Make sure your policy will pass muster with the National Labor Relations Board (NLRB). In recent months, the NLRB has come down hard on employers with social media policies that might restrict discussion of working conditions. Policy language that many companies have used for years has been struck down as too likely to lead employees to believe that they may not criticize the company's policies and practices online, in violation of the right employees have to freely discuss working conditions with each other. The Board has objected to policies that prohibit disparagement or criticism of others; policies that require employees not to post "confidential" or "nonpublic" information (unless the policy illustrates the types of information covered, so as not to dissuade employees from discussing wages or other terms of employment); policies that require employees to avoid picking fights or discussing topics that are objectionable or inflammatory; and policies that require employees to check with a supervisor before posting. This is a rapidly changing area of law, so check your social media policy with a lawyer to make sure it complies with the most recent legal decisions.

Personal Blogs and Online Posts

Our Company recognizes that some of our employees may choose to express themselves by posting personal information on the Internet through personal websites, social media, blogs, or chat rooms, by uploading content, or by making comments at other websites or blogs. We value our employees' creativity and honor your interest in engaging in these forms of personal expression on your own time, should you choose to do so.

However, problems can arise when a personal posting identifies or appears to be associated with our Company, or when a personal posting is used in ways that violate the Company's rights or the rights of other employees.

No Posting Using Company Resources

You may not use Company resources to create or maintain a personal blog, personal website, or personal page on a social networking site, or to upload content or make personal postings online, nor may you do so on Company time.

Guidelines for Online Posting

You are legally responsible for content you post to the Internet, in a blog, social media site, or otherwise. You can be held personally liable for defaming others, revealing trade secrets, and copyright infringement, among other things.

All of our Company policies apply to anything you write in a personal blog, post to the Internet, or upload to the Internet. This means, for example, that you may not use personal postings to harass or threaten other employees or reveal Company trade secrets or confidential information, such as internal reports or confidential company communications.

If, in the process of making a personal post or upload on the Internet, you identify yourself as an employee of our Company, whether by explicit statement or by implication, you must clearly state that the views expressed in your post, or at your blog, social media page, or website, are your own, and do not reflect the views of the Company.

You may not use the Company's trademarks, logos, copyrighted material, branding, or other intellectual property in a way that violates intellectual property law.

The company may have a legal duty not to disclose certain facts, such as information on stock offerings. Employees must follow the law and refrain from making any prohibited financial disclosures.

Promoting the Company or Its Products or Services

Do not engage in covert marketing or endorsements for the Company or its products or services. If you post anything about the Company, you must identify yourself as a Company employee. You are legally required to identify your employment relationship if it might be relevant to a consumer's decision to patronize our company or if your failure to do so could be misleading to readers. This means, for example, that employees may not post anonymous online reviews of Company products or promotional statements about the Company in which they fail to identify themselves as employees.

You must also identify yourself as an employee in your online post if you endorse or review Company products or services on social media. It is not enough to identify the Company as your employer in your profile page, for example.

Interacting Online With Colleagues

The Company does not tolerate conduct or communications toward work colleagues that violate company policies—such as sexual harassment, bullying, or threats—whether they take place online or off.

Employee Records

If you are like many employers, you keep all of the records pertaining to an employee in one place: a manila folder in a file cabinet labeled "personnel files." Typically, these files contain documents such as the employee's job application and résumé, letters of reference, offer letter, IRS W-4 Form, records of performance and discipline, emergency contacts, benefit forms, signed handbook acknowledgment, and so on.

Prudent employers keep these files under lock and key (and the electronic versions behind a firewall). After all, personnel records contain highly sensitive, personal information. Sometimes, however, it is appropriate for an employee, manager, or supervisor to review some or all of the file's contents.

The records section of your handbook should inform employees that you maintain personnel files, explain that the files are confidential, and indicate whether—and under what circumstances—employees and others can inspect them.

16:1 Your Personnel File

File Name: 16_Records.rtf

Include This Policy?

☐ Yes

☐ No

☐ Use our existing policy

☐ Other _____

Alternate Modifications

None

Additional Clauses

None

Related Policies

None

Notes

_____
_____
_____
_____
_____
_____
_____
_____
_____
_____
_____
_____
_____
_____
_____
_____
_____
_____

16:1 Personnel Records

Your personnel file policy should start with some general information to lay the foundation for the policies to come, particularly, the policy requiring employees to notify you of changes to personal information and the policy alerting employees of their right to inspect personnel records. After all, employees can understand their rights and obligations regarding personnel records only if they know about the records in the first place.

The following policy notifies employees that you maintain personnel files, and it gives employees an idea of what records you do—and do not—keep in the file.

Your Personnel File

This Company maintains a personnel file on each employee. The purpose of this file is to allow us to make decisions and take actions that are personally important to you, including notifying your family in case of an emergency, calculating income tax deductions and withholdings, and paying for appropriate insurance coverage.

Although we cannot list here all of the types of documents that we keep in your personnel file, examples include: _____

_____ .

We do not keep medical records or work eligibility forms in your personnel file. Those are kept separately. To find out more about those types of records, see Section _____ and Section _____, respectively, of this Handbook.

Your personnel file is physically kept by _____

_____ .

If you have any questions about your personnel file, contact

_____

16:2 Confidentiality

An employer always should treat employee personnel records as private. To do otherwise is to risk embarrassment for the employee and a lawsuit for the company. Employees need to feel confident that their personal information won't become public knowledge just because it is in a file. Otherwise, employees might be reticent to provide personal information.

The need for confidentiality must sometimes give way to other considerations, however. For example, an employee's supervisor might want to look at the employee's résumé when it becomes clear that the employee is not able to do his or her job. Or an office manager might need an employee's emergency contact information if the employee becomes incapacitated at work. You want a confidentiality policy that gives you the flexibility to reveal information in the file to people in the organization who need to know it.

The following policy gives the confidentiality assurance employees need while keeping things flexible.

Confidentiality of Personnel Files

Because the information in your personnel file is by its nature personal, we keep the file as confidential as possible. We allow access to your file only on a need-to-know basis.

16:2 Confidentiality of Personnel Files

File Name: 16_Records.rtf

Include This Policy?
- ☐ Yes
- ☐ No
- ☐ Use our existing policy
- ☐ Other _____

Alternate Modifications
None

Additional Clauses
None

Related Policies
None

Notes

**16:3 Please Notify Us If Your
Information Changes**

File Name: 16_Records.rtf

Include This Policy?
- ☐ Yes
- ☐ No
- ☐ Use our existing policy
- ☐ Other _____

Alternate Modifications

None

Additional Clauses

None

Related Policies

None

Notes

_____
_____
_____
_____
_____
_____
_____
_____
_____
_____
_____
_____
_____
_____
_____
_____
_____
_____
_____
_____
_____
_____

16:3 Changes in Personal Information

Personnel records are only as good as the information that's in them. Take good care to keep the information up to date. Obviously, the employee is in the best position to keep the records from becoming stale. As things happen in their personal lives, however, it may not occur to employees to let their employer know of the changes, which could have implications at work.

For example, the boss may not be the first person an employee thinks to tell when the employee's spouse files for divorce. If the employee is badly injured at work, however, and the office manager calls the soon-to-be-ex spouse (who is still listed as an emergency contact), the situation could turn awkward at best and medically dangerous at worst.

This policy reminds employees of the importance of keeping your company posted about certain changes in their personal information.

Please Notify Us If Your Information Changes

Because we use the information in your personnel file to take actions on your behalf, it is important that the information in that file be accurate. Please notify _____ _____ whenever any of the following changes:

- your name
- your mailing address
- your phone number
- your dependents
- the number of dependents you are designating for income tax withholding
- your marital status
- the name and phone number of the individual whom we should notify in case of an emergency, or
- restrictions on your driver's license.

16:4 Inspection of Personnel Records

Although many employers would rather not have employees inspecting their own personnel records, state laws may require that employees be granted access. These laws vary greatly in the details. In some states, employees may review their files only at specified hours. In other states, only past employees, not current employees, have the right to inspect their files.

Typically, these laws state who can inspect, when they can inspect, whether they have to give notice, whether they can photocopy their file, and whether they have to pay for the copies. To find out about your state's law, refer to "State Laws on Access to Personnel Records" at the end of this chapter. You can also check with your state labor department. (See Appendix B for contact information.)

Because the laws vary so much, we cannot provide a standard policy for you to use. The following is an example of what your policy might look like.

SAMPLE POLICY LANGUAGE

Current employees who want to inspect their personnel files must make an appointment with the Human Resources Department. Appointments will typically take place Monday through Friday between 1 p.m. and 5 p.m. Although we will make every effort to give employees an appointment quickly, it may take up to 48 hours. If an employee would like a representative to view his or her file, the employee must make the request in writing.

Former employees who would like to inspect their files must make a written request to do so. Upon receiving the written request, the Human Resources Department will call the former employee to schedule an appointment.

We do not allow current or former employees to photocopy their file. If you would like a copy of a document in the file, the Human Resources Department will copy it for you at a price of 10¢ per page.

If you have any questions about this policy, please contact the Human Resources Manager.

Drafting Your Own Policy

When drafting your own policy on employee access to personnel records, be sure to check your state's law so that you don't create a policy that is contrary to legal requirements. A typical inspection policy will state:

16:4 Inspecting Your Records

File Name: 16_Records.rtf

Include This Policy?
- ☐ Yes
- ☐ No
- ☐ Use our existing policy
- ☐ Other _____

Alternate Modifications
None

Additional Clauses
None

Related Policies
None

Notes

_____
_____
_____
_____
_____
_____
_____
_____
_____
_____
_____
_____
_____
_____
_____
_____
_____
_____

- who can inspect the file (current employees, former employees, designated representatives, and so on)
- when they can inspect the file
- where they can inspect the file
- whether they need to make a request
- whether their request must be in writing
- whether they can photocopy the file, and
- how much you will charge for photocopying.

16:5 Work Eligibility Records

Federal law requires employers to make sure their employees are legally authorized to work in the United States. As part of this process, the employer has to complete a form issued by a federal agency, the United States Citizenship and Immigration Services ("USCIS"), called Form I-9. Employers should not keep Form I-9 or other work eligibility forms in employee personnel files. The USCIS is entitled to inspect these forms. If the forms are kept in a worker's personnel file, the USCIS will be able to see all the other documents in the file as well. Not only does this compromise a worker's privacy, but it could also open the company up to additional questions and investigation.

The following policy reassures employees that their work status records will not be kept in their personnel files.

Work Eligibility Records

In compliance with federal law, all newly hired employees must present proof that they are legally eligible to work in the United States. We must keep records related to that proof, including a copy of the USCIS Form I-9 that each employee completes for us.

Those forms are kept as confidential as possible. We do not keep them in your personnel file.

If you would like more information about your I-9 Form, see Section _____ of this Handbook or contact _____

_____ .

16:5 Work Eligibility Records

File Name: 16_Records.rtf

Include This Policy?
☐ Yes
☐ No
☐ Use our existing policy
☐ Other _____

Alternate Modifications
None

Additional Clauses
None

Related Policies
4:3   Proof of Work Eligibility

Notes

16:6 Medical Records

File Name: 16_Records.rtf

Include This Policy?
- ☐ Yes
- ☐ No
- ☐ Use our existing policy
- ☐ Other _____

Alternate Modifications

None

Additional Clauses

None

Related Policies

None

Notes

_____
_____
_____
_____
_____
_____
_____
_____
_____
_____
_____
_____
_____
_____
_____
_____
_____
_____
_____
_____

16:6 Medical Records

Employers come into possession of worker medical records for a variety of reasons. Perhaps a worker has requested an accommodation for a disability and has presented your company with a medical evaluation verifying the disability. Or maybe a worker has requested medical leave and has given your company documentation to show the seriousness of the medical condition.

Medical records should not go into a worker's personnel file. The federal Americans with Disabilities Act includes strict rules on how to handle records relating to an employee's disability: Medical information must be kept separate from nonmedical records, and medical files must be stored in a locked cabinet. Your state might have a similar, or perhaps even stricter, law requiring confidential handling of employee medical records. Whether your state's law goes beyond the federal requirements or not, it's a good practice to keep all medical records confidential and in a separate, locked file cabinet.

The following standard policy informs employees that their medical records will be kept separate from their personnel files.

Medical Records

Employee medical records, including but not limited to workers' compensation information, medical certifications and authorizations, and information pertaining to disabilities and accommodations, are not kept in an employee's regular personnel file. Instead, we keep each employee's medical records in a separate, confidential file. We make these records available only as required or allowed by law.

If you have any questions about the storage of your medical records or about inspecting your medical records, contact

_____ .

State Laws on Access to Personnel Records

This chart deals with only those states that authorize access to personnel files. Generally, an employee is allowed to see evaluations, performance reviews, and other documents that determine a promotion, bonus, or raise; access usually does not include letters of reference, test results, or records of a criminal or workplace violation investigation. Under other state laws, employees may have access to their medical records and records of exposure to hazardous substances; these laws are not included in this chart.

Alaska

Alaska Stat. § 23.10.430

Employers affected: All.

Employee access to records: Employee or former employee may view and copy personnel files.

Conditions for viewing records: Employee may view records during regular business hours under reasonable rules.

Copying records: Employee pays (if employer requests).

California

Cal. Lab. Code §§ 1198.5; 432

Employers affected: All employers subject to wage and hour laws.

Employee access to records: Employee or former employee has right to inspect personnel records relating to performance or to a grievance proceeding, within 30 days of making a written request for records. Employer may redact the names of any nonmanagerial employees. Employer need not comply with more than one request per year from a former employee. If employee files a lawsuit against employer that relates to a personnel matter, the right to review personnel records ceases while the suit is pending.

Written request required: Yes. If employee makes an oral request, the employer must supply a form to make a written request.

Conditions for viewing records: Employee may view personnel file at reasonable times, during break or nonwork hours. If records are kept offsite or employer does not make them available at the workplace, then employee must be allowed to view them at the storage location without loss of pay. If former employee was terminated for reasons relating to harassment or workplace violence, employer may provide copy of records or make them available offsite.

Copying records: Employee or former employee also has a right to a copy of personnel records, at the employee's cost, within 30 days of making a written request.

Colorado

Colo. Rev. Stat. Ann. § 8-2-129

Employers affected: All.

Employee access to records: Upon request, current employee may inspect personnel file at least once per year. Former employee may inspect personnel file once after termination of employment.

Conditions for viewing records: Employer must make personnel file available at its place of business at a time convenient to employee and employer. Employer may have a designated representative present at the time of inspection.

Copying records: Employee or former employee may request a copy of the personnel file. Employer can require the employee to pay reasonable copying costs.

Connecticut

Conn. Gen. Stat. Ann. §§ 31-128a to 31-128h

Employers affected: All.

Employee access to records: Employee has right to inspect personnel files within 7 business days after making a request, but not more than twice a year. Former employee has right to inspect personnel files within 10 business days after making a request.

Written request required: Yes.

Conditions for viewing records: Employee may view records during regular business hours in a location at or near worksite. Employer may require that files be viewed in the presence of designated official.

Copying records: Employer must provide copies within 7 days (current employee) or 10 days (former employee) after receiving employee's written request; request must identify the materials employee wants copied. Employer may charge a fee that is based on the cost of supplying documents. Employee is entitled to a copy of any disciplinary action against the employee within 1 business day after it is imposed; employer must immediately provide terminated employee with a copy of the termination notice.

Employee's right to insert rebuttal: If employee disagrees with information in personnel file and cannot reach an agreement with employer to remove or correct it, employee may submit an explanatory written statement (a "rebuttal"). Rebuttal must be maintained as part of the file. Employer must inform employee of the right to submit a rebuttal in evaluation, discipline, or termination paperwork.

Delaware

Del. Code Ann. tit. 19, §§ 730 to 735

Employers affected: All.

Employee access to records: Current employee, employee who is laid off with reemployment rights, or employee on leave of absence may inspect personnel record; employee's agent is not entitled to have access to records. Unless there is reasonable cause, employer may limit access to once a year.

Written request required: At employer's discretion. Employer may require employee to file a form and indicate either the purpose of the review or what parts of the record employee wants to inspect.

Conditions for viewing records: Records may be viewed during employer's regular business hours. Employer may require that employees view files on their own time and may also require that files be viewed on the premises and in the presence of a designated official.

Copying records: Employer is not required to permit employee to copy records. Employee may take notes.

Employee's right to insert rebuttal: If employee disagrees with information in personnel file and cannot reach an agreement with employer to remove or correct it, employee may submit an explanatory written statement (a "rebuttal"). Rebuttal must be maintained as part of the personnel file.

Illinois

820 Ill. Comp. Stat. §§ 40/1 to 40/12

Employers affected: Employers with 5 or more employees.

Employee access to records: Current employee, or former employee terminated within the past year, is permitted to inspect records twice a year at reasonable intervals, unless a collective bargaining agreement provides otherwise. An employee involved in a current grievance may designate a representative of the union or collective bargaining unit, or other agent, to inspect personnel records that may be relevant to resolving the grievance. Employer must make records available within 7 working days after employee makes request (if employer cannot meet deadline, may be allowed an additional 7 days).

Written request required: At employer's discretion. Employer may require use of a form.

Conditions for viewing records: Records may be viewed during normal business hours at or near worksite or, at employer's discretion, during nonworking hours at a different location if more convenient for employee.

Copying records: After reviewing records, employee may get a copy. Employer may charge only actual cost of duplication. If employee is unable to view files at worksite, employer, upon receipt of a written request, must mail employee a copy.

Employee's right to insert rebuttal: If employee disagrees with any information in the personnel file and cannot reach an agreement with employer to remove or correct it, employee may submit an explanatory written statement (a "rebuttal"). Rebuttal must remain in file with no additional comment by employer.

Iowa

Iowa Code §§ 91A.2, 91B.1

Employers affected: All employers with salaried employees or commissioned salespeople.

Employee access to records: Employee may have access to personnel file at time agreed upon by employer and employee.

Conditions for viewing records: Employer's representative may be present.

Copying records: Employer may charge copying fee for each page that is equivalent to a commercial copying service fee.

Maine

Me. Rev. Stat. Ann. tit. 26, § 631

Employers affected: All.

Employee access to records: Within 10 days of submitting request, employee, former employee, or authorized representative may view and copy personnel files.

Written request required: Yes.

Conditions for viewing records: Employee may view records during normal business hours at the location where the files are kept, unless employer, at own discretion, arranges a time and place more convenient for employee. If files are in electronic or any other nonprint format, employer must provide equipment for viewing and copying.

Copying records: Employee entitled to one free copy of personnel file during each calendar year, including any material added to file during that year. Employee must pay for any additional copies.

State Laws on Access to Personnel Records (continued)

Massachusetts

Mass. Gen. Laws ch. 149, § 52C

Employers affected: All.

Employee access to records: Employee or former employee must have opportunity to review personnel files within 5 business days of submitting request, but not more than twice a calendar year. (Law does not apply to tenured or tenure-track employees in private colleges and universities.) Employer must notify an employee within 10 days of placing in the employee's personnel record any information to the extent that the information is, has been, or may be used, to negatively affect the employee's qualification for employment, promotion, transfer, additional compensation, or the possibility that the employee will be subject to disciplinary action. (This notification does not count toward employee's two allotted opportunities to view personnel file.)

Written request required: Yes.

Conditions for viewing records: Employee may view records at workplace during normal business hours.

Copying records: Employee must be given a copy of record within 5 business days of submitting a written request.

Employee's right to insert rebuttal: If employee disagrees with any information in personnel record and cannot reach an agreement with employer to remove or correct it, employee may submit an explanatory written statement (a "rebuttal"). Rebuttal becomes a part of the personnel file.

Michigan

Mich. Comp. Laws §§ 423.501 to 423.505

Employers affected: Employers with 4 or more employees.

Employee access to records: Current or former employee is entitled to review personnel records at reasonable intervals, generally not more than twice a year, unless a collective bargaining agreement provides otherwise.

Written request required: Yes. Request must describe the record employee wants to review.

Conditions for viewing records: Employee may view records during normal office hours either at or reasonably near the worksite. If these hours would require employee to take time off work, employer must provide another reasonable time for review.

Copying records: After reviewing files, employee may get a copy; employer may charge only actual cost of duplication. If employee is unable to view files at the worksite, employer, upon receipt of a written request, must mail employee a copy.

Employee's right to insert rebuttal: If employee disagrees with any information in personnel record and cannot reach an agreement with employer to remove or correct it, employee may submit a written statement explaining his or her position. Statement may be no longer than five 8½" by 11" pages.

Minnesota

Minn. Stat. Ann. §§ 181.960 to 181.966

Employers affected: 20 or more employees.

Employee access to records: Current employee may review files once per 6-month period; former employee may have access to records once only during the first year after termination. Employer must comply with written request within 7 working days (14 working days if personnel records kept out of state). Employer may not retaliate against an employee who asserts rights under these laws.

Written request required: Yes.

Conditions for viewing records: Current employee may view records during employer's normal business hours at worksite or a nearby location; does not have to take place during employee's working hours. Employer or employer's representative may be present.

Copying records: Employer must provide copy free of charge. Current employee must first review record and then submit written request for copies. Former employee must submit written request; providing former employee with a copy fulfills employer's obligation to allow access to records.

Employee's right to insert rebuttal: If employee disputes specific information in the personnel record, and cannot reach an agreement with employer to remove or revise it, employee may submit a written statement identifying the disputed information and explaining his or her position. Statement may be no longer than 5 pages and must be kept with personnel record as long as it is maintained.

Nevada

Nev. Rev. Stat. Ann. § 613.075

Employers affected: All.

Employee access to records: An employee who has worked at least 60 days, and a former employee, within 60 days of termination, must be given a reasonable opportunity to inspect personnel records.

Conditions for viewing records: Employee may view records during employer's normal business hours.

State Laws on Access to Personnel Records (continued)

Copying records: Employer may charge only actual cost of providing access and copies.

Employee's right to insert rebuttal: Employee may submit a reasonable written explanation in direct response to any entry in personnel record. Statement must be of reasonable length; employer may specify the format; employer must maintain statement in personnel records.

New Hampshire

N.H. Rev. Stat. Ann. § 275:56

Employers affected: All.

Employee access to records: Employer must provide employees with a reasonable opportunity to inspect records.

Copying records: Employer may charge a fee reasonably related to cost of supplying copies.

Employee's right to insert rebuttal: If employee disagrees with any of the information in personnel record and cannot reach an agreement with the employer to remove or correct it, employee may submit an explanatory written statement along with supporting evidence. Statement must be maintained as part of personnel file.

Oregon

Ore. Rev. Stat. § 652.750

Employers affected: All.

Employee access to records: Within 45 days after receipt of request, employer must provide employee a reasonable opportunity to inspect payroll records and personnel records used to determine qualifications for employment, promotion, or additional compensation, termination, or other disciplinary action.

Conditions for viewing records: Employee may view records at worksite or place of work assignment.

Copying records: Within 45 days after receipt of request, employer must provide a certified copy of requested record to current or former employee (if request made within 60 days of termination). If employee makes request after 60 days from termination, employer shall provide a certified copy of requested records if employer has records at time of the request. May charge amount reasonably calculated to recover actual cost of providing copy.

Pennsylvania

43 Pa. Cons. Stat. Ann. §§ 1321 to 1324

Employers affected: All.

Employee access to records: Employer must allow employee to inspect personnel record at reasonable times. (Employee's agent, or employee who is laid off with reemployment rights or on leave of absence, must also be given access.) Unless there is reasonable cause, employer may limit review to once a year by employee and once a year by employee's agent.

Written request required: At employer's discretion. Employer may require the use of a form as well as a written indication of the parts of the record employee wants to inspect or the purpose of the inspection. For employee's agent: Employee must provide signed authorization designating agent; must be for a specific date and indicate the reason for the inspection or the parts of the record the agent is authorized to inspect.

Conditions for viewing records: Employee may view records during regular business hours at the office where records are maintained, when there is enough time for employee to complete the review. Employer may require that employee or agent view records on their own time and may also require that inspection take place on the premises and in the presence of employer's designated official.

Copying records: Employer not obligated to permit copying. Employee may take notes.

Employee's right to insert rebuttal: The Bureau of Labor Standards, after a petition and hearing, may allow employee to place a counterstatement in the personnel file, if employee claims that the file contains an error.

Rhode Island

R.I. Gen. Laws § 28-6.4-1

Employers affected: All.

Employee access to records: Employer must permit employee to inspect personnel file when given at least 7 days' advance notice (excluding weekends and holidays). Employer may limit access to no more than 3 times a year.

Written request required: Yes.

Conditions for viewing records: Employee may view records at any reasonable time other than employee's work hours. Inspection must take place in presence of employer or employer's representative.

Copying records: Employee may not make copies or remove files from place of inspection. Employer may charge a fee reasonably related to cost of supplying copies.

State Laws on Access to Personnel Records (continued)

Washington

Wash. Rev. Code Ann. §§ 49.12.240 to 49.12.260

Employers affected: All.

Employee access to records: Employee may have access to personnel records at least once a year within a reasonable time after making a request.

Employee's right to insert rebuttal: Employee may petition annually that employer review all information in employee's personnel file. If there is any irrelevant or incorrect information in the file, employer must remove it. If employee does not agree with employer's review, employee may request to have a statement of rebuttal or correction placed in file. Former employee has right of rebuttal for two years after termination.

Wisconsin

Wis. Stat. Ann. § 103.13

Employers affected: All employers who maintain personnel records.

Employee access to records: Employee and former employee must be allowed to inspect personnel records within 7 working days of making request. Access is permitted twice per calendar year unless a collective bargaining agreement provides otherwise. Employee involved in a current grievance may designate a representative of the union or collective bargaining unit, or other agent, to inspect records that may be relevant to resolving the grievance.

Written request required: At employer's discretion.

Conditions for viewing records: Employee may view records during normal working hours at a location reasonably near worksite. If this would require employee to take time off work, employer may provide another reasonable time and place for review.

Copying records: Employee's right of inspection includes the right to make or receive copies. If employer provides copies, may charge only actual cost of reproduction.

Employee's right to insert rebuttal: If employee disagrees with any information in the personnel record and cannot come to an agreement with the employer to remove or correct it, employee may submit an explanatory written statement. Employer must attach the statement to the disputed portion of the personnel record.

Drugs and Alcohol

Employee drug and alcohol problems can take a toll on a workplace in many ways. Employees who abuse alcohol and drugs (including illegal drugs, prescription drugs, and over-the-counter drugs) pose significant problems for their employers, managers, and coworkers, from diminished job performance and low productivity to excessive absenteeism and tardiness. Out-of-pocket costs include increased workers' compensation claims, increased occupational health claims, and higher health insurance premiums.

As a result, most employers include in their handbook a policy or set of policies designed to combat substance abuse. These policies range from simple statements prohibiting alcohol and drug use to complicated frameworks that include rehabilitation, employee searches, and drug testing.

From a legal standpoint, the simple approach is the easiest, because the law clearly gives employers the right to prohibit illegal drug and alcohol use in the workplace. If you confine your policies to conduct and activities in which you have a legitimate business interest—for example, performance and safety—you should be on safe legal ground.

If you decide to enter the world of employee searches and drug testing, however, you'll have a number of legal obstacles to face. Remember that your employees have a right to privacy. Depending on the state in which you live, the law may be more or less aggressive in protecting this right. We address these legal issues in more detail in the individual policy discussions below.

The set of policies you choose will depend on your company's values and type of business. In this chapter, we help you tailor your company's policies to its business needs by explaining your options.

CONTENTS

This chapter provides information about substance abuse policies that you can include in your handbook. It does not discuss in detail the legal issues involved in actually dealing with an employee who abuses substances. Both state and federal law have a lot to say about what employers can and cannot do when faced with such an employee, and prudent employers familiarize themselves with these laws before taking action. For comprehensive information and resources on this issue, go to the website of the Division of Workplace Programs of the federal government's Substance Abuse and Mental Health Services Administration (SAMHSA), www.samhsa.gov/workplace.

17:1 Policy Against Drug and Alcohol Use at Work

Given the amount of social drinking and drug use in our culture, there's no room for ambiguity in a substance use policy; it must be clear as to when employees may and may not partake. Although illegal drug use is always unacceptable, there are times when a drink on company time may be appropriate (see the modifications, below).

Your drug and alcohol use policy should explain to employees when they can and cannot use alcohol and legal drugs, that your company prohibits substance use for their own safety and well-being, and that your company can discipline or even terminate them for violating the policy.

This policy does not prohibit legal drug use. When crafting any substance abuse policy, it is important to understand the difference between legal drug use and illegal drug use. You can prohibit the latter, but not the former. This is because an employee's legal drug use—for example, taking prescription or over-the-counter drugs according to a doctor's orders—may be protected by state and federal disability laws. (For more information on this issue, see Chapter 1 of *Dealing With Problem Employees: A Legal Guide*, by Amy DelPo and Lisa Guerin (Nolo).) To learn more about federal disability law, contact the U.S. Equal Employment Opportunity Commission; to learn more about your state's disability law, contact your state labor department. (See Appendix B for contact information.)

Who Needs This Policy

Federal law requires federal contractors to have policies that ensure a drug-free workplace. (See "The Drug-Free Workplace Act of 1988," below.) Some state laws offer employers discounts on their workers' compensation premiums if they adopt drug-free workplace policies. To find out if your state has such a law, contact your state labor department. (See Appendix B for contact information.) If you are an employer covered by these laws, then you will need some type of drug and alcohol policy. That policy might look like the one below or, depending on the legal requirements, it might be more comprehensive.

All other employers are free to choose whether to have this type of policy. Given the negative impact of drugs and alcohol on morale, performance, and productivity, we cannot imagine a reason for failing to include such a policy in a handbook. As explained above, there are no murky legal issues involved in such a bare-bones policy, and including one gives employers more leeway in combating any drug and alcohol problems that arise in their workplace.

17:1 Policy Against Alcohol and Illegal Drug Use

File Name: 17_Drugs Alcohol.rtf

Include This Policy?
- ☐ Yes
- ☐ No
- ☐ Use our existing policy
- ☐ Other _____

Alternate Modifications
None

Additional Clauses
Serving Alcohol at Functions
  Insert?:   ☐ Yes ☐ No
Entertaining Clients
  Insert?:   ☐ Yes ☐ No

Related Policies
None

Notes
_____
_____
_____
_____
_____
_____
_____
_____
_____
_____
_____
_____
_____
_____
_____
_____

Policy Against Alcohol and Illegal Drug Use

This Company is committed to providing a safe, comfortable, and productive work environment for its employees. We recognize that employees who abuse drugs or alcohol at work—or who appear at work under the influence of alcohol or illegal drugs—harm both themselves and the work environment.

As a result, we prohibit employees from doing the following:

- appearing at work under the influence of alcohol or illegal drugs
- conducting Company business while under the influence of alcohol or illegal drugs (whether or not the employee is actually on work premises at the time)
- using alcohol or illegal drugs on the worksite
- using alcohol or illegal drugs while conducting Company business (whether or not the employee is actually on work premises at the time)
- possessing, buying, selling, or distributing alcohol or illegal drugs on the worksite, and
- possessing, buying, selling, or distributing alcohol or illegal drugs while conducting Company business (whether or not the employee is actually on work premises at the time).

Illegal drug use includes more than just outlawed drugs such as amphetamines, cocaine, or opiates. It also includes the misuse of otherwise legal prescription and over-the-counter drugs.

This policy covers times when employees are on call but not working and times when employees are driving Company vehicles or using Company equipment.

Employees who violate this policy may face disciplinary action, up to and including termination.

The Drug-Free Workplace Act of 1988

If your company is a federal government contractor or grant recipient, it must abide by the federal Drug-Free Workplace Act of 1988. (41 U.S.C. §§ 701 and following.) This law requires such companies to do a number of things, including publish an antidrug-use statement (perhaps in a handbook) and establish a drug awareness program.

While the specifics of the Drug-Free Workplace Act are beyond the scope of this book, the U.S. Department of Labor (DOL) enforces the Act and can provide you with the information you need to comply with its requirements. (See Appendix B for contact information.) You can find detailed information about the Drug-Free Workplace Act and other workplace substance abuse programs at the SAMHSA website, www.samhsa.gov/workplace.

Be aware that many states have similar drug-free workplace laws. (To find out about your state's law, see "State Drug and Alcohol Testing Laws" at the end of this chapter.) You can also contact your state department of labor. (See Appendix B for contact details.)

Additional Clause for Serving Alcohol at Functions

Some companies sponsor functions, such as holiday parties or anniversary celebrations, at which the company serves alcohol. Those companies will have to modify the policy above to allow alcohol use sometimes. Otherwise, the company is sending employees contradictory and confusing messages, serving them alcohol while at the same time prohibiting them from drinking it.

There are certain legal risks involved whenever a company allows employees to consume alcohol, either because the company has served them the alcohol or because the company has sanctioned their drinking while on the job. For example, if an employee consumes alcohol and then hurts himself or someone else, the company might be liable for those injuries; the company's workers' compensation policy might not provide coverage. (Check your company's insurance policy before serving alcohol or allowing employees to consume alcohol at a company function.) If your company plans to serve alcohol to employees or sanction employee drinking on the job, consider consulting legal counsel to learn ways to shield your company from liability.

If you think that your company will serve alcohol, either on site or during work hours, consider adding the following paragraph to the policy.

Additional Clause

> We do not prohibit employees from consuming alcohol at social or business functions that we sponsor where alcohol is served. Even at these functions, however, employees may not consume alcohol to the point of intoxication or to the point where they endanger their own safety or the safety of others. In addition, employees involved in security and employees who work with heavy or dangerous machinery or materials may not consume any alcohol at these functions if they will be returning to work that same day.

Additional Clause for Entertaining Clients

Some employees must entertain clients and customers as part of their job. For example, a salesman might take a buyer to dinner to seal a deal, or an attorney might celebrate with a client after winning a big case. Often, entertainment includes sharing a drink or two.

If you'd like your employees to be able to consume alcohol while entertaining clients, consider adding the following paragraph to your policy.

Additional Clause

> This policy does not prohibit employees from consuming alcohol while entertaining clients or prospective clients. However, employees may not consume alcohol to the point of intoxication, nor may they consume alcohol if they are going to drive. In addition, employees must always conduct themselves professionally and appropriately while on Company business.

17:2 Inspections to Enforce Policy Against Drugs and Alcohol

Some employers choose to inspect the workplace and their employees to enforce their policy against alcohol and illegal drug use. Although most state laws allow inspections in some form, these same laws impose strict limits on how and when employers can conduct these inspections. Most often, these laws seek to balance the employer's right to keep the workplace free of drugs and alcohol against the employee's right to privacy. Exactly how to strike this balance varies from state to state.

Because the legal rules regarding inspections are so varied and complicated, we recommend you consult with an attorney before your company conducts an inspection.

The sample policy below reserves your company's right to inspect without going into detail, thereby giving you the flexibility to use procedures that comply with your state's law.

Inspections to Enforce Drug and Alcohol Policy

This Company reserves the right to inspect employees, their possessions, and their workspaces to enforce our policy against alcohol and illegal drug use.

Who Needs This Policy

Not every employer needs to inspect the workplace, but if you would like to have the option of searching employees and their workspaces for drugs and alcohol, then you should probably include this type of policy in your handbook.

Whether you want to have this option depends in large part on your company's needs and values as an employer. One drawback of the policy is that it sends a message of mistrust to employees. If your company is a large employer that has experienced large-scale problems with employees' abusing drugs and alcohol, however, you might be willing to live with that drawback in exchange for being able to aggressively address drug and alcohol use in the workplace. On the other hand, if your company is a small employer that has not had many problems with substance-abusing employees, you probably do not need to include this type of policy in the handbook.

17:2 Inspections to Enforce Drug and Alcohol Policy

File Name: 17_Drugs Alcohol.rtf

Include This Policy?
- ☐ Yes
- ☐ No
- ☐ Use our existing policy
- ☐ Other _____

Alternate Modifications
None

Additional Clauses
None

Related Policies
None

Notes

17:3   Drug Testing

File Name: 17_Drugs Alcohol.rtf

Include This Policy?
☐ Yes
☐ No
☐ Use our existing policy
☐ Other _____

Alternate Modifications
None

Additional Clauses
None

Related Policies
None

Notes
_____
_____
_____
_____
_____
_____
_____
_____
_____
_____
_____
_____
_____
_____
_____
_____
_____
_____
_____
_____

17:3 Drug Testing

In recent years, drug tests have become cheaper and more reliable, spurring more and more employers to use drug testing as a tool in trying to create a drug-free workplace. Employers test for drugs in a variety of contexts: Some test all prospective hires, others test only when an employee seems to be under the influence, and still others randomly test employees who are in jobs where safety or security is an issue.

Your state's laws will determine whether, when, and how your company can test employees. In addition, state privacy laws regulate how and when an employer can conduct the test.

To learn more about your state's rules on drug testing, contact your state labor department. (See Appendix B for contact information.) You can also refer to "State Drug and Alcohol Testing Laws" at the end of this chapter.

Although the varied nature of state laws means that we cannot provide a standard drug testing policy, here is an example of what such a policy might look like.

> **SAMPLE POLICY LANGUAGE**
>
> As part of our efforts to keep this workplace safe and free of illegal drug use, we will conduct random and intermittent drug tests of all employees who work in safety-sensitive positions.
>
> In addition, we may ask any employee, regardless of job responsibilities, to submit to a drug test in the following circumstances:
> - when we reasonably suspect that the employee is under the influence of illegal drugs
> - when we reasonably suspect that the employee has been involved in the sale, purchase, use, or distribution of illegal drugs on the worksite or while performing job duties
> - when the employee has been involved in a workplace accident or incident
> - when the employee has been involved in an accident or incident off site but while on company business, or
> - when the employee has violated a safety rule.

Who Needs This Policy

The U.S. Department of Transportation (DOT) requires drug testing in certain transportation industries, including aviation, trucking, railway, maritime, and mass transit. Those regulations are beyond the scope of this book. If your business uses trucks or boats or is involved in transporting goods or people, you can find out more by contacting the Department of Transportation. Contact details and other helpful information are available on the DOT's website, at www.transportation.gov. (From the home page, select "Resources for Partners," then "Drug and Alcohol Testing.")

There are considerable legal challenges and procedural hurdles involved in drug testing. Employers other than those covered by DOT regulations—or similar state regulations—should think twice before taking this step. Nonetheless, if you do want to have the option of drug testing employees, be sure to include this type of policy in the handbook. In addition, you should consult with an attorney when drafting a drug-testing policy and before conducting any drug test.

Medical and Recreational Marijuana Laws

Currently, about half the states and the District of Columbia have passed laws allowing medical use of marijuana. Although these laws vary in the details, the main intent behind them is to allow people to use marijuana for medical purposes (for example, to relieve the pain of migraine headaches, ameliorate the effects of glaucoma, or provide relief from the nausea that is caused by certain cancer treatments). In addition, eight states have legalized marijuana for purely recreational uses.

Despite these state laws, however, it is still a crime under federal law to use marijuana, for medical or any other purposes. If you operate in a state with a medical or recreational marijuana law, you have some tricky issues to deal with. For example, is marijuana a legal drug or an illegal one? If you fire an employee for failing a drug test because of marijuana use, is the firing valid or is it wrongful termination? And, if your state protects employees from workplace discrimination based on their legal off-duty activities, may you discipline or terminate an employee for the legal use of marijuana during nonwork hours?

Some courts have ruled in favor of employers who terminate employees for testing positive for marijuana, even if the employee has a legally valid prescription. But a few states, including Arizona and Delaware, protect employees with valid prescriptions for medical marijuana from being fired for a positive drug test, unless the employee uses, possesses, or is impaired by marijuana at work or during work hours. The law is generally too varied—and too unsettled—to provide firm guidance here.

If your state has a medical or recreational marijuana law, consult with an attorney to find out how it affects your ability to regulate drug use in your workplace. And, make sure your handbook policies on drug use and drug testing deal with this emerging issue.

Include This Policy?
- ☐ Yes
- ☐ No
- ☐ Use our existing policy
- ☐ Other _____

Alternate Modifications

None

Additional Clauses

None

Related Policies

None

Notes

_____
_____
_____
_____
_____
_____
_____
_____
_____
_____
_____
_____
_____
_____
_____
_____
_____
_____
_____

17:4 Leave for Rehabilitation

Although some employers take a zero tolerance approach to employee substance abuse problems, others recognize that they can help employees who have fallen prey to alcohol and drug abuse kick their habits, and become valuable, productive, and loyal workers in the process. For some employers, this means something as small and inexpensive as giving employees paid or unpaid leave to participate in a rehabilitation program.

Your rehabilitation policy should let employees know that their employer cares about them and their well-being and that, as a result, your company may allow them to take leave to deal with their substance abuse problem. It should not, however, promise such leave to anyone who requests it. Your policy should also remind employees who have a substance abuse problem that they must meet the same performance, productivity, and conduct standards as everyone else.

Leave to Participate in Rehabilitation Program

We believe that employees who have a substance abuse problem can help themselves by enrolling in a rehabilitation program. Not only will overcoming their problem help these employees in their personal lives, it will help them to be more effective and productive workers.

Although we cannot guarantee that we will grant this leave to all employees who request it, employees who would like to participate in a rehabilitation program may, subject to approval, be able to use up to _____ weeks of [paid _or_ unpaid] leave from work to attend the program.

Employees [will _or_ will not] be entitled to health and other benefits while on rehabilitation leave.

Employees [will _or_ will not] be allowed to accrue vacation and other benefits while on rehabilitation leave.

At the end of the rehabilitation leave, we [will _or_ will not] require proof that the employee successfully completed the program.

To learn more about this type of leave, including whether you qualify for it, the circumstances under which we will grant it, and the requirements that you must meet, contact _____ .
We will keep all conversations regarding employee substance abuse problems as confidential as possible.

Please note that even as you might be seeking assistance for your substance abuse problem, we still expect you to meet the same standards of performance, productivity, and conduct that we expect of all employees, including our prohibition on alcohol or illegal drug use at work. We reserve the right to discipline you—up to and including termination—for failing to meet those standards.

Who Needs This Policy

Some states require employers to allow employees to take leave to participate in a rehabilitation program. If you operate in such a state, include this policy (or one similar to it) in your handbook. To find out about your state's law, contact your state department of labor. (See Appendix B for contact information.)

If you don't operate in a state that requires rehabilitation leave, you can still benefit from this type of policy. The expense of the policy may be small when compared to the potential reward of assisting problem employees in becoming valuable and productive members of the workforce.

How to Complete This Policy

As you can see from reading the standard rehabilitation leave policy, above, you will have to make a number of decisions when drafting your leave policy. You will have to decide:

- which employees qualify for the leave. For example, will you have a length-of-service requirement: a requirement that employees have worked for your company for a certain amount of time before they qualify? Will only full-time employees be eligible? Will you require employees to provide medical proof of the substance abuse problem?
- the amount of leave you will allow. When making this decision, you might consult with rehabilitation programs in your area to get an estimate of what is reasonable.
- whether you will require employees to provide proof that they successfully completed the program
- whether the leave will be paid or unpaid, and
- whether you will allow employees to accrue benefits while on leave.

In most states, the law does not provide you with much direction on these issues. The way you answer these questions will depend on your company's values and what it can afford.

In the states that require this type of leave, however, the law may also have rules about issues relating to the leave. These rules typically mandate such things as whether employees are entitled to benefits while on leave and whether the leave is paid or unpaid. If your state has such a law, you may have to modify the policy that we provide above.

17:5 Rehabilitation and Your EAP

File Name: 17_Drugs Alcohol.rtf

Include This Policy?
- ☐ Yes
- ☐ No
- ☐ Use our existing policy
- ☐ Other _____

Alternate Modifications

None

Additional Clauses

None

Related Policies

None

Notes

_____
_____
_____
_____
_____
_____
_____
_____
_____
_____
_____
_____
_____
_____
_____
_____
_____
_____
_____
_____
_____

17:5 Rehabilitation and Your EAP

Most employee assistance plans (EAPs) include drug and alcohol rehabilitation and counseling services. If you offer an EAP as a benefit to your employees, check to see whether your plan includes these things. If it does, inform employees of this fact either through the policy below or through a policy provided by your EAP administrator.

Rehabilitation and Your EAP

Because we care about the health and welfare of our employees, your benefits package includes an Employee Assistance Program (EAP) that provides assistance to employees who suffer from substance abuse problems, personal problems, or emotional problems.

If you would like assistance in dealing with your substance abuse problem, see _____ for information about our EAP program. Your request for assistance will be kept as confidential as possible.

[*If you will have a policy allowing leave to participate in a rehabilitation program, refer to that policy here.*]

Please note that even as you might be seeking assistance for your substance abuse problem, we still expect you to meet the same standards of performance, productivity, and conduct that we expect of all employees, including our prohibition on alcohol or illegal drug use at work. We reserve the right to discipline or terminate you for failing to meet those standards.

State Drug and Alcohol Testing Laws

Note: The states of California, Colorado, Delaware, Kansas, Massachusetts, Michigan, Missouri, Nevada, New Hampshire, New Jersey, New Mexico, New York, Pennsylvania, South Dakota, Texas, Washington, West Virginia, Wisconsin, and the District of Columbia are not included in this chart because they do not have specific drug and alcohol testing laws governing private employers. Additional laws may apply. Check with your state department of labor for more information.

Alabama

Ala. Code §§ 25-5-330 to 25-5-340

Employers affected: Employers who establish a drug-free workplace program to qualify for a workers' compensation rate discount.

Testing applicants: Employer must test applicants upon conditional offer of employment. May test only those applying for certain positions, if based on reasonable job classifications. Job ads must include notice that drug and alcohol testing required.

Testing employees: Random testing permitted. Must test after an accident that results in lost work time; upon reasonable suspicion (reasons for suspicion must be documented and made available to employee upon request); as required by employer's routinely scheduled fitness for duty exams; and as follow-up to a required rehabilitation program.

Employee rights: Employees have 5 days to contest or explain a positive test result. Employer must have an employee assistance program or maintain a resource file of outside programs.

Notice and policy requirements: All employees must have written notice of drug policy. Must give 60 days' advance notice before implementing testing program. Policy must include consequences of refusing to take test or testing positive.

Alaska

Alaska Stat. §§ 23.10.600 to 23.10.699

Employers affected: Employers with one or more full-time employees.

Testing applicants: Employer may test applicants for any job-related purpose consistent with business necessity and the terms of the employer's policy.

Testing employees: Employers are not required to test. Random testing permitted. Employer may test: for any job-related purpose consistent with business necessity;

to maintain productivity or safety; as part of an accident investigation or investigation of possible employee impairment; or upon reasonable suspicion.

Employee rights: Employer must provide written test results within 5 working days. Employee has 10 working days to request opportunity to explain positive test results; employer must grant request within 72 hours or before taking any adverse employment action.

Notice and policy requirements: Before implementing a testing program employer must distribute a written drug policy to all employees and must give 30 days' advance notice. Policy must include consequences of a positive test or refusal to submit to testing.

Arizona

Ariz. Rev. Stat. §§ 23-493 to 23-493.11

Employers affected: Employers with one or more full-time employees.

Testing applicants: Employer must inform prospective hires if they will undergo drug testing as a condition of employment.

Testing employees: Statute does not encourage, discourage, restrict, prohibit or require testing. Random testing permitted. Employees may be tested: for any job-related purpose; to maintain productivity or safety; as part of an accident investigation or investigation of individual employee impairment; or upon reasonable suspicion. If employer tests, all compensated employees must be included in the program, including officers, directors, and supervisors.

Employee rights: Policy must inform employees of their right to explain positive results.

Notice and policy requirements: Before conducting tests employer must give employees a copy of the written policy. Policy must include the consequences of a positive test or refusal to submit to testing.

Arkansas

Ark. Code Ann. §§ 11-3-203, 11-14-101 to 11-14-112

Testing applicants: Employers who establish a drug-free workplace program to qualify for a workers' compensation rate discount: must test for drug use upon conditional offer of employment. May test only those applying for certain positions, if based on reasonable job classifications. Employer may test for alcohol. Job ads must include notice that testing is required.

All employers: may not test applicant unless employer pays for the cost of the test, and upon written request, provides a free copy of the report to the employee or applicant.

Testing employees: Employers who establish a drug-free workplace program to qualify for a workers' compensation rate discount: employer must test any employee

- upon reasonable suspicion
- as part of a routine fitness-for-duty medical exam
- after an accident that results in injury, and
- as follow-up to a required rehabilitation program.

Employer may test for any other lawful reason.

All employers: may not test employee unless employer pays for the cost of the test, and upon written request, provides a free copy of the report to the employee or applicant.

Employee rights: Employer may not refuse to hire applicant or take adverse personnel action against an employee on the basis of a single positive test that has not been verified by a confirmation test and a medical review officer. An applicant or employee has 5 days after receiving test results to contest or explain them.

Notice and policy requirements: Employer must give all employees a written statement of drug policy, including the consequences of a positive test or refusal to submit to testing. Employer must give 60 days' advance notice before implementing program.

Connecticut

Conn. Gen. Stat. Ann. §§ 31-51t to 31-51bb

Employers affected: All employers.

Testing applicants: Employer must inform job applicants in writing if drug testing is required as a condition of employment. Employer must provide copy of positive test result.

Testing employees: Employer may test: when there is reasonable suspicion that employee is under the influence of drugs or alcohol and job performance is or could be impaired.

Random testing is allowed only:

- when authorized by federal law
- when employee's position is dangerous or safety sensitive
- when employee drives a school bus or student transportation vehicle, or
- as part of a voluntary employee-assistance program.

Employee rights: Employer may not take any adverse personnel action on the basis of a single positive test that has not been verified by a confirmation test.

Florida

Fla. Stat. Ann. §§ 440.101 to 440.102

Employers affected: Employers who establish a drug-free workplace program to qualify for a workers' compensation rate discount.

Testing applicants: Employers must test job applicants upon conditional employment offer. May test only those applying for certain positions, if based on reasonable job classifications. Job ads must include notice that testing is required.

Testing employees: Must test employee:

- upon reasonable suspicion
- as part of a routine fitness-for-duty medical exam, or
- as part of a required rehabilitation program.

Random testing and testing for any other reason is neither required nor precluded by the law.

Employee rights: Employees who voluntarily seek treatment for substance abuse cannot be fired, disciplined, or discriminated against, unless they have tested positive or have been in treatment in the past. All employees have the right to explain positive results within 5 days. Employer may not take any adverse personnel action on the basis of an initial positive result that has not been verified by a confirmation test and a medical review officer.

Notice and policy requirements: Prior to implementing testing, employer must give 60 days' advance notice and must give employees written copy of drug policy. Policy must include consequences of a positive test result or refusal to submit to testing.

Georgia

Ga. Code Ann. §§ 34-9-410 to 34-9-421

Employers affected: Employers who establish a drug-free workplace program to qualify for a workers' compensation rate discount.

Testing applicants: Employer must test on conditional offer of employment. May test only those applying for certain positions, if based on reasonable job classifications. Job ads must include notice that testing is required.

Testing employees: Must test any employee:

- upon reasonable suspicion
- as part of a routine fitness-for-duty medical exam
- after an accident that results in an injury, or
- as part of a required rehabilitation program.

State Drug and Alcohol Testing Laws (continued)

Random testing and testing for any other lawful reason is neither required nor prohibited.

Employee rights: Employees have 5 days to explain or contest a positive result. Employer must have an employee assistance program or maintain a resource file of outside programs. Initial positive result must be confirmed.

Notice and policy requirements: Employer must give applicants and employees notice of testing and must give 60 days' notice before implementing program. All employees must receive a written policy statement; policy must state the consequences of refusing to submit to a drug test or of testing positive.

Hawaii

Haw. Rev. Stat. §§ 329B-1 to 329B-5.5

Employers affected: All employers.

Testing applicants: Same conditions as current employees.

Testing employees: Employer may test employees only if these conditions are met:

- Employer pays all costs including confirming test.
- Tests are performed by a licensed laboratory.
- Employee receives a list of the substances being tested for (and medications that could cause a positive result).
- There is a form for disclosing medicines and legal drugs.
- The results are kept confidential.

Notice and policy requirements: If employer uses an on-site screening test, it must follow the instructions on the package. If an employee or applicant tests positive in an on-site test, the employer must direct the employee or applicant to go to a licensed laboratory, within four hours, for a follow-up test. If the employee or applicant doesn't go to the lab, the employer can fire, refuse to hire, or take other adverse action against the employee or applicant only if the employer provided written notice that: the employer followed the required procedures for the on-site test; and the employee or applicant could refuse to take the test. If the employee or applicant refused or failed to take the test, the employer can take adverse action.

Idaho

Idaho Code §§ 72-1701 to 72-1716

Employers affected: Employers who establish a drug-free workplace program to qualify for a workers' compensation rate discount and/or prohibit employees fired for drug

or alcohol use from qualifying for unemployment compensation.

Testing applicants: Employer may test as a condition of hiring.

Testing employees: May test for variety of reasons, including: following a workplace accident; based on reasonable suspicion; as part of a return-to-duty exam; at random; and as a condition of continued employment. An employer who follows drug-free workplace guidelines may fire employees who refuse to submit to testing or who test positive for drugs or alcohol. Employees will be fired for misconduct and denied unemployment benefits.

Employee rights: An employee or applicant who receives notice of a positive test may request a retest within 7 working days. Employee must have opportunity to explain positive result. If the retest results are negative, the employer must pay for the cost; if they are positive, the employee must pay. Employer may not take any adverse employment action on the basis of an initial positive result that has not been verified by a confirmation test.

Notice and policy requirements: Employer must have a written policy that includes a statement that violation of the policy may result in termination due to misconduct, as well as what types of testing employees may be subject to.

Illinois

775 Ill. Comp. Stat. § 5/2-104(C)(2)

Employers affected: Employers with 15 or more employees.

Testing employees: Statute does not "encourage, prohibit, or authorize" drug testing, but employers may test employees who have been in rehabilitation.

Indiana

Ind. Code Ann. §§ 22-9-5-6(b), 22-9-5-24

Employers affected: Employers with 15 or more employees.

Testing employees: Statute does not "encourage, prohibit, or authorize" drug testing, but employers may test employees who have been in rehabilitation.

Iowa

Iowa Code § 730.5

Employers affected: Employers with one or more full-time employees.

Testing applicants: Employer may test as a condition of hiring.

Testing employees: Statute does not encourage, discourage, restrict, limit, prohibit, or require testing. Employer may conduct unannounced, random testing of employees

State Drug and Alcohol Testing Laws (continued)

selected from the entire workforce at one site, all full-time employees at one site, or all employees in safety-sensitive positions. Employers may also test: upon reasonable suspicion; during and after rehabilitation; or following an accident that caused a reportable injury or more than $1,000 property damage.

Employee rights: Employee has 7 days to request a retest. Employers with 50 or more employees must provide rehabilitation for any employee testing positive for alcohol use who has worked for at least 12 of the last 18 months and has not previously violated the substance abuse policy. Employer must have an employee assistance program or maintain a resource file of outside programs.

Notice and Policy Requirements: Must have written drug test policy that includes consequences of positive result and refusal to take test. Employer may take action only on confirmed positive result.

Kentucky

Ky. Rev. Stat. 304.13-167; 803 Ky. Admin. Code 25:280

Employers affected: Employers who establish a drug-free workplace to qualify for a workers' compensation premium discount.

Testing applicants: Must test for drugs and alcohol after conditional offer of employment.

Testing employees: Must test for drugs:
- upon reasonable suspicion
- following a workplace accident that requires medical care
- as a follow-up to an Employee Assistance Program (EAP) or rehabilitation program for drug use, and
- upon being selected using a statistically valid, random, unannounced selection procedure.

Must test for alcohol:
- upon reasonable suspicion, following a workplace accident that required medical care, and
- as a follow-up to an EAP or rehabilitation program for alcohol use.

Employee rights: Employee must have an opportunity to report use of prescription or over-the-counter medicines after receiving a positive test result.

Notice and Policy Requirements: Employer must have a written drug-free workplace policy. Employer must distribute and post notice of how it will determine whether employees have violated the policy and the consequences of violating the policy.

Louisiana

La. Rev. Stat. Ann. §§ 49:1001 to 49:1012

Employers affected: Employers with one or more full-time employees. (Does not apply to oil drilling, exploration, or production.)

Testing applicants: Employer may require all applicants to submit to drug and alcohol test. An employer must use certified laboratories and specified procedures for testing if it will base its hiring decisions on the results of the test.

Testing employees: Employer may require employees to submit to drug and alcohol test. An employer that will take negative action against an employee based on a positive test result must use certified laboratories and specified procedures for testing.

Employee rights: Employees with confirmed positive results have 7 working days to request access to all records relating to the drug test. Employer may allow employee to undergo rehabilitation without termination of employment.

Maine

Me. Rev. Stat. Ann. tit. 26, §§ 681 to 690

Employers affected: Employers with one or more full-time employees.

Testing applicants: Employer may require applicant to take a drug test only if offered employment or placed on an eligibility list.

Testing employees: Statute does not require or encourage testing. Employer may test based upon probable cause but may not base belief on a single accident, an anonymous informant, or off-duty possession or use (unless it occurs on the employer's premises or nearby, during or right before work hours); must document the facts and give employee a copy. May test randomly when there could be an unreasonable threat to the health and safety of coworkers or the public. Testing is also allowed when an employee returns to work following a positive test.

Employee rights: Employee who tests positive has 3 days to explain or contest results. Employee must be given an opportunity to participate in a rehabilitation program for up to 6 months; an employer with more than 20 full-time employees must pay for half of any out-of-pocket costs. After successfully completing the program, employee is entitled to return to previous job with full pay and benefits.

State Drug and Alcohol Testing Laws (continued)

Notice and policy requirements: All employers must have a written policy, which includes the consequences of a positive result or refusing to submit to testing. Policy must be approved by the state department of labor. Policy must be distributed to each employee at least 30 days before it takes effect. Any changes to policy require 60 days' advance notice. An employer with more than 20 full-time employees must have an employee assistance program certified by the state office of substance abuse before implementing a testing program.

Maryland

Md. Code Ann., [Health-Gen.] § 17-214

Employers affected: All employers.

Testing applicants: May use preliminary screening to test applicant. If initial result is positive, may make job offer conditional on confirmation of test results.

Testing employees: Employer may require substance abuse testing for legitimate business purposes only.

Employee rights: The sample must be tested by a certified laboratory; at the time of testing employee may request laboratory's name and address. An employee who tests positive must be given:
- a copy of the test results
- a copy of the employer's written drug and alcohol policy
- a written notice of any adverse action employer intends to take, and
- a statement of employee's right to an independent confirmation test at own expense.

Minnesota

Minn. Stat. Ann. §§ 181.950 to 181.957

Employers affected: Employers with one or more employees.

Testing applicants: Employers may require applicants to submit to a drug or alcohol test only after they have been given a job offer and have seen a written notice of testing policy. May only test if required of all applicants for same position.

Testing employees: Employers are not required to test. Employers may require drug or alcohol testing only according to a written testing policy. Testing may be done if there is a reasonable suspicion that employee:
- is under the influence of drugs or alcohol
- has violated drug and alcohol policy
- has been involved in a work-related accident; or

- has sustained or caused another employee to sustain a personal injury.

Random tests permitted only for employees in safety-sensitive positions. With 2 weeks' notice, employers may also test as part of an annual routine physical exam. Employer may test, without notice, an employee referred by the employer for chemical dependency treatment or evaluation or participating in a chemical dependency treatment program under an employee benefit plan. Testing is allowed during and for two years following treatment.

Employee rights: If test is positive, employee has 3 days to explain the results; employee must notify employer within 5 days of intention to obtain a retest. Employer may not discharge employee for a first-time positive test without offering counseling or rehabilitation; employee who refuses or does not complete program successfully may be discharged.

Notice and policy requirements: Employees must be given a written notice of testing policy that includes consequences of refusing to take test or having a positive test result. Two weeks' notice required before testing as part of an annual routine physical exam.

Mississippi

Miss. Code Ann. §§ 71-7-1 to 71-7-33, 71-3-121, 71-3-205 to 71-3-225

Employers affected: Employers with one or more full-time employees. Employers who establish a drug-free workplace program to qualify for a workers' compensation rate discount must implement testing procedures.

Testing applicants: May test all applicants as part of employment application process. Employer may request a signed statement that applicant has read and understands the drug and alcohol testing policy or notice.

Testing employees: May require drug and alcohol testing of all employees:
- upon reasonable suspicion
- as part of a routinely scheduled fitness-for-duty medical examination
- as a follow-up to a rehabilitation program, or
- if they have tested positive within the previous 12 months.

May also require drug and alcohol testing following an employee's work-related injury, for purposes of determining workers' compensation coverage. Testing is also allowed on a neutral selection basis.

State Drug and Alcohol Testing Laws (continued)

Employee rights: Employer must inform an employee in writing within 5 working days of receipt of a positive confirmed test result; employee may request and receive a copy of the test result report. Employee has 10 working days after receiving notice to explain the positive test results. Employer may not discharge or take any adverse personnel action on the basis of an initial positive test result that has not been verified by a confirmation test. Private employer who elects to establish a drug-free workplace program must have an employee assistance program or maintain a resource file of outside programs.

Notice and policy requirements: 30 days before implementing testing program employer must give employees written notice of drug and alcohol policy that includes consequences:

- of a positive confirmed result
- of refusing to take test, and
- of other violations of the policy.

Montana

Mont. Code Ann. §§ 39-2-205 to 39-2-211

Employers affected: Employers with one or more employees.

Testing applicants: May test as a condition of hire, but only for applicants who will work in a hazardous work environment; a security position; a position that affects public safety or health; a position with a fiduciary relationship to the employer, or a position that requires driving.

Testing employees: Same job restrictions apply to employees as to applicants. Employees in these positions may be tested:

- upon reasonable suspicion
- after involvement in an accident that causes personal injury or more than $1,500 property damage
- as a follow-up to a previous positive test, or
- as a follow-up to treatment or a rehabilitation program.

Employer may conduct random tests as long as there is an established date, all personnel are subject to testing, the employer has signed statements from each employee confirming receipt of a written description of the random selection process, and the random selection process is conducted by a scientifically valid method. Employer may require an employee who tests positive to undergo treatment as a condition of continued employment.

Employee rights: After a positive result, employee may request additional confirmation by an independent laboratory; if the results are negative, employer must pay the test costs. Employer may not take action or conduct follow-up testing if the employee presents a reasonable explanation or medical opinion that the original results were not caused by illegal drug use; employer must also remove results from employee's record.

Notice and policy requirements: Written policy must be available for review 60 days before testing. Policy must include consequences of a positive test result.

Nebraska

Neb. Rev. Stat. §§ 48-1901 to 48-1910

Employers affected: Employers with 6 or more full-time and part-time employees.

Testing employees: Employers are not required to test. Employer may require employees to submit to drug or alcohol testing and may discipline or discharge any employee who refuses, tests positive, or tampers with the test sample.

Employee rights: Employer may not take adverse action on the basis of an initial positive result unless it is confirmed according to state and federal guidelines.

North Carolina

N.C. Gen. Stat. §§ 95-230 to 95-235

Employers affected: All employers.

Testing applicants: May test as a condition of hire. Applicant has right to retest a confirmed positive sample at own expense. If first screening test produces a positive result, applicant may waive a second examination that is intended to confirm the results.

Testing employees: Employers may, but are not required to, test. Testing must be performed under reasonable, sanitary conditions, and must respect individual dignity to the extent possible. Employer must preserve samples for at least 90 days after confirmed test results are released.

Employee rights: Employee has right to retest a confirmed positive sample at own expense.

North Dakota

N.D. Cent. Code §§ 34-01-15, 65-01-11

Employers affected: All employers.

Testing applicants: May test as a condition of hire.

Testing employees: Employer may test following an accident or injury that will result in a workers' compensation claim, if employer has a mandatory policy of testing under these

State Drug and Alcohol Testing Laws (continued)

circumstances, or if employer or physician has reasonable grounds to suspect injury was caused by impairment due to alcohol or drug use.

Employee rights: Employer who requires drug testing must pay for the test.

Ohio

Ohio Admin. Code § 4123-17-58

Employers affected: Employers who establish a drug-free safety program may qualify for a workers' compensation rate bonus.

Testing applicants: Must test all applicants and new hires.

Testing employees: Must test employees:

- upon reasonable suspicion
- following a return to work after a positive test
- after an accident that results in an injury requiring off-site medical attention or property damage.

Employers must test at random to meet requirements for greater discounts.

Employee rights: Employer must have an employee assistance plan. Employers who test at random to qualify for greater discount must not terminate employee who tests positive for the first time, comes forward voluntarily, or is referred by a supervisor. For these employees, employer must pay costs of substance abuse assessment.

Notice and policy requirements: Policy must state consequences for refusing to submit to testing or for violating guidelines. Policy must include a commitment to rehabilitation.

Oklahoma

Okla. Stat. Ann. tit. 40, §§ 551 to 565

Employers affected: Employers with one or more employees.

Testing applicants: May test applicants.

Testing employees: Statute does not require or encourage testing. Before requiring testing, employer must provide an employee assistance program. Random testing is allowed. May test employees:

- upon reasonable suspicion
- after an accident resulting in injury or property damage
- on a random selection basis
- as part of a routine fitness-for-duty examination, or
- as follow-up to a rehabilitation program.

Employee rights: Employee has right to retest a positive result at own expense; if the confirmation test is negative, employer must reimburse costs.

Notice and policy requirements: Before requiring testing employer must: adopt a written policy; give a copy to each employee and to any applicant offered a job; and allow 10 days' notice. Policy must state consequences of a positive test result or refusing to submit to testing.

Oregon

Or. Rev. Stat. §§ 659.840, 659A.300, 438.435

Employers affected: All employers.

Testing applicants: Unless there is reasonable suspicion that an applicant is under the influence of alcohol, no employer may require a breathalyzer test as a condition of employment. Employer is not prohibited from conducting a test if applicant consents.

Testing employees: Unless there is reasonable suspicion that an employee is under the influence of alcohol, no employer may require a breathalyzer or blood alcohol test as a condition of continuing employment. Employer is not prohibited from conducting a test if employee consents.

Employee rights: No action may be taken based on the results of an on-site drug test without a confirming test performed according to state health division regulations. Upon written request, test results will be reported to the employee.

Rhode Island

R.I. Gen. Laws §§ 28-6.5-1 to 28-6.5-2

Employers affected: All employers.

Testing applicants: May test as a condition of hire.

Testing employees: May require employee to submit to a drug test only if there are reasonable grounds, based on specific, documented observations, to believe employee may be under the influence of a controlled substance that is impairing job performance.

Employee rights: Employee must be allowed to provide sample in private, outside the presence of any person. Employee who tests positive may have the sample retested at employer's expense and must be given opportunity to explain or refute results. Employee may not be terminated on the basis of a positive result but must be referred to a licensed substance abuse professional. After referral, employer may require additional testing and may terminate employee if test results are positive.

State Drug and Alcohol Testing Laws (continued)

South Carolina

S.C. Code Ann. §§ 41-1-15, 38-73-500

Employers affected: Employers who establish a drug-free workplace program to qualify for a workers' compensation rate discount.

Testing applicants: Employer is not required to test applicants to qualify for discount.

Testing employees: Must conduct random testing among all employees.

Employee rights: Employee must receive positive test results in writing within 24 hours.

Notice and policy requirements: Employer must notify all employees of the drug-free workplace program at the time it is established or at the time of hiring, whichever is earlier. Program must include a policy statement that balances respect for individuals with the need to maintain a safe, drug-free environment.

Tennessee

Tenn. Code Ann. §§ 50-9-101 to 50-9-114

Employers affected: Employers who establish a drug-free workplace program to qualify for a workers' compensation rate discount.

Testing applicants: Must test applicants for drugs upon conditional offer of employment. May test only those applying for certain positions, if based on reasonable job classifications. May test for alcohol after conditional offer of employment. Job ads must include notice that drug and alcohol testing is required.

Testing employees: Employer must test upon reasonable suspicion; must document behavior on which the suspicion is based within 24 hours or before test results are released, whichever is earlier; and must give a copy to the employee upon request. Employer must test employees:

- if required by employer policy as part of a routine fitness-for-duty medical exam
- after an accident that results in injury, or
- as a follow-up to a required rehabilitation program.

May test employees who are not in safety-sensitive positions for alcohol only if based on reasonable suspicion.

Employee rights: Employee has the right to explain or contest a positive result within 5 days. Employee may not be fired, disciplined, or discriminated against for voluntarily seeking treatment unless employee has previously tested positive or been in a rehabilitation program.

Notice and policy requirements: Before implementing testing program, employer must provide 60 days' notice and must give all employees a written drug and alcohol policy statement. Policy must include consequences of a positive test or refusing to submit to testing.

Utah

Utah Code Ann. §§ 34-38-1 to 34-38-15

Employers affected: Employers with one or more employees.

Testing applicants: Employer may test any applicant for drugs or alcohol as long as management and employer also submit to periodic testing.

Testing employees: Employer may test employee for drugs or alcohol as long as management also submits to periodic testing. Employer may require testing to:

- investigate possible individual employee impairment
- investigate an accident or theft
- maintain employee or public safety, or
- ensure productivity, quality, or security.

Employer may suspend, discipline, discharge, or require treatment on the basis of a failed test (confirmed positive result, adulterated sample, or substituted sample) or a refusal to take test.

Notice and policy requirements: Testing must be conducted according to a written policy that has been distributed to employees and is available for review by prospective employees.

Vermont

Vt. Stat. Ann. tit. 21, §§ 511 to 520

Employers affected: Employers with one or more employees.

Testing applicants: Employer may not test applicants for drugs or alcohol unless there is a job offer conditional on a negative test result and applicant is given written notice of the testing procedure and a list of the drugs to be tested for.

Testing employees: Random testing not permitted unless required by federal law. Employer may not require testing unless:

- There is probable cause to believe an employee is using or is under the influence.
- Employer has an employee assistance program that provides rehabilitation.
- Employee who tests positive and agrees to enter employee assistance program is not terminated.

State Drug and Alcohol Testing Laws (continued)

Employee rights: Employer must contract with a medical review officer who will review all test results and keep them confidential. Medical review officer is to contact employee or applicant to explain a positive test result. Employee or applicant has right to an independent retest at own expense. Employee who successfully completes employee assistance program may not be terminated, although employee may be suspended for up to 3 months to complete program. Employee who tests positive after completing treatment may be fired.

Notice and policy requirements: Must provide written policy that states consequences of a positive test.

Virginia

Va. Code Ann. § 65.2-813.2

Employers affected: Employers that establish drug-free workplace programs to qualify for workers' compensation insurance discount.

Testing applicants: State law gives insurers the authority to establish guidelines and criteria for testing.

Testing employees: State law gives insurers the authority to establish guidelines and criteria for testing.

Wyoming

Wy. Stat. Ann. 27-14-201; Wy. Rules & Regulations, WSD WCD Ch. 2, § 8

Employers affected: Employers that establish a drug and alcohol testing program approved by the state Department of Workforce Services may receive a workers' compensation discount of up to 5% of the base rate for the employer's classification.

Testing applicants: Must test applicants for drugs; may test applicants for alcohol. Job announcements must state that testing is required.

Testing employees: Must test employees:
- upon reasonable suspicion
- following a workplace accident, or
- at random.

Must follow testing protocols prescribed in regulations (including "strong recommendation" that post-accident testing be done by blood sample).

Employee rights: Employee has 5 days to contest or explain a positive result.

Notice and Policy Requirements: Employer must have written policy including consequence of positive result or refusing to submit to test. Must give notice 60 days prior to testing.

Trade Secrets and Conflicts of Interest

Often, what gives a company a competitive advantage is the specialized knowledge that it has gained through the ingenuity, innovation, or just plain hard work of its owners and employees. This specialized knowledge could be something as mundane as a list of customers who have a specific need for your company's services or as glamorous as the top-secret formula for your company's product. The law of trade secrets protects this specialized knowledge from disclosure to, and use by, your competitors.

Employees pose a thorny dilemma for businesses with valuable trade secrets. After all, a business has to let some workers in on its trade secrets, either because they need the information to do their jobs or because they helped develop the information in the first place. Yet these same people may harm the business— either accidentally or through bad intentions—by revealing trade secrets to competitors.

Most states impose a duty of loyalty on employees that includes keeping their employer's trade secrets confidential. Nonetheless, it doesn't hurt to specifically inform employees in the handbook that they must keep mum.

A similar issue arises with regard to conflicts of interest. Most employers do not want their current employees also working for competitors. Such work inherently divides an employee's loyalties and creates a risk that the employee will reveal trade secrets to the competitor. By the same token, such work creates the risk that the employee will reveal the competitor's trade secrets to someone in your company. Although having a double agent on your team might not sound so bad at first, it's illegal. A competitor could drag your company into court.

One of the first steps in protecting your company is to put employees on notice about what is expected of them in this area, something that the policies included in this chapter will do for you. If your company has valuable information to protect, however, it will need more than a few handbook policies to do the job. It will need policies and procedures in place to identify confidential information and limit access to it, among other things.

18:1 Confidentiality and Trade Secrets

File Name: 18_Trade Secrets.rtf

Include This Policy?
- ☐ Yes
- ☐ No
- ☐ Use our existing policy
- ☐ Other _____

Alternate Modifications
None

Additional Clauses
Companies With Confidentiality
Procedures in Place
Insert?:   ☐ Yes   ☐ No

Related Policies
None

Notes
_____
_____
_____
_____
_____
_____
_____
_____
_____
_____
_____
_____
_____
_____
_____
_____
_____
_____
_____
_____

18:1 Confidentiality and Trade Secrets

Often, ensuring that employees don't disclose sensitive information is as simple as cluing them in to the importance of keeping quiet and the consequences of failing to do so. The sample policy in this section serves these purposes.

Confidentiality and Trade Secrets

Information is part of what makes this Company competitive. During your employment here, you may periodically learn trade secrets and other protected proprietary and confidential information about the Company, such as _____ . Some employees may need this information to do their jobs; others may be responsible for developing this type of information for the Company.

Employees may not disclose trade secrets and other protected proprietary and confidential information to anyone outside of the Company. If you have any questions about your obligations or what types of information this policy covers, please contact _____ . Employees who violate this policy will face disciplinary action, up to and including termination.

After you leave this Company, you are still legally prohibited from disclosing trade secrets and similarly protected proprietary and confidential information.

How to Complete This Policy

In the first blank, you will need to provide some examples of the types of information your Company might treat as proprietary or confidential. For example, an investment company might insert "financial and personal information about clients, business plans, and investment strategies." A chain of fitness centers might insert "customer personal and financial information, marketing strategies, business plans, and internal memoranda regarding the development of our personal training programs."

In the second blank, insert the position of someone who can help employees with questions about confidentiality and trade secrets, such as "your human resources representative" or "the Chief Information Officer."

CAUTION

You can't prohibit employees from discussing wages and other terms of employment. The National Labor Relations Act (NLRA) protects employee rights to discuss the terms and conditions of their employment with each other. This includes information about wages, schedules, and so on. The National Labor Relations Board (NLRB) has recently found that employer confidentiality policies an employee might interpret as infringing on this right are illegal. Confidentiality policies may not prohibit employees from discussing wages and salary, explicitly or implicitly. And, a policy that is too broad in defining confidential information might also run afoul of this protection.

Additional Clause for Companies With Confidentiality Procedures in Place

If you have procedures in place to protect your confidential information, pat yourself on the back. Then modify the standard policy above to inform employees of this fact. You don't need to give exhaustive detail about the procedures. It is sufficient to alert employees to their existence and tell employees where they can go for more information. Consider adding the following paragraph to the standard policy above.

Additional Clause

Because of the grave importance of keeping certain information confidential, this Company follows practices designed to alert employees to confidential, proprietary, and trade secret information, to limit access to that information, and to inform employees about what disclosures are and are not acceptable. We expect employees to follow these procedures. Employees who fail to do so face discipline, up to and including termination. To find out more about these procedures, refer to _____ .

If you have any questions about these procedures, contact

_____ .

Reality Check: Use Confidentiality Agreements and Designate Confidential Information

If your business depends on trade secret information to keep a competitive advantage, it behooves you to develop confidentiality procedures to protect valuable information from disclosure. These procedures typically include fairly simple means—such as labeling certain documents as "confidential"—of letting employees know what information is confidential and what information isn't. Your company's right to prevent others from using its trade secrets depends, in part, on whether you have taken adequate steps to keep that information confidential. The more you do to protect your company's trade secret, the stronger your legal claims will be if a competitor somehow gets its hands on them.

If your company has employees who will learn or develop confidential information while working there, consider having them sign a confidentiality agreement (also called a "nondisclosure agreement"). Although the duty of loyalty that we mentioned above should be technically sufficient to protect your company's trade secrets, nondisclosure agreements underscore the importance of confidentiality and clear up any ambiguity about what information your company considers a trade secret. They can also be helpful if your company ever has to haul an employee into court for revealing a trade secret, whether the employee is still working for your company or not.

18:2 Conflicts of Interest

Your company wants and expects its employees to be loyal to the company, not to its competitors. After all, a company and its employees work together as a team to compete in the marketplace and create a healthy, thriving business.

In most instances, the fact that an employee has a little job on the side isn't going to do much—if any—damage to your company. If that job is with a competitor, however, there is a risk that the side job will divide the employee's loyalties.

Similarly, employee investments will pose little harm to your company, unless those investments make the employee act in a way that is contrary to your company's interests.

Although your company has a legal right to protect itself from conflicts of interest, your employees also have legal rights to invest as they see fit and to work for whomever they want. The law balances your company's rights against those of its employees. If you need to discipline an employee or terminate someone for violating this policy, consult with an attorney first to make sure that your actions don't violate a law designed to protect employees.

This policy tells employees that loyalty is part of their job description. It also informs them that they will face consequences if they act in ways that could harm the company.

This policy applies to current employees only. It does not prohibit former employees from working for competitors. No handbook policy can do that. Instead, you'll need a contract called a noncompete agreement, which limits a former employee's ability to work for or start a competing company for a period of time. The rules on noncompete agreements vary from state to state. To find out how to draft a noncompete agreement that will be enforceable, talk to an employment lawyer.

18:2 Conflicts of Interest

File Name: 18_Trade Secrets.rtf

Include This Policy?
- ☐ Yes
- ☐ No
- ☐ Use our existing policy
- ☐ Other _____

Alternate Modifications
None

Additional Clauses
None

Related Policies
None

Notes

Conflicts of Interest

Employees may not engage in any activities or relationships that create either an actual conflict of interest or the potential for a conflict of interest.

Although we cannot list every activity or relationship that would create either an actual or potential conflict of interest, examples of activities that violate this policy include the following:

- working for a competitor or customer or vendor as a part-time employee, full-time employee, consultant, or independent contractor, or in any other capacity
- owning an interest in a competitor, customer, vendor, or anyone else who seeks to do business with this Company
- using the resources of this Company for personal gain, and
- using your position in this Company for personal gain.

Employees who violate this policy face disciplinary action, up to and including termination.

If you are unsure about whether an activity might violate this policy, or if you have any questions at all about this policy, please talk to _____ .

Discrimination and Harassment

Most employers are required to follow federal antidiscrimination laws, including laws prohibiting sexual harassment. Depending on where your company does business, it may also have to follow state and even local laws banning discrimination. An employer's obligation to comply with these laws has nothing to do with its personnel policies. Whether a company has an antidiscrimination policy or not, it must follow the law.

So why include policies prohibiting discrimination and harassment in an employee handbook? First, these policies educate employees and managers about what constitutes discrimination or harassment, what types of conduct are prohibited, and what the company will do to stop it. Armed with this information, employees and managers will know what to do if they are victims of, or witnesses to, illegal behavior. They will also know that the company believes in equal employment opportunity for everyone, a philosophy that can help a business build solid relations with its workers.

Second, stated policies against discrimination and harassment will encourage workers to bring misconduct to the company's attention immediately. Unless your company is very small, this could be the only way management finds out that a potentially troublesome situation is brewing. If employees complain quickly, the company has a chance to deal with the problems right away, before they poison the workplace environment.

Finally, a well-crafted policy against harassment buys the company some legal protection, should it ever be sued by an employee. If your company has a clear written policy prohibiting harassment and spelling out a complaint procedure, employees must follow these procedures to make complaints. If they fail to alert the company to a problem, courts might not let them sue the company for failing to deal with it.

19:1 Our Commitment to Equal Employment Opportunity

File Name: 19_Discrimination.rtf

Include This Policy?
- ☐ Yes
- ☐ No
- ☐ Use our existing policy
- ☐ Other _____

Alternate Modifications
None

Additional Clauses
Emphasize Company's Commitment
Insert?: ☐ Yes ☐ No

Related Policies
Chapter 20 covers policies for making a discrimination or harassment complaint.

Notes

_____
_____
_____
_____
_____
_____
_____
_____
_____
_____
_____
_____
_____
_____
_____
_____

19:1 Antidiscrimination Policy

Your antidiscrimination policy should explain the company's commitment to equal opportunity. It should describe what is prohibited, let employees know what to do if they witness or suffer discrimination, and tell employees how the company will deal with discrimination in the workplace.

Our Commitment to Equal Employment Opportunity

Our Company is strongly committed to providing equal employment opportunity for all employees and all applicants for employment. For us, this is the only acceptable way to do business.

All employment decisions at our Company—including those relating to hiring, promotion, transfers, benefits, compensation, placement, and termination—will be made without regard to

_____
_____ .

Any employee or applicant who believes that he or she has been discriminated against in violation of this policy should immediately file a complaint with _____
_____ ,

as explained in our Complaint Policy. We encourage you to come forward if you have suffered or witnessed what you believe to be discrimination; we cannot solve the problem until you let us know about it. The Company will not retaliate, or allow retaliation, against any employee or applicant who complains of discrimination, assists in an investigation of possible discrimination, or files an administrative charge or lawsuit alleging discrimination.

Managers are required to report any discriminatory conduct or incidents, as described in our Complaint Policy.

Our Company will not tolerate discrimination against any employee or applicant. We will take immediate and appropriate disciplinary action against any employee who violates this policy.

Who Needs This Policy

No law requires an employer to include an antidiscrimination policy in its handbook. Because of the benefits such a policy can provide, however, all employers who are subject to antidiscrimination laws should have one. (For details on which employers have a legal obligation not to discriminate, see "Which Federal Antidiscrimination Laws Apply to Your Company," below.)

How to Complete This Policy

Before you can complete our sample policy, you will need to know what antidiscrimination laws your company is required to follow under both federal and state law. This will tell you what to put in the blank in our sample policy, above, where you list prohibited bases for discrimination at your company.

Federal laws require many employers not to discriminate on the basis of race, color, national origin, religion, sex, age, disability, or citizenship status. However, these laws don't apply to every employer; they apply only to employers who have a specified minimum number of employees. To find out which federal laws your company has to follow—and, therefore, which characteristics to list in your policy—refer to "Which Federal Antidiscrimination Laws Apply to Your Company," below.

In addition, most states and some municipalities have their own antidiscrimination laws. Some of these laws duplicate the federal protections, while others apply to smaller employers or prohibit discrimination based on additional characteristics that federal law does not include, such as marital status or sexual orientation. To find out whether your state imposes any additional obligations, consult "State Laws Prohibiting Discrimination in Employment" at the end of this chapter. You can find out whether any local laws apply by getting in touch with your state fair employment department (see Appendix B for contact information) or your local government offices.

Which Federal Antidiscrimination Laws Apply to Your Company

Not every antidiscrimination law applies to every employer. For the most part, whether your company has to follow these laws depends on its size and location. Federal antidiscrimination laws apply only to employers with more than a minimum number of employees; this minimum number is different for each law.

Name of Law:	Discrimination Prohibited on the Basis of:	Applies to:
Title VII	Race, color, national origin, religion, sex*	Employers with 15 or more employees
Age Discrimination in Employment Act	Age (over 40 only)	Employers with 20 or more employees
Americans with Disabilities Act	Physical or mental disability	Employers with 15 or more employees
Equal Pay Act	Sex (applies only to wage discrimination)	All employers
Civil Rights Act of 1866	Race, ethnicity	All employers
Immigration Reform and Control Act	Citizenship status, national origin	Employers with 4 or more employees
Genetic Information Nondiscrimination Act	Genetic information	Employers with at least 15 employees

* In 2016, the EEOC announced that it interprets Title VII's prohibition on sex discrimination to also prohibit discrimination based on gender identity and sexual orientation.

Your handbook should refer only to those types of discrimination that are prohibited for your company. For example, if your company does business in a state that outlaws discrimination based on marital status, you should include marital status in the list of prohibited bases for discrimination. Similarly, if your company has only 15 employees, it does not have to comply with the federal Age Discrimination in Employment Act. Unless a separate state law prohibits age discrimination in companies of your size, you should not include age in your list.

You will also have to decide who in your company will receive complaints of discrimination. In this blank in the sample policy, designate the positions named in your complaint policy. (See Chapter 20 for complaint policies and related discussions.) If you have a human resources department, you can refer employees there.

Additional Clause to Emphasize Company's Commitment

You may want to include additional language to further explain and emphasize your company's commitment to equal employment opportunity. Some employers take special pride in their efforts to combat discrimination, to provide goods or services to traditionally underserved communities, or to honor cultural diversity. Consider the following examples of additions based on the purpose each company serves.

SAMPLE POLICY LANGUAGE

Our Company was founded to help women achieve equal opportunity in the field of sports. This commitment to equal opportunity for everyone extends to our workplace and the way we treat each other. Discrimination of any kind is contrary to the principles for which our Company stands.

SAMPLE POLICY LANGUAGE

Our mission is to bring fresh, high-quality food products from around the world to customers in the United States. We take pride in the great diversity of our customers and our employees. We treat our employees, and expect our employees to treat each other, with respect and dignity. Discrimination of any kind is against our Company philosophy and policies and will not be tolerated.

RESOURCE

Developing a comprehensive policy for transgender employees. In the past few years, employers and legislators have paid more attention to discrimination against transgender employees: employees whose gender identity differs from the gender they were assigned at birth. As of July 2016, the EEOC, which enforces Title VII, announced that sex discrimination includes discrimination based on gender identity. If your company wants to go beyond including gender identity as a protected trait in its discrimination policy and adopt a policy on how it will treat transgender and transitioning employees, there are a number of helpful resources available, including:

- *A Guide to Restroom Access for Transgender Workers*, an OSHA publication available at https://www.osha.gov/Publications/OSHA3795.pdf, which includes model employer practices for providing equal access to facilities.
- *Model Transgender Employment Policy*, available from the Transgender Law Center, https://transgenderlawcenter.org.
- *Transgender Inclusion in the Workplace*, available from the Human Rights Campaign, www.hrc.org.

19:2 Reasonable Accommodation for Disabilities

File Name: 19_Discrimination.rtf

Include This Policy?
- ☐ Yes
- ☐ No
- ☐ Use our existing policy
- ☐ Other _____

Alternate Modifications

None

Additional Clauses

Reasonable Accommodation for Pregnancy

Insert?:   ☐ Yes   ☐ No

Related Policies

None

Notes

_____
_____
_____
_____
_____
_____
_____
_____
_____
_____
_____
_____
_____
_____
_____
_____

19:2 Reasonable Accommodation for Disabilities

If your company is subject to the Americans with Disabilities Act (ADA) or to a state or local law prohibiting disability discrimination, you have an obligation to provide reasonable accommodations to allow qualified employees with disabilities to do their jobs. Even if you aren't legally required to do so, accommodating an employee with a disability can make good business sense: It allows you to retain employees and help them succeed, often at very low expense.

You aren't legally required to have a written policy letting employees know how to request an accommodation, but it's a very good idea. Allowing employees to come forward as soon as they know they need assistance will minimize disruptions and downtime and allow everyone to work quickly to solve the problem and get back to work.

In recent years, about a dozen states have passed laws that require employers to provide reasonable accommodation to employees who are temporarily unable to work due to pregnancy. These laws differ slightly in the details. Generally, however, they require employers to accommodate an employee's medical limits during pregnancy and/or to transfer an employee to a less strenuous or less hazardous position. For example, an employee whose doctor has imposed a lifting restriction might request a transfer to a job that doesn't require her to lift more than 20 pounds.

Most states that have adopted laws requiring employers to accommodate an employee's pregnancy require employers to give employees written notice of their rights under the law. A couple of states have gone further, explicitly requiring employers to include these rights in their employee handbook.

Your reasonable accommodation policy should explain who is entitled to an accommodation, how to request one, and what will happen after the employee makes the request.

> ### Reasonable Accommodation for Disabilities
>
> Our Company will provide reasonable accommodations to enable qualified employees with disabilities to perform their jobs and to enjoy the benefits and privileges of employment here, unless doing so would cause undue hardship.
>
> If you believe you need a reasonable accommodation, please submit your request to _____
>
> _____ .
>
> You may make your request orally or in writing. If you know of a particular accommodation that you believe will help, please mention it in your request. Although we cannot guarantee that we will grant your specific request, we will certainly consider it.
>
> Once you make your request, the Company will engage in a flexible, interactive dialogue with you to come up with an effective accommodation that does not create undue hardship. As part of this process, we may request medical records or information from your medical provider regarding your disability and possible accommodations. In this event, we will treat this information as a confidential medical record.

How to Complete This Policy

In the blank space, name the position responsible for taking requests for reasonable accommodations (for example, "the HR director").

Additional Clause on Accommodations for Pregnant Employees

If you do business in a state that requires employers to accommodate pregnant employees, you should add this clause to your policy. As noted above, some states require employers to include this information in their employment handbooks.

Additional Clause

> If you need a reasonable accommodation due to pregnancy, childbirth, or related conditions, please submit your request to
>
> _____ .
>
> You may submit your request orally or in writing.
>
> If your physician has given you job restrictions, we will try to accommodate them. We will also consider transferring you to a less hazardous or less strenuous job. However, we will not provide an accommodation if it creates undue hardship for the Company.
>
> As part of the reasonable accommodation process, we may ask your physician to provide a medical certification or other information regarding your medical limitations. In this event, we will treat this information as a confidential medical record.

CAUTION

Your state law may require more or different language. The language above can be used in most states that require employers to accommodate pregnancy, and by employers who wish to provide this accommodation even if it isn't legally mandated. However, state regulations and new state laws may dictate that you use particular language in your handbook. This is an issue your lawyer can help you with when you get a legal review of your finished draft of the handbook.

19:3 Reasonable Accommodation for Religious Practices or Beliefs

Companies that are subject to Title VII of the Civil Rights Act of 1964 or to a state or local law prohibiting discrimination based on religion must provide reasonable accommodations for employees whose religious beliefs, observances, or practices conflict with their job duties or workplace rules. For example, an employee may need an exception to the usual dress code for a headscarf or turban, may need Saturdays off to observe a Sabbath, or may need time off and a quiet, private room during the work day for prayer.

Your company does not have to grant an employee's accommodation request if doing so would create undue hardship. In the context of religious accommodations, an undue hardship is anything more than a minimal cost on the employer's business operations, whether in actual dollars and cents or in lost efficiency, safety risks, or shifting job duties to other employees. (The standard for undue burden is different—and harder to meet—for disabilities.)

Your policy should explain that your company will provide a religious accommodation, how employees should request one, and how that request will be handled.

Reasonable Accommodation for Religious Practices or Beliefs

Our Company will provide reasonable accommodations to employees whose religious beliefs, practices, or observances require them, unless doing so would cause undue hardship.

If you believe you need a reasonable accommodation (for example, because your religious beliefs or practices create a conflict with your job duties, schedule, dress code, or other Company policies or practices), please submit your request to _____ _____. You may make your request orally or in writing. If you know of a particular accommodation that you believe will be effective, please mention it in your request. Although we cannot guarantee that we will grant your specific request, we will certainly consider it.

Once you make your request, the Company will engage in a flexible, interactive dialogue with you to come up with an effective accommodation that does not create undue hardship. As part of this process, we may request information from you regarding your religious beliefs or practices.

19:3 Reasonable Accommodation for Religious Practices or Beliefs

File Name: 19_ReligiousPractices.rtf

Include This Policy?
- ☐ Yes
- ☐ No
- ☐ Use our existing policy
- ☐ Other _____

Alternate Modifications
None

Additional Clauses
None

Related Policies
Chapter 20 covers policies for making a discrimination or harassment complaint.

Notes

How to Complete This Policy

Complete this policy by filling in the position responsible for handling employee reasonable accommodation requests (for example, "your manager" or "your HR representative").

19:4 Harassment

Legally, harassment is a form of discrimination. The same laws that prohibit discrimination also require employers to stop harassment. Therefore, every employer who is subject to the antidiscrimination laws discussed above should also have a policy against harassment.

No law requires an employer to have a policy prohibiting harassment. However, in addition to the practical benefits such a policy can provide, a harassment policy creates one very substantial legal benefit: protection against certain harassment lawsuits. If your company has a policy prohibiting harassment that includes the essential elements we discuss below (and include in our sample policy), and the company fully investigates complaints of harassment and takes appropriate disciplinary action against those who violate the policy, a court may decide that an employee who failed to complain of harassment cannot sue the company.

This protection applies only to certain types of harassment cases, however. If management was aware of the harassment even though the employee did not complain (for example, there were lewd posters and X-rated graffiti displayed prominently throughout the workplace), the employee's failure to complain won't get the company off the hook. And if the harassment was committed by a manager or supervisor and resulted in a serious, negative job action against the employee (for example, the employee was fired or denied a promotion because she refused to have a sexual relationship with a supervisor), the company will be responsible whether or not the employee complained. However, if no negative job action was taken against the employee (for example, an employee was repeatedly teased or subjected to lewd jokes and stories but was not demoted or fired), she can sue the company for harassment by a manager or supervisor only if she first complained, using the company's harassment and complaint policies.

Your harassment policy should explain what harassment is, let workers know that harassment will not be tolerated, tell workers and managers what to do if they witness or suffer harassment, and assure everyone that retaliation against those who complain of harassment or participate in a harassment investigation is strictly prohibited.

19:4 Harassment Will Not Be Tolerated

File Name: 19_Discrimination.rtf

Include This Policy?
- [ ] Yes
- [ ] No
- [ ] Use our existing policy
- [ ] Other _____

Alternate Modifications
None

Additional Clauses
None

Related Policies
Chapter 20 covers policies for making a discrimination or harassment complaint.

Notes

_____
_____
_____
_____
_____
_____
_____
_____
_____
_____
_____
_____
_____
_____
_____
_____
_____

Harassment Will Not Be Tolerated

It is our policy and our responsibility to provide our employees with a workplace free from harassment. Harassment on the basis of

_____

_____

undermines out workplace morale and our commitment to treat each other with dignity and respect. Accordingly, harassment will not be tolerated at our Company.

Harassment can take many forms, including but not limited to touching or other unwanted physical contact, posting offensive cartoons or pictures, using slurs or other derogatory terms, telling offensive or lewd jokes and stories, and sending email messages with offensive content. Unwanted sexual advances, requests for sexual favors, and sexually suggestive gestures, jokes, propositions, email messages, or other communications all constitute harassment.

If you experience or witness any form of harassment in the workplace, please immediately notify the Company by following the steps outlined in our Complaint Policy (see Section _____ of this Handbook). We encourage you to come forward with complaints; the sooner we learn about the problem, the sooner we can take steps to resolve it. The Company will not retaliate, or allow retaliation, against anyone who complains of harassment, assists in a harassment investigation, or files an administrative charge or lawsuit alleging harassment. All managers are required to immediately report any incidents of harassment, as set forth in our Complaint Policy.

Complaints will be investigated quickly. Those who are found to have violated this policy will be subject to appropriate disciplinary action, up to and including termination.

How to Complete This Policy

Because harassment is legally considered to be a type of discrimination, a company's obligation to prevent and remedy harassment tracks its obligation not to discriminate. For example, if the law protects employees from discrimination on the basis of race, they are also protected from racial harassment. In the blank space, fill in the same prohibited bases for harassment that you included in your antidiscrimination policy.

RESOURCE

For more information on federal antidiscrimination laws, see *The Essential Guide to Federal Employment Laws,* by Lisa Guerin and Sachi Barreiro (Nolo). This helpful resource devotes an entire chapter to each of the major federal employment laws, including the antidiscrimination laws listed above. You can also find helpful fact sheets, posters, compliance assistance, and more on the website of the Equal Employment Opportunity Commission—the federal agency that interprets and enforces federal antidiscrimination laws—at www.eeoc.gov.

State Laws Prohibiting Discrimination in Employment

Alabama

Ala. Code §§ 25-1-20, 25-1-21

Law applies to employers with: 20 or more employees

Private employers may not make employment decisions based on:

- Age (40 and older)

Alaska

Alaska Stat. §§ 18.80.220, 18.80.300, 47.30.865

Law applies to employers with: One or more employees

Private employers may not make employment decisions based on:

- Age
- Ancestry or national origin
- Physical or mental disability
- Gender
- Marital status, including changes in status
- Pregnancy, childbirth, and related medical conditions, including parenthood
- Race or color
- Religion or creed
- Mental illness

Arizona

Ariz. Rev. Stat. §§ 41-1461, 41-1463, 41-1465

Law applies to employers with: 15 or more employees

Private employers may not make employment decisions based on:

- Age (40 and older)
- Ancestry or national origin
- Physical or mental disability
- AIDS/HIV
- Gender
- Race or color
- Religion or creed
- Genetic testing information

Arkansas

Ark. Code Ann. §§ 11-4-601, 11-5-403, 16-123-102, 16-123-107

Law applies to employers with: Nine or more employees

Private employers may not make employment decisions based on:

- Ancestry or national origin
- Physical, mental, or sensory disability
- Gender

- Pregnancy, childbirth, and related medical conditions
- Race or color
- Religion or creed
- Genetic testing information

California

Cal. Gov't. Code §§ 12920, 12926.1, 12940, 12941, 12945; Cal. Lab. Code § 1101

Law applies to employers with: Five or more employees

Private employers may not make employment decisions based on:

- Age (40 and older)
- Ancestry or national origin
- Physical or mental disability
- AIDS/HIV
- Gender
- Marital status
- Pregnancy, childbirth, and related medical conditions
- Race or color
- Religion or creed
- Sexual orientation
- Genetic testing information
- Gender identity
- Medical condition
- Political activities or affiliations
- Status as victim of domestic violence, sexual assault, or stalking
- Military and veteran status

Colorado

Colo. Rev. Stat. §§ 24-34-301, 24-34-401, 24-34-402, 24-34-402.5, 27-65-115; Colo. Code Regs. 708-1:60.1, 708-1:80.8

Law applies to employers with: One or more employees; 25 or more employees (marital status only)

Private employers may not make employment decisions based on:

- Age (40 and older)
- Ancestry or national origin
- Physical, mental, or learning disability
- AIDS/HIV
- Gender
- Marital status (only applies to marriage to a coworker or plans to marry a coworker)
- Pregnancy, childbirth, and related medical conditions
- Race or color
- Religion or creed

State Laws Prohibiting Discrimination in Employment (continued)

- Sexual orientation, including perceived sexual orientation
- Lawful conduct outside of work
- Mental illness
- Transgender status

Connecticut

Conn. Gen. Stat. Ann. §§ 25-4-1401, 46a-51, 46a-60, 46a-81a, 46a-81c

Law applies to employers with: Three or more employees

Private employers may not make employment decisions based on:

- Age
- Ancestry or national origin
- Present or past physical, mental, learning, or intellectual disability
- Gender
- Marital status, including civil unions
- Pregnancy, childbirth, and related medical conditions
- Race or color
- Religion or creed
- Sexual orientation, including having a history of being identified with a preference
- Genetic testing information
- Gender identity or expression
- Arrests or convictions that have been erased, pardoned, or rehabilitated

Delaware

Del. Code Ann. tit. 19, §§ 710, 711, 724

Law applies to employers with: Four or more employees

Private employers may not make employment decisions based on:

- Age (40 and older)
- Ancestry or national origin
- Physical or mental disability
- AIDS/HIV
- Gender
- Marital status
- Pregnancy, childbirth, and related medical conditions
- Race or color
- Religion or creed
- Sexual orientation
- Genetic testing information
- Gender identity
- status as victim of domestic violence, sexual offense, or stalking

- family responsibilities (effective December 2016)
- "reproductive health decisions" (effective December 2016)

District of Columbia

D.C. Code Ann. §§ 2-1401.01, 2-1401.02, 2-1401.05, 2-1402.82, 7-1703.03, 32-131.08

Law applies to employers with: One or more employees

Private employers may not make employment decisions based on:

- Age (18 and older)
- Ancestry or national origin
- Physical or mental disability
- Gender
- Marital status, including domestic partnership
- Pregnancy, childbirth, and related medical conditions, including parenthood
- Race or color
- Religion or creed
- Sexual orientation
- Genetic testing information
- Enrollment in vocational, professional, or college education
- Family duties
- Source of income
- Place of residence or business
- Personal appearance
- Political affiliation
- Victim of intrafamily offense
- Gender identity or expression
- Status as unemployed
- Tobacco use
- Any reason other than individual merit

Florida

Fla. Stat. Ann. §§ 448.075, 760.01, 760.02, 760.10, 760.50

Law applies to employers with: 15 or more employees

Private employers may not make employment decisions based on:

- Age
- Ancestry or national origin
- "Handicap"
- AIDS/HIV
- Gender
- Marital status
- Pregnancy, childbirth, and related medical conditions
- Race or color

State Laws Prohibiting Discrimination in Employment (continued)

- Religion or creed
- Sickle cell trait

Georgia

Ga. Code Ann. §§ 34-1-2, 34-5-1, 34-5-2, 34-6A-1 and following

Law applies to employers with: 15 or more employees (disability); 10 or more employees (gender) (domestic and agricultural employees not protected); one or more employee (age)

Private employers may not make employment decisions based on:
- Age (40 to 70)
- Physical, mental, or learning disability
- Gender (wage discrimination only)

Hawaii

Haw. Rev. Stat. §§ 378-1, 378-2, 378-2.5;
Hawaii Admin Rules § 12-46-182

Law applies to employers with: One or more employees

Private employers may not make employment decisions based on:
- Age
- Ancestry or national origin
- Physical or mental disability
- AIDS/HIV
- Gender
- Marital status
- Pregnancy, childbirth, and related medical conditions, including breast-feeding
- Race or color
- Religion or creed
- Sexual orientation
- Genetic testing information
- Arrest and court record (unless there is a conviction directly related to job)
- Credit history or credit report, unless the information in the individual's credit history or credit report directly relates to a bona fide occupational qualification
- Gender identity and gender expression
- Status as a victim of domestic or sexual violence (if employer has knowledge or is notified of this status)

Idaho

Idaho Code §§ 39-8303, 67-5902, 67-5909, 67-5910

Law applies to employers with: Five or more employees

Private employers may not make employment decisions based on:
- Age (40 and older)
- Ancestry or national origin
- Physical or mental disability
- Gender
- Pregnancy, childbirth, and related medical conditions
- Race or color
- Religion or creed
- Genetic testing information

Illinois

410 Ill. Comp. Stat. § 513/25; 775 Ill. Comp. Stat. §§ 5/1-102, 5/1-103, 5/1-105, 5/2-101, 5/2-102, 5/2-103; 820 Ill. Comp. Stat. §§ 105/4, 180/30; Ill. Admin. Code tit. 56, § 5210.110

Law applies to employers with: 15 or more employees; one or more employees (disability)

Private employers may not make employment decisions based on:
- Age (40 and older)
- Ancestry or national origin
- Physical or mental disability
- Gender
- Marital status
- Pregnancy, childbirth, and related medical conditions
- Race or color
- Religion or creed
- Sexual orientation
- Genetic testing information
- Citizenship status
- Military status
- Unfavorable military discharge
- Gender identity
- Arrest record
- Victims of domestic violence
- Order of protection status
- Lack of permanent mailing address or having a mailing address of a shelter or social service provider

Indiana

Ind. Code Ann. §§ 22-9-1-2, 22-9-2-1, 22-9-2-2, 22-9-5-1 and following

Law applies to employers with: 6 or more employees; 1 or more employees (age only); 15 or more employees (disability only)

State Laws Prohibiting Discrimination in Employment (continued)

Private employers may not make employment decisions based on:

- Age (40 to 75—applies to employers with one or more employees)
- Ancestry or national origin
- Physical or mental disability (15 or more employees)
- Gender
- Race or color
- Religion or creed
- Status as a veteran
- Off-duty tobacco use
- Sealed or expunged arrest or conviction record

Iowa

Iowa Code §§ 216.2, 216.6, 216.6A, 729.6

Law applies to employers with: Four or more employees

Private employers may not make employment decisions based on:

- Age (18 or older)
- Ancestry or national origin
- Physical or mental disability
- AIDS/HIV
- Gender
- Pregnancy, childbirth, and related medical conditions
- Race or color
- Religion or creed
- Sexual orientation
- Genetic testing information
- Gender identity
- Wage discrimination

Kansas

Kan. Stat. Ann. §§ 44-1002, 44-1009, 44-1112, 44-1113, 44-1125, 44-1126, 65-6002(e)

Law applies to employers with: Four or more employees

Private employers may not make employment decisions based on:

- Age (40 or older)
- Ancestry or national origin
- Physical or mental disability
- AIDS/HIV
- Gender
- Race or color
- Religion or creed
- Genetic testing information
- Military service or status

Kentucky

Ky. Rev. Stat. Ann. §§ 207.130, 207.135, 207.150, 342.197, 344.010, 344.030, 344.040

Law applies to employers with: Eight or more employees

Private employers may not make employment decisions based on:

- Age (40 or older)
- Ancestry or national origin
- Physical or mental disability
- AIDS/HIV
- Gender
- Pregnancy, childbirth, and related medical conditions
- Race or color
- Religion or creed
- Occupational pneumoconiosis with no respiratory impairment resulting from exposure to coal dust
- Off-duty tobacco use

Louisiana

La. Rev. Stat. Ann. §§ 23:301 to 23:368

Law applies to employers with: 20 or more employees

Private employers may not make employment decisions based on:

- Age (40 or older)
- Ancestry or national origin
- Physical or mental disability
- Gender
- Pregnancy, childbirth, and related medical conditions (applies to employers with 25 or more employees)
- Race or color
- Religion or creed
- Genetic testing information
- Sickle cell trait
- Being a smoker or nonsmoker

Maine

Me. Rev. Stat. Ann. tit. 5, §§ 19302, 4552, 4553, 4571 to 4576, 23; tit. 26, § 833; tit. 39-A, § 353

Law applies to employers with: One or more employees

Private employers may not make employment decisions based on:

- Age
- Ancestry or national origin
- Physical or mental disability
- AIDS/HIV

State Laws Prohibiting Discrimination in Employment (continued)

- Gender
- Pregnancy, childbirth, and related medical conditions
- Race or color
- Religion or creed
- Sexual orientation, including perceived sexual orientation
- Genetic testing information
- Gender identity or expression
- Past workers' compensation claim
- Past whistle-blowing
- Medical support notice for child

Maryland

Md. Code, [State Government], §§ 20-101, 20-601 to 20-608

Law applies to employers with: 15 or more employees

Private employers may not make employment decisions based on:
- Age
- Ancestry or national origin
- Physical or mental disability
- Gender
- Marital status
- Pregnancy, childbirth, and related medical conditions
- Race or color
- Religion or creed
- Sexual orientation
- Genetic testing information
- Civil Air Patrol membership
- Gender identity

Massachusetts

Mass. Gen. Laws ch. 149, § 24A, ch. 151B, §§ 1, 4; Code of Massachusetts Regulations 804 CMR 3.01

Law applies to employers with: Six or more employees

Private employers may not make employment decisions based on:
- Age (40 or older)
- Ancestry or national origin
- Physical or mental disability
- Gender
- Marital status
- Race or color
- Religion or creed
- Sexual orientation
- Genetic testing information
- Military service

- Arrest record
- Gender identity
- status as a veteran

Michigan

Mich. Comp. Laws §§ 37.1103, 37.1201, 37.1202, 37.2201, 37.2202, 37.2205a, 750.556

Law applies to employers with: One or more employees

Private employers may not make employment decisions based on:
- Age
- Ancestry or national origin
- Physical or mental disability
- AIDS/HIV
- Gender
- Marital status
- Pregnancy, childbirth, and related medical conditions
- Race or color
- Religion or creed
- Genetic testing information
- Height or weight
- Misdemeanor arrest record
- Civil Air Patrol membership

Minnesota

Minn. Stat. Ann. §§ 144.417, 181.81, 181.974, 363A.03, 363A.08

Law applies to employers with: One or more employees

Private employers may not make employment decisions based on:
- Age (18 to 70)
- Ancestry or national origin
- Physical, sensory, or mental disability
- Gender
- Marital status
- Pregnancy, childbirth, and related medical conditions
- Race or color
- Religion or creed
- Sexual orientation, including perceived sexual orientation
- Genetic testing information
- Gender identity
- Member of local commission
- Receiving public assistance
- Familial status (protects parents or guardians living with a minor child)

State Laws Prohibiting Discrimination in Employment (continued)

Mississippi

Miss. Code Ann. § 33-1-15

Law applies to employers with: One or more employees

Private employers may not make employment decisions based on:

- Military status
- No other protected categories unless employer receives public funding

Missouri

Mo. Rev. Stat. §§ 191.665, 213.010, 213.055, 375.1306

Law applies to employers with: Six or more employees

Private employers may not make employment decisions based on:

- Age (40 to 70)
- Ancestry or national origin
- Physical or mental disability
- AIDS/HIV
- Gender
- Race or color
- Religion or creed
- Genetic testing information
- Off-duty use of alcohol or tobacco

Montana

Mont. Code Ann. §§ 49-2-101, 49-2-303, 49-2-310

Law applies to employers with: One or more employees

Private employers may not make employment decisions based on:

- Age
- Ancestry or national origin
- Physical or mental disability
- Gender
- Marital status
- Pregnancy, childbirth, and related medical conditions
- Race or color
- Religion or creed

Nebraska

Neb. Rev. Stat. §§ 20-168, 48-236, 48-1001 to 48-1010, 48-1102, 48-1104

Law applies to employers with: 15 or more employees

Private employers may not make employment decisions based on:

- Age (40 or older—applies to employers with 20 or more employees)

- Ancestry or national origin
- Physical or mental disability
- AIDS/HIV
- Gender
- Pregnancy, childbirth, and related medical conditions
- Race or color
- Religion or creed
- Genetic testing information (applies to all employers)

Nevada

Nev. Rev. Stat. Ann. §§ 613.310 and following

Law applies to employers with: 15 or more employees

Private employers may not make employment decisions based on:

- Age (40 or older)
- Ancestry or national origin
- Physical or mental disability
- AIDS/HIV
- Gender
- Pregnancy, childbirth, and related medical conditions
- Race or color
- Religion or creed
- Sexual orientation, including perceived sexual orientation
- Genetic testing information
- Use of service animal
- Gender identity or expression
- Opposing unlawful employment practices
- Credit report or credit information (with some exceptions)

New Hampshire

N.H. Rev. Stat. Ann. §§ 141-H:3, 354-A:2, 354-A:6, 354-A:7

Law applies to employers with: Six or more employees

Private employers may not make employment decisions based on:

- Age
- Ancestry or national origin
- Physical or mental disability
- Gender
- Marital status
- Pregnancy, childbirth, and related medical conditions
- Race or color
- Religion or creed
- Sexual orientation
- Genetic testing information

State Laws Prohibiting Discrimination in Employment (continued)

- Victims of domestic violence, harassment, sexual assault, or stalking
- Off-duty use of tobacco products

New Jersey

N.J. Stat. Ann. §§ 10:5-1, 10:5-4.1, 10:5-5, 10:5-12, 10:5-29.1, 34:6B-1, 43:21-49

Law applies to employers with: One or more employees

Private employers may not make employment decisions based on:

- Age (18 to 70)
- Ancestry or national origin
- Past or present physical or mental disability
- AIDS/HIV
- Gender
- Marital status, including civil union or domestic partnership status
- Pregnancy, childbirth, and related medical conditions
- Race or color
- Religion or creed
- Sexual orientation, including affectional orientation and perceived sexual orientation
- Genetic testing information
- Atypical heredity cellular or blood trait
- Accompanied by service or guide dog
- Military service
- Gender identity
- Unemployed status

New Mexico

N.M. Stat. Ann. §§ 24-21-4, 28-1-2, 28-1-7, 50-4A-4
N.M. Admin. Code 9.1.1

Law applies to employers with: Four or more employees

Private employers may not make employment decisions based on:

- Age (40 or older)
- Ancestry or national origin
- Physical or mental disability
- Gender
- Marital status (applies to employers with 50 or more employees)
- Pregnancy, childbirth, and related medical conditions
- Race or color
- Religion or creed
- Sexual orientation, including perceived sexual orientation (applies to employers with 15 or more employees)
- Genetic testing information

- Gender identity (employers with 15 or more employees)
- Serious medical condition
- Domestic abuse leave

New York

N.Y. Exec. Law §§ 292, 296; N.Y. Lab. Law § 201-d

Law applies to employers with: Four or more employees; all employers (sexual harassment only)

Private employers may not make employment decisions based on:

- Age (18 and over)
- Ancestry or national origin
- Physical or mental disability
- Gender
- Marital status
- Pregnancy, childbirth, and related medical conditions
- Race or color
- Religion or creed
- Sexual orientation, including perceived sexual orientation
- Genetic testing information
- Lawful recreational activities when not at work
- Military status or service
- Observance of Sabbath
- Political activities
- Use of service dog
- Arrest or criminal accusation
- Domestic violence victim status
- Familial status

North Carolina

N.C. Gen. Stat. §§ 95-28.1, 95-28.1A, 127B-11, 130A-148, 143-422.2, 168A-5

Law applies to employers with: 15 or more employees

Private employers may not make employment decisions based on:

- Age
- Ancestry or national origin
- Physical or mental disability
- AIDS/HIV
- Gender
- Race or color
- Religion or creed
- Genetic testing information
- Military status or service
- Sickle cell or hemoglobin C trait
- Lawful use of lawful products off site and off duty

State Laws Prohibiting Discrimination in Employment (continued)

North Dakota

N.D. Cent. Code §§ 14-02.4-02, 14-02.4-03, 34-01-17

Law applies to employers with: One or more employees

Private employers may not make employment decisions based on:

- Age (40 or older)
- Ancestry or national origin
- Physical or mental disability
- Gender
- Marital status
- Pregnancy, childbirth, and related medical conditions
- Race or color
- Religion or creed
- Lawful conduct outside of work
- Receiving public assistance
- Keeping and bearing arms (as long as firearm is never exhibited on company property except for lawful defensive purposes)
- Status as a volunteer emergency responder

Ohio

Ohio Rev. Code Ann. §§ 4111.17, 4112.01, 4112.02

Law applies to employers with: Four or more employees

Private employers may not make employment decisions based on:

- Age (40 or older)
- Ancestry or national origin
- Physical, mental, or learning disability
- AIDS/HIV
- Gender
- Pregnancy, childbirth, and related medical conditions
- Race or color
- Religion or creed
- Military status
- Caring for a sibling, child, parent, or spouse injured while in the armed service

Oklahoma

Okla. Stat. Ann. tit. 25, §§ 1301, 1302; tit. 36, § 3614.2; tit. 40, § 500; tit. 44, § 208

Law applies to employers with: 1 or more employees

Private employers may not make employment decisions based on:

- Age (40 or older)
- Ancestry or national origin
- Physical or mental disability

- Gender
- Pregnancy, childbirth, and related medical conditions (except abortions where the woman is not in "imminent danger of death")
- Race or color
- Religion or creed
- Genetic testing information
- Military service
- Being a smoker or nonsmoker or using tobacco off duty

Oregon

Ore. Rev. Stat. §§ 25-337, 659A.030, 659A.122 and following, 659A.303

Law applies to employers with: One or more employees

Private employers may not make employment decisions based on:

- Age (18 or older)
- Ancestry or national origin
- Physical or mental disability (applies to employers with 6 or more employees)
- Gender
- Marital status
- Pregnancy, childbirth, and related medical conditions
- Race or color
- Religion or creed
- Sexual orientation
- Genetic testing information
- Parent who has medical support order imposed by court
- Domestic violence victim status
- Refusal to attend an employer-sponsored meeting with the primary purpose of communicating the employer's opinion on religious or political matters
- Credit history
- Whistle-blowers
- Off-duty use of tobacco products

Pennsylvania

43 Pa. Cons. Stat. Ann. §§ 954 to 955

Law applies to employers with: Four or more employees

Private employers may not make employment decisions based on:

- Age (40 to 70)
- Ancestry or national origin
- Physical or mental disability
- Gender
- Pregnancy, childbirth, and related medical conditions

State Laws Prohibiting Discrimination in Employment (continued)

- Race or color
- Religion or creed
- Relationship or association with a person with a disability
- GED rather than high school diploma
- Use of service animal

Rhode Island

R.I. Gen. Laws §§ 12-28-10, 23-6.3-11, 28-5-6, 28-5-7, 28-6-18, 28-6.7-1

Law applies to employers with: Four or more employees; one or more employees (gender-based wage discrimination)

Private employers may not make employment decisions based on:

- Age (40 or older)
- Ancestry or national origin
- Physical or mental disability
- AIDS/HIV
- Gender
- Pregnancy, childbirth, and related medical conditions
- Race or color
- Religion or creed
- Sexual orientation, including perceived sexual orientation
- Genetic testing information
- Domestic abuse victim
- Gender identity or expression
- Homelessness

South Carolina

S.C. Code §§ 1-13-30, 1-13-80

Law applies to employers with: 15 or more employees

Private employers may not make employment decisions based on:

- Age (40 or older)
- Ancestry or national origin
- Physical or mental disability
- AIDS/HIV
- Gender
- Pregnancy, childbirth, and related medical conditions
- Race or color
- Religion or creed

South Dakota

S.D. Codified Laws Ann. §§ 20-13-1, 20-13-10, 60-2-20, 60-12-15,

62-1-17

Law applies to employers with: One or more employees

Private employers may not make employment decisions based on:

- Ancestry or national origin
- Physical or mental disability
- Gender
- Race or color
- Religion or creed
- Genetic testing information
- Preexisting injury
- Off-duty use of tobacco products

Tennessee

Tenn. Code Ann. §§ 4-21-102, 4-21-401 and following, 8-50-103, 50-2-201, 50-2-202

Law applies to employers with: Eight or more employees; one or more employees (gender-based wage discrimination)

Private employers may not make employment decisions based on:

- Age (40 or older)
- Ancestry or national origin
- Physical, mental, or visual disability
- Gender
- Pregnancy, childbirth, and related medical conditions (refer to chart on Family and Medical Leave)
- Race or color
- Religion or creed
- Use of guide dog
- Volunteer rescue squad worker responding to an emergency

Texas

Tex. Lab. Code Ann. §§ 21.002, 21.051, 21.082, 21.101, 21.106, 21.402

Law applies to employers with: 15 or more employees

Private employers may not make employment decisions based on:

- Age (40 or older)
- Ancestry or national origin
- Physical or mental disability
- Gender
- Pregnancy, childbirth, and related medical conditions
- Race or color
- Religion or creed
- Genetic testing information

State Laws Prohibiting Discrimination in Employment (continued)

Utah

Utah Code Ann. §§ 26-45-103, 34A-5-102, 34A-5-106

Law applies to employers with: 15 or more employees

Private employers may not make employment decisions based on:

- Age (40 or older)
- Ancestry or national origin
- Physical or mental disability
- AIDS/HIV
- Gender
- Pregnancy, childbirth, and related medical conditions including breastfeeding
- Race or color
- Religion or creed
- Sexual orientation
- Gender identity
- Genetic testing information

Vermont

Vt. Stat. Ann. tit. 21, §§ 495, 495d; tit. 18, § 9333

Law applies to employers with: One or more employees

Private employers may not make employment decisions based on:

- Age (18 or older)
- Ancestry or national origin
- Physical, mental, or emotional disability
- AIDS/HIV
- Gender
- Race or color
- Religion or creed
- Sexual orientation
- Genetic testing information
- Gender identity
- Place of birth
- Credit report or credit history

Virginia

Va. Code Ann. §§ 2.2-3900, 2.2-3901, 40.1-28.6, 40.1-28.7:1, 51.5-41

Law applies to employers with: One or more employees

Private employers may not make employment decisions based on:

- Age
- Ancestry or national origin
- Physical or mental disability
- AIDS/HIV
- Gender
- Marital status
- Pregnancy, childbirth, and related medical conditions
- Race or color
- Religion or creed
- Genetic testing information

Washington

Wash. Rev. Code Ann. §§ 38.40.110, 49.12.175, 49.44.090, 49.44.180, 49.60.030, 49.60.040, 49.60.172, 49.60.180, 49.76.120; Wash. Admin. Code § 162-30-020

Law applies to employers with: Eight or more employees; one or more employees (gender-based wage discrimination)

Private employers may not make employment decisions based on:

- Age (40 or older)
- Ancestry or national origin
- Physical, mental, or sensory disability
- AIDS/HIV
- Gender
- Marital status
- Pregnancy, childbirth, and related medical conditions, including breast-feeding
- Race or color
- Religion or creed
- Sexual orientation
- Genetic testing information
- Hepatitis C infection
- Member of state militia
- Use of service animal
- Gender identity
- Domestic violence victim

West Virginia

W.Va. Code §§ 5-11-3, 5-11-9, 16-3C-3, 21-5B-1, 21-5B-3

Law applies to employers with: 12 or more employees; one or more employees (gender-based wage discrimination)

Private employers may not make employment decisions based on:

- Age (40 or older)
- Ancestry or national origin
- Physical or mental disability, or blindness
- AIDS/HIV
- Gender
- Race or color
- Religion or creed
- Off-duty use of tobacco products

State Laws Prohibiting Discrimination in Employment (continued)

Wisconsin

Wis. Stat. Ann. §§ 111.32 and following

Law applies to employers with: One or more employees

Private employers may not make employment decisions based on:

- Age (40 or older)
- Ancestry or national origin
- Physical or mental disability
- Gender
- Marital status
- Pregnancy, childbirth, and related medical conditions
- Race or color
- Religion or creed
- Sexual orientation, including having a history of or being identified with a preference
- Genetic testing information
- Arrest or conviction record
- Military service

- Declining to attend a meeting or to participate in any communication about religious matters or political matters
- Use or nonuse of lawful products off duty and off site

Wyoming

Wyo. Stat. §§ 27-9-102, 27-9-105, 19-11-104

Law applies to employers with: Two or more employees

Private employers may not make employment decisions based on:

- Age (40 or older)
- Ancestry or national origin
- Disability
- Gender
- Pregnancy, childbirth, and related medical conditions
- Race or color
- Religion or creed
- Military service or status

Complaint Policies

The purpose of a complaint policy is simple: to encourage employees to come forward with concerns and problems. If employees let managers know when trouble is brewing, the company will have an opportunity to resolve workplace difficulties right away, before morale suffers or workers start siding with or against each other. And a complaint policy helps managers and supervisors, by letting them know what their responsibilities are if they observe misconduct or receive a complaint.

As mentioned in Chapter 19 (on antidiscrimination and harassment policies), a complaint policy also offers companies an important legal bonus: some protection against harassment lawsuits brought by current or former employees. If your company has a clear complaint policy, and an employee who did not complain according to this policy later sues the company for harassment, the company can use the employee's failure to make a complaint as a legal defense in the harassment lawsuit. This might lead a court to decide that the employee cannot proceed with the lawsuit. The idea behind this is that an employee who fails to complain when a company has a clear complaint policy deprives the company of the chance to fix the problem.

However, these legal protections kick in only if your policy is user-friendly and genuinely encourages employees to make problems known and make a complaint. In this chapter, we'll show you how to put together policies that do just that.

CONTENTS

20:1 Complaint Procedures

File Name: 20_Complaints.rtf

Include This Policy?

☐ Yes

☐ No

☐ Use our existing policy

☐ Other _____

Alternate Modifications

None

Additional Clauses

Accounting Irregularities And
Shareholder Fraud

Insert?:   ☐ Yes   ☐ No

Related Policies

Chapter 19 includes policies against
discrimination and harassment (often
the subject of complaints).

Notes

_____
_____
_____
_____
_____
_____
_____
_____
_____
_____
_____
_____
_____
_____
_____
_____
_____

20:1 Complaint Procedures

Your complaint policy should describe the conduct about which employees can complain, explain how to make a complaint, and let workers know what will happen once a complaint is filed.

Complaint Procedures

Our Company is committed to providing a safe and productive work environment, free of threats to the health, safety, and well-being of our workers. These threats include, but are not limited to, harassment, discrimination, violations of health and safety rules, and violence.

Any employee who witnesses or is subject to inappropriate conduct in the workplace may complain to _____ _____ or to any Company officer. Any supervisor, manager, or Company officer who receives a complaint about, hears of, or witnesses any inappropriate conduct is required to immediately notify _____ _____ . Inappropriate conduct includes any conduct prohibited by our policies about harassment, discrimination, discipline, workplace violence, health and safety, wages and hours, and drug and alcohol use. In addition, we encourage employees to come forward with any workplace complaint, even if the subject of the complaint is not explicitly covered by our written policies.

We encourage you to come forward with complaints immediately, so we can take whatever action is needed to handle the problem. Once a complaint has been made, _____ will determine how to handle it. For serious complaints, we will immediately conduct a complete and impartial investigation.

We expect all employees to cooperate fully in Company investigations by, for example, answering questions completely and honestly and giving the investigator all documents and other material that might be relevant. All complaints will be handled as confidentially as possible. When the investigation is complete, the company will take corrective action, if appropriate.

We will not engage in or allow retaliation against any employee who makes a good-faith complaint or participates in an investigation. If you believe that you are being subjected to any kind of negative treatment because you made or were questioned about a complaint, report the conduct immediately to _____ _____ .

Who Needs This Policy

There are really no drawbacks to having a complaint policy, and plenty of good reasons to adopt one. From a legal standpoint, a complaint policy provides a possible legal defense against claims of harassment, as explained above. There are also many practical advantages of encouraging employees to make workplace problems known: The policy will give the company an opportunity to correct problems before they get out of hand, will promote communication and teamwork, and will let employees know that management cares about their concerns. Because of these benefits, we recommend that every employer adopt a complaint policy.

How to Complete This Policy

Our sample policy leaves you a space to designate the person or department that will be available to receive complaints. If your company has a human resource function, you can simply fill in all these blanks with "the human resources department."

If, like many smaller companies, your company doesn't have a dedicated human resources department, you will need to modify this policy to let employees know where to direct their complaints and who will deal with them. If you ask workers to complain to their direct supervisor or manager, make sure that employees can also complain to someone outside their chain of command, such as another supervisor or officer or even the head of the company. If an employee is being harassed or mistreated by his or her own supervisor, this allows the worker to bypass that person and complain to someone who isn't part of the problem. Even if the employee's direct supervisor is not the source of the complaint, some employees feel more comfortable talking to someone who won't be responsible for evaluating their performance and making decisions on promotions, raises, and assignments.

Because complaints—particularly complaints of harassment, discrimination, violence, or safety concerns—are a serious matter, many companies prefer to designate someone at the top of the company ladder, such as the president or CEO.

Make sure that the people whom you designate to take complaints are accessible to employees. For example, if the human resources department is located in a distant office or the company president spends most workdays traveling to promote the company, you should choose alternate people to accept complaints who are local and available.

⊘ CAUTION

Confidentiality requirements are under scrutiny. Recently, both the National Labor Relations Board and the Equal Employment Opportunity Commission have challenged employers who imposed confidentiality requirements on employees who participate in investigations. Prohibiting employees from discussing workplace problems with each other could violate laws prohibiting employers from retaliating against their employees and from punishing workers for talking to each other about the terms and conditions of their employment. If you have this type of provision in your policies or you make an oral demand that employees keep investigations confidential, have the language you are using vetted by a lawyer who is up on the latest developments in this area.

Additional Clause Regarding Complaints of Accounting Irregularities and Shareholder Fraud

In the wake of corporate scandals involving WorldCom, Enron, and other large companies accused of defrauding shareholders, Congress passed the Sarbanes-Oxley Act of 2002 (SOX). The stated purpose of SOX is to protect investors in publicly traded companies by improving the accuracy and reliability of corporate disclosures, and the law seeks to further this goal by imposing strict rules for audits and auditors of publicly traded companies, preventing insider trading, requiring companies to adopt strict internal controls, and enhancing the penalties for white-collar crimes relating to investor fraud.

SOX also includes provisions intended to encourage employees to come forward with information about questionable accounting practices and potential shareholder fraud. These provisions do two things: They prohibit retaliation against employee whistle-blowers who complain of possible shareholder fraud to government agencies or company officials, and they require publicly traded companies to establish a system to allow employees to submit confidential, anonymous complaints about questionable accounting or auditing matters. Companies must also develop record-keeping procedures for handling and maintaining any complaints they receive.

If your company is publicly traded, you must include the clause below to alert employees to the rights created by SOX. Insert the clause immediately before the final paragraph of the policy. Complete the clause by describing your company's procedures for submitting anonymous, confidential complaints. For example, you might insert "calling our hotline at 800-555-1212, where you can submit your concerns confidentially," or "going to our confidential complaint reporting website, which is operated and maintained by an independent, third-party company, at www. ourcompanyconfidentialcomplaint.com."

SEE AN EXPERT

Get some help with SOX compliance. SOX is a notoriously complicated law that imposes significant burdens on the companies it covers. Although the whistle-blowing and complaint mechanism provisions are among the simpler passages in this lengthy statute, they also raise a number of compliance questions, including what types of complaint procedures are sufficiently anonymous and confidential, how complaints should be handled once they are received, and exactly what type of complaints qualify for SOX protection. We advise you to consult with a lawyer to make sure your company meets its obligations under this law.

Additional Clause

We also encourage employees to come forward with complaints or concerns regarding the Company's accounting, auditing, or internal controls procedures, and complaints or concerns regarding possible shareholder fraud. You may raise these issues through the complaint procedures described in this policy, or you may do so anonymously by _____
_____ .

20:2 Our Doors Are Open to You

File Name: 20_Complaints.rtf

Include This Policy?
- ☐ Yes
- ☐ No
- ☐ Use our existing policy
- ☐ Other _____

Alternate Modifications
None

Additional Clauses
None

Related Policies
None

Notes
_____
_____
_____
_____
_____
_____
_____
_____
_____
_____
_____
_____
_____
_____
_____
_____
_____

20:2 Open-Door Policy

Many employers choose to adopt an open-door policy in addition to a more formal complaint policy. While your complaint policy will encourage employees to come forward with big problems, such as serious misconduct and violations of company rules, an open-door policy serves a slightly different purpose. It encourages employees to keep in touch with their supervisors about day-to-day work issues. An employee who has, for example, a personality conflict with a client, a creative idea to boost profits, or a concern that his or her work group isn't coming together as a team, probably wouldn't think of filing a formal complaint. But an open-door policy will encourage employees to bring these issues to the attention of management, thereby giving the company a chance to make improvements by, for example, changing work assignments, adopting that good idea, or offering training to the team.

Our Doors Are Open to You

We want to maintain a positive and pleasant environment for all of our employees. To help us meet this goal, our Company has an open-door policy, by which employees are encouraged to report work-related concerns.

If something about your job is bothering you, or if you have a question, concern, idea, or problem related to your work, please discuss it with your immediate supervisor as soon as possible. If for any reason you don't feel comfortable bringing the matter to your supervisor, feel free to raise the issue with any company officer.

We encourage you to come forward and make your concerns known to the Company. We can't solve the problem if we don't know about it.

Who Needs This Policy

An open-door policy doesn't offer the legal benefit of a complaint policy, but its practical advantages are similar: It helps managers learn what's going on in the workplace, encourages communication, and promotes goodwill.

The potential disadvantage of an open-door policy is wasted time. If workers feel compelled to keep management apprised of their every thought and feeling, managers might soon be tempted to close their doors and lock them. However, this problem can usually be handled effectively through individual counseling. If necessary, tell the one or two employees who might abuse the policy that their enthusiasm is appreciated, but they need to use more discretion in deciding which matters are important enough to bring to a manager's attention.

In our opinion, the benefits of having an open-door policy outweigh this potential downside. However, this is a decision each company will have to make for itself, based on the character of its workforce and the amount of time managers can afford to spend listening to whoever comes through their open doors.

RESOURCE

For more information on investigating complaints and problems, see *The Essential Guide to Workplace Investigations,* by Lisa Guerin (Nolo), a step-by-step guide to investigating common workplace situations.

Ending Employment

Ending the employment relationship can be difficult for employer and employee alike. An employer's goals are to keep operations running smoothly as employees come and go, and to make sure that any employees who have to be fired or laid off don't decide to respond with a lawsuit.

If your company has adopted an at-will policy, discussed in Chapter 2, it has already gone a long way toward accomplishing this second goal. The company has warned workers that their employment can be terminated at any time and for any reason. And, for those workers who didn't hear it the first time, other policies throughout your handbook give them fair warning that they can expect to be disciplined or fired for taking part in certain types of prohibited conduct.

Policies about ending employment serve a slightly different purpose: to tell employees how the company will handle the practical concerns that may arise when an employee leaves, such as severance packages, references, and insurance coverage. Explaining these matters up front will help smooth the transition when employees leave: They'll know exactly what to expect and be able to plan accordingly. End-of-employment policies can also help you make sure that the company has met its legal obligations (to offer health insurance continuation and cut final paychecks on time, for example). By adopting uniform policies and applying them evenhandedly when employees leave, employers can also avoid claims of unfairness, as well as the lawsuits that these feelings sometimes fuel.

21:1 Resignation

File Name: 21_Ending Employment.rtf

Include This Policy?
- ☐ Yes
- ☐ No
- ☐ Use our existing policy
- ☐ Other _____

Alternate Modifications

None

Additional Clauses

None

Related Policies

None

Notes

_____
_____
_____
_____
_____
_____
_____
_____
_____
_____
_____
_____
_____
_____
_____
_____
_____
_____
_____

21:1 Resignation

No employment relationship lasts forever, and often it is the employee, not the employer, who decides that the time has come to move on. When that happens, you will no doubt want the employee to notify the right people and to give you plenty of notice. The policy below reminds employees that they must return company property and that they must continue to maintain the confidentiality of your company's trade secrets.

If You Resign

If you decide to leave our Company for another position, we wish you well. Please notify _____ in writing about your plans. If you can, please give us _____ weeks notice. This will give us time to calculate your final paycheck and accrued overtime, vacation pay, and any other money that we owe you. Please see Section _____ of this handbook for more information about final paychecks.

You must return all company property in good condition. Please see Section _____ of this handbook for more about company property.

Even as you leave this Company and move on to future endeavors, you still have an obligation to keep confidential this Company's trade secrets and other protected proprietary and confidential information. Please see Section _____ of this handbook for more about this obligation.

21:2 Final Paychecks

Although no federal law requires employers to pay terminated employees by a particular date, the laws of most states impose fairly tight deadlines for final paychecks. Often, these deadlines vary depending on whether the employee quits or is fired. In some states, employers must pay a fired employee immediately. Other states allow employers to wait until the next payday.

Adopting a final paycheck policy that includes these deadlines will help ensure that your company complies with these laws. And employees will know when they can expect that check, especially if they don't have another job lined up right away.

Final Paychecks

Employees who resign from their job will receive their final paycheck
_____ . Employees whose employment
is terminated involuntarily will receive their final paycheck _____
_____ .

Final paychecks will include all compensation earned but not paid through the date of termination.

How to Complete This Policy

This policy includes 2 blanks for you to complete based on your state's law. The chart at the end of this chapter, "State Laws That Control Final Paychecks," lists employer requirements for final paychecks by state. In the first blank, insert the time limit for paying an employee who is fired (for example, within 2 weeks after termination). In the second blank, insert the time limit for paying an employee who quits.

Additional Clause to Specify Compensation Included in Final Paycheck

As you'll see from the chart at the end of this chapter, some states require employers to include unused vacation pay in an employee's final check. However, these laws apply only to vacation pay that has already been earned or accrued. For example, if employees accrue 1 day of vacation leave per month, and the company fires someone who has worked for a year without taking any vacation, that employee would be entitled to 12 additional days of pay in his or her final paycheck. But an employee who is fired after only 2 months gets only 2 days of vacation pay, assuming those days haven't been used.

21:2 Final Paychecks

File Name: 21_Ending Employment.rtf

Include This Policy?
- [ ] Yes
- [ ] No
- [ ] Use our existing policy
- [ ] Other _____

Alternate Modifications
None

Additional Clauses
Specify Compensation Included in Final Paycheck
Insert?: [ ] Yes [ ] No

Related Policies
Chapter 7 provides information and policies on pay.

Notes

_____
_____
_____
_____
_____
_____
_____
_____
_____
_____
_____
_____
_____
_____
_____

In addition to vacation pay, some employers choose to pay out unused sick leave or personal leave, some portion of a discretionary bonus, or other forms of compensation. No law requires this. Employers who follow this route generally do so to maintain a good relationship with the departing employee and the workers who remain, and to create incentives for solid performance. By paying out unused sick time, for example, employers encourage their employees not to take sick leave unless it's absolutely necessary. And paying out a portion of a discretionary bonus encourages employees to do their best right up until their last day of work.

If your state requires employers to pay out unused vacation time, or if your company wants to pay this or other types of compensation even though it's not legally required, add the sentence below to the end of our sample policy. In the blank space, insert the type of additional compensation employees will receive (for example, all unused vacation time that the employee has earned as of the date of termination, or a pro rata share of any discretionary bonus for which the employee is eligible, based on the length of the employee's employment during the bonus period and the employee's performance).

Additional Clause

Final paychecks will also include _____ .

Seek Legal Advice for Layoffs and Layoff Policies

In a layoff, an employer generally terminates the employment of a group of employees for reasons related to business productivity, such as economic problems or shifts in the company's direction. When an employer lays workers off, it is legally required to provide them with a certain amount of notice and, in a few states, severance pay. If you wish to adopt a layoff policy, you'll have to consider a number of factors, such as how employees will be chosen for layoff, what benefits (if any) laid-off workers will receive, whether laid-off workers are eligible for rehire if circumstances turn around, and how employees will be informed of the layoff. Because these issues can get fairly complicated, we advise you to consult with a lawyer if you plan to adopt a layoff policy.

21:3 Severance Pay

Except for a few states that require severance pay when laying workers off, no law says that employers must give their employees severance pay. Unless the company promises severance pay or leads employees to believe they will receive it—for example, by saying so in a written contract or policy—there is no obligation to pay severance to terminated employees.

For many employers, that's all they need to know: If it isn't required, they aren't going to pay it. But before your company decides to join their ranks, consider the benefits of paying severance. For starters, it helps a fired worker get by until another job comes along, which sends the message that the company cares about its workers and wants to help out. This can go a long way not only toward building employee morale, but also toward nipping potential lawsuits in the bud. Studies have shown that the way in which employment terminations are handled plays a big role in determining whether a fired employee will sue the employer. Thus, a company will have to weigh these very tangible benefits against the eminently sensible desire not to pay out money unnecessarily.

Your severance policy should let employees know whether and under what circumstances the company offers severance pay. If your company will offer severance, the policy should tell employees who is eligible and how severance pay will be calculated.

We offer you several alternative sample policies below. Policy A is a simple no-severance policy. Policy B provides that a company will pay severance at its own discretion. Policy C is a severance policy with eligibility requirements and a formula for determining severance pay.

CAUTION

Severance plans can be tricky. If your company plans to adopt a policy to pay severance, whether according to a formula or other criteria, ask a lawyer to review it for you and to let you know whether your company has to follow the requirements of the federal law known as ERISA (the Employees Retirement Income Security Act, 29 U.S.C. §§ 1001 and following). This highly technical law imposes a number of requirements on employers who provide certain types of benefit plans to their employees. Severance plans may or may not be subject to these requirements, depending on the plan's features and the way courts in your state have interpreted the law.

21:3 Severance Pay

File Name: 21_Ending Employment.rtf

Include This Policy?
☐ Yes
    Choose one: ☐ A ☐ B ☐ C
☐ No
☐ Use our existing policy
☐ Other _____

Alternate Modifications
None

Additional Clauses
None

Related Policies
None

Notes

_____
_____
_____
_____
_____
_____
_____
_____
_____
_____
_____
_____
_____
_____
_____
_____
_____
_____
_____
_____

Alternate Policy A

> ## No Severance Pay
>
> Our Company does not pay severance to departing employees, whether they quit, are laid off, or are fired for any reason.

Alternate Policy B

> ## Severance Pay Is Discretionary
>
> Generally, our Company does not pay severance to departing employees, whether they quit, are laid off, or are fired for any reason. However, we reserve the right to pay severance. Decisions about severance pay will be made on a case-by-case basis and are entirely within the discretion of the Company. No employee has a right to severance pay, and you should not expect to receive it.

Alternate Policy C

> ## Severance Pay
>
> Employees may be eligible for severance pay upon the end of their employment. Employees must meet <u>all</u> of the following criteria to be eligible:
>
> - They must have worked for the Company for at least 1 year prior to their termination.
> - They must not have quit or resigned.
> - Their employment must have been terminated for reasons other than misconduct or violation of Company rules.
>
> Eligible employees will receive _____ of severance pay for every full year of employment with the Company.

How to Complete This Policy

If you adopt Sample Policy C, simply fill in the blank with the amount of severance the company plans to offer. Most employers offer 1 or 2 weeks of pay, at the employee's current rate, for every year of work. You can do the same by inserting "one week" or "two weeks" in the blank.

21:4 Continuing Your Health Insurance Coverage

If your company offers employees health insurance coverage under a group health plan, it may be required to offer them continued coverage under the circumstances outlined in the sample policy below. A federal law known as COBRA (the Consolidated Omnibus Budget Reconciliation Act) mandates that employees who quit, suffer a reduction in hours, or are fired for reasons other than serious misconduct are entitled to choose to continue on the employer's group health care plan for up to 18 months, and employees' dependents may continue their coverage for up to 36 months. COBRA applies only to employers with at least 20 employees.

Many states also have their own health insurance continuation laws. These laws generally apply to smaller employers. Some echo most of COBRA's provisions; others provide for shorter periods of insurance continuation and/or place limits on the types of benefits that must be provided. A chart of these state laws, entitled "State Health Insurance Continuation Laws," is included at the end of this chapter.

Your insurance continuation policy should tell employees:

- whether, and under what circumstances, they will be able to continue their insurance coverage after termination
- how long the continued coverage will last, and
- who will pay for the coverage.

How to Complete This Policy

In the blanks in this policy, insert the length of time for which employees and their dependents can continue their health insurance coverage. If your company is covered by COBRA, employees are entitled to continue their coverage for 18 months (insert this in the first blank), and dependents for 36 months (insert this in the second blank).

Smaller employers that are not covered by COBRA may nevertheless have to comply with a state insurance continuation law. Some of these laws also provide for 18 and 36 months of coverage; others provide for shorter periods of coverage. Consult the chart "State Health Insurance Continuation Laws," at the end of this chapter, to find out what your state requires.

21:4 Continuing Your Health Insurance Coverage

File Name: 21_Ending Employment.rtf

Include This Policy?
☐ Yes
☐ No
☐ Use our existing policy
☐ Other _____

Alternate Modifications
None

Additional Clauses
Include Eligibility Requirements
Insert?: ☐ Yes ☐ No

Related Policies
8:3 Health Care Benefits

Notes

Continuing Your Health Insurance Coverage

Our Company offers employees group health insurance coverage as a benefit of employment. If you are no longer eligible for insurance coverage because of a reduction in hours, because you quit, or because your employment is terminated for reasons other than serious misconduct, you have the right to continue your health insurance coverage for up to _____ .
You will have to pay the cost of this coverage.

Others covered by your insurance (your spouse and children, for example) also have the right to continue coverage if they are no longer eligible for certain reasons. If you and your spouse divorce or legally separate, or if you die while in our employ, your spouse may continue coverage under our group health plan. And once your children lose their dependent status, they may continue their health care as well. In any of these situations, your family members are entitled to up to _____ of continued health care. They must pay the cost of this coverage.

You will receive an initial notice of your right to continued health insurance coverage when you first become eligible for health insurance under the Company's group plan. You will receive an additional notice when your hours are reduced, you quit, or your employment is terminated. This second notice will tell you how to choose continuation coverage, what your obligations will be, whether you are entitled to a partial subsidy, and how much you will have to pay for coverage. You must notify us if any of your family members become eligible for continued coverage due to divorce, separation, or reaching the age of majority.

Who Needs This Policy

If your company is covered by COBRA or a state health insurance continuation law, including this policy can alleviate a lot of anxiety for workers. one of the first questions a departing employee is likely to ask is, "What about my health insurance?" As the costs of medical care skyrocket, many employees cannot afford to go without health insurance until they find another job. Even if they line up new work quickly, their new employer might not offer insurance coverage or there may be a waiting period before coverage begins. And those who forego health insurance face fines under Obamacare.

COBRA used to be the only (or at least, the least expensive) game in town for employees who lost their employer-provided health insurance coverage. It could be difficult for employees to qualify for or afford an individual policy on the open market. These days, however, Obamacare gives everyone access to health insurance through the online health insurance exchange marketplace. (At least this was the case when this book went to press.) Often, these plans (under Obamacare) are less expensive than continuing health insurance through COBRA. However, many employees still choose to use COBRA because their employer-based plan offers more generous benefits, allows the employee to continue to use familiar medical professionals, or otherwise is simply a better fit.

If your company is not covered by COBRA or a similar state law or doesn't offer health insurance coverage to your employees (see Chapter 8 for information on benefits policies), leave this policy out of the handbook.

Additional Clause to Include Eligibility Requirements

Some states require employers to offer continued coverage only to certain employees. Most commonly, employees are eligible only if they have worked for the employer and been covered by the employer's health insurance plan for at least 3 months. If your company is not covered by COBRA (which protects all employees who are covered by the employer's plan) but is covered by a state health insurance continuation law that protects only certain employees, modify our policy by adding the following language after the first sentence. In the blank, insert your state's eligibility requirements (for example, "have been covered continuously under our insurance policy for at least 3 months" or "work at least 25 hours a week").

Additional Clause

Only employees who _____ are entitled to continue their health insurance coverage under this policy.

21:5 Exit Interviews

File Name: 21_Ending Employment.rtf

Include This Policy?

☐ Yes
☐ No
☐ Use our existing policy
☐ Other _____

Alternate Modifications

None

Additional Clauses

None

Related Policies

None

Notes

_____
_____
_____
_____
_____
_____
_____
_____
_____
_____
_____
_____
_____
_____
_____
_____
_____
_____
_____
_____

21:5 Exit Interviews

Exit interviews are a great way to learn valuable information about your company; they can also help diffuse the tension of an involuntary termination. Former employees can provide the lowdown on dozens of issues, from workplace morale and teamwork to how well (or poorly) managers and supervisors are doing their jobs. An employee on the way out the door is more likely to be candid in offering opinions, maybe brutally so. Although employers should certainly take these parting comments with a healthy dose of salt, they may get some helpful information about how the company is perceived by its workers and where it has room to improve.

The person who interviews employees who quit should try to find out why that employee is moving on: Did your company fail to offer opportunities to advance? Are the company's pay scales in line with those of other businesses in your industry? Are there problems in the company that management doesn't know about?

It can be equally valuable to interview employees you fire, although for a slightly different reason. These employees are probably somewhat upset about losing their jobs, and they may have a long list of negative comments about the company as a result. But they will have a chance to air these complaints during the interview, which allows the company to demonstrate that it cares about their concerns. If a fired employee feels that the company "gets it," that employee is less likely to seek a courtroom forum for his or her grievances. Adopting an exit interview policy tells these employees that there will be a time and a place for their voices to be heard.

Some employers hold exit interviews with every departing employee, while others schedule interviews only if the departing employee wants one. Adopting an optional interview policy has the benefit of drastically reducing the time spent conducting these interviews. Very few employees, other than those with a large ax to grind, will bother to take the time to share their opinions on the way out the door. The corresponding drawback is that a company that holds voluntary interviews won't be able to gather as much valuable information, because the interviewer will probably be hearing only from those whose employment experience was negative.

Exit Interviews

We will hold an exit interview with every employee who leaves the Company, for any reason. During the interview, you will have the opportunity to tell us about your employment experience here: what you liked, what you didn't like, and where you think we can improve. We greatly value these comments.

The exit interview also gives us a chance to handle some practical matters relating to the end of your employment. You will be expected to return all Company property at the interview. You will also have an opportunity to ask any questions you might have about insurance, benefits, final paychecks, references, or any other matter relating to your employment.

21:6 References

File Name: 21_Ending Employment.rtf

Include This Policy?
☐ Yes
  Choose one: ☐ A ☐ B
☐ No
☐ Use our existing policy
☐ Other _____

Alternate Modifications
None

Additional Clauses
None

Related Policies
None

Notes
_____
_____
_____
_____
_____
_____
_____
_____
_____
_____
_____
_____
_____
_____
_____
_____
_____
_____

21:6 References

Reference requests are fraught with legal and practical dangers for employers. If an employer criticizes a former employee unduly, or unfairly prevents that employee from getting a job, it could face a lawsuit for defamation or blacklisting. If an employer gives a reference that is too positive for an employee it knows to be dangerous or grossly unqualified, it risks legal trouble from the new employer if the truth comes out.

Given these risks, many employers choose to take a "name, rank, and serial number" approach, giving prospective new employers only the dates of employment, title, and salary of a former employee. If your company decides to go this route, our sample Policy A, below—a minimal reference policy to confirm dates of employment, salary, and positions held—will work for you.

But before deciding to adopt this type of policy, consider the purpose of a reference. Former employees count on them to find new work; and the sooner a fired employee finds new work, the less likely you are to face a wrongful termination claim. Prospective employers use references to figure out whom to hire and to read between the lines of carefully prepared résumés and interview responses. Both of these tasks are made a lot tougher by employers who adopt a minimal reference approach.

Employers can give an informative reference without undue risk of legal trouble if they insist on a written release from the employee, giving the former employer permission to talk to a prospective employer. And your company can protect itself further by insisting on written reference requests and responding to them only in writing. This gives the company a clear record of exactly what was said if a company representative is later accused of making a false statement. This approach also gives the person providing the reference time to craft a careful response. If your company decides to go this route, you can use our sample Policy B, below.

Alternate Policy A

> ### References
>
> When we are contacted by prospective employers seeking information about former employees, we will release the following data only: the position(s) the employee held, the dates the employee worked for our Company, and the employee's salary or rate of pay.

Alternate Policy B

References

When we are contacted by prospective employers seeking information about former employees, we will release the following data only: the position(s) the employee held, the dates the employee worked for our Company, and the employee's salary or rate of pay.

If you would like us to give a more detailed reference, you will have to provide us with a written release—a consent form giving us your permission to respond to a reference request. We will respond only to written reference requests, and we will respond only in writing. Please direct all reference requests to _____

_____ .

RESOURCE

For information on providing references, see *Dealing With Problem Employees*, by Amy DelPo and Lisa Guerin (Nolo).

State Laws That Control Final Paychecks

Note: The states of Alabama, Florida, Georgia, and Mississippi are not included in this chart because they do not have laws specifically controlling final paychecks. Contact your state department of labor for more information. (See Appendix B for contact list.)

Alaska
Alaska Stat. § 23.05.140(b)

Paycheck due when employee is fired: Within 3 working days after termination.

Paycheck due when employee quits: Next regular payday at least 3 days after employee gives notice.

Unused vacation pay due: Only if agreed to by employer or required by company policy or practice.

Arizona
Ariz. Rev. Stat. §§ 23-350, 23-353

Paycheck due when employee is fired: Next payday or within 7 working days, whichever is sooner.

Paycheck due when employee quits: Next regular payday or by mail at employee's request.

Unused vacation pay due: No provision.

Arkansas
Ark. Code Ann. § 11-4-405

Paycheck due when employee is fired: Upon request, within 7 days of discharge; otherwise, next regular payday.

Paycheck due when employee quits: No provision.

Unused vacation pay due: No provision.

Special employment situations: Railroad or railroad construction: day of discharge.

California
Cal. Lab. Code §§ 201 to 202, 227.3

Paycheck due when employee is fired: Immediately.

Paycheck due when employee quits: Immediately if employee has given 72 hours' notice; otherwise, within 72 hours.

Unused vacation pay due: Yes.
Special employment situations: Motion picture business: next payday.

Oil drilling industry: within 24 hours (excluding weekends and holidays) of termination.

Seasonal agricultural workers: within 72 hours of termination.

Colorado
Colo. Rev. Stat. § 8-4-109

Paycheck due when employee is fired: Immediately. (Within 6 hours of start of next workday, if payroll unit is closed; 24 hours if unit is offsite.) When paycheck is not due immediately, employer may make the check available at the work site, the employer's local office, or the employee's last-known mailing address.

Paycheck due when employee quits: Next payday.

Unused vacation pay due: Yes.

Connecticut
Conn. Gen. Stat. Ann. §§ 31-71c, 31-76k

Paycheck due when employee is fired: Next business day after discharge.

Paycheck due when employee quits: Next payday.

Unused vacation pay due: Only if policy or collective bargaining agreement requires payment on termination.

Delaware
Del. Code Ann. tit. 19, § 1103

Paycheck due when employee is fired: Next payday.

Paycheck due when employee quits: Next payday.

Unused vacation pay due: Only if required by employer policy or agreement, in which case vacation must be paid within 30 days after it becomes due.

District of Columbia
D.C. Code Ann. § 32-1303

Paycheck due when employee is fired: Next business day.

Paycheck due when employee quits: Next payday or 7 days after quitting, whichever is sooner.

Unused vacation pay due: Yes, unless there is an agreement to the contrary.

Hawaii
Haw. Rev. Stat. § 388-3

Paycheck due when employee is fired: Immediately or next business day, if timing or conditions prevent immediate payment.

Paycheck due when employee quits: Next payday or immediately, if employee gives 1 pay period's notice.

Unused vacation pay due: No.

State Laws That Control Final Paychecks (continued)

Idaho
Idaho Code §§ 45-606, 45-617

Paycheck due when employee is fired: Next payday or within 10 days (excluding weekends and holidays), whichever is sooner. If employee makes written request for earlier payment, within 48 hours of receipt of request (excluding weekends and holidays).

Paycheck due when employee quits: Next payday or within 10 days (excluding weekends and holidays), whichever is sooner. If employee makes written request for earlier payment, within 48 hours of receipt of request (excluding weekends and holidays).

Unused vacation pay due: No provision.

Illinois
820 Ill. Comp. Stat. § 115/5

Paycheck due when employee is fired: At time of separation if possible, but no later than next payday. Employer must comply with employee's written request to mail final paycheck.

Paycheck due when employee quits: At time of separation if possible, but no later than next payday. Employer must comply with employee's written request to mail final paycheck.

Unused vacation pay due: Yes.

Indiana
Ind. Code Ann. §§ 22-2-5-1, 22-2-9-1, 22-2-9-2

Paycheck due when employee is fired: Next payday.

Paycheck due when employee quits: Next payday. (If employee has not left address, (1) 10 business days after employee demands wages or (2) when employee provides address where check may be mailed.)

Unused vacation pay due: If employer agrees to vacation pay, absent an agreement to the contrary, employer must pay out accrued unused vacation upon termination.

Special employment situations: Does not apply to railroad employees.

Iowa
Iowa Code §§ 91A.4, 91A.2(7)(b)

Paycheck due when employee is fired: Next payday.

Paycheck due when employee quits: Next payday.

Unused vacation pay due: Yes.

Special employment situations: If employee is owed commission, employer has 30 days to pay.

Kansas
Kan. Stat. Ann. § 44-315

Paycheck due when employee is fired: Next payday.

Paycheck due when employee quits: Next payday.

Unused vacation pay due: Only if required by employer's policies or practice.

Kentucky
Ky. Rev. Stat. Ann. §§ 337.010, 337.055

Paycheck due when employee is fired: Next payday or within 14 days, whichever is later.

Paycheck due when employee quits: Next payday or within 14 days, whichever is later.

Unused vacation pay due: Yes.

Louisiana
La. Rev. Stat. Ann. § 23:631

Paycheck due when employee is fired: Next payday or within 15 days, whichever is earlier.

Paycheck due when employee quits: Next payday or within 15 days, whichever is earlier.

Unused vacation pay due: Yes.

Maine
Me. Rev. Stat. Ann. tit. 26, § 626

Paycheck due when employee is fired: Next payday or within 2 weeks of requesting final pay, whichever is sooner.

Paycheck due when employee quits: Next payday or within 2 weeks of requesting final pay, whichever is sooner.

Unused vacation pay due: Yes, accrued vacation is considered wages and must be paid out upon termination.

Special employment situations: Employer must pay employees all wages due within 2 weeks of the sale of a business.

Maryland
Md. Code Ann., [Lab. & Empl.] § 3-505

Paycheck due when employee is fired: Next scheduled payday.

Paycheck due when employee quits: Next scheduled payday.

Unused vacation pay due: Yes.

State Laws That Control Final Paychecks (continued)

Massachusetts
Mass. Gen. Laws ch. 149, § 148

Paycheck due when employee is fired: Day of discharge.

Paycheck due when employee quits: Next payday. If no scheduled payday, then following Saturday.

Unused vacation pay due: Yes.

Michigan
Mich. Comp. Laws §§ 408.471 to 408.475; Mich. Admin. Code § 408.9007

Paycheck due when employee is fired: Next payday.

Paycheck due when employee quits: Next payday.

Unused vacation pay due: Only if required by written policy or contract.

Special employment situations: Hand-harvesters of crops: within 1 working day of termination.

Minnesota
Minn. Stat. Ann. §§ 181.13, 181.14, 181.74

Paycheck due when employee is fired: Within 24 hours.

Paycheck due when employee quits: Next regular payday. If next payday is less than 5 days after employee's last day, employer may delay payment until payday after that. But in no event may payment exceed 20 days from employee's last day.

Unused vacation pay due: Only if required by written policy or contract.

Special employment situations: If employee was responsible for collecting or handling money or property, employer has 10 days after termination or resignation to audit and adjust employee accounts before making payment.

Commissions must be paid to sales employees within 3 days if employee is fired or quits with at least 5 days' notice. Otherwise, commissions must be paid within 6 days. Migrant agricultural workers who resign: within 5 days..

Missouri
Mo. Rev. Stat. § 290.110

Paycheck due when employee is fired: Day of discharge.

Paycheck due when employee quits: No provision.

Unused vacation pay due: No.

Special employment situations: Requirements do not apply if employee is paid primarily based on commission and an audit is necessary or customary to determine the amount due.

Montana
Mont. Code Ann. § 39-3-205; Mont. Admin. Code § 24.16.7521

Paycheck due when employee is fired: Immediately if fired for cause or laid off (unless there is a written policy extending time to earlier of next payday or 15 days).

Paycheck due when employee quits: Next payday or within 15 days, whichever comes first.

Unused vacation pay due: Yes.

Nebraska
Neb. Rev. Stat. §§ 48-1229 to 48-1230

Paycheck due when employee is fired: Next payday or within 2 weeks, whichever is earlier.

Paycheck due when employee quits: Next payday or within 2 weeks, whichever is earlier.

Unused vacation pay due: Only if required by agreement.

Special employment situations: Commissions due on next payday following receipt.

Nevada
Nev. Rev. Stat. Ann. §§ 608.020, 608.030

Paycheck due when employee is fired: Immediately.

Paycheck due when employee quits: Next payday or within 7 days, whichever is earlier.

Unused vacation pay due: No.

New Hampshire
N.H. Rev. Stat. Ann. §§ 275:43(V), 275:44

Paycheck due when employee is fired: Within 72 hours. If laid off, next payday.

Paycheck due when employee quits: Next payday, or within 72 hours if employee gives 1 pay period's notice.

Unused vacation pay due: Yes.

New Jersey
N.J. Stat. Ann. § 34:11-4.3

Paycheck due when employee is fired: Next payday.

Paycheck due when employee quits: Next payday.

Unused vacation pay due: Only if required by policy.

New Mexico
N.M. Stat. Ann. §§ 50-4-4, 50-4-5

Paycheck due when employee is fired: Within 5 days.

Paycheck due when employee quits: Next payday.

Unused vacation pay due: No provision.

State Laws That Control Final Paychecks (continued)

Special employment situations: If paid by task or commission, 10 days after discharge.

New York
N.Y. Lab. Law §§ 191(3), 198-c(2)

Paycheck due when employee is fired: Next payday.

Paycheck due when employee quits: Next payday.

Unused vacation pay due: Yes, unless employer has a contrary policy.

North Carolina
N.C. Gen. Stat. §§ 95-25.7, 95-25.12

Paycheck due when employee is fired: Next payday.

Paycheck due when employee quits: Next payday.

Unused vacation pay due: Yes, unless employer has a contrary policy.

Special employment situations: If paid by commission or bonus, on next payday after amount calculated.

North Dakota
N.D. Cent. Code § 34-14-03; N.D. Admin. Code § 46-02-07-02(12)

Paycheck due when employee is fired: Next payday.

Paycheck due when employee quits: Next payday.

Unused vacation pay due: Yes. However, if an employer provides written notice at the time of hire, employer need not pay out vacation that has been awarded, but not yet earned. And, if an employee quits with less than 5 days notice, employer may withhold accrued vacation, as long as the employer gave written notice of the limitation at the time of hire and the employee was employed for less than one year.

Ohio
Ohio Rev. Code Ann. § 4113.15

Paycheck due when employee is fired: First of month for wages earned in first half of prior month; 15th of month for wages earned in second half of prior month.

Paycheck due when employee quits: First of month for wages earned in first half of prior month; 15th of month for wages earned in second half of prior month.

Unused vacation pay due: Yes, if company has policy or practice of making such payments.

Oklahoma
Okla. Stat. Ann. tit. 40, §§ 165.1(4), 165.3

Paycheck due when employee is fired: Next payday.

Paycheck due when employee quits: Next payday.

Unused vacation pay due: Yes.

Oregon
Or. Rev. Stat. §§ 652.140, 652.145

Paycheck due when employee is fired: End of first business day after termination.

Paycheck due when employee quits: Immediately, with 48 hours' notice (excluding weekends and holidays); without notice, within 5 business days or next payday, whichever comes first (must be within 5 days if employee submits time records to determine wages due).

Unused vacation pay due: Only if required by policy.

Special employment situations: Seasonal farmworkers: fired or quitting with 48 hours' notice, immediately; quitting without notice, within 48 hours or next payday, whichever comes first. If the termination occurs at the end of harvest season, the employer is a farmworker camp operator, and the farmworker is provided housing at no cost until wages are paid, employer must pay by noon on the day after termination.

Pennsylvania
43 Pa. Cons. Stat. Ann. §§ 260.2a, 260.5

Paycheck due when employee is fired: Next payday.

Paycheck due when employee quits: Next payday.

Unused vacation pay due: Only if required by policy or contract.

Rhode Island
R.I. Gen. Laws § 28-14-4

Paycheck due when employee is fired: Next payday. Paycheck is due within 24 hours if employer liquidates, merges, or disposes of the business, or moves it out of state.

Paycheck due when employee quits: Next payday.

Unused vacation pay due: Yes, if employee has worked for 1 full year and the company has verbally or in writing awarded vacation.

South Carolina
S.C. Code Ann. §§ 41-10-10(2), 41-10-50

Paycheck due when employee is fired: Within 48 hours or next payday, but not more than 30 days.

Paycheck due when employee quits: No provision.

Unused vacation pay due: Only if required by policy or contract.

State Laws That Control Final Paychecks (continued)

South Dakota
S.D. Codified Laws Ann. §§ 60-11-10, 60-11-11, 60-11-14

Paycheck due when employee is fired: Next payday (or until employee returns employer's property).

Paycheck due when employee quits: Next payday (or until employee returns employer's property).

Unused vacation pay due: No.

Tennessee
Tenn. Code Ann. § 50-2-103

Paycheck due when employee is fired: Next payday or within 21 days, whichever is later.

Paycheck due when employee quits: Next payday or within 21 days, whichever is later.

Unused vacation pay due: Only if required by policy or contract.

Special employment situations: Applies to employers with 5 or more employees.

Texas
Tex. Lab. Code Ann. §§ 61.001, 61.014

Paycheck due when employee is fired: Within 6 days.

Paycheck due when employee quits: Next payday.

Unused vacation pay due: Only if required by policy or contract.

Utah
Utah Code Ann. §§ 34-28-5; Utah Admin. Code § 610-3

Paycheck due when employee is fired: Within 24 hours.

Paycheck due when employee quits: Next payday.

Unused vacation pay due: Only if required by policy or contract.

Special employment situations: Requirements do not apply to commissioned sales employees if audit is necessary to determine the amount due.

Vermont
Vt. Stat. Ann. tit. 21, § 342(c)

Paycheck due when employee is fired: Within 72 hours.

Paycheck due when employee quits: Next regular payday or next Friday, if there is no regular payday.

Unused vacation pay due: No provision.

Virginia
Va. Code Ann. § 40.1-29(A.1)

Paycheck due when employee is fired: Next payday.

Paycheck due when employee quits: Next payday.

Unused vacation pay due: Only if agreed to in a written statement.

Washington
Wash. Rev. Code Ann. § 49.48.010

Paycheck due when employee is fired: End of pay period.

Paycheck due when employee quits: End of pay period.

Unused vacation pay due: No provision.

West Virginia
W.Va. Code §§ 21-5-1, 21-5-4

Paycheck due when employee is fired: Next regular payday.

Paycheck due when employee quits: Next regular payday.

Unused vacation pay due: Only if required by policy or contract.

Wisconsin
Wis. Stat. Ann. §§ 109.01(3), 109.03

Paycheck due when employee is fired: Next payday or within 1 month, whichever is earlier. If termination is due to merger, relocation, or liquidation of business, within 24 hours.

Paycheck due when employee quits: Next payday.

Unused vacation pay due: Yes.

Special employment situations: Does not apply to managers, executives, or sales agents working on commission basis.

Wyoming
Wyo. Stat. Ann. §§ 27-4-104, 27-4-501, 27-4-507(c)

Paycheck due when employee is fired: Next regular payday.

Paycheck due when employee quits: Next regular payday.

Unused vacation pay due: No, if employer's policies state that vacation is fortfeited upon termination of employment and the employee acknowledged the policy in writing.

Special employment situations: Requirements do not apply to commissioned sales employees if audit is necessary to determine the amount due.

State Health Insurance Continuation Laws

Alabama

Ala. Code § 27-55-3(a)(4)

Special Situations: 18 months for subjects of domestic abuse who have lost coverage they had under abuser's insurance and who do not qualify for COBRA.

Arizona

Ariz. Rev. Stat. §§ 20-1377, 20-1408

Employers affected: All employers who offer group disability insurance.

Length of coverage for dependents: Insurer must either continue coverage for dependents or convert to individual policy upon death of covered employee or divorce. Coverage must be the same unless the insured chooses a lesser plan.

Qualifying event: Death of an employee; change in marital status; any other reason stated in policy (other than failure to pay premium).

Time employer has to notify employee: No provisions for employer. Insurance policy must include notice of conversion privilege. Clerk of court must provide notice to anyone filing for divorce that dependent spouse entitled to convert health insurance coverage.

Time employee has to apply: 31 days after termination of existing coverage.

Arkansas

Ark. Code Ann. §§ 23-86-114 to 23-86-116

Employers affected: All employers who offer group health insurance.

Eligible employees: Employees continuously insured for previous 3 months.

Length of coverage for employee: 120 days.

Length of coverage for dependents: 120 days.

Qualifying event: Termination of employment; change in insured's marital status. Employer may—but is not required to—continue benefits on death of employee.

Time employee has to apply: 10 days.

California

Cal. Health & Safety Code §§ 1373.6, 1373.621; Cal. Ins. Code §§ 10128.50 to 10128.59

Employers affected: Employers who offer group health insurance and have 2 to 19 employees.

Eligible employees: All covered employees are eligible.

Length of coverage for employee: 36 months.

Length of coverage for dependents: 36 months.

Qualifying event: Termination of employment; reduction in hours; death of employee; change in marital status; loss of dependent status; covered employee's eligibility for Medicare (for dependents only)

Time employer has to notify employee: 15 days.

Time employee has to apply: 60 days.

Special situations: Employee who is at least 60 years old and has worked for employer for previous 5 years may continue benefits for self and spouse beyond COBRA or Cal-COBRA limits (also applies to COBRA employers). Employee who began receiving COBRA coverage on or after 1/1/03 and whose COBRA coverage is for less than 36 months may use Cal-COBRA to bring total coverage up to 36 months.

Colorado

Colo. Rev. Stat. § 10-16-108

Employers affected: All employers who offer group health insurance.

Eligible employees: Employees continuously insured for previous 6 months.

Length of coverage for employee: 18 months.

Length of coverage for dependents: 18 months.

Qualifying event: Termination of employment; reduction in hours; death of employee; change in marital status.

Time employer has to notify employee: 60 days.

Time employee has to apply: 30 days after termination; 60 days if employer fails to give notice.

Connecticut

Conn. Gen. Stat. Ann. §§ 38a-512a, 31-51n, 31-51o

Employers affected: All employers who offer group health insurance.

Eligible employees: All covered employees are eligible.

Length of coverage for employee: 30 months, or until eligible for Medicare benefits.

Length of coverage for dependents: 30 months, or until eligible for Medicare benefits; 36 months in case of employee's death, divorce, or loss of dependent status.

Qualifying event: Layoff; reduction in hours; termination of employment; death of employee; change in marital status; loss of dependent status.

Special situations: When facility closes or relocates, employers with 100 or more employees must pay for insurance for

State Health Insurance Continuation Laws (continued)

employee and dependents for 120 days or until employee is eligible for other group coverage, whichever comes first (does not affect employee's right to conventional continuation coverage, which begins when 120-day period ends).

Delaware

18 Del. Code Ann. § 3571F

Employers affected: Employers that offer group health insurance and have 1 to 19 employees.

Eligible employees: Employees continuously insured for previous 3 months

Length of coverage for employee: 9 months.

Length of coverage for dependents: 9 months.

Qualifying event: Employee's death; termination of employment; divorce or legal separation; employee's eligibility for Medicare; loss of dependent status.

Time employer has to notify employee: Within 30 days of the qualifying event.

Time employee has to apply: 30 days.

District of Columbia

D.C. Code Ann. §§ 32-731 to 32-732

Employers affected: Employers with fewer than 20 employees.

Eligible employees: All covered employees are eligible.

Length of coverage for employee: 3 months.

Length of coverage for dependents: 3 months.

Qualifying event: Any reason employee or dependent becomes ineligible for coverage, except employee's termination for gross misconduct.

Time employer has to notify employee: Within 15 days of termination of coverage.

Time employee has to apply: 45 days after termination of coverage.

Florida

Fla. Stat. Ann. § 627.6692

Employers affected: Employers with fewer than 20 employees.

Eligible employees: Full-time (25 or more hours per week) employees covered by employer's health insurance plan.

Length of coverage for employee: 18 months.

Length of coverage for dependents: 18 months.

Qualifying event: Layoff; reduction in hours; termination of employment; death of employee; change in marital status.

Time employer has to notify employee: Carrier notifies within 14 days of learning of qualifying event (beneficiary has 63 days to notify carrier of qualifying event).

Time employee has to apply: 30 days from receipt of carrier's notice.

Georgia

Ga. Code Ann. §§ 33-24-21.1 to 33-24-21.2

Employers affected: All employers who offer group health insurance.

Eligible employees: Employees continuously insured for previous 6 months.

Length of coverage for employee: 3 months plus any part of the month remaining at termination.

Length of coverage for dependents: 3 months plus any part of the month remaining at termination.

Qualifying event: Termination of employment (except for cause).

Special situations: Employee, spouse, or former spouse who is 60 years old and who has been covered for previous 6 months may continue coverage until eligible for Medicare. (Applies to companies with more than 20 employees; does not apply when employee quits for reasons other than health.)

Hawaii

Haw. Rev. Stat. §§ 393-11, 393-15

Employers affected: All employers required to offer health insurance (those paying a regular employee a monthly wage at least 86.67 times state hourly minimum—about $542).

Length of coverage for employee: If employee is hospitalized or prevented from working by sickness, employer must pay insurance premiums for 3 months or for as long employer continues to pay wages, whichever is longer.

Qualifying event: Employee is hospitalized or prevented by sickness from working.

Idaho

Idaho Code § 41-2213

Employers affected: All employers that offer group disability insurance.

Eligible employees: Employees or dependents who are totally disabled at the time the policy ends. (Applies to policies that provide benefits for loss of time during periods of hospitalization, benefits for hospital or medical expenses, or benefits for dismemberment.)

State Health Insurance Continuation Laws (continued)

Length of coverage for employee: Must provide a reasonable extension of coverage (in the case of medical and hospital expenses, a reasonable extension is at least 12 months).

Length of coverage for dependents: Must provide a reasonable extension of coverage (in the case of medical and hospital expenses, a reasonable extension is at least 12 months).

Illinois

215 Ill. Comp. Stat. §§ 5/367e, 5/367.2, 5/367.2-5

Employers affected: All employers who offer group health insurance.

Eligible employees: Employees continuously insured for previous 3 months.

Length of coverage for employee: 12 months.

Length of coverage for dependents: Upon death or divorce, 2 years' coverage for spouse under 55 and eligible dependents who were on employee's plan; until eligible for Medicare or other group coverage for spouse over 55 and eligible dependents who were on employee's plan. A dependent child who has reached plan age limit or who was not already covered by plan, is also entitled to 2 years' continuation coverage.

Qualifying event: Termination of employment; reduction in hours; death of employee; divorce.

Time employer has to notify employee: 10 days.

Time employee has to apply: 30 days after termination or reduction in hours or receiving notice from employer, whichever is later, but not more than 60 days from termination or reduction in hours.

Iowa

Iowa Code §§ 509B.3, 509B.5

Employers affected: All employers who offer group health insurance.

Eligible employees: Employees continuously insured for previous 3 months.

Length of coverage for employee: 9 months.

Length of coverage for dependents: 9 months.

Qualifying event: Any reason employee or dependent becomes ineligible for coverage.

Time employer has to notify employee: 10 days after termination of coverage.

Time employee has to apply: 10 days after termination of coverage or receiving notice from employer, whichever is later, but not more than 31 days from termination of coverage.

Kansas

Kan. Stat. Ann. § 40-2209(i)

Employers affected: All employers who offer group health insurance.

Eligible employees: Employees continuously insured for previous 3 months.

Length of coverage for employee: 18 months.

Length of coverage for dependents: 18 months.

Qualifying event: Any reason employee or dependent becomes ineligible for coverage.

Time employer has to notify employee: Reasonable notice.

Kentucky

Ky. Rev. Stat. Ann. § 304.18-110

Employers affected: All employers who offer group health insurance.

Eligible employees: Employees continuously insured for previous 3 months.

Length of coverage for employee: 18 months.

Length of coverage for dependents: 18 months.

Qualifying event: Any reason employee or dependent becomes ineligible for coverage.

Time employer has to notify employee: Employer must notify insurer as soon as employee's coverage ends; insurer then notifies employee.

Time employee has to apply: 31 days from receipt of insurer's notice, but not more than 90 days after termination of group coverage.

Louisiana

La. Rev. Stat. Ann. §§ 22:1045, 22:1046

Employers affected: All employers who offer group health insurance and have fewer than 20 employees.

Eligible employees: Employees continuously insured for previous 3 months.

Length of coverage for employee: 12 months.

Length of coverage for dependents: 12 months.

Qualifying event: Termination of employment; death of insured; divorce.

Time employee has to apply: By the end of the month following the month in which the qualifying event occurred.

Special situations: Surviving spouse who is 50 or older may have coverage until remarriage or eligibility for Medicare or other insurance.

State Health Insurance Continuation Laws (continued)

Maine

Me. Rev. Stat. Ann. tit. 24-A, § 2809-A

Employers affected: All employers who offer group health insurance and are not subject to COBRA.

Eligible employees: Employees employed for at least 6 months.

Length of coverage for employee: 1 year.

Length of coverage for dependents: 1 year.

Qualifying event: Temporary layoff; permanent layoff if employee is eligible for federal premium assistance for laid-off employees who continue coverage; loss of employment because of a work-related injury or disease.

Time employee has to apply: 31 days from termination of coverage.

Maryland

Md. Code Ann., [Ins.] §§ 15-407 to 15-409

Employers affected: All employers who offer group health insurance.

Eligible employees: Employees continuously insured for previous 3 months.

Length of coverage for employee: 18 months.

Length of coverage for dependents: 18 months upon death of employee; upon change in marital status, 18 months or until spouse remarries or becomes eligible for other coverage.

Qualifying event: Termination of employment; death of employee; change in marital status.

Time employer has to notify employee: Must notify insurer within 14 days of receiving employee's continuation request.

Time employee has to apply: 45 days from termination of coverage. Employee begins application process by requesting an election of continuation notification form from employer.

Massachusetts

Mass. Gen. Laws ch. 175, §§ 110G, 110I; ch. 176J, § 9

Employers affected: All employers who offer group health insurance and have fewer than 20 employees.

Eligible employees: All covered employees are eligible.

Length of coverage for employee: 18 months; 29 months if disabled.

Length of coverage for dependents: 18 months upon termination or reduction in hours; 29 months if disabled; 36 months on divorce, death of employee, employee's eligibility for Medicare, or employer's bankruptcy.

Qualifying event: Involuntary layoff; death of insured employee; change in marital status.

Time employer has to notify employee: Carrier must notify beneficiary within 14 days of learning of qualifying event.

Time employee has to apply: 60 days.

Special situations: Termination due to plant closing: 90 days' coverage for employee and dependents, at the same payment terms as before closing.

Minnesota

Minn. Stat. Ann. §§ 62A.17; 62A.20; 62A.21

Employers affected: All employers who offer group health insurance and have 2 or more employees.

Eligible employees: All covered employees are eligible.

Length of coverage for employee: 18 months; indefinitely if employee becomes totally disabled while employed.

Length of coverage for dependents: 18 months for current spouse or child after termination of employment; divorced or widowed spouse can continue until eligible for Medicare or other group health insurance. Upon divorce or death of employee, dependent children can continue until they no longer qualify as dependents under plan.

Qualifying event: Termination of employment; reduction in hours.

Time employer has to notify employee: Within 14 days of termination of coverage.

Time employee has to apply: 60 days from termination of coverage or receipt of employer's notice, whichever is later.

Mississippi

Miss. Code Ann. § 83-9-51

Employers affected: All employers who offer group health insurance and have fewer than 20 employees.

Eligible employees: Employees continuously insured for previous 3 months.

Length of coverage for employee: 12 months.

Length of coverage for dependents: 12 months.

Qualifying event: Termination of employment; divorce; employee's death; employee's eligibility for Medicare; loss of dependent status.

Time employer has to notify employee: Insurer must notify former or deceased employee's dependent child or divorced spouse of option to continue insurance within 14 days of their becoming ineligible for coverage on employee's policy.

State Health Insurance Continuation Laws (continued)

Time employee has to apply: Employee must apply and submit payment before group coverage ends; dependents or former spouse must elect continuation coverage within 30 days of receiving insurer's notice.

Missouri

Mo. Rev. Stat. § 376.428

Employers affected: All employers who offer group health insurance and are not subject to COBRA.

Eligible employees: All employees.

Length of coverage for employee: 18 months.

Length of coverage for dependents: 18 months if eligible due to termination or reduction in hours; 36 months if eligible due to death or divorce.

Qualifying event: Termination of employment; death of employee; divorce; reduction in hours; employee's eligibility for Medicare; loss of dependent status.

Time employer has to notify employee: Same rules as COBRA.

Time employee has to apply: Same rules as COBRA.

Montana

Mont. Code Ann. §§ 33-22-506 to 33-22-507

Employers affected: All employers who offer group disability insurance.

Eligible employees: All employees.

Length of coverage for employee: 1 year (with employer's consent).

Qualifying event: Reduction in hours.

Special situations: Insurer may not discontinue benefits to child with a disability after child exceeds age limit for dependent status.

Nebraska

Neb. Rev. Stat. §§ 44-1640 and following, 44-7406

Employers affected: Employers not subject to federal COBRA laws.

Eligible employees: All covered employees.

Length of coverage for employee: 6 months.

Length of coverage for dependents: 1 year upon death of insured employee. Subjects of domestic abuse who have lost coverage under abuser's plan and who do not qualify for COBRA may have 18 months' coverage (applies to all employers).

Qualifying event: Involuntary termination of employment (layoff due to labor dispute not considered involuntary).

Time employer has to notify employee: Within 10 days of termination of employment must send notice by certified mail.

Time employee has to apply: 10 days from receipt of employer's notice.

Nevada

Nev. Rev. Stat. Ann. § 689B.0345; Nev. Rev. Stat. Ann. § 689B.245 to 689B.249, (repealed 2014)

Employers affected: All employers that offer group health insurance.

Eligible employees: Employees who are on unpaid leave due to total disability.

Length of coverage for employee: Coverage must continue for 12 months, unless 1 of the following events occurs sooner: the employee is terminated, the employee obtains another health insurance policy, or the group health insurance policy is terminated.

Length of coverage for dependents: Coverage must continue for 12 months, unless 1 of the following events occurs sooner: the employee is terminated, the employee obtains another health insurance policy, or the group health insurance policy is terminated.

New Hampshire

N.H. Rev. Stat. Ann. §§ 415:18

Employers affected: All employers who offer group health insurance.

Eligible employees: All insured employees are eligible.

Length of coverage for employee: 18 months; 29 months if disabled at termination or during first 60 days of continuation coverage.

Length of coverage for dependents: 18 months; 29 months if disabled at termination or during first 60 days of continuation coverage; 36 months upon death of employee, divorce or legal separation, loss of dependent status, or employee's eligibility for Medicare.

Qualifying event: Any reason employee or dependent becomes ineligible for coverage.

Time employer has to notify employee: Carrier must notify beneficiary within 30 days of receiving notice of loss of coverage.

State Health Insurance Continuation Laws (continued)

Time employee has to apply: Within 45 days of receipt of notice.

Special situations: Layoff or termination due to strike: 6 months' coverage with option to extend for an additional 12 months. Surviving, divorced, or legally separated spouse who is 55 or older may continue benefits available until eligible for Medicare or another employer-based group insurance.

New Jersey

N.J. Stat. Ann. §§ 17B:27-51.12, 17B:27A-27

Employers affected: Employers with 2 to 50 employees.

Eligible employees: Employed full time (25 or more hours).

Length of coverage for employee: 18 months; 29 months if disabled at termination or during first 60 days of continuation coverage.

Length of coverage for dependents: 18 months; 36 months upon death of employee, divorce or legal separation, loss of dependent status, or employee's eligibility for Medicare.

Qualifying event: Termination of employment; reduction in hours; change in marital status; death.

Time employer has to notify employee: At time of qualifying event.

Time employee has to apply: Within 30 days of qualifying event.

Special benefits: Coverage must be identical to that offered to current employees.

Special situations: Total disability: employee who has been insured for previous 3 months and employee's dependents entitled to continuation coverage that includes all benefits offered by group policy (applies to all employers).

New Mexico

N.M. Stat. Ann. § 59A-18-16

Employers affected: All employers who offer group health insurance.

Eligible employees: All insured employees are eligible.

Length of coverage for employee: 6 months.

Length of coverage for dependents: 6 months for termination of employment; may continue group coverage or convert to individual policies upon death of covered employee or divorce or legal separation.

Qualifying event: Termination of employment.

Time employer has to notify employee: Insurer or employer must give written notice at time of termination.

Time employee has to apply: 30 days after receiving notice.

New York

N.Y. Ins. Law § 3221(m)

Employers affected: All employers who offer group health insurance.

Eligible employees: All covered employees are eligible.

Length of coverage for employee: 36 months.

Length of coverage for dependents: 36 months.

Qualifying event: Termination of employment; death of employee; divorce or legal separation; loss of dependent status; employee's eligibility for Medicare.

Time employee has to apply: 60 days after termination or receipt of notice, whichever is later.

North Carolina

N.C. Gen. Stat. §§ 58-53-5 to 58-53-40

Employers affected: All employers who offer group health insurance.

Eligible employees: Employees continuously insured for previous 3 months.

Length of coverage for employee: 18 months.

Length of coverage for dependents: 18 months.

Qualifying event: Termination of employment.

Time employer has to notify employee: Employer has option of notifying employee as part of the exit process..

Time employee has to apply: 60 days.

North Dakota

N.D. Cent. Code §§ 26.1-36-23, 26.1-36-23.1

Employers affected: All employers who offer group health insurance.

Eligible employees: Employees continuously insured for previous 3 months.

Length of coverage for employee: 39 weeks.

Length of coverage for dependents: 39 weeks; 36 months if required by divorce or annulment decree.

Qualifying event: Termination of employment; change in marital status, if divorce or annulment decree requires employee to continue coverage.

Time employee has to apply: Within 10 days of termination or of receiving notice of continuation rights, whichever is later, but not more than 31 days from termination.

State Health Insurance Continuation Laws (continued)

Ohio

Ohio Rev. Code Ann. §§ 3923.38, 1751.53

Employers affected: All employers who offer group health insurance.

Eligible employees: Employees continuously insured for previous 3 months who were involuntarily terminated for reasons other than gross misconduct on the part of the employee.

Length of coverage for employee: 12 months.

Length of coverage for dependents: 12 months.

Qualifying event: Involuntary termination of employment.

Time employer has to notify employee: At termination of employment.

Time employee has to apply: Whichever is earlier: 31 days after coverage terminates; 10 days after coverage terminates if employer notified employee of continuation rights prior to termination; 10 days after employer notified employee of continuation rights, if notice was given after coverage terminated.

Oklahoma

Okla. Stat. Ann. tit. 36, § 4509

Employers affected: All employers who offer group health insurance.

Eligible employees: Employees insured for at least 6 months; (all other employees and their dependents entitled to 30 days' continuation coverage).

Length of coverage for employee: 63 days for basic coverage; 6 months for major medical at the same premium rate prior to termination of coverage (only for losses or conditions that began while group policy in effect).

Length of coverage for dependents: 63 days for basic coverage; 6 months for major medical at the same premium rate prior to termination of coverage (only for losses or conditions that began while group policy in effect).

Qualifying event: Any reason coverage terminates (except employment termination for gross misconduct).

Time employer has to notify employee: Carrier must notify employee in writing within 30 days of receiving notice of termination of employee's coverage.

Time employee has to apply: 31 days after receipt of notice.

Special benefits: Includes maternity care for pregnancy begun while group policy was in effect.

Oregon

Ore. Rev. Stat. §§ 743B.343 to 743B.347

Employers affected: Employers not subject to federal COBRA laws.

Eligible employees: Employees continuously insured for previous 3 months.

Length of coverage for employee: 9 months.

Length of coverage for dependents: 9 months.

Qualifying event: Termination of employment; reduction in hours; employee's eligibility for Medicare; loss of dependent status; termination of membership in group covered by policy; death of employee.

Time employer has to notify employee: 10 days after qualifying event.

Time employee has to apply: Within the time limit determined by the insurer, which must be at least 10 days after the qualifying event or employee's receipt of notice, whichever is later.

Special situations: Surviving, divorced, or legally separated spouse who is 55 or older and dependent children entitled to continuation coverage until spouse remarries or is eligible for other coverage; must include dental, vision, or prescription drug benefits, if they were offered in original plan (applies to employers with 20 or more employees).

Pennsylvania

Pa. Stat. 40 P.S. § 764j

Employers affected: Employers that offer group health insurance and have 2 to 19 employees.

Eligible employees: Employees continuously insured for at least 3 months.

Length of coverage for employee: 9 months.

Length of coverage for dependents: 9 months.

Qualifying event: Termination of employment; reduction in hours; death of employee; change in marital status; employer's bankruptcy.

Time employer has to notify employee: 30 days after qualifying event.

Time employee has to apply: 30 days after receiving notice.

Rhode Island

R.I. Gen. Laws §§ 27-19.1-1, 27-20.4-1 to 27-20-4-2

Employers affected: All employers who offer group health insurance.

State Health Insurance Continuation Laws (continued)

Eligible employees: All insured employees are eligible.

Length of coverage for employee: 18 months (but not longer than continuous employment); cannot be required to pay more than 1 month premium at a time.

Length of coverage for dependents: 18 months (but not longer than continuous employment); cannot be required to pay more than 1 month premium at a time.

Qualifying event: Involuntary termination of employment; death of employee; change in marital status; permanent reduction in workforce; employer's going out of business.

Time employer has to notify employee: Employers must post a conspicuous notice of employee continuation rights.

Time employee has to apply: 30 days from termination of coverage.

Special situations: If right to receiving continuing health insurance is stated in the divorce judgment, divorced spouse has right to continue coverage as long as employee remains covered or until divorced spouse remarries or becomes eligible for other group insurance.

South Carolina

S.C. Code Ann. § 38-71-770

Employers affected: All employers who offer group health insurance.

Eligible employees: Employees continuously insured for previous 6 months.

Length of coverage for employee: 6 months (in addition to part of month remaining at termination).

Length of coverage for dependents: 6 months (in addition to part of month remaining at termination).

Qualifying event: Any reason employee or dependent becomes ineligible for coverage.

Time employer has to notify employee: At time of termination, employer must clearly and meaningfully advise employee of continuation rights.

South Dakota

S.D. Codified Laws Ann. §§ 58-18-7.5, 58-18-7.12; 58-18C-1

Employers affected: All employers who offer group health insurance.

Eligible employees: All covered employees.

Length of coverage for employee: 18 months; 29 months if disabled at termination or during first 60 days of continuation coverage.

Length of coverage for dependents: 18 months; 29 months if disabled at termination or during first 60 days of continuation coverage; 36 months upon death of employee, divorce or legal separation, loss of dependent status, or employee's eligibility for Medicare.

Qualifying event: Termination of employment; death of employee; divorce or legal separation; loss of dependent status; employee's eligibility for Medicare.

Special situations: When employer goes out of business: 12 months' continuation coverage available to all employees. Employer must notify employees within 10 days of termination of benefits; employees must apply within 60 days of receipt of employer's notice or within 90 days of termination of benefits if no notice given.

Tennessee

Tenn. Code Ann. § 56-7-2312

Employers affected: All employers who offer group health insurance.

Eligible employees: Employees continuously insured for previous 3 months.

Length of coverage for employee: 3 months (in addition to part of month remaining at termination).

Length of coverage for dependents: 3 months (in addition to part of month remaining at termination); 15 months upon death of employee or divorce (in addition to part of month remaining at termination).

Qualifying event: Termination of employment; death of employee; change in marital status.

Special situations: Employee or dependent who is pregnant at time of termination entitled to continuation benefits for 6 months following the end of pregnancy.

Texas

Tex. Ins. Code Ann. §§ 1251.252 to 1251.255; 1251.301 to 1251.310

Employers affected: All employers who offer group health insurance.

Eligible employees: Employees continuously insured for previous 3 months.

Length of coverage for employee: 9 months; for employees eligible for COBRA, 6 months after COBRA coverage ends.

Length of coverage for dependents: 9 months; for employees eligible for COBRA, 6 months after COBRA coverage ends. 3 years for dependents with coverage due to the death or retirement of employee or severance of the family relationship.

State Health Insurance Continuation Laws (continued)

Qualifying event: Termination of employment (except for cause); employee leaves for health reasons; severance of family relationship; retirement or death of employee.

Time employee has to apply: 60 days from termination of coverage or receiving notice of continuation rights from employer or insurer, whichever is later. Must give notice within 15 days of severance of family relationship. Within 60 days of death or retirement of family member or severance of family relationship, dependent must give notice of intent to continue coverage.

Utah

Utah Code Ann. § 31A-22-722

Employers affected: All employers who offer group health insurance.

Eligible employees: Employees continuously insured for previous 3 months.

Length of coverage for employee: 12 months.

Length of coverage for dependents: 12 months.

Qualifying event: Termination of employment; retirement; death; divorce; reduction in hours; sabbatical; disability; loss of dependent status.

Time employer has to notify employee: In writing within 30 days of termination of coverage.

Time employee has to apply: Within 60 days of qualifying event.

Vermont

Vt. Stat. Ann. tit. 8, §§ 4090a to 4090c

Employers affected: All employers who offer group health insurance.

Eligible employees: All covered employees are eligible.

Length of coverage for employee: 18 months.

Length of coverage for dependents: 18 months.

Qualifying event: Termination of employment; reduction in hours; death of employee; change of marital status; loss of dependent status.

Time employer has to notify employee: Within 30 days of qualifying event.

Time employee has to apply: Within 60 days of receiving notice following the occurrence of a qualifying event.

Virginia

Va. Code Ann. §§ 38.2-3541 to 38.2-3452

Employers affected: All employers who offer group health insurance.

Eligible employees: Employees continuously insured for previous 3 months.

Length of coverage for employee: 12 months.

Length of coverage for dependents: 12 months.

Qualifying event: Any reason employee or dependent becomes ineligible for coverage.

Time employer has to notify employee: 14 days from termination of coverage.

Time employee has to apply: Within 31 days of receiving notice of eligibility, but no more than 60 days following termination.

Special situations: Employee may convert to an individual policy instead of applying for continuation coverage (must apply within 31 days of termination of coverage).

Washington

Wash. Rev. Code Ann. § 48.21.075

Employers affected: All employers who offer disability insurance.

Eligible employees: Insured employees on strike.

Length of coverage for employee: 6 months if employee goes on strike.

Length of coverage for dependents: 6 months if employee goes on strike.

Qualifying event: If employee goes on strike.

Special situations: All employers have option of offering continued group health benefits.

West Virginia

W.Va. Code §§ 33-16-2, 33-16-3(e); W. Va. Code R. § 114-93-3

Employers affected: Employers providing insurance for between 2 and 20 employees.

Eligible employees: All employees are eligible.

Length of coverage for employee: 18 months in case of involuntary layoff.

Qualifying event: Involuntary layoff.

Time employer has to notify employee: Carrier must notify beneficiaries within 15 days of receiving notice from beneficiary of intent to apply.

Time employee has to apply: 20 days to send notice of intention to apply; 30 days to apply after receiving election and premium notice.

State Health Insurance Continuation Laws (continued)

Wisconsin

Wis. Stat. Ann. § 632.897

Employers affected: All employers who offer group health insurance.

Eligible employees: Employees continuously insured for previous 3 months.

Length of coverage for employee: 18 months (or longer at insurer's option).

Length of coverage for dependents: 18 months (or longer at insurer's option).

Qualifying event: Any reason employee or dependent becomes ineligible for coverage (except employment termination due to misconduct).

Time employer has to notify employee: 5 days from termination of coverage.

Time employee has to apply: 30 days after receiving employer's notice.

Wyoming

Wyo. Stat. § 26-19-113

Employers affected: Employers not subject to federal COBRA laws.

Eligible employees: Employees continuously insured for previous 3 months.

Length of coverage for employee: 12 months.

Length of coverage for dependents: 12 months.

Time employee has to apply: 31 days from termination of coverage.

Creating Your Handbook

This book comes with interactive files that you can access online at:

www.nolo.com/back-of-book/EMHA.html

This page (called the book's companion page) provides all of the forms and policies in this book, as well as legal updates, blog posts, and more.

To use the files, your computer must have specific software programs installed. The files in this book are provided as RTFs. You can open, edit, print, and save these form files with most word processing programs such as Microsoft *Word*, Windows *WordPad*, and recent versions of *WordPerfect*.

Each file includes the policies from a particular chapter of the book. The companion page also includes separate files for each of the forms included in the book.

Editing Handbook Sections

When you are ready to start preparing your handbook, open the file for the chapter of policies you'd like to include, then begin working your way through the policies, referring back to the chapter's discussion for instructions and help completing the policies. Here are tips for working on your document:

- **Underlines.** Underlines indicate where to enter information. After filling in the needed text, delete the underline. In most word processing programs you can do this by highlighting the underlined portion and typing CTRL-U.
- **Bracketed and italicized text.** Bracketed and italicized text indicates instructions. Be sure to remove all instructional text before you finalize your document.
- **Alternative text.** Alternative text gives you the choice between two or more text options. Delete those options you don't want to use. Renumber numbered items, if necessary.

- **Optional text.** Optional text allows you to choose whether or not to include the text. Delete optional text you do not want to include; keep optional text you want in your handbook. In either case, delete the italicized instructions. If you choose to delete an optional numbered clause, renumber subsequent clauses.
- **Signature lines.** Signature lines should appear on a page with at least some text from the document itself.

Every word processing program uses different commands to open, format, save, and print documents, so refer to your software's help documents for help using your program. Nolo cannot provide technical support for questions about how to use your computer or your software.

CAUTION

In accordance with U.S. copyright laws, the forms provided by this book are for your personal use only.

Assembling Your Employee Handbook

When you've edited the handbook sections to your satisfaction and are ready to begin assembling your employee handbook, open the Employee Handbook Outline. You can then start opening, copying, and pasting from your completed handbook section files into the Employee Handbook Outline. Be sure to delete the bracketed instructions from the Employee Handbook Outline as you paste in your handbook sections. After you've finished pasting in your handbook sections, save your final document following the instructions above.

List of Forms

The following files are available for download at:
www.nolo.com/back-of-book/EMHA.html

Planner Section Name	File Name
Employee Handbook Outline	00_Outline.rtf
Introduction	01_Introduction.rtf
The Employment Relationship	02_Employment.rtf
Hiring	03_Hiring.rtf
New Employee Information	04_NewEmployeeInfo.rtf
Employee Classifications	05_EmployeeClass.rtf
Hours	06_Hours.rtf
Pay Policies	07_PayPolicies.rtf
Employee Benefits	08_EmployeeBenefits.rtf
Use of Company Property	09_CompanyProperty.rtf
Leave and Time Off	10_TimeOff.rtf
Performance	11_Performance.rtf
Workplace Behavior	12_WorkBehavior.rtf
Health and Safety	13_HealthSafety.rtf
Employee Privacy	14_Privacy.rtf
Computers, Email, and the Internet	15_Computers.rtf

Planner Section Name	File Name
Employee Records	16_Records.rtf
Drugs and Alcohol	17_DrugsAlcohol.rtf
Trade Secrets and Conflicts of Interest	18_TradeSecrets.rtf
Discrimination and Harassment	19_Discrimination.rtf
Complaint Policies	20_Complaints.rtf
Ending Employment	21_EndingEmployment.rtf
Handbook Acknowledgment Form	Acknowledgment.rtf
Payroll Deduction Authorization Form	PayrollDeduction.rtf
Tip Credit Notice Form	TipCredit.rtf
Expense Reimbursement Form	Reimbursement.rtf
Telephone Monitoring Policy Acknowledgment	PhoneAcknowledgment.rtf
Email and Internet Policy Acknowledgment Form	EmailAcknowledgment.rtf

Where to Go for Further Information

CONTENTS

State Departments of Labor

Note: Phone numbers listed are for each department's headquarters. Check the website for regional office locations and numbers.

Alabama
Department of Labor
Montgomery, AL
334-242-8055
www.labor.alabama.gov

Alaska
Department of Labor and Workforce
  Development
Juneau, AK
907-465-2700
www.labor.state.ak.us

Arizona
Industrial Commission
Phoenix, AZ
602-542-4661
www.azica.gov

Arkansas
Department of Labor
Little Rock, AR
501-682-4500
www. labor.arkansas.gov

California
Labor Commissioner's Office
Department of Industrial Relations
Oakland, CA
510-285-2118
www.dir.ca.gov/DLSE/dlse.html

Colorado
Department of Labor and
  Employment
Denver, CO
303-318-8441
www.colorado.gov/CDLE

Connecticut
Department of Labor
Wethersfield, CT
860-263-6000
www.ctdol.state.ct.us

Delaware
Department of Labor
Wilmington, DE
302-761-8000
http://dol.delaware.gov

District of Columbia
Department of Employment Services
Washington, DC
202-724-7000
www.does.dc.gov

Florida
Department of Economic
  Opportunity
Tallahassee, FL
850-245-7105
www.floridajobs.org

Georgia
Department of Labor
Atlanta, GA
404-232-7300
www.dol.georgia.gov

Hawaii
Department of Labor and Industrial
  Relations
Honolulu, HI
808-586-8844
http://labor.hawaii.gov

Idaho
Department of Labor
Boise, ID
208-332-3570
http://labor.idaho.gov

Illinois
Department of Labor
Chicago, IL
312-793-2800
www.state.il.us/agency/idol

Indiana
Department of Labor
Indianapolis, IN
317-232-2655
www.in.gov/dol

Iowa
Division of Labor
Des Moines, IA
515-281-3606
www.iowadivisionoflabor.gov

Kansas
Department of Labor
Topeka, KS
785-296-5000
www.dol.ks.gov

Kentucky
Labor Cabinet
Frankfort, KY
502-564-0684
www.labor.ky.gov

Louisiana
Louisiana Workforce Commission
Baton Rouge, LA
225-342-3111
www.ldol.state.la.us

Maine
Department of Labor
Augusta, ME
207-623-7900
www.state.me.us/labor

State Departments of Labor (continued)

Maryland
Division of Labor, Licensing, and
   Regulation
Baltimore, MD
410-767-2241
www.dllr.state.md.us/labor

Massachusetts
Labor and Workforce Development
Boston, MA
617-626-7122
www.mass.gov/lwd

Michigan
Department of Licensing and
   Regulatory Affairs
Lansing, MI
517-373-1820
www.michigan.gov/lara

Minnesota
Department of Labor and Industry
St. Paul, MN
800-342-5354
651-284-5005
www.dli.mn.gov

Mississippi
Department of Employment Security
Jackson, MS
601-321-6000
www.mdes.ms.gov

Missouri
Department of Labor and Industrial
   Relations
Jefferson City, MO
573-751-3215
www.labor.mo.gov

Montana
Department of Labor and Industry
Helena, MT
406-444-2840
www.dli.mt.gov

Nebraska
Department of Labor
Lincoln, NE
402-471-9000
www.dol.nebraska.gov

Nevada
Office of the Labor Commissioner
Las Vegas, NV
702-486-2650
http://labor.nv.gov

New Hampshire
Department of Labor
Concord, NH
603-271-3176
800-272-4353
www.nh.gov/labor

New Jersey
Department of Labor and Workforce
   Development
Trenton, NJ
609-659-9045
http://lwd.state.nj.us/labor

New Mexico
Department of Workforce Solutions
Albuquerque, NM
505-841-8405
www.dws.state.nm.us

New York
Department of Labor
Albany, NY
518-457-9000
888-469-7365
www.labor.ny.gov/home

North Carolina
Department of Labor
Raleigh, NC
919-807-2796
800-625-2267
www.nclabor.com

North Dakota
Department of Labor and
   Human Rights
Bismarck, ND
701-328-2660
800-582-8032
www.nd.gov/labor

Ohio
Division of Industrial Compliance
Reynoldsburg, OH
614-644-2223
www.com.ohio.gov/dico

Oklahoma
Department of Labor
Oklahoma City, OK
405-521-6100
www.ok.gov/odol

Oregon
Bureau of Labor and Industries
Portland, OR
971-637-0761
www.oregon.gov/boli

Pennsylvania
Department of Labor and Industry
Harrisburg, PA
800-932-0665
www.dli.pa.gov

Rhode Island
Department of Labor and Training
Cranston, RI
401-462-8000
www.dlt.state.ri.us

South Carolina
Department of Labor, Licensing, and
   Regulation
Columbia, SC
803-896-4300
www.llr.state.sc.us/labor

State Departments of Labor (continued)

South Dakota
Department of Labor and Regulation
Pierre, SD
605-773-3101
www.dlr.sd.gov

Tennessee
Department of Labor and Workforce
    Development
Nashville, TN
844-224-5818
www.tn.gov/workforce

Texas
Texas Workforce Commission
Austin, TX
512-463-2222
www.twc.state.tx.us

Utah
Labor Commission
Salt Lake City, UT
801-530-6800
800-530-5090
www.laborcommission.utah.gov

Vermont
Department of Labor
Montpelier, VT
802-828-4000
www.labor.vermont.gov

Virginia
Department of Labor and Industry
Richmond, VA
804-371-2327
www.doli.virginia.gov

Washington
Department of Labor and Industries
Tumwater, WA
360-902-5800
www.lni.wa.gov

West Virginia
Division of Labor
Charleston, WV
304-558-7890
www.wv/labor.com

Wisconsin
Department of Workforce
    Development
Madison, WI
608-266-3131
http://dwd.wisconsin.gov

Wyoming
Department of Workforce Services
Cheyenne, WY
307-777-7261
www.wyomingworkforce.org

Agencies That Enforce Laws Prohibiting Discrimination in Employment

Note: Phone numbers listed are for each department's headquarters. Check the website for regional office locations and numbers.

United States
Equal Employment Opportunity Commission
131 M Street, NW
Washington, DC 20507
800-669-4000
TTY: 800-669-6820
www.eeoc.gov

Alabama
Birmingham District Office
Equal Employment Opportunity Commission
Birmingham, AL
800-669-4000
http://eeoc.gov/field/birmingham/index.cfm

Alaska
Commission for Human Rights
Anchorage, AK
907-274-4692
800-478-4692
http://humanrights.alaska.gov

Arizona
Civil Rights Division
Arizona Attorney General
Phoenix, AZ
602-542-5263
877-491-5742
www.azag.gov/civil-rights

Arkansas
Little Rock Area Office
Equal Employment Opportunity Commission
Little Rock, AR
800-669-4000
www.eeoc.gov/field/littlerock/index.cfm

California
Department of Fair Employment and Housing
Elk Grove, CA
800-884-1684
www.dfeh.ca.gov

Colorado
Civil Rights Division
Denver, CO
303-894-2997
www.colorado.gov/dora/civil-rights

Connecticut
Commission on Human Rights and Opportunities
Hartford, CT
860-541-3400
www.ct.gov/chro/site

Delaware
Division of Industrial Affairs
Department of Labor
Wilmington, DE
302-761-8200
http://dia.delawareworks.com/discrimination

District of Columbia
Office of Human Rights
Washington, DC
202-727-4559
http://ohr.dc.gov

Florida
Commission on Human Relations
Tallahassee, FL
850-488-7082
800-342-8170
http://fchr.state.fl.us

Georgia
Atlanta District Office
Equal Employment Opportunity Commission
Atlanta, GA
800-669-4000
www.eeoc.gov/field/atlanta

Hawaii
Hawaii Civil Rights Commission
Honolulu, HI
808-586-8636
http://labor.hawaii.gov/hcrc

Idaho
Idaho Commission on Human Rights
Boise, ID
208-334-2873
888-249-7025
http://humanrights.idaho.gov

Illinois
Department of Human Rights
Chicago, IL
312-814-6200
www2.illinois.gov/dhr

Indiana
Civil Rights Commission
Indianapolis, IN
317-232-2600
800-628-2909
www.in.gov/icrc

Iowa
Civil Rights Commission
Des Moines, IA
515-281-4121
800-457-4416
https://icrc.iowa.gov

Kansas
Human Rights Commission
Topeka, KS
785-296-3206
www.khrc.net

Agencies That Enforce Laws Prohibiting Discrimination in Employment (continued)

Kentucky
Commission on Human Rights
Louisville, KY
502-595-4024
800-292-5566
www.kchr.ky.gov

Louisiana
Commission on Human Rights
Baton Rouge, LA
225-342-6969
http://gov.louisiana.gov/page/louisiana-
commission-on-human-rights

Maine
Human Rights Commission
Augusta, ME
207-624-6290
www.maine.gov/mhrc

Maryland
Commission on Civil Rights
Baltimore, MD
410-767-8600
800-637-6247 (in-state only)
www.mccr.maryland.gov

Massachusetts
Commission Against Discrimination
Boston, MA
617-994-6000
www.mass.gov/mcad

Michigan
Department of Civil Rights
Detroit, MI
313-456-3700
800-482-3604
www.michigan.gov/mdcr

Minnesota
Department of Human Rights
St. Paul, MN
651-539-1100
800-657-3704
http://mn.gov/mdhr

Mississippi
Jackson Area Office
Equal Employment Opportunity
Commission
Jackson, MS
800-699-4000
www.eeoc.gov/field/jackson

Missouri
Commission on Human Rights
Jefferson City, MO
573-751-3325
877-781-4236
www.labor.mo.gov/mohumanrights

Montana
Human Rights Bureau
Employment Relations Division
Department of Labor and Industry
Helena, MT
800-542-0807
http://erd.dli.mt.gov/human-rights/
human-rights

Nebraska
Nebraska Equal Opportunity
Commission
Lincoln, NE
402-471-2024
800-642-6112
www.neoc.ne.gov

Nevada
Equal Rights Commission
Las Vegas, NV
702-486-7161
www.detr.state.nv.us/nerc.htm

New Hampshire
Commission for Human Rights
Concord, NH
603-271-2767
www.nh.gov/hrc

New Jersey
Division on Civil Rights
Office of the Attorney General
Trenton, NJ
609-292-4605
www.nj.gov/oag/dcr/index.htm

New Mexico
Human Rights Bureau
Santa Fe, NM
505-827-6838
800-566-9471
www.dws.state.nm.us/
LaborRelations/HumanRights/
Information

New York
Division of Human Rights
Bronx, NY
888-392-3644
www.dhr.ny.gov

North Carolina
Employment Discrimination Bureau
Department of Labor
Raleigh, NC
919-807-2796
800-NC-LABOR
www.nclabor.com/edb/edb.htm

North Dakota
Human Rights Division
Department of Labor and Human
Rights
Bismarck, ND
701-328-2660
800-582-8032
www.nd.gov/labor/human-rights/
index.html

Ohio
Civil Rights Commission
Columbus, OH
614-466-2785
888-278-7101
www.crc.ohio.gov

Agencies That Enforce Laws Prohibiting Discrimination in Employment (continued)

Oklahoma
Office of Civil Rights Enforcement
Office of the Attorney General
Tulsa, OK
918-581-2910
www.ok.gov/oag/About_the_Office/
  OCRE.html

Oregon
Civil Rights Division
Bureau of Labor and Industries
Portland, OR
971-673-0764
www.oregon.gov/BOLI/CRD

Pennsylvania
Human Relations Commission
Harrisburg, PA
717-787-4410
www.phrc.state.pa.us

Rhode Island
Commission for Human Rights
Providence, RI
401-222-2661
http://sos.ri.gov/govdirectory/index.ph
  p?page=DetailDeptAgency&eid=189

South Carolina
Human Affairs Commission
Columbia, SC
803-737-7800
800-521-0725
www.schac.sc.gov

South Dakota
Division of Human Rights
Department of Labor and Regulation
Pierre, SD
605-773-3681
www.dlr.sd.gov/humanrights/default.
  aspx

Tennessee
Human Rights Commission
Nashville, TN
800-251-3589
www.tennessee.gov/humanrights

Texas
Civil Rights Division
Texas Workforce Commission
Austin, TX
512-463-2642
888-452-4778
www.twc.state.tx.us/customers/
  jsemp/jsempsubcrd.html

Utah
Antidiscrimination and Labor
  Division
Labor Commission
Salt Lake City, UT
801-530-6801
800-222-1238
www.laborcommission.utah.gov/
  divisions/Antidiscrimination
  AndLabor/index.html

Vermont
Attorney General's Office
Civil Rights Unit
Montpelier, VT
802-828-3657
888-745-9195
http://ago.vermont.gov/divisions/
  civil-rights.php

Virginia
Office of the Attorney General
Division of Human Rights
Richmond, VA
804-225-2292
www.oag.state.va.us/index.php/
  programs-initiatives/human-rights

Washington
Human Rights Commission
Olympia, WA
800-233-3247
www.hum.wa.gov

West Virginia
Human Rights Commission
Charleston, WV
304-558-2616
888-676-5546
www.hrc.wv.gov

Wisconsin
Division of Equal Rights
Department of Workforce
  Development
Madison, WI
608-266-6860
http://dwd.wisconsin.gov/er

Wyoming
Labor Standards Office
Department of Workforce Services
Cheyenne, WY
307-777-7261
www.wyomingworkforce.org/
  workers/labor/

Index

sick leave and, 152

on telephone monitoring, 271, 272

tip pools and, 100

on work eligibility, 307

See also Affordable Care Act
(Obamacare); Americans with
Disabilities Act (ADA); COBRA
(Consolidated Omnibus Budget
Reconciliation Act); ERISA
(Employee Retirement Income
Security Act); Fair Labor Standards
Act (FLSA); Family and Medical
Leave Act (FMLA); Federal Trade
Commission (FTC); Immigration
Reform and Control Act (IRCA);
National Labor Relations Board
(NLRB); Occupational Safety and
Health Act (OSHA); Sarbanes-
Oxley Act (SOX); USERRA
(Uniformed Services Employment
and Reemployment Rights Act)

Federal Trade Commission (FTC),
297–298

FICA tax, deduction from paycheck
for, 106

Fighting, 225, 231. *See also* Violence

Files available online, 404–405

Final paychecks, 377–378, 388–392

Financial disclosures, prohibited, 300

Fire, 240

Fire drills, 240

Fire extinguishers, 241

Firing of employee

at-will policy and, 27–31, 230

for comments about violence, 247

employment contracts and, 27, 31

exit interview and, 384–385

final paycheck and, 377, 388–392

health insurance continuation and,
381–383

immediate for certain conduct, 231

Montana law and, 27, 49

progressive discipline and, 230–232

reference and, 386

severance pay and, 379

unused paid time off and, 158

unused vacation time and, 148

See also At-will policy

Flexible scheduling, 66–67

Flexible spending accounts, payroll
deductions for, 106

Floating holidays, 149–150

unified paid time off and, 155, 156, 158

FLSA. *See* Fair Labor Standards Act
(FLSA)

FMLA. *See* Family and Medical Leave
Act (FMLA)

Formatting the handbook, 9–10

at-will policy and, 29

Forms available online, 404–405

401(k)s, payroll deductions for, 106

FTC (Federal Trade Commission),
297–298

Full-time employees, 60

G

Gambling websites, 288

Garnishment of wages, 107–108

for lost, stolen, or damaged company
property, 144

Gender identity discrimination, 347

Goals of company, 16, 17, 20

Government employees, 4

Grooming, 217–221

Guns, 248–249

immediate termination and, 231

searches for, 269

See also Violence

H

Handbook. *See* Employee handbook

Handbook Acknowledgment Form,
32–34

distribution of, 11

for electronic handbook, 10

for employees with disabilities, 10

not for reading entire handbook, 34

rtf file containing, 405

Harassment

complaint procedures for, 368, 369

by email, 281

as form of discrimination, 353, 354

lawsuits for, 343, 353, 354, 367

in online posts, 297, 299

by personal mobile device, 295

by photos or recordings, 276

policy on, 353–354

reasons for including policy on, 343

searches related to, 269–270

termination for, 231

See also Antidiscrimination laws;
Sexual harassment

Health care benefits

classifications of employees and,
129–130

continuation of, 381–383, 393–402

coverage for spouses under, 130

during family and medical leave,
164–165

mental health, 251

during military leave, 174

policy on, 128–130

smoking cessation and, 244–245

waiting period for, 51

See also Affordable Care Act
(Obamacare)

Hidden cameras, 270

Hiring

antidiscrimination policy in, 36–37,
343, 344–347

from within the company, 38–39, 40

recruitment for, 38–39, 41–43

of relatives, 44–46

History of the company, 14, 16, 19–20

Holidays

designation of, 149

falling on a weekend, 149

floating, 149–150, 155, 156, 158

in overtime calculation, 73

payday falling on, 88, 89

premium for working on, 74

Home

work done from, 72

See also Conduct outside of work

Horseplay, 224, 235, 247

Hours of work, 64–65

breaks and, 68–71, 76–81

flexible, 66–67

See also Overtime

Human resources department, 22, 25

NOLO *Online Legal Forms*

Nolo offers a large library of legal solutions and forms, created by Nolo's in-house legal staff. These reliable documents can be prepared in minutes.

Create a Document

- **Incorporation.** Incorporate your business in any state.
- **LLC Formations.** Gain asset protection and pass-through tax status in any state.
- **Wills.** Nolo has helped people make over 2 million wills. Is it time to make or revise yours?
- **Living Trust (avoid probate).** Plan now to save your family the cost, delays, and hassle of probate.
- **Trademark.** Protect the name of your business or product.
- **Provisional Patent.** Preserve your rights under patent law and claim "patent pending" status.

Download a Legal Form

Nolo.com has hundreds of top quality legal forms available for download—bills of sale, promissory notes, nondisclosure agreements, LLC operating agreements, corporate minutes, commercial lease and sublease, motor vehicle bill of sale, consignment agreements and many, many more.

Review Your Documents

Many lawyers in Nolo's consumer-friendly lawyer directory will review Nolo documents for a very reasonable fee. Check their detailed profiles at **Nolo.com/lawyers**.